# An account of the people called Shakers, their faith, doctrines and practice, exemplified in the life, conversations and experience of the author during the time that he belonged to the Society;

Thomas Brown

BIBLIOLIFE

# AN ACCOUNT OF THE PEOPLE CALLED SHAKERS:

THEIR

## FAITH, DOCTRINES, AND PRACTICE,

EXEMPLIFIED IN THE

LIFE, CONVERSATIONS, AND EXPERIENCE OF THE AUTHOR DURING THE TIME HE BELONGED TO THE SOCIETY.

TO WHICH IS AFFIXED A

## HISTORY OF THEIR RISE AND PROGRESS TO THE PRESENT DAY.

BY THOMAS BROWN,

Of Cornwall, Orange County, State of New-York.

Prove all things, hold faſt to that which is good. *Apoſtle Paul.*

An hiſtorian ſhould not dare to tell a falſehood, or leave a truth untold. *Cicero.*

TROY

*PRINTED BY PARKER AND BLISS.*

SOLD AT THE TROY BOOKSTORE; BY WEBSTERS AND SKINNERS, ALBANY: AND BY S. WOOD, NEW-YORK.

1812.

# PREFACE.

As a full and impartial account of the people called Shakers, has never yet been presented to the publick, although the attention and inquiry of a large portion of the community, has been excited to an unusual degree, by their novel appearance and unexpected increase, the author of the following work, has been prevailed upon to give the world the result of his experience and investigation among them. He is confident, that their rise, tenets, and practices are more singular (the present state of the world, and general information of mankind being taken into consideration) than those of any religious sect which has taken its rise in the christian world since the first promulgation of the gospel.

The following correspondence which took place between the author and the church, when the ensuing publication was nearly finished, will, I doubt not, be accepted as being properly adapted for a prefatory introduction.

*To the Church called Shakers.*

Friends,

I think proper to give you the following information, viz. since I withdrew from your society, I have written for publication, and have now nearly finished, an account of my life and experience among you; in which I have given a statement of the many conversations we have had respecting your faith, doctrines, and practices, with the most authentick account of the rise of the church that can be obtained.

I feel not, and therefore write not as an enemy; but merely give an impartial statement according to the best of my ability and knowledge; which knowledge, I have spared no pains nor expence to obtain from every credible source of information. I wish to publish nothing but what is strictly the truth; and I have studiously avoided using one word that would have a tendency to misrepresent, or convey a wrong idea.

Notwithstanding, that there may be no room left for undue animadversions, I hereby make you the offer, if you please to accept it, of examining the work, in manuscript, previous to publication; and if it can be clearly pointed out to me, wherein I have not given a correct account, I shall be willing to alter and correct, as it is only my intention to act the part of a faithful historian.

Having once had a privilege among you, and being now what you term a backslider, you may therefore consider me as an individual beneath attention; but you will pay some deference to mankind in general, and as what I offer for your examination is of a publick nature, I conclude you may think it worthy your attention.

Deference to you as a religious society, together with the advice of some of your members, and several other people, has induced me to make you this offer; if it should meet with your approbation, I will thank you to let me know it in due season.

I shall at present add no more, but that I remain, with sentiments of esteem, Your Friend,

THOMAS BROWN.

Lucy Wright and Abiathar Babbot,
First in the Ministration.
*Cornwall, November*, 1808.

A short time after, I received from the Church, the following answer.

*To Thomas Brown.*

" Professed Friend,

" A letter with thy subscription, has been put into my " hands, directed to " Abiathar Babbot," purporting, that thou " art about publishing thy Life, Experience, &c. with a full ac- " count of our Faith, Doctrines, &c. proposing to offer the man- " uscript for our examination, previous to publication. So far " from wishing to offend thee with a reply incongruous with thy " feelings, it is with much regret that we have any thing to say " or do in the matter, but since we are called upon in a cir- " cumstance like this, we deem it expedient to reply, That we " have no desire to examine thy writings. It is sufficient that we " know thee, Thomas; and be thy opinion whatever it may " concerning thy own abilities, we must candidly tell thee. that " we are far from considering thee competent to the task thou "hast undertaken relative to the subject of *our faith*, either as "it respects thy knowledge of the work of God among us, or "thy understanding of our doctrines; and we think we may "add with propriety and candour, that thy letter presents no "very favourable specimen of literary talents; therefore, we "explicitly declare our disapprobation of thy undertaking yet "be assured, that this declaration is not made from any appre-"hension of harm that may accrue to us from thy publication; "but a regard to truth, and respect to the world of mankind, "who are unacqainted with us or thee, and who are liable to "be led into error by ignorant pretenders to a knowledge of "our doctrines, urge us to withhold our sanction from publi-"cations of that description emanating from such authors.

"We hope these plain reasons will be sufficient to induce thee "to relinquish thy design without any further trouble, for we "don't wish to be urged to the disagreeable necessity of expos-"ing this correspondence to the publick, in order to prevent seri-"ous inquirers from being imposed upon by such like publications.

"Respecting the publication of thy own life, abstractedly "considered, we have nothing to do. In that thou hast an un-"doubted right to act thy pleasure; charity, however, induces "us to suggest to thee, as our candid opinion, that it would be "much more to thy credit to lay aside thy pen, and turn thy "attention to some better employment than to expose thy life "to the world by thy writings.

"We hope the plainness of this reply to the subject of thy "letter, will not be imputed to any desire in us to give offence; "but to the privilege we claim of expressing our sentiments free-"ly on that subject.

"In behalf of the Church, Signed,

"DAVID OSBORN.

"*Watervliet, December* 21, 1808."

ANSWER.

RESPECTED FRIENDS,

Your letter of December 21, 1808, purporting to be an answer to mine of November last, was lately received; and had you barely expressed in your reply, that you had "no "desire to examine my writings," you would probably have heard no more from me in this way; but you have chosen, it seems, to sit in judgment on me and my abilities, and to dictate for me. It was my wish that you might see the work I had written, before you would undertake to condemn it. If you had seen it, you would then have been able to judge whether I was competent to the task or not, and you would have had it in your power to point out to me any errours it might contain; but no, you wait not for that, but at once, and in terms not altogether pleasing, say, "*That be my opinion whatever it may* "*of my own abilities, you must candidly tell me, that you are far from consid-* "*ering me competent to the task I have undertaken.*" You likewise preface this with an expression, which, by its ambiguity and vulgar use, is an insinuation either of immorality in my conduct, insincerity in my heart, or ignorance in my head. To which of these, or whether to all, you have not thought fit to confine yourselves. Your expression is—"*We have no desire to examine thy writings: it is* "*sufficient that we know thee, Thomas.*" It obviously appears by this expression (as I intimated above) that you mean to imply something prejudicial to my character, something too bad to mention, as there is no evil conduct but what is implied in that expression. And from the opinion I entertained of your civility, I could not have believed you would have so imitated the vulgar part of mankind; and that when they are displeased, as it is then common for them to say, "Ah, I know you; I know what you have done." Why, my friends, what do you know of me? Speak out, for such sarcasms and dark implications are unkind and ungenerous, and do not belong to a people making the profession which you do, of mildness and plainness of speech. But you know in truth, you cannot alledge any thing prejudicial to my character; and therefore you would imply every thing bad in a laconic, sarcastical sentence. And I could not have believed you would have treated me thus for the kindness of my offer.

You observe, that "*my letter presents no very favourable specimen* "*of literary talents.*" I confess it does not. I have no pretensions to such talents. But though I boast not of literary talents, nor of ſplendid abilities, I ſtill truſt I am capable of relating in writing ſuch matters of fact as my eyes have ſeen and my ears have heard. You have alſo blended my want of literary talents, with inability as to the ſubject of your faith, "*underſtanding* "*your doctrines, or having any knowledge of the work of God among* "*you*" This is what I did not expect, in as much as I hoped that a ſacred regard to truth would have been adhered to in all your correſpondence As to the work of God among you, I ſhall leave the reader to judge for himſelf.

You explicitly declare your diſapprobation of my work even before you have examined it. This mode of deſtroying the authenticity of a book, will be accepted by thoſe only who pin their faith on your ſleeves: and I truſt you cannot have the boldneſs to publiſh to the world, that it is impoſſible for a man to obtain a knowledge of your faith and doctrines, who has been a member of your Church upwards of ſix years, and who has ſpent much of his time in diſcourſes with the Elders and others who had an underſtanding of the faith, in order to procure that knowledge. But I perceive you have not written particularly for me, but hereafter for the publick, in order to rebut or invalidate my publication whenever it may make its appearance; and therefore you wiſh to make people believe, I have not an *underſtanding of your faith and doctrines*, and am not *competent to the taſk I have undertaken*; but the underſtanding reader will then ſee, that I have a thorough knowledge thereof. likewiſe, a competent knowledge of the Hiſtory of the Church from the earlieſt time to the period in which my work ends, and will be able to judge whether or not I have written with candour.

As to the world of mankind being ignorant of me, as you mention, it concerns me little: where I am known, however, I have the ſatisfaction to think I ſhall be believed

I ſhall adhere ſtrictly to truth in my repreſentations of you, your faith and practice; and I am conſcious to myſelf of having conducted this undertaking with upright intentions. And though you, in part of your letter, ſeem apprehenſive that my "*writings may impoſe on ſerious inquirers,*" yet in another part you aſſure me "*there is no apprehenſion of harm to you from my publica-*

"*tion.*" If you are of God, and led by him as you profess to be, my publication cannot hurt you, but will (agreeable to the scriptures) work for your good

Towards the close of your letter, you allow that "*I have an* "*undoubted right to publish an account of my own life, and with that ab*- "*stractedly considered*, you say you *have nothing to do.*" These expressions are so vague that I am at a loss to know what you really intend by them. If you mean to say, that in the publication of my life, I have no right to treat of my experience and connection with you, of your faith, &c. I candidly think you are mistaken Almost all authors, whose lives I have read, have given the religious opinions, &c. of the sect or sects they have been connected with, and I presume it will not be thought arrogance in me to follow their steps. I would further observe, that the proposition I made to you to examine my book, was in order that you might have an opportunity to point out to me your objections, and seasonably testify against whatever might be found amiss; and likewise, that you might have less plausibility to censure me in future of speaking untruths, as you have others who have separated from your society.

I still remain, with sentiments of respect,

Your Friend,

THOMAS BROWN.

*Cornwall, May* 12, 1809.

To this letter I received no reply. A few observations will conclude this prefatory introduction.

In relating the conversations I had with the Elders and others of the society, and the discourses I heard both in public and private, I have given them in their own words, except where their remarks were short, or not sufficiently explicit: to give the reader a just idea of their meaning I have enlarged, and wherein they were too prolix, I have abridged them; in every particular taking the utmost care not to misrepresent their real sentiments If the reader should find any seeming contradictions in the several discourses and explanations of their doctrines and faith, given in the ensuing publication, I am not chargeable with them, having only scrupulously related matters of fact.

In the Hiſtory annexed to this work, to avoid repetitions, I have omitted ſeveral things which are inſerted in the narration of my life; and I have been careful not to record any thing but what has been procured from authentick ſources, and the truth of which has been well ſubſtantiated. Though this ſociety may deem ſeveral of the tranſactions related, prejudicial to their cauſe, and on this accout will condemn both the work and its author, yet this, however, has not in the leaſt deterred me from my undertaking, and particularly from keeping cloſe to well authenticated facts, excluſive of every other conſideration; and I feel perſuaded that the unprejudiced reader will obſerve that candour pervades the whole. I am far from thinking I have made no miſtakes, notwithſtanding I have uſed all the care and precaution that I could. If any ſuch be pointed out to me, I ſhall be thankful for the intimation, eſpecially if there ſhould be a demand for a ſecond edition. I might add more, but nothing more is neceſſary to enable thoſe to judge of this work, who judge with underſtanding, impartiality, and candour. I therefore conclude by expreſſing my gratitude to God for his continued kindneſs and mercy through every period of my life, and for his gracious aid and benediction in enabling me to bring this arduous undertaking to a cloſe.

## ERRATA.

N. B. (b) ſignifies from the bottom of the page.

Page 61, line 3, for *we*, read *I*—p. 71 l. 6 (b) f. Matt. r. *Luke*—page 99, line 22, for cannot, read *can*—p. 134, l. 10 (b) f. in, r. *into*—p. 139, l. 7 (b) f. mortal, r. *immortal*—p. 140, l. 4 (b) f. thou, r. *though*—p. 158, l. 20 f. and, r. *that is*—p. 169, l. 8 (b) f. 1803, r. 1802—p. 230, l. 2 (b) f. pales, r. *pale*—p. 257, l. 9, f. March, r. *January*—p. 266, l. 7 (b) f. hat, r. *that*—p. 319, l. 2, f. companions, r. *companion*—p. 345, l. 9, dele *that*—p. 346, l. 18 (b) f. that, r. *his*—p. 347, l. 13 (b) f. barked, r. *acted*—p. 347, l. 14, f. lie, r. *lay*—p. 347, l. 17 (b) r. *with* after accompanied, and *by* after ſucceeded.

For Neſkauna, wherever it occurs, read *Niſkeuna*.

There are ſeveral other typographical errors, but not of ſufficient importance to be noted here.

# SUBSCRIBERS' NAMES.

*Cornwall, Orange Co.*
WM A CLARK, Esq. 24 copies,
Dr. Elihu Hedges,
David Sands,
Samuel Sayre, Esq.
Obadiah Smith, Esq.
William Jackson,
Wm Townsend,
Noah Townsend
Samuel H. Purdy,
Richard B Williams,
Wm Vail jun
John Coffey, Esq.
Edward Coffey,
Wm Brown, 6 cop.
Nathaniel Brown,
Jarvis R Brown,
Charles Southerland,
Margaret Mills,
Mary Brown,
Martin Hallock,
Mary Willet,
Samuel Sayre, jun
Wm Denniston,
John Arthur,
James Roe,
Henry Clark,
Cornelius H. Clark,
Reuben Clark,
Nathan Clark,
David Clark,
Francis Clark,
Joshua Clark,
Rev. J. Robertson,
Rev William Jewitt,
Elijah Horton,
Nathaniel Palmer,
Nathaniel Sacket,
Nathaniel S Sacket,
Sylvanus Wood,
Capt R Reynolds,
Durell Williams,
Capt Nath Ring,
Samuel Savage,
Wyatt Carr,
Stephen Crissey,
John Crissey,
Amos Whitmore,
Jabesh Green,
John Green,
Bartholomew Miller,
Nathaniel Barton,
Thos Carpenter, jr.
James Smith,
John Ketchum,
Samuel Reynolds,
Thos. Coleman,
Lewis Barret,
John Buckley,
Thos Walton
Josiah Tompkins
Samuel Allen
Cornelius Travis
Wm Southerland
Horace S Belden
O Cunningham
Thomas Willis
Gilbert Dean
Gilbert Webb
Joseph Southerland
Nathaniel Fuller
Elias Hand
Oliver Farrington
Isaac Vanduzer
John Hammond
John Brundage
Joseph Wood
Andrew J Caldwell
Abraham Finch
Shadrach Cooper

*Monroe*
Abraham Lett, Esq
John L O'Grady
A Southerland
Wm. Moffitt, Esq.

*Blooming-Grove.*
Capt. J M'Laughlin
Samuel Moffitt
Benjamin Brewster
J. Horton, Esq.

*Goshen.*
Thomas Thorne
Nath H White, Esq.
Reuben Hopkins, Esq.
Benj. Strong, Esq.
Thomas Waters
Edward Ely, Esq.
James G Horton
David Westcott
John G Hurton
Steph. Jackson, Esq
Michael A. Jones
Dr Thos. Wickham
Dr. Daniel Seward
George Moore
Wm Thompson, Esq.
James Everitt, Esq.
E. N. James, Esq.
Archibald Smith
Josiah Ketchum
Charles F Snover
Sidney A Knownton

*Minisink*
Joseph Smith, Esq
Nathan Arthur
P. E. Gumaer, Esq.

*West-Point.*
Lieut R. E Dansy
Lieut. A. Larrabee
Wm F. Hobart
Thomas North

*Warwick*
Samuel Ketchum
James Burt, Esq.

*Newburgh.*
Selah Reeve
David Mubois
Gilbert H Clement
J Fisk Esq
Benj. S Reeves, Esq.
I. Cooley, Esq
Wm Ross, Esq
Charles Dundall
Joseph Robertson

Wm H. Smith
Chauncy Grifwold
Ward M Gazlay
Daniel Belknap
William Pike
Afa Rutzer
Chefter Clark
David Wolf, Efq.
Wm. W. Sacket
Hiram Wells
Jas. Hamilton, Efq.
Chauncy Woodin
B. F Lewis, 2 cop.
John H. Walfh
Leonard Smith

*New-Windfor.*

A. Shultys, Efq.
Jos Morrice, Efq.
Jeffe Hulfe
Mofes Ely
Daniel B Moore

*Montgomery.*

John Blake, Efq.
David Mafon, Efq.
David Ruggles, Efq.
Wm. M Wells
J H Jackfon, Efq
Cornelius H. Dirker

*Wallkill*

Thos Brunfon
John Morrell
Horace Swezy
Thos. M. Clark
Ifaac Seely

*New-York.*

William Bufh
Sam. Wood, 50 cop.
Mary Hazard
Wm T. Robertfon
Rev John Boyd
John Hammond, jun.
J. H Shyres, 6 cop
G. Hodgfon, 2 cop.
William Elliot

*Raway*

Andrew Alfton.
Azel Roe
Elizabeth Edgar
Samuel Moore
Dr. Lewis Morgan
Ifaac Moore
Edward Moore

*Long-Ifland.*

John Everitt
Mary Everitt

*Mount-Pleafant.*

Solomon Underhill
John Hubbart

*Cortland-Town.*

John Green
Caleb Sutten
John Conklin

*Peekskill.*

Charles Dufenbury
Caleb Brown

*Poughkeepfie*

Hallock Patten
James Sands
Ifaac Everitt
James Reynolds
Jacob Noble

*Rhinebeck.*

Ebenezer Wood

*Hudfon.*

A. Woodworth, jun.
Benj. Cooper
Abner Auftin
Alanfon Carpenter
Alpheus Adams
Wm I Ofterhout
Edward Hulbert
Oliver H Allen
Wm E. Norman
Enoch Barnard
Oliver Wifwall
Daniel R. Waldo
Jared Plumb
W. Aylefworth
John Munfon
Henry Ludlow
G. Van Volkenburgh

*Claverack*

I Ten Broeck
Julia S. Ludlow
Phineas Freeland
Daniel B. Stow
Abm Jordan, Efq.
James Barnes
Wm. D. Miller
John Thompfon
Charles Price
Charles Smith
Wm. P. Snyder
Timothy Turner
John Martin

*Hillfdale.*

Samuel Bryan
Aaron Reed
Jonathan Turner
Apollo Robertfon
Gaius Stebbens
Benjamin Dakain

*Athens.*

Thomas Howe
Nathan Clark, 12 c.
Thos. Lawrence
Alexander Frazer
Ruffel Leffingwell
John T Nutterwell
Aaron Reed
Wm. Dobfon
A. G. Barnard
Timothy Witherell
Samuel Doxey
John W. Hays
David Shaw
Eben. Thornton
Matthias Van Loon
John Colefon
Zacheus Roache
Nich. I. Van Loon
Samuel Hamilton
Calvin Balis
Henry White
John Hull, jun.
John Williams
Benj. A. Howland
Wm. Hallenbeck

*Loonenburgh.*

Henry Wells, jun.

*Coxfakie*

Richard M'Carty
Wm Murry
J & C Cock

*Kinderhook.*

Caleb Finch
Wm. S. Gardenier

*Schodack*

Wm. I. Van Alftine
Jacob Baurhyte
Charles C Frink
R. B. Springfted
John Johnfon
Roelof Johnfon
S. Tompkins, Efq.
James Van Derpoel
Samuel Hitchcock
Wm Jacobee
Abm C Huyck
Howard A Simmons

*Coeymans.*

Jacob Parifh

*Caftleton.*

James M'Clafkey

*Albany.*

Michael Flack
James Daniel
James Thorne
Jofeph P. Barney
Samuel P Penny
Philip Barnop
John Taylor
Weeden Lincoln
Juftus Cafe
Jacob Eaton
Levi Perry
Caleb Mathews
Levi Page
Seth Watkins
Ephraim Mandell
Henry Carpenter
Alfred Parker
V Auftin
Henry Dickinfon
Ifaac Van Bufkirk
Wm. M'Harg
Philip Talbot
Nathaniel Niles
Jofeph Golden
Wm. G Taylor
Edward Hunter
Wm Lamb
Dennis Allen
Henry Vifher
Eliakim Ford
Wm. W. Manfill

*Troy.*

Parker & Blifs, 50 c.
Henry Townfend
George Lent
John Nafew
Aaron Rider, jun.
Benjamin Vail
Nathaniel Hazard
Rev. David Butler
E. Oftrander, M. D.
Job Collins
Jofiah Chapman
Samuel Scobey
Caleb Curtis
Mary Campbell
Lewis Richards
Afa Sheldon
James Wallace
Henry Fero
Jonathan Warren
Abner Fofter
Abijah Fowler
C. J. Newcomb, 6 c.
Abraham Eager, 12 c.
Nathan Eaftman

*Balfton.*

James Clark
John Kelley
Daniel Rathbone
Reuben Thurfton
Adonijah Skinner
Beriah Palmer

*Lanfingburgh.*

Levinus R. Winne

*Greenbufh.*

Jere. Clark, jun.
Jacob Wood, Efq.

*Canaan.*

Mehitable Bramhall

*Clinton, Dutchefs Co.*

Capt. Ifaac Ruffell
Jacob Noble

*Camden, Oneida Co.*

Allen Sperry

*New-Rochell.*

Rev. Eben Smith

*Schenectady.*

John B. Clute, jun.

*Water-Vliet*

E. Van Denburgh
Daniel Fort
Wm. James
Aaron D. Barrows
Abraham Males
Henry Mansfield
John Gaddes
John Truefdell
Ifaac Van Denburgh
Jacob Lanfing, jun.
John Mafcraft
Wm Kane
Jofeph Whittaker
Ifaac Fowler

*Nifkeuna.*

Rev. Thos. Romaine
Derick Groat
Nicholas Groat
John G. Clute
Thomas Slats
Michael Freligh
Tobias Putman
Philip Linderbecker
Eldan F. Goodin
Seth Veeder

*Coventry, Conn.*

Leon. Handee, 20 c.

*Hebron, Conn.*

Benj. Davenport

*Kingfton, Canada.*

John Hodgfon

N B. The names of many fubfcribers in feveral of the above mentioned and other places have not yet come to hand; but as in printing the work it has amounted to above forty pages more than was expected, the deficiency in this lift of fubfcribers, it is prefumed, will be readily excufed.

AN

# ACCOUNT, &c.

## PART I.

*From the time of the Author's acquaintance with the people called Shakers, and joining their Society, until he began to doubt; and more minutely examine into the propriety of their Faith, Doctrines, and Practice.*

A FEW ſketches of my life, previouſly to my becoming acquainted with the people who are the ſubject of this *hiſtory*, may, perhaps, be acceptable to my readers.

I was born the 26th day of May, 1766, of reputable parents, who then reſided in the city of New-York. Soon after my father joined the Society of the people called *Quakers*; and with an acquaintance and ſome connection with this people I was brought up. In my juvenile years, I was much diſpoſed to ſerious inquiry and reflection; and thought if I lived to be a man, I would not be wicked as I ſaw many were. But when I attained the age of fourteen years, I became immoral and wicked, and continued ſo until my eighteenth year.—Then I became *thoughtful* and *ſerious*, which produced a reformation in my life and practice; and at length I was brought to experience what I had been an utter ſtranger to before, and which was what is believed by Chriſtians in general to be that converſion which entitles the ſoul to the kingdom of heaven. But loſing a feeling ſenſe of what I had enjoyed, I again had my trials, as I could not reſt in any thing ſhort of true peace of mind. About three years after I had become ſeriouſly diſpoſed, it was impressed on my mind as a duty, to appoint meetings, and to speak by way of exhortation to those who assembled to hear me. In the year 1787, I joined the people called Quakers, and was admitted as a member of their society: with them I continued about three years, and spoke several times in their meetings. Then I left that society, so far as related to particular membership; but still continued to hold meetings occasionally in a separate standing, and often preached among the Methodists. In the year 1793, I was received a member of that society. Soon after they gave me a certificate to officiate in public, by way of exhortation. Accordingly I travelled, in connection with that society, about two years; in which time I became so much reduced in my circumstances, that I was necessitated to engage in some business to support my family. Notwithstanding, I did not wholly neglect that which I conceived to be my duty in the ministerial line.

For about two years previously to my joining the people who are the subject of the ensuing publication, I was not, in a strict sense, a member of any sect, and thought I would never again join any, unless I could find a society whose practices, in my view, were more conformable with the precepts of Christianity. In short, for the space of a year before I became acquainted with the people called Shakers, I entertained an opinion, that the millennium was near at hand, and that I should live to see it: and I wished to find a people prepared, according to the scripture account, to meet Christ at his second coming.

I had often heard of the people called Shakers, by verbal accounts, as a strange people; but on the 13th of April, 1798, (on a journey to Philadelphia) I saw a small pamphlet, written by V Rathbone, which gave an account of them, which surpassed every thing I had heard or read before respecting any people professing religion. I thought it not possible, that any sect in this enlightened age of the world, especially in this country, could answer that description. I thought that they might be very different from what they were represented, as truly religious people have always been misrepresented. I had understood they held to some doctrines, which appeared to me more pure than professed by others. I was therefore determined, (if God pleased) to go and see them, and examine for myself. Accordingly, some time in August, (the same year) I was at *Albany*, and the first Sabbath after I arrived in the city, I went to see them; a number of whom resided at *Watervliet*, commonly called *Neskauna*, (eight miles north-west from *Albany*) I attended their meeting: they sat silent a few minutes, then arose and stood in their order, and sung a tune without words; after which, four or five sung a more lively tune, to which the others *danced*. After dancing about half an hour, they all kneeled in silence a few minutes; as soon as they arose, their leader spoke of an intermission. During which, they retired to a dwelling-house on the other side of the road, opposite to the meeting-house, and left me ruminating what kind of a people and religion this could be; for they appeared to me very solemn, and I thought they were a sincere people. At the conclusion of the afternoon meeting, I wished to converse with some of them; as I began, from their solemn appearance, to conceive a favourable opinion of them. But as no one spoke to me, I hardly knew how to introduce myself. However, I was determined not to leave them, without farther information respecting their faith, &c. I saw I was losing an opportunity to speak to them, (as they were silently returning to their places of abode.) I therefore immediately spoke to a young man, and said, I have often heard of these people, and believe I have heard many things which are *false*; I have now come some distance to see them, and cannot feel satisfied to return without having some conversation, in order to a better understanding of their religious principles, than I have hitherto had from hearsay and flying reports, and I would thank you to inform me where, and of whom I may gain this information? He pleasantly replied, "Your request can be granted: go with me to my *father's*, and he will give you whatever information you desire."

I gladly accepted of his invitation, and went home with him. I was kindly received, and soon invited to dine. After which, I had an agreeable conversation with the young man's father, (Benjamin Youngs.) Towards evening he invited me to tarry all night. I did so; and we conversed till two o'clock in the morning, on various points of their faith; of which, for the sake of brevity, I think best to give now only the substance, as these subjects will be treated of hereafter. I shall state our discourses by way of questions (for many I asked) and answers, which may serve as the contents of all that follows to be treated of in the course of this work, respecting their doctrines; for he possessed as much information as any one I ever conversed with among them, and was as able to communicate his ideas. And I the more willingly insert the substance of our discourses here, as the account I received from him, corresponded with what I heard from the *Elders*, and others in their faith, for near two years afterwards. At which time, they began to hold forth to me the real doctrines and practice of the church; which appeared to me (and will hereafter to the reader) somewhat different, particularly from those passages which I have, for this reason, inclosed in brackets—thus, [ ].

## *THE SUBSTANCE OF MY ADDRESS.*

I have come to see you, and to have a little conversation (if agreeable) concerning your faith and religious profession; as I sincerely desire to know the way of life and salvation To prove all things; hold fast that which is good—1 *Thess.* v 21.

The reply was, "To those who come sincerely to in-" quire of us respecting our faith, we are willing, accord-" ing to our ability, to give all the information they de-" sire."

1. *What is your fundamental principle?*

"We believe it is *sin* which has separated all souls " from God, his favour, and true happiness Therefore " our fundamental principle is, to *confess and forsake all* " *sin*, and live an holy, upright, just life. Believing that " this is the only way we can return to God, be heard " by him, have his favour, and enjoy true happiness."

2. *As this is the fundamental principle of all religious people, wherein do you materially differ from others?*

"We materially differ from others in not only con-
"fessing our sins, but in receiving power to *forsake them.*
"We have experienced the second coming of Christ, and
"are in (what is called) the millennium*; a time that
"has been prophecied of, in which Satan shall be bound†,
"and a dispensation of greater power and grace given
"than ever hath been before. It being now the time
"the Lord is searching Jerusalem (i. e. the church) as
"with candles.‡ Therefore, no hypocrite can abide in
"this church, continuing in hypocrisy, or in the com-
"mission of any private sin whatever, as such may in
"other churches."

He gave me all the information he could respecting the first revelation, and preaching of the gospel of the second coming of Christ. He also discoursed of the chosen witnesses and servants of God, (*Ann Lee, Wm. Lee,* and *James Whittaker*) who received the first gifts of the gospel. In the next place he gave a history of their coming from England in the year 1774, to America, and settling here in the wilderness. Then he recited the poverty, difficulties, trials, labours, and persecutions, they passed through; and mentioned a variety of miracles wrought in support of their mission, and the gospel they preached, (a more particular account of the whole of which will be seen hereafter.) He mentioned many scripture prophecies that spake of this day and work: and I thought he gave many good reasons for all he advanced.

3. *What reasons, or rather proof, have you, to believe that Christ has made his second appearance, and that you are in a superior dispensation to all others?*

He answered—"We have abundant proof, both ex-
"ternal and internal. Outwardly we know by the fruit;
"as Christ said, *By their fruits ye shall know them*—(Math.
"vii. 16.) Also, *by this shall all men know that ye are my*

* *This was what I did not expect to hear. Glorious news, indeed! thought I, if true. I was almost in transports.*

† *Rev. xx. 2.* ‡ *Zeph. i. 12.*

" *disciples, if ye have love one to another*—(John xiii. 35.)
" And further, all the apostolic gifts are in the church,
" as the gifts of miracles, &c. According to the prom-
" ise, *These signs shall follow them that believe; in my name*
" *they shall cast out devils, they shall speak with new tongues.*
" Matt. xvi. 17. (This being a proof with us, that oth-
" er churches are not the churches of Christ; these signs
" follow not; miracles are all ceased among them)—
" And inwardly we have greater evidence By *confes-*
" *sing our sins*, according to to the *gift* of God, we receive
" power to forsake and to feel forgiveness of all our sins.
" In consequence of which, in our spiritual travail we
" know the promise is fulfilled, *I will cleanse them from all*
" *unrighteousness.*" 1 John, i. 9.

4. *How and on what condition are persons received as members?*

" By making an honest confession of all their sins in
" thought, word, and deed, which they can at the time
" remember to have ever committed. The confession is
" made to one or two of the Elders—[and they tell no
" person what has been told them, but endeavour to bu-
" ry all in oblivion.] This was the gift of God to the
" church in the first opening of the gospel, or dawning
" of this dispensation, and likewise the practice of the an-
" cient people of God, as we read in Josh. vii. 19. Prov.
" xxii. 13. James v. 16."

5. *What is done if sins are committed after confession, and what is your order of excommunication?*

" Such among us who fall into sin, confess the same,
" and are laboured with by the Elders accordingly.—
" But they cannot hold any in union, who, contrary to
" their own faith, and counsel of the Elders, continue to
" live in the practice of any known sin, [on any other
" accounts they disown none.] We believe it is as ne-
" cessary to forsake as to confess"

6. *What is your method of church government?*

" By a ministration, according to the Mosaic dis-
" pensation. God spake to Moses, and he delivered the
" words he received to the people. So in this church,
" Christ is the head: his second coming is spiritual in his
" people. The first in the ministration is, (her we call)

" the Mother of the church. She, immediately receiv-
" ing the revelation of the mind and will of God, com-
" municates the same to the Elders, whom, in this gift,
" she has appointed to preside over, or to have the care
" of the church and families, in the several places where
" they are settled. Those Elders are obedient to her;
" those they have the care of, are obedient to them.
" [Though all have the privilege to act their own faith,
" as the gospel don't bind creatures any farther than to
" forsake all sin, and every practice each individual feels
" condemned for. As to civil, immaterial, or non-essen-
" tial matters, we let all think, and act for themselves;
" and do not differ with, and excommunicate for senti-
" ments or conduct, that does not immediately concern
" our salvation. The Elders do not usurp authority
" over any, only advise, and leave them to act their own
" faith without censure] We are to do what we are
" conscious is right, and refrain from what we are con-
" scious is wrong?"

7. *What is your faith concerning worship?* I see you dif-
fer from all others in praying and singing; *and what scripture or reasons have you for dancing?*

" True and acceptable worship is performed by those
" only who keep the commandments of God: accord-
" ing to the words of Christ, *If ye love me, keep my com-*
" *mandments*—(John xiv. 15.) Prayer is the sincere de-
" sire and breathing of the soul; therefore, we seldom
" pray vocally; as, God knows the language and desires
" of our hearts, a composition of words, expressive there-
" of, is, to him (who knows best what we stand in need
" of,) not necessary. As to singing, though we sing
" vocally, we seldom sing hymns, or a composition of
" words. Every soul praises God according to its state,
" and travail. Our singing is that which St. John
" heard, (Rev. xiv. 3, 4.) that no man could learn, (or
" understand) but those who were redeemed from the
" earth, and not defiled with women, or rather (accord-
" ing to our travail) the song of redemption and com-
" plete salvation. Vocal prayer, and singing a compo-
" sition of words, are accepted when done in the gift of

" God ;* and at some future time we may be so led to " pray and praise. Dancing is the gift of God to the " church, or the way in which it has been led. In this " exercise we receive that strength, and consolation, to " which the world are total strangers. This is reason " sufficient for us, if we could produce no other. But " it may be clearly proved that it was a worship among " the ancient people of God ; and prophecied of, that it " should be again restored to the people of God ; partic- " ularly by Jeremiah, xxxi. 13."

8. *I have understood you forbid marriage, and that you separate man and wife ; what is your faith and conduct herein ?*

" We forbid no one ; we say, *It is better to marry than* " *to burn ;* that is, it is better to marry than to do worse. " *All men cannot receive this saying, save they to whom it* " *is given.* Christ says farther, *He that is able to receive* " *it, let him receive it*—(Matt. xix. 11, 12.) It is given " unto us, and we are able. We have come out of the " order of natural generation, to travail in regeneration. " *In the resurrection, they neither marry, nor are given in mar-* " *riage*—(Matt. xxii. 30.) This second coming of Christ, " and last dispensation, is that resurrection.

" And as to separating man and wife, they are not " separated against their feelings and faith ; [but are " left to act their own faith, and live together if they " choose, or think best so to do.] You have proof of " this before your eyes ; it is now seven years since I " joined this people ; I still live with my wife and fam- " ily, and transact business for myself. The gospel " does not bind creatures ; the Elders usurp author- " ity over no one, but the church can hold no husband " and wife in union, who live together after the course " of the world. We believe the gospel requires us, not " only to forsake all the vain pomps and vanities of the " world, but likewise all the carnal desires, and incli- " nations of the flesh."

In order that I might have a clear understanding of the doctrine respecting marriage, he gave me an account,

* *At this time I little knew what they meant by the gift of God.*

according to their faith, of the increasing work of God, in order for man's complete salvation and redemption, in the different dispensations of God's grace, from the fall of our first parents to the present day; particularly represented, or signified in Ezekiel's vision of the holy waters—chap. +v.47. Also an increasing purity in heart and practice, being required in a succeeding and superior dispensation, which was not required in an antecedent, and inferior.

As these are the principal subjects on which we conversed at that time, I shall proceed with my narative until our next conference. I parted with this kind family in the morning, the father of which, earnestly invited me to come and see them again. I told him, I thought I should. I returned to *Albany*, and first went to see my friend *Wm. Carter*; I told him I had been to see the people called *Shakers*. He invited me into a private room, and desired me to inform him what I thought of them.

I told him I had a more favourable opinion of them, than I had before I saw them I gave him an account of the meeting, my kind reception, and principal part of the conversation with *B. Youngs*, with the reasons he advanced for their faith; and concluded by saying, I am surprised you should live many years, so nigh such good people, and never once go to see them: I wish you now to go, and you will hear such preaching, and doctrine, and see such practice as you never heard, nor saw before; and afterwards you will be glad you went.

He said, "I will go." I bid him farewell, and in a few days arrived at home. But the Shakers, and the millennium doctrine, my friend B. Youngs had preached to me, was daily in my thoughts; for I had already caught some of their spirit, and could not be easy without seeing them again.

I left home on the 14th of November, and walked to *Albany*, (one hundred miles,) where I arrived the 19th. I first went to see my friend *John Taylor*; he soon told me "I must go to *Wm. Carter's*, and make a confession, for I had ruined the family." I told him I knew not what he meant. He said, "Try and recollect" I replied, I am not conscious of doing any wrong, so I shall make myſelf eaſy. He did not keep me in ſuſpenſe long, but informed me, that "in conſequence of my preaching to *Carter* about the Shakers, he had been up to ſee them, confeſſed his ſins, and joined them; on account of which, his wife and children were very much diſſatisfied."

Next morning I went to ſee him; as ſoon as I entered his houſe, his wife was all in a rage; ſhe ordered me out of the houſe, got the horſe whip, ſhook it over my head, round and about me with many threats, and ordered one of her children to go and tell her eldeſt ſon, (who was in town,) to come home, and he would do ſo and ſo. In ſhort, ſhe abuſed me, and uſed very harſh expreſſions. I tried to moderate her anger with mild words, and to reaſon with her, but ſhe was quite outrageous, and *Carter* ſat ſilent, not daring, apparently, to ſpeak a word. I told her, I hoped ſhe would ſee her error, and left her with a conſciouſneſs that I had done no wrong, having only complied with the earneſt requeſt of her huſband. Afterwards their eldeſt ſon threatened to ſhoot me, or ſome way take my life. I wrote to him on the conſequences of ſuch threats, informing him if I heard the leaſt whiſper more of the like kind, I would proceed as the law directed.

I left *Albany* 21ſt of November, 3 o'clock, P. M in order to pay *B. Youngs* another viſit. Here I may obſerve that at that time, there was not a houſe on the road from the ſuburbs of the city, to the Shaker ſettlement; and by reaſon of a deep ſnow, which fell the preceding evening, I got loſt in the woods, and froze both my feet, and did not get to my deſtined place till 3 o'clock in the morning, when I was quite exhauſted, and on the point of periſhing. The family received me with tenderneſs, and adminiſtered to my neceſſities. But notwithſtanding every attention which was paid to me, it was eight or nine days before I was able to walk. I tarried ten days, during which time, and for ſeven years afterwards, their kindneſs to me, was ſuch as to cauſe me to remember them with gratitude and affection.

B. Youngs being a man of a friendly, ſociable turn, we had much converſation on the faith, as profeſſed by him and his brethren; to all which I made no objections, except wherein it was neceſſary to gain a clear underſtanding of any ſubject or point, on which he was treating. Indeed I did not go to ſee them to object and diſpute, but to aſk queſtions, and gain information. I ſhall treat the ſubjects reſpecting the doctrines of the church, as in the firſt conference.

Previouſly to our entering on particular ſubjects, reſpecting their faith and practice, I obſerved to him that having conſidered the ſubject of our former diſcourſe, and having thereby been enabled to think favourably of the people with whom he was in union, I had come to have ſome farther converſation, and if he was in a ſuperior diſpenſation of light and grace, I hoped I might become convinced thereof, and then I ſhould be willing to take up my croſs and follow Chriſt in the way that he profeſſed

He replied, "I am happy to ſee you, and am willing "to give you all the ſatisfaction in my power; and "hope your labour and ſuffering, in coming to ſee us, "and our converſation, will not be in vain, but wiſh "you may be richly rewarded"

9. *I have underſtood there are ſome among you, who have all temporal things in common, ſomewhat like unto the primitive chriſtians?*

"The principal motive, deſire, and labour, of the "children of this world, is to gain a temporal intereſt, "to accumulate wealth for themſelves and poſterity, "to conſume it, as the apoſtle expreſſes it, *upon their* "*luſts*—(James iv. 3.) But the principal motive, deſire, "and labour, of the people of God, and true followers "of Chriſt, is to *lay up a treaſure in heaven*, and to labour "for the ſupport of the goſpel, and thoſe who are obe- "dient thereto; become willing when taught, or re- "quired, by the gift of God, to give up their temporal "intereſt, and join in a united one; or, in other words, "to ſupport a joint intereſt, and gather into family and "church order, having all things common.

"The church is made up of many families, (though "in ſpirit and practice, all are one.) The number in "each family, is according to the convenience of houſes,

"and circumſtances. A deacon in each family, tranſ-
"acts the temporal buſineſs: others have no worldly
"concern, as food, raiment, and all things neceſſary,
"are by him provided; and what each family has to
"ſpare, is carried to the office, and depoſited in the care
"of the deacon of the church, to be by him given for
"charitable purpoſes, to thoſe who are in want, and for
"the ſupport of the goſpel. Thus it is among us, (i. e.
"thoſe who are brought into family, or church order, as
"before mentioned.) according as it was under the
"power of the goſpel formerly: *all that believed, were*
"*together, and had all things common*."—Acts ii. 44.

10. *Is it particularly required of all to come into this joint intereſt and give up their property? and are perſons who have no property, as willingly received, and made equal ſharers?*

"[None are required contrary to their feelings and
"faith; each one acts his own faith, particularly in
"all civil things, that do not obſtruct the growth, or in-
"creaſe of the ſoul's ſalvation; and thoſe who are poor,
"are as willingly received as the rich.]"

11. *If thoſe who have depoſited intereſt in common ſtock, and laboured faithfully for a longer, or ſhorter time, and finally loſe their faith, or for ſome cauſe, chooſe to go away, is what they depoſited, returned?*

"The church do what is juſt, and right, in all caſes.
"I have known inſtances of it being returned, and
"compenſation made for their labours."

12. *What do you believe, particularly, concerning the ſcriptures?*

"We believe they are a true record of the work of
"God in paſt diſpenſations, written by inſpiration, and
"profitable to thoſe to whom they were directed, and
"to thoſe under the diſpenſation in which they were
"written; and that they end under the diſpenſation of
"the firſt coming of Chriſt. Nevertheleſs, we believe
"them fraught with prophecies, from beginning to end,
"of a further, and final diſplay of God's grace in a fu-
"ture day, when the *man of ſin* would be revealed, and
"a full, complete, and finiſhed ſalvation obtained."

13. *What do you believe concerning (what ſome profeſſors call) univerſal and ſaving light?*

" We believe Chriſt has *enlightened every man that com-*
" *eth into the world*—(John 49,) and that a talent, or tal-
" ents, is *given to every man to improve*—(Matt. 25,) and
" all who live according to their light, and improve the
" talents that God has given, have found juſtification,
" and acceptance with God. For as the ſcriptures ex-
" preſs it, a manifeſtation of the ſpirit, is given to every
" man to profit withal—(1 Cor. xii. 7,) and diſobedi-
" ence thereto, is the cauſe of condemnation."

14. *What is your faith concerning juſtification?*

" We believe all thoſe have found juſtification, who
" have been obedient to their light, and knowledge; and
" as we are obedient to the goſpel of the ſecond coming
" of Chriſt, we find juſtification, and ſanctification."

15 *Then do you believe in perfection, or a ſtate of freedom from ſin, attainable in this life?*

" Such who are obedient to the goſpel of the ſecond
" coming of Chriſt, and abiding in the travail of regen-
" eration, overcome all evil, ſo as not to ſin in thought,
" word, or deed, and the wicked one toucheth them
" not."—1 John :v. 18.

16. *What do you believe concerning perſeverance, and falling from grace?*

" We believe creatures may receive the grace of God,
" and experience a good degree of the power of the
" goſpel; nevertheleſs fall away, and become darker in
" their minds than ever they were before. Though we
" believe a ſtate attainable, from whence there will be
" no more going out."—Rev. iii. 12.

17. *What is your faith reſpecting the condition of man in the fall?*

" Mankind in a ſtate of nature, (or before they hear
" the goſpel, and yield obedience to it,) are ſpiritually
" dead, loſt and ſunk far from God; and of their own
" nature, inclined to evil continually. But as the natural
" ſun ſhineth on the world, giving warmth and life, ſo
" doth the ſun of righteouſneſs ſhine on the hearts of all;
" and according to the light and warmth received, they
" have power to improve; and when they hear the goſ-
" pel in the gift of God. they have power given to chooſe
" or refuſe. The goſpel, according to the diſpenſation

" of it, is the power of God unto ſalvation, raiſing ſuch " out of the fall as believe, receive, and obey it."

18. *What do you believe concerning the doctrine of election and reprobation?*

" We believe in election. Chriſt is the elect of God, " and all men in him are elect. He is the head of eve- " ry man. They are not created machines, but have a " will and power given to chooſe or refuſe; and when " they believe in, and receive the goſpel, particularly of " Chriſt's ſecond coming, they are benefitted by this " election. We deny that God ever decreed to ſhut " any ſoul eternally from his mercy and favour."

19. *It appears to me you believe in the final reſtoration?*

" We believe the goſpel in the power of it, will be " offered to every ſoul, if not in time, in eternity, and " finally will prevail, and conquer, and bring all crea- " tures back from whence they are fallen; and *every knee* " *ſhall bow, and every tongue confeſs Chriſt to the glory of* " *God.*"

20. *What is your faith concerning the divinity of Chriſt and his ſufferings?*

*Do you believe he was co-equal and co-eternal with the Father?*

" We believe him to have been what the ſcriptures " teſtify of him; that is, the *ſecond Adam*, like unto the " firſt, before he ſinned; and by Chriſt the ſecond Adam, " was in a meaſure reſtored, (and now is fully reſtored " in the true ſenſe, by Chriſt's ſecond coming,) that gift " of God, and revelation, which, by diſobedience, the " firſt Adam loſt. And by the revelation of the power " and ſpirit of God to the man Chriſt, he was enabled " to keep out of all ſin, *though in all points tempted as we* " *are*—(Heb. vii. 15) becauſe he took upon him our " fallen nature. Hence we believe Chriſt was like other " men, ſin excepted: but he being endowed with the " ſpirit and power of God, according to the apoſtle; " *God giveth not the ſpirit by meaſure unto him*—(John iii. 34) " that is, God, by his ſpirit, dwelt in the man Chriſt Je- " ſus, and in this reſpect he was God and man.

" As to his being co-eternal, and co-equal with the " Father, as man he was not ſo; but the ſpirit of God

" that was in him, (as before mentioned,) and by which " he was actuated, was so. Therefore, in the begin- " ning, was what St. John calls the *Word;* and this " word that dwelt in the man Christ, *was God;* and by " this all-powerful word, *all things were made, and without* " *it, was not any thing made, that was made.* And in this " *word was life,* and by Christ's abiding in this life, he " destroyed the sinful, or fallen nature, which he took " upon him; and he then became the first born in the " new creation, the light of the world, and an example " to all men.

" Now as by this *word,* all things were made, so by " the same, did Christ perform all the miracles of which " we read. This *word* or spirit was the same that ap- " peared to the patriarchs, and by which the prophets " spake. And though Christ was, as hath been repre- " sented, nevertheless, he passed through heavy trials, and " deep sufferings. For example, his being tempted of " the devil, or the evil nature, the flesh, the old man of " sin; which after his trials and sufferings in resisting " the same in all its cravings, *angels came and ministered* " *unto him.* Like unto other men, he was dependent on " God, and prayed to him. Of himself he had no abil- " ity to work miracles; *But the Father,* saith he, *that* " *dwelleth in me, he doth the works*—(John xx. 10.) As a " man, when he was on earth, he knew not, and now he " is in heaven, he knows not the secrets of the Father, " (Matt. xxvii. 36,) any farther than they are commu- " nicated unto him. Wherefore we have that expression " in the Revelations: *The revelation of Jesus Christ, which* " *God gave unto him*—Rev. i. 1.

" As a man, he wept over Jerusalem. As a man, he " was in an agony and prayed. As a man, on the cross " he cries, *My God, my God, why hast thou forsaken me?* " Here we see clearly no part of the deity, or divine " nature suffered. If God had forsaken him, how then " could he be God in any other sense than I have al- " ready described.

" We do not believe as Dr. Watts expresses it, that,

" *God the mighty maker died,*
" *For man the creature's sin.*

" He opened a way for all to follow him, in that line " of obedience to his Father, by a daily crofs, even to " the death of the crofs—(Phil. ii. 8.) In confequence " of which he was accepted of the Father, and became " the firft born among many brethren.—Rom. viii. 29.

" God cannot, nor ever will be known any further " than he manifefts himfelf. Chrift was the greateft " manifeftation, or revelation of God, that had ever " been made. According to his own words, *He that* " *hath feen me, hath feen the Father*. That is, his wifdom, " power, holinefs, forbearance, kindnefs, benevolence, " compaffion, and love. In fhort, he is our example; " and in every refpect, whereunto we are called, we " muft follow him in that path which he has marked " out for us; and even to become, according to the " apoftle, *partakers of his fufferings*, and in order to reign " with him, we muft fuffer with him—(1 Peter vii. 13. " 2 Tim. ii. 12) We do not believe in imputed right- " eoufnefs, the doctrine of atonement, nor Chrift's mak- " ing fatisfaction for fin."

21. *What is your faith refpecting what is called the facrament of bread and wine?*

" We believe it may be right for all fuch as are under " the difpenfation of the firft coming of Chrift, or have " not heard the gofpel of his fecond coming, to partake " of it, if they do it confcientioufly and in fincerity.— " For we read, *As often as ye eat of this bread, and drink* " *of this cup, ye do fhew the Lord's death till he come*—(1 Cor. " xi 26. And we know he has come; and we drink " with him of that new wine, which he promifed to give " when he fhould come in his Father's kingdom."

22. *What do you believe concerning war?*

" It belongs to thofe who are of the fpirit of this " world, to fight. *Chrift's kingdom is not of this world;* " (John xviii. 36) therefore his fervants cannot fight. " And the apoftle James fays, *Wars and fighting come from* " *your lufts, that war in your members*"—iv. 1.

23. *What is your faith and practice concerning fwearing before the civil magiftrate?*

" Our faith and practice is according to the precept " of Chrift, *Not to fwear at all*, neither by one thing nor "the other; but to let our communication be *yea, yea;* "*and nay, nay: for whatsoever is more than these, cometh of* "*evil.*—(Matt. v. 34.) And when called upon, we af- "firm; and speak the truth on all occasions."

24. *What is your faith respecting the ministry, or in what manner are persons qualified and authorised to preach?*

"We believe no one can preach the gospel, who has "it not. That no one can administer that to others, "to profit, which he has not known and experienced "himself. Likewise, none are true gospel ministers, ex- "cept they be qualified and sent of God, according to "Romans x. 15. And any persons, whose conduct and "conversation becometh the gospel, and feeling it im- "pressed on their minds, and believing it to be their du- "ty, or what is required of them, and have the gift and "and ability to administer the gospel; and the church "feeling union with them therein, they are then allowed "to act accordingly."

25. *What do you believe concerning the resurrection?*

"We believe, that, *By man came death; by man* (Christ) "*came also the resurrection from the dead,* (1 Cor. xv. 21) "viz. a resurrection from a death in sin, i. e. out of the "evil nature, to a life of righteousness. It is the soul "of man in the fall, in a state of sin, and lost from God, "that is the subject of the resurrection, and not these "vile corruptible bodies. According to the apostle, "*It is sown a natural body, it is raised a spiritual body.* If "fallen, lost creatures, while they are talking and deter- "mining, in their carnal imaginations, with respect to "the resurrection, were careful to forsake their sins, and "know a resurrection from a state of sin to a state of "righteousness, they would then be more able to judge "concerning it. Now, though we thus endeavour to "give honest, inquiring minds a *reason of the hope that is* "*in us,* (1 Pet. iii. 15) and of our faith, doctrines, and "practice, nevertheless, they are all such as we have "been led into by the *gift of God:* In which gift we ex- "perience that redemption and salvation, peace and con- "solation, we cannot communicate unto those who have "never had faith. Which is sufficiently convincing, and

" much more ſatisfactory to us, than all outward argu-
" ments and reaſons that can poſſibly be produced."

Thus I have thrown together a ſummary of their doctrines, faith, and practice; and in giving the account, I have ſcrupulouſly retained their dialect, and ſhall endeavour to do it, where neceſſary, throughout this work.

This man appeared very deſirous to gain me to the faith He had ſacrificed conſiderable of his intereſt and friendſhip for the ſake of it. Therefore he was zealous to gain me to that, for which he had *counted all things but as droſs*—(Phil. iii 7) It appeared to be his delight to expatiate on the bleſſings and privileges of this glorious goſpel, (as he often called it) the glorious riſing of the ſun of righteouſneſs, for the complete ſalvation and redemption of fallen man. He appeared to be exceedingly happy in the contemplation of his having lived to ſee the day which has been the ſubject of prophecy and prayer.

He recommended the Shakers as a *peculiar people, zealous of good works*—(Titus ii. 4) labouring after holineſs; *heavenly in all their converſation;* (Phil. iii. 20) exemplary in all their conduct. He often inſiſted on the following portions of ſcripture, as a rule to judge who are the people of God; viz. " By their fruits ye ſhall know them. And by this ſhall all men know that ye are my diſciples, if ye have love one to another."

He invited me to ſtay two or three weeks, and go among them and ſee for myſelf, till I was fully ſatisfied. He wiſhed me to become acquainted with ſome of the large families, who were brought into family and church order, that I might ſee what union, love, peace, and quietneſs, prevailed among them; and how different they were from the people and profeſſors of the world. He aſſerted, that " all thoſe reports that had circulated a-
" bout them were falſe; and what I had read in V. Rath-
" bone's pamphlet, were miſrepreſentations; all which
" was no more than what Chriſt foretold, that *They ſhould*
" *say all manner of evil, againſt his followers, falſely for his*
" *sake.* But he told them to *rejoice and be exceeding glad,*
" *for great ſhould be their reward in heaven.*" Matt. v. 11.

According to his advice, I went to see some of the large families, or those who had all things in common, or supported a joint interest. I conversed with divers persons concerning the faith.

I returned to B. Youngs' family. He asked me what hindered me from joining them I told him, they held to some doctrines with which I could not fully unite. He said, "That is of little consequence; we do not dif-"fer with one another because we cannot believe alike "in every respect; neither shall we with you. And "those things you cannot see into, leave them, and em-"brace or unite with what you do believe is right."

I considered of all I had heard and seen; I thought assuredly I saw that order, peace, and union, I never saw before. I felt a love towards the people for the love and kindness they had manifested to me. I thought if they were what they professed to be, they were just such a Christian people as I long had wanted to find. Therefore, in order to be initiated as a member of the church, I saw no impropriety in telling one or two persons in the church, all the sins I had committed; and thought of a precept in the epistle of St. James: "Confess your "faults one to another;" and of several other passages of scripture on this subject. Finally, the evening before I left them, I came to a conclusion; and spake to one of the brethren, who stood in the appointment to hear openings, (as they call it) and we retired into a private room. Before I began to confess, I kneeled, (seeing me do so, he did the same) with silent desires and breathing to God, that I might be enabled to confess in a right spirit, and that he would bless me in my undertaking. And in as much sincerity as ever I did any thing in my life, I opened every sin and every thing wherein I believed I had done wrong, that I could remember.

Now nearly all who had heard of these people, believed them to be very enthusiastic, and their religion unscriptural; therefore I expected to be counted a fool for joining them; but this I did not regard; as religion and the salvation of my soul I regarded (and do still) above all things in this world. Therefore I was willing to take up any cross, and make trial, with them, of that power over all ſin, and a continual peace and ſenſe of the love of God, of which they teſtified. This is what I long had deſired and prayed for. Therefore I felt willing to forſake the world, to live with a people who enjoyed this Chriſtian privilege And as there was no other way thoroughly to know what theſe people were in their faith and practice, but by becoming one of them; and to prove the truth of what they profeſſed, I made a beginning, and entered in by faith and confeſſion.

Now if the reader proceeds regularly, from page to page, he will ſee an exact ſtatement of all matters as they happened, and how I came out at laſt.

On the 30th of November, I left this kind family, and on the 8th of December arrived at home.

After my return, I ſpent two or three weeks in writing, as a memorandum, what I received from B. Youngs and others, concerning the riſe of this church, their doctrines, faith, and practice.

I was not yet myſelf a full believer. I had many doubts and reaſonings within myſelf, as ſome things looked very dark; but I imputed it to my want of light; for they had ſaid, "The things of God were a myſtery "to the natural man; and that I could not underſtand "the goſpel and way of ſalvation, any further than I "travailed therein, and obtained a victory over ſin." Alſo, "it was ſin which had blinded the mind, and ſtu-"pified the ſenſes of all the human race."

Now, in order that the reader may have a right and thorough underſtanding reſpecting the faith, and to repreſent it in as true a light as poſſible, I think beſt to inſert a ſhort treatiſe, which contains the ground-work of their faith, written by their eſteemed Elder, Joſeph Meacham. A copy of which I obtained from a manuſcript, by the favour of B. Youngs, while I reſided at his houſe. This, with a letter annexed, written by their Elder, James Whittaker, are the only writings reſpecting their faith I ever found among them. I often inquired why they did not publiſh their faith and practice in general, as other churches had done, that the world might have an authentick account thereof; and that the fallacy of many reports that had gone abroad reſpecting their faith and practice might be contradicted. The anfwer I always received was, "There has never been any gift fo "to do; and that the true church and people of God, "in all their proceedings, were different from the pro- "feffors and anti-chriftian churches of the world."

The following I give verbatim as I received it.

"A concife ftatement of the principles of the only "true church, according to the gofpel of the prefent ap- "pearance of Chrift; as held to, and practifed upon, by "the true followers of the living Saviour, at New-Leb- "anon and a number of other places. Likewife, a let- "ter annexed, written by James Whittaker, minifter of "the gofpel in this day of Chrift's fecond appearing, to "his natural relations in England, dated October 9, 1785. "A fhort information of what we believe of the difpen- "fation of God's grace to fallen man: and in what "manner they have found acceptance with God, and "falvation from fin in former difpenfations: with par- "ticular references to the prefent difplay of God's grace "unto us; and in what manner we find acceptance with "God, and hopes of eternal life, through our Lord Je- "fus Chrift, in obedience to the gofpel of his prefent ap- "pearance."

## *A CONCISE STATEMENT, &c.*

"1ft. We believe that the firft light of falvation was "given or made known to the Patriarchs by promife; "and they that believed in the promife of Chrift, and "were obedient to the command of God made known "unto them, were the people of God; and were accept- "ed by him as righteous, or perfect in their generation, "according to the meafure of light and truth manifeft- "ed unto them; which were as waters to the ankles; "fignified by Ezekiel's vifion of the holy waters, chap. "xlvii. And although they could not receive regene- "ration, or the fulnefs of falvation, from the flefhly or "fallen nature in this life; becaufe the fulnefs of time "was not yet come that they fhould receive the baptifm "of the Holy Ghoft and fire, for the deftruction of the

" body of sin, and purification of the soul. But Abraham " being called and chosen of God, as the father of the " faithful, was received into covenant relation with God " by promise; that in him, and his seed, all the fami- " lies of the earth should be blessed. And the earth- " ly blessings, which were promised to Abraham, were " a shadow of gospel or spiritual blessings to come. " And circumcission, or outward cutting of the foreskin " of the flesh, did not cleanse the man from sin, but was " a sign of the spiritual baptism of the Holy Ghost and " fire. Which is by the power of God manifested in " divers operations and gifts of the spirit, as in the days " of the apostles, which does indeed destroy the body of " sin or fleshly nature, and purify the man from all sin, " both soul and body. So that Abraham, though in " the full faith of the promise, yet as he did not receive " the substance of the thing promised, his hopes of eter- " nal salvation was in Christ, by the gospel to be attain- " ed in the resurrection from the dead."

" 2d. The second dispensation was the law that was " given of God to Israel, by the hand of Moses; which " was a farther manifestation of that salvation, which " was promised through Christ by the gospel, both in " the order and ordinances which was instituted and giv- " en to Israel, as the church and people of God, accord- " ing to that dispensation which was as *waters to the* " *knees*—(Ezek. xlvii. 4) by which they were distinguish- " ed from all the families of the earth. For while they " were faithful and strictly obedient to all the com- " mands, ordinances, and statutes that God gave; ap- " probated of God according to the promise for life, " and blessing promised unto them in the line of obedi- " ence; cursing and death in disobedience—(Deut. xxviii. " 2, 15.) For God, who is ever jealous for the honor " and glory of his own great name, always dealt with " them according to his word. For while they were o- " bedient to the commands of God, and purged out sin " from among them, God was with them, according to " his promise. But when they disobeyed the commands " of God, and committed sin, and became like other " people, the hand of the Lord was turned against them;

" and those evils came upon them which God had " threatened. So we see that they that were wholly o- " bedient to the will of God, made known in that dis- " pensation were accepted as just or righteous. Yet as " that dispensation was short, they did not attain that " salvation which was promised in the gospel; so that, " as it respected the new birth, or real purification of the " man from all sin, the *law made nothing perfect*—(Heb. " vii. 19) *but was a shadow of good things to come*—(1 Cor. " ii. 17. Heb. x. 1.) Their only hope of eternal re- " demption was in the promise of Christ by the gospel, " to be attained in the resurrection from the dead

" 3d. The third dispensation was the gospel of Christ's " first appearance in the flesh, which was as *waters to the* " *loins*—(Ezek. xlvii. 4) and that salvation which took " place in consequence of his life, death, resurrection, " and ascension to the right hand of the Father, being " accepted in his obedience, as the *first born among many* " *brethren*—(Rom. viii. 29) he received power and au- " thority to administer the power of the resurrection and " eternal judgment to all the children of men. So that " he has become the *author of eternal salvation unto all that* " *obey him*—(Heb. iv. 9.) And as Christ had this power " in himself, he did administer power and authority to " his church at the day of Pentecost, as his body, with " all the gifts that he had promised them; which was " the first gifts of the Holy Ghost, as an in-dwelling com- " forter, to abide with them for ever; and by which they " were *baptized into Christ's death*; death to all sin: and " were in the hope of the resurrection from the dead, " through the operation of the power of God, which " wrought in them. And as they had received the sub- " stance of the promise of Christ's coming in the flesh, " by the gift and power of the Holy Ghost, they had " power to preach the gospel, in Christ's name, to *every* " *creature*; and to administer the power of God to as " many as believed, and were obedient to the gospel " which they preached; and to remit and retain " sins in the power and authority of Christ on earth. " So that they that believed in the gospel, and were obe- " dient to that form of doctrine which was taught them,

" *by denying all ungodliness and worldly lust*, and became
" entirely dead to the law, by the body of Christ, or
" power of the Holy Ghost, were in the travail of the
" resurrection from the dead, or the *redemption of the*
" *body*—(Rom. viii. 23) So that they who took up
" a full cross against the world, flesh, and devil, and who
" forsook all for Christ's sake, and followed him in the
" regeneration, by persevering in that line of obedience
" to the end, found the resurrection from the dead, and
" eternal salvation in that dispensation. But as the na-
" ture of that dispensation was only as water to the loins,
" (Ezek. 47) the mystery of God was not finished, but
" there was another day prophesied of, called the sec-
" ond appearance of Christ, or final and last display of
" God's grace to a lost world, in which the *mystery of*
" *God should be finished*, (Rev. x. 7) as he has spoken by
" his prophets, *since the world began*—(Luke i. 70):
" which day could not come, except there was a falling
" away from that faith and power that the Church then
" stood in—(2 Thess. ii. 3 2 Tim iv 3. Dan. xi. 36,
" to 38. See Dan. chap. xii) In which Anti-Christ
" was to have his reign, whom Christ should destroy with
" the spirit of his mouth, and brightness of his appear-
" ance—(2 Thess. ii 8.) Which falling away, began
" soon after the apostles, and gradually increased in the
" Church, until about 457 years, (or thereabouts); at
" which time the power of the holy people, or church of
" Christ was scattered or lost, by reason of transgression,
" (Dan. xii. 7. viii. 12.); and Anti Christ, or false reli-
" gion, got to be established Since that time, the wit-
" nesses of Christ have prophesied in sackcloth, or under
" darkness—(Rev. xi 3.) And although many have
" been faithful to testify against sin, even to the laying
" down of their lives for the testimony which they held,
" so that God accepted them in their obedience, which
" they were faithful and just to live, or walk up to the
" measure of light and truth of God, revealed or made
" known unto them. But as it is written, that all they
" that will live godly in Christ Jesus, shall suffer persecu-
" tion; and so it has been: and those faithful witnesses
" lost their lives by those falsely called the church of

"Christ, which is anti-christ. For the true church of "Christ never persecuted any; but were inoffensive, "harmless, separate from sin. For the true church of "Christ, taking up their cross against the world, flesh, "and devil, and all sin; living in obedience to God, "they earnestly contend for the same. Therefore, it "may be plainly seen and known where the true church "is But as it is written anti-christ, or false churches, "should prevail against the saints, and overcome them, "before Christ's second appearance—(2 Thess. ii. 3,) "*Let no man deceive you by any means, for that day shall not* "*come, except there come a falling away first, and that man of* "*sin be revealed, the son of perdition.* And it was given "unto him to *overcome all kindreds, tongues, and nations*— "(Rev. 13, 7.) And this is the state Christ prophesied "the world of mankind should be in, at his second ap-"pearance. (See Luke xvii. 22, to end of the chap.) "*And as it was in the days of Noah, so shall it be in the days* "*of the Son of man,* (ver. 30.) Even so shall it be in-the "days *when the Son of Man is revealed:* Plainly refering "to his second appearing, to consume and destroy anti-"christ, and make a final end of sin, and establish his "kingdom upon earth—(Isa. lxv 25. Jer. xxxi. 33, 34. "Dan. ii. 44, and vii. 18, 27, and ix. 24. Oba. 21. Rev. "xi. 15, &c.) But as the revelation of Christ is spiritu-"al, consequently must be in his people, whom he had "chosen to be his body, to give testimony of him, and "to preach his gospel to a lost world.

"4th. The fourth dispensation is the second appear-"ance of Christ, or final and last display of God's grace "to a lost world; in which the mystery of God will be "finished, and a decisive work, to the final salvation or "damnation of all the children of men: which accord-"ing to the prophecies, rightly calculated and truly un-"derstood, began in the year of our Saviour 1747, (see "Daniel and the Revelations) in the manner following: "To a number, in the manifestation of great light, and "mighty trembling, by the invisible power of God, and "visions, revelations, miracles, and prophecies. Which "has progressively increased with administrations of all "those spiritual gifts that was administered to the apos-

" ties at the day of pentecoſt : which is the comforter " that has led us into all truth ; and which was prom- " iſed to abide with the true church of Chriſt unto the " end of the world. And by which we find *baptiſm into* " *Chriſt's death*—(Rom. vi. 4) death to all ſin : become " alive to God, by the power of Chriſt's reſurrection, " which worketh in us mightily. By which a diſpenſa- " tion of the goſpel is committed unto us, and woe be " unto us if we preach not the goſpel of Chriſt ; for in " ſending ſo great a ſalvation and deliverance from the " law of ſin and death, in believing and obeying this " goſpel, which is the goſpel of Chriſt ; in confeſſing and " forſaking all ſin, and denying ourſelves, and bearing " the croſs of Chriſt againſt the world, fleſh, and devil, " we have found *forgiveneſs* of all our ſins, and are made " partakers of the grace of God, wherein we now ſtand. " Which all others, in believing and obeying, have ac- " ceptance with God, and find ſalvation from their ſins " as well as we. God being no reſpecter of perſons, but " willing that all men ſhould come to the knowledge of " the truth and be ſaved.

" Thus we have given a ſhort information of what we " believe of the diſpenſations of God's grace to mankind, " both paſt and preſent ; and in what manner the people " of God have found juſtification, or acceptance with " God Which was, and is ſtill, in believing and obey- " ing the light and truth of God revealed or made known " in the day or diſpenſation in which they live. *For as* " *the wrath of God is revealed from heaven, againſt all un-* " *godlineſs, worldly luſts, and unrighteouſneſs of men, who* " *hold the truth in unrighteouſneſs*—(Rom i. 18) or live in " any known ſin againſt him : ſo his mercy and grace " is towards all them who truly love and fear him, and " turn from all their ſins by repentance, *confeſſing, and* " *forſaking* : which is the way and manner in which all " have, and muſt find forgiveneſs of their ſins, and ac- " ceptance with God, through our Lord Jeſus Chriſt ; " or finally fail of the grace of God, and that ſalvation " brought to light by the goſpel. But to conclude, in " ſhort, as we believe and do teſtify, that the preſent " goſpel of God's grace unto us, is the day which in the

" ſcriptures is ſpoken or propheſied of, as the ſecond ap-
" pearing of Chriſt to conſume, or deſtroy anti-chriſt, or
" falſe religion; and to make an end of the reigning
" power of ſin over the children of men; and to eſtab-
" liſh his kingdom, and that righteouſneſs that will ſtand
" forever; and that the preſent diſplay of the work and
" power of God, will increaſe until it is manifeſted to
" all; which it muſt be in due time. For every eye
" ſhall ſee him, and he will reward every man accord-
" ing to his deeds—(Rev. i. 7. Matt. xvi. 27. Rom.
" ii 6) and none can ſtand in ſin, or unrighteouſneſs;
" but in that righteouſneſs which is pure and holy, even
" without fault before the throne of God—(Rev. xiv. 5)
" which is obtained by grace, through faith, in obedi-
" ence to the truth of the everlaſting goſpel of our Lord
" Jeſus Chriſt; in denying all ungodlineſs and worldly
" luſts, by confeſſing all ſin, and taking up the croſs of
" Chriſt againſt the world, fleſh, and devil. We deſire,
" therefore, that the children of men would believe the
" teſtimony of truth, and turn from their ſins by repent-
" ance, that they may obtain the mercy of God, and
" ſalvation from ſin, before it be too late."

## A LETTER

### *WRITTEN BY JAMES WHITTAKER.*

" I have written to you a letter, in anſwer to one you
" wrote me laſt winter. I have ſignified my mind part-
" ly to you, heretofore; it remains now that I declare
" unto you my whole heart, which I cannot tell at preſ-
" ent; but it will be a final cloſe between you and me,
" through time and eternity.

" Flattering titles I am not about to uſe towards you,
" or to ſooth you with lies; but with the truth will I
" come forth, whether you will hear or forbear. Be not
" ſo unwiſe as the ſcribes and phariſees, who ſaid to
" Chriſt, *Thou beareſt record of thyſelf; thy record is not*
" *true;* when I teſtify unto you what God has done
" for my ſoul. Bleſſed be God for evermore, who has
" ſeparated me from the world, and made me a miniſter

" of the gospel in the day of Christ's second appearance. " All earthly profits and pleasures, all earthly generation, and propagation, which are the delights of all men " in their natural state: all these, I say, have I forsaken " for Christ's sake; and I have already received an hundred fold, in this present time, according as the holy " Son of God promised in the day of his first appearance, and much more abundantly. A death to the " man of sin have I found; a total spoiling of the strong " man's goods; and redemption from the bondage of " corruption; which is that sordid propensity to, or ardent desire of copulation with woman; which has not " been understood in that sense many ages, but now is " made manifest in this dispensation, to all them that " believe and obey the gospel of Christ's second appearance, which God has committed to my trust. *I daily* " *feel a fountain of love, life, joy, and heavenly glory, flowing in my soul, like a river of living water, pure and clean.* " *My soul is constantly replenished with rich supplies from* " *the heavenly glory; and my heart constantly flows with* " *charity and benevolence to all mankind. With a broken heart,* " *God has blessed me; and the image of the Lord of Glory is* " *formed in my soul. Plenty of the dew of heaven is distilled in my soul from day to day; and the divine nature doth* " *infold me, like a delightful sea of pleasant waters, full of* " *glory* What think ye; if I were to seek friends in " this world, should I not cleave to my own blood; " should I not make you the objects of my first pursuit? " But I am weaned from all terrestrial connections, and " in lieu thereof, I have joined the host of heaven; with " open vision do I behold the angelic company of the " spiritual world, and join the melodious songs of the " new Jerusalem.

" Why tell ye me of your increasing and multiplying " after the flesh? Your vessels are *marred in the potters* " *hands*—(Jer xviii. 4.) and they must be made over again by regeneration, or go down to the pit. Say ye, " it is a command to *increase and multiply;* but I say it " never was a command to corrupt the earth, and fill it " with a double condemnation, and then plead the commands of God to *increase and multiply,* as though you "had been doing his will; when you are conſcious to "yourſelves, or know in your own hearts, that you never "had any other will but your own in ſo doing; a will "proceeding from the luſts of the fleſh. God has given "me the power to increaſe and multiply in its true myſ- "tical, typical, and evangelical ſenſe; which I go forth "to do. I have begotten many thouſands of children, "and repleniſhed them with many good things I hate "your fleſhly lives, and your fleſhly generations, as I "hate the ſmoke of the bottomleſs pit; and your plead- "ing the commands of God to *increaſe and multiply*, to "cover your beaſtly conduct and doleful corruption, "and inverting the order of heaven. Think ye that I "will look toward you, while you live after the fleſh, "defiling yourſelves with effeminate deſires, and profan- "ing the commands of God for a cover? It is in my "power, indeed, to help you greatly, in a temporal ſenſe, "and many others who live as corrupt lives as you do "this day; as much without God in the world. But "be it known unto you, and all men, that I will not do "it, except you forſake your wicked lives, and ſerve the "living and true God. Which I have no expectation "you will do, if I ſhould nouriſh and cheriſh you, as a "tender father does his children. Stay in England, till "you go down into your graves—as long as you are for "following natural generation, and the courſe of this "world I know that your greateſt oppreſſion is your "living after the fleſh; which is your own chooſing, and "is the very reaſon I will not help you, though I have "it in my power. Away with your looking towards "me for help, ſince you are ſunk in my ſoul for your "diſobedience to God, and your lying hopes, that you "are in favour with God, while you corrupt the law "and trample the pure goſpel under foot. Were it ſo "indeed, that you had it in your hearts to turn to God, "and obey the goſpel, I would look towards you with "charity and compaſſion; and would take care of you, "ſoul and body, as much as lay in my power But that "is far from you; and it is in your hearts to enlarge "your liberty after the fleſh, and to provide living for "yourſelves and poſterity; therefore you are but a ſtink "in my nostrils; instead of your having a pardon for "your sins, you are deceived, and I feel that you are "powerfully alienated from the life of God, and become "carnal, sensual, and unwise; therefore, as you have "chosen your own ways, see what the God you serve "will do for you; and your false hopes, what they will "bring you to. All we that are of that community who "worship God in spirit, and rejoice in Christ Jesus, be-"ing separated from all effeminate desires, and sensual "pleasures, are in possession of the only true hope of e-"ternal life. My God has delivered me, redeemed my "soul, filled it with heavenly joy, and the power of an "endless life, as well as made me able to help many in "a temporal sense; and you might have been sharers "with me in all this unmerited munificence, had you "obeyed the gospel with me * As, therefore, you have "forsaken God, I also have forsaken you; and will nev-"er give you any encouragement to come into this land, "till once for all you resolve to turn to God, and obey "the gospel. I feel the compassion of God to warn you "of what you are losing in this great day of the second "appearance of the Son of Man. You are losing no "less than the only means of salvation that ever will be "offered again in this world. The power of the gospel "does prosper in my soul, in bowels and compassion, for "the poor lost children of men. And I desire that you "would be warned by a faithful friend, not to outstand "the great day of God's final visitation, for the sake of "your false hopes, which will leave your soul desolate "and barren, or for the fading things of this life, which "are but vanity and vexation of spirit. Oh that you "would hearken! for then there is the same door for "your escape, as for the rest of the children of men. "At which door if you enter, I feel to receive you with "charity. And the severity of this letter is the charity "of God to your souls, and his abhorrence of your false "hopes. JAMES WHITTAKER."

* Those whom he wrote to, had heard this gospel, but would not be obedient to it; and likewise come with those who came to America.

February, 1799. Having no companions in the faith, in Cornwall, the place where I resided, I wished to gain some proselytes. Accordingly I visited a neighbour of mine, Ralph Hodgson, by name, an honest man, with whom I had been, for some time, intimately acquainted. He was a member of the society of the people called Quakers, and a man who was much esteemed and respected. I had often conversed with him respecting the prevailing vices of the times, and the carelessness and indifference of religious professors. I now began to open to him new subjects of religion. I preached the millennium; and told him I had found a people who were in it; and represented them as the most religious and exemplary of any that had ever been before. He was all attention; and, in two hours, concluded to make a journey with me to Neskauna, and see for himself.

Accordingly, on the 20th of the month, we entered on our journey, and three days afterwards arrived at Neskauna. In the evening, said Hodgson conversed with B. Youngs, concerning the faith; and the next day we went to see those in church order, i. e. the old believers. He began to think he had got into the millennium indeed; and in a few days confessed his sins; on account of which, I was glad I had a brother companion with whom I could converse respecting the blessed faith (as we called it) when we again got home. Before I parted with the Elders at this time, it was requested of me to confess my sins again; which I did to Elder Hezekiah and John Scott. These Elders were appointed, because there appeared to be then an ingathering, as they called it, or another opening of the gospel; for, they said, the church had been shut up, as but few had joined it for years before that time.

Here it may be observed, that the first time I ever saw John Scott, he spake to me in a very imprudent and abrupt manner; which was the first instance of their conduct I disliked. Sitting in company with Hodgson and a few brethren, he came into the room and abruptly asked me, in very uncouth and indecorous language, if I had not been in the commission of sin since I was there laſt. This abrupt, indecent queſtion, from a man I had never ſeen before, I thought bore no mark of the gentleneſs and decency of the goſpel. I therefore ſaid—Friend, you have a zeal, but not according to knowledge: look to your own ſins; I anſwer no ſuch queſtions. It may be expected that I ſhall open my mind, as ſoon as I have an opportunity, according to order. You are out of order, in thus queſtioning me before company. He made no reply; and immediately retired. Afterwards I aſked Elder Hezekiah the man's name, by whom I was thus imprudently queſtioned. He told me his name, and ſaid, his zeal was ſuch againſt ſin, that he ſometimes ſpake when he ſhould not; and that I muſt take no offence, for he meant no harm.

When we were about to part, Elder Hezekiah told me, if at any time hereafter I felt deſirous to open my mind again, I might have the privilege to do it.

From hence we went to what was called the elderly family, conſiſting of about twenty in number. Thither I frequently reſorted, till there was a family of young believers gathered. There I had conſiderable converſation with the old believers; the moſt of whom had belonged to the church ever ſince their firſt ſettlement in America. We converſed, chiefly, on the riſe of the church, the firſt miniſters, the gifts, various operations, and miracles, that had been wrought, (as they ſaid,) in the church from time to time. Theſe were not altogether what they had heard, but what they ſaid they had ſeen and experienced; ſome of the miracles being wrought upon their own bodies. One man, in particular, told me, that "he had been a cripple, and that he was inſtantly healed by the power of God, through the inſtrumentality of one of his brethren."

I was informed there was a woman* in this family, who came with the firſt Elders from England; and wiſhing to have the account reſpecting their riſe and proceedings in former times, as correct as poſſible, I ſpake to him who was the head of the family, requeſting of

* Mary Hocknell, born July the 9th, 1759, and was fifteen years old when ſhe came to America.

him her company, if agreeable, giving my reaſons. He went and informed her; ſhe ſoon came into our room, accompanied by two aged women, and they took their ſeats; the ſubſtance of our diſcourſe was as follows:

I addreſſed her thus—I have underſtood thou haſt* been in the faith from thy youth; and, as Paul ſaid to Timothy, from a child haſt thou known the holy ſcriptures, or in other words, the faith; and that thou cameſt from England with the firſt Elders and brethren. Now, though I have heard ſomething of the riſe of the church, yet wiſhing to have further and more correct information, I have made free to requeſt thy company, which I take kindly of thee in granting; and will thank thee, if thou wilt inform me of what thou knoweſt, or haſt ſeen and heard concerning the faith and people in the firſt opening of the goſpel; as there have been many reports circulated, and much ſaid, pro and con. reſpecting the people when they firſt ſettled here; and of Ann Lee, and ſome others, being in the practice of uſing ſpirituous liquors to exceſs. Now if theſe and ſome other reports are falſe. I wiſh to be able, from correct information and good authority, to contradict them; eſpecially when they are brought forward to invalidate my faith in the goſpel, as profeſſed by theſe people.

She anſwered—"I am very willing to give you what "information I am able. As to my knowledge of "mother Ann Lee, I was very intimate with her from the "time I was eight or ten years old. till ſhe died. I was "her companion by day, and her bed-fellow by night; "and if there were any truth in the aſſertion of her uſing "liquor to exceſs, ſurely I ſhould have ſeen ſomething "of it. I never knew that ſhe made any more uſe of "it, than women in general. At all times it appeared "to be her greateſt labour and delight to ſerve God, "and promote the good of mankind. She was a great "enemy to, and hater of ſin; and at all opportunities

* The reader will obſerve, that in ſome places in this work, the ſingular language is uſed, and in other places the plural. This has been done in order that the converſations might be written exactly as they were ſpoken.

" teſtified againſt it. She had the firſt and greateſt gifts " of God of any in her day; and I believe Chriſt was " in, and with her of a truth As to particulars in Eng- " land, I was too young then to give now much account. " But this I well remember; that they were much a- " buſed and perſecuted, Mother in particular. At one " time, the worldly authority held a trial reſpecting her; " when ſhe was ſo endued with the ſpirit and power of " God, that ſhe ſpake before the court and a large con- " courſe of people, in twelve different languages, to the " aſtoniſhment of many preſent; particularly ſome of " the learned, who underſtood her, when ſhe ſpake in " French, Hebrew, Greek, and Latin: alſo ſome being " preſent who underſtood other languages. Thus it was " a time like unto the day of Pentecoſt, when every man " heard the apoſtles ſpeak in his own language—(Acts " ii 6.) Concerning her ſo ſpeaking there was much " talk and wondering for ſome time.

" About this time, ſhe was confined two or three " months in priſon; moſt of the time ſhe had no other " ſubſiſtence than milk, which I conveyed to her by " means of a quill through the key-hole; for they would " not open the door to let any of her friends ſee her. " They ſaid ſhe was a witch, and I know not what all. " Theſe things I well remember, being then twelve years " old. Shortly after this time, Mother ſaid, it was the " gift of God, for all who had faith to prepare for to " go to America. Accordingly, twelve of us came; " three or four of which were but children, and ſettled " here in the wilderneſs, twenty-three or twenty-four " years ago.

" When I look back and ſee our poverty, (living at " firſt in a ſmall log-houſe, and ſeveral of the brethren " under the neceſſity of going among the people of the " world to work) perſecutions, and various trials we " paſſed through, and compare our condition then with " the church at preſent, I am filled with admiration at " the goodneſs of God, and the bleſſings and proſperity " that have attended us"

I replied, it is admirable; and the hand of God appears ſo conſpicuous, that it is needleſs to regard any reports to invalidate it. But that I may be able to satisfy honest, inquiring minds, who may have heard false reports, not knowing but what they were true, and be able to contradict them, or represent things in a true light, from good authority, and information received from eye, and ear witnesses, I make free to ask thee a question concerning a report which has been, and still is asserted to be a fact by many who have been among the people, and have left them; which is, that these people, in Mother's day, by her gift, or by order of some of the other Elders, were repeatedly in the practice of dancing naked, men and women together, in their meetings.

She answered, "I am sure Mother was a very modest woman; and if there had been any such conduct, "I should have seen, or known it, which I never did. "There were many operations by the power of God, "and wonderful gifts; as speaking in unknown tongues, "trembling, groaning, and sometimes turning round; "on account of which, people would report we were "drunk, as they did formerly about the apostles, who "had similar gifts and operations—(Acts, chap. ii.) "And because the brethren pulled of their coats, or outside garments, to labour, or as the world call it, dancing; and in warm weather the sisters being lightly "clothed, they would report we danced naked. And "you know how apt the ignorant and vulgar part of "mankind, are to misrepresent what they see. If one "told they danced part naked, or with but few clothes "on, another in telling the story, would leave out the "part, or few, and so it was reported we danced naked"

I replied, It is very probable; and wicked people often wilfully and intentionally, misrepresent what they see, especially of religious people. They reported of George Fox, the first Quaker, that he got drunk, and carried a bottle of rum with him, which made the people follow him; and many other foolish, ridiculous stories. Similar stories have been reported of many other religious societies, when they first arose; and it would be singular if this society should escape false reports. For my part, I am satisfied, and thank you for the present conference.

An aged woman and old man, head of the family, who were in company with us, informed me of more of their proceedings, preaching, gifts, operations, and miracles, that had been in the church. One miracle in particular, the old man related; which was, " A few years " after they settled here, there was an opening of the " gospel, and the people flocked from all parts to see " them; they entertained all as well as they could; " Mother often told the brethren and sisters not to be " uneasy, for God would provide. At a certain time, " when about fifty of them sat at the table to eat, they " had not provision enough for five; but by a miracle, " similar to that in Matt. xiv. 20, *they did all eat, and* " *were filled; and they took up of the fragments that remain-* " *ed*, more than all they put upon the table." Any further I think best not to relate at present

The next day, two aged women favoured me with their company, and brought with them a large bible, and read several prophesies, which they said, " pointed " to, and meant first Mother: viz. Psal. xlv. 9, to 17. " Jer xxxiii 16. Rev chap. 12; and that Solomon also " spake of her in the Canticles." They also pointed out many other prophesies concerning the church; particularly, " Jer xxxi. 12, 13. Dan ii. 45 and vii. 22 to 27. " Rev. xii. 10 and xx 6. and xxi. and xxii. chap. and of " those passages speaking of the gospel work in this day; " which are, Isa xxviii. 18, 20, 21. Habak. i. 5." Some of these quotations were feeding me with very strong meat, which I had not faith enough yet, to believe they were all properly applied. They believe that the fulfilment of most of the prophesies, centres in the first and this second coming of Christ.

I should not mention these things, if they were only the faith, or opinions of a few individuals; for this would not be giving a correct account of the rise, faith and doctrines of a church, unless we know such an individual account accorded with what is given by the church in general, or by the heads, or leaders of it As it would not be right to charge a church with the conduct of, and with what a few (perhaps ignorant) members might assert as truth. Therefore, I relate nothing in this work of the conduct, faith, opinions, or speeches of individuals, unless it is what I know they have been taught by the leaders of the church, except I mention the heads of the church had no unity therewith, or what is not according to the faith.

I tarried at this time, four or five days with this and other families, all of whom I found exceedingly kind and friendly. I left them with regret, and by the last of the month, arrived at home. Hodgson was so zealous, he preached the faith to almost every one he met; and it now became known among my acquaintance, that I had joined the Shakers. After I returned home (in travelling to Pennsylvania and Wilmington) I was much exercised respecting this faith, and had many arguments in my own mind, concerning the truth of it, and the doctrines professed. Nevertheless, I was satisfied with what I had done. I thought at least, since they made such a profession, and were so circumspect in their conduct, they deserved a trial, and it was no more than right and reasonable to prove whether they were the people they professed to be. About the first of September, I left home again, in company with Hodgson. In the evening of the third day, we arrived at B Youngs', and next day we went to the church. After two or three days visiting among the brethren and sisters, who all appeared glad to see us increasing in our faith; by seeing (as then appeared to us) their sober, and in every respect, christ-like deportment.

My companion going a journey near Canada, I accompanied him ten or twelve miles, to see an uncle of mine, and his family. After I had been here a few hours, I felt desirous to hold a meeting in the neighbourhood, as I had been in the practice of so doing some years past; and I knew of nothing contrary to the faith or order of the church, of which I was now a member, to hinder me. I opened my feelings to a few serious neighbours, to which they willingly agreed; and accordingly gave notice to their neighbours for an evening meeting: to which came near two hundred people; to whom I spake about an hour an half. All appeared to be attentive and solemn. I said nothing about a new dispensation, the faith, or people, I had joined; but preached the good old gospel. After I had concluded and sat down, I arose again, not wishing to deceive the people, or act the part of a hypocrite, thinking they might conclude I was, what I was not.

I informed them, in few words, concerning my faith, and the society I belonged to; and concluded by saying, they are not the people you conceive them to be; neither are they such as you have heard from report. Some said afterwards, my telling I belonged to the Shakers, and recommending them as a good people, destroyed all the good I had done.

I returned back in three days to the church, called on the Elders, and informed them I had held a meeting in my absence, which I had no thoughts of before I went. Had my mind been impressed with the idea previously to my departure, I should have mentioned it, to know their mind, as I wished to act in union; and desired to know if they had unity with what I had done; and whether they would have union with my continuing to appoint meetings, at convenient opportunities: if not, I would desist. They retired, I suppose, to know the mind of the superior Elder, or to consult what reply they should make. In about half an hour, one of them, viz. Elder Hezekiah, returned.

Now I shall be particular in relating the substance of this discourse that followed; because, on it much depends respecting the representation of the faith hereafter; and I shall have to make frequent references to it in the course of this history.

He said—"Thomas, we have union with what you "have done respecting the meeting, and feel willing you "should hold meetings, for the time to come, at con-"venient opportunities, when and where you feel dis-"posed; for the gospel does not bind creatures, but "gives liberty to all religious acts; as preaching, pray-"ing, singing, &c. whenever we feel disposed We "cannot direct or tell you what you must do, or not do, "in every respect. All we desire and teach is for crea-"tures to act according to the dictates of conscience, "and not violate it in any respect; but do what they "feel and believe to be their duty. Above all, we "counsel creatures not to violate their consciences in "committing sin; neither to do any thing they believe "to be wrong; but to do what they have faith in. "Each one should act according to his own faith. If you "have faith in, and believe it your duty to appoint "meetings, and speak to the people, what right have "we to forbid you? We dare not, we do not set up to "be judges of other men's consciences. And according "to the apostle John, *If our heart, or consciences condemn "us not, then have we confidence towards God*—(1 John iii. "21.) Therefore we advise all to keep a justified con-"science, and to live up to that light which God has "given them. *Christ has enlightened every man that cometh "into the world, and a measure of the spirit is given to every "man to profit withal.* Therefore, this light that shineth "in all men's hearts, and the spirit of God that striveth "with, and teacheth all, is every man's rule to walk by, "and to whom all should be obedient."

This is a doctrine I then believed, and his preaching it to me, brought me into a nearer union, and much strengthened my faith in them, as we are the more ready to believe those right who are of the same opinion; and I expect this was his motive in treating thus on this subject, though I had heard the same before, from others; but this was only feeding me with milk. The real faith of the church was insisted upon sometime afterwards, as will be seen in the sequel. I state every thing according to the order of time, as they happened

Before he parted with me at this time, he spake on various other subjects; particularly the mercy of God in the final restoration of all the posterity of Adam, in the following manner:

"We believe this to be a dispensation of the greatest "light, and the final and last display of God's grace to "a lost world; in which the mystery of God will be "finished, and in the increasing work of it, Christ will "deliver up *all things* to the Father; and *every knee* will "have to *bow*, and *every tongue confess to the glory of God.* "And as *by one man's disobedience, many*, i e all, *were "made sinners; so by the obedience of one, shall many*, (i. e.

" the ſame number that were made ſinners) *be made* " *righteous* —(Rom. v. 19.) We believe that Chriſt, in " the end, will become a complete conqueror: for, *as in* " *Adam all die, even ſo in Chriſt ſhall all be made alive* — " (1 Cor. xv. 22.) *He is the Saviour of all men, eſpecially* " *of those that believe.*—(1 Tim. iv. 10.) He will *reign* " *till he hath put all enemies under his feet*—(1 Cor. xv. 25) " until he has brought *all things in ſubjection to his gov-* " *ernment*—(Heb. ii. 8.) *The laſt enemy that ſhall be de-* " *ſtroyed, is death*—(ver. 26) not the natural death, which " all men die; but a ſpiritual death, a death to God: " and he will in the *end deliver up the kingdom to God, when* " *he ſhall have put down all rule, authority, and power*— " (1. Cor. xv. 24.) Therefore if all authority and pow- " er be put down or deſtroyed, then ſurely the power of " darkneſs, the ſecond death, will not always reign and " have authority and power over fallen creatures. The " firſt promulgation of the goſpel was, *Peace on earth,* " *and good will towards men* —(Luke ii. 14.) But with " many who pretend to publiſh the goſpel, it is hell-fire, " brimſtone, and eternal damnation; of which they " will have more in one ſermon, than is to be found " in the whole Bible. Now any perſon who believes in " the final reſtoration, could not frame words more full, " pertinent, and concluſive, that all will be ſaved, than " the foregoing quotations.

" Chriſt's kingdom, in the book of Daniel, is repre- " ſented as overcoming and deſtroying all other king- " doms; and alſo, that all ſhall ſerve and obey him. " Will he not, therefore, overcome and deſtroy the king- " dom and power of Satan, and deliver creatures from " under his power and thraldom, when the ſcriptures " declare that he was manifeſted for this very purpoſe? " *For this purpoſe was the Son of God manifeſted, that he* " *might deſtroy the works of the devil*—(1 John, iii. 8.) " Can any thing be plainer? Suppoſe we were informed " of two kings, who were at open war; one repreſented " as very powerful, and his throne eſtabliſhed in right- " eouſneſs; and the happineſs of his ſubjects, and of " mankind in general, was his greateſt deſire: ſuppoſe " the other to be repreſented as a tyrant, who is weak,

" cruel, and unjust; and who does all he can to injure " the subjects of the righteous king. Again, being also " informed, that this powerful and righteous king did " not make a complete conquest of the unjust and cruel " one; and that he never designed to do it, but meant " to rescue only a few of the sufferers from under his " tyranny and oppression; what should we think of " this righteous king, of the happiness of his subjects, and " of his desire to promote the felicity of mankind in gen" eral?

" Now those who believe only in partial salvation, re" present Christ to be like this king. They make him " appear but a petty conqueror. The devil, the power " of darkness, and hell, reigns eternally victorious over " the greatest part of poor lost men. In truth, astonish" ing to tell, some say, that *God Almighty has given the* " *devil a great number of Adam's posterity, by an irreversible* " *decree, from all eternity to all eternity; and let them do what* " *they will, or can, they cannot help themselves.* This is the " most astonishing present, that ever was made; and for " injustice, there never has been any thing on earth equal " to it. But to return to partial salvation: Christ came " into the world, to save the world; but, alas! few are " saved by him. He died, according to their faith, *to* " *atone for the sins of the world, and pay the debt that fallen* " *man could not pay;* and yet the debt of the greatest part " eternally remain unpaid. What inconsistencies! Oh! " but say they, *he did pay the debt for all; yet all would not* " *accept of the payment, or offer; therefore, must eternally a*" *bide by the consequences of their folly.* So they represent " him as a powerful monarch, who makes no conquest " of his opponent's, or adversary's subjects, but those who " please to come to him. He goes round upon his walls, " or sends some among them, calling and inviting them " to quit the service of a tyrant; and a few, or as many " as become sensible of their slavery, and can accept his " invitation, make their escape What sort of a power " is this? Can such a king be worthy of the title of con" queror? Is he not like the one I represented, who had " power sufficient, and did not make use of it? In truth, " a wise, powerful monarch, would go forward, *conquer-*

" *ing and to conquer*—(Rev. vi. 2) till he had made death " and hell give up their miserable captives—(Isa. xlv. " 13 Ps. lxviii. 18.) and till he had taken all their death " weapons from them, and destroyed their strong holds, " (2 Cor. x. 4) forts and garrisons—(Ezek. xxvi. 11.) " Now we believe, *The last enemy that shall be destroyed, is* " *death*—(1 Cor. xv. 26) Which is not the death of " the body, as I said before, for all will die. But that " spiritual death, which is an enemy that will hold all " souls in captivity, until it is destroyed by the conquer-" ing power of Christ. Nevertheless, we believe, that " all who have been favoured here with the privilege and " light of the gospel, and have been disobedient thereto, " their loss and torment hereafter will be inexpressible; " and every one will be punished according to the resist-" ance of the light received." This is the most I ever heard the Elders say on this subject; for it is a doctrine seldom advanced by them. Indeed, they say but little about a futurity, either of happiness or misery. They say, " We need not concern ourselves what is to be, or " how it will be with us hereafter, (leaving it to God, " who will do perfectly just by all his creatures) but " make it the principal concern and business of our lives, " to forsake, and travel out of all sin; living a *just and* " *holy life*, which is the only way any creature ever found " peace in this world: also, by so doing, we shall feel a " confidence in God, and have a comfortable hope of a " happy immortality." He advised me to " do what I " believed to be right; and if I preached to others, to " live the life I preached. Not to preach one thing and " do another, like unto many preachers in the world." Observing, that " if I lived the life I preached, they " were willing I should preach any where, and at any " time" They proposed, that " I should go to the " Methodist meeting, (nigh by) the Sabbath following, " and speak to the people, after their preacher had con-" cluded; and wished me, for the time to come, to man-" ifest my faith more than I had yet done; and let peo-" ple see there was a reality in it, by a sober, circumspect " life."

After I left the houſe, walking in company with Seth Wells, a young believer, who opened his mind about the time I did, I told him what the Elders had propoſed, but that I felt no impreſſion of mind ſo to do. He replied—"If the Elders had made the ſame propoſal to "me, I ſhould go, whether I had a deſire or not; "for though we may not feel it our duty (ſaid he) to do "as they adviſe, yet we ſhould find, that going forth in "obedience, would be attended with a bleſſing. When "they teach or counſel me (ſaid he) to do any thing, I "do not wait to conſult my own mind or feelings about "it; believing they have the gift of God, and going "forth in obedience to what they teach, without any "heſitation, or conſulting my own natural feelings and "reaſonings whether it be right or not, I find a bleſſing." I ſaid, I had no ſuch faith; and it is contrary to what I have heard Elder Hezekiah preach this day. So he ſaid no more. But I have ſince ſeen, that he underſtood the nature of the faith, much better than I did; and had that faith then, to which I have never attained.

I continued viſiting the brethren near two weeks, (who were all exceeding kind and friendly) converſing with them concerning the increaſing work of God; the different diſpenſations; the condition of mankind; the loſt ſtate of profeſſors in the preſent day, and concerning the propheſies; the fulfilment of them reſpecting the ſecond coming of Chriſt; the political revolutions, wars, ſigns, and forebodings, in the preſent age; the firſt opening, preaching, and reception of the goſpel; the propheſies that had been delivered by the former miniſters, and other brethren, and ſiſters, in the church, concerning its future increaſe. We alſo diſcourſed of the lives of ſome ſince they embraced the faith; and concerning various points of doctrine, eſpecially, as they term it, the works of the fleſh. But the greateſt topic of converſation was, concerning the direful effects of ſin, and the neceſſity of living a holy, juſt, upright, honeſt life. By ſeeing the latter ſo much in practice; beholding ſuch order, neatneſs, peace, love, and union, as I never ſaw before, I often thought, ſurely Chriſt is with theſe people: and I became much ſtrengthened in my faith, and much ſatisfied that they were the people they professed to be, i. e. in the second coming of Christ, the long promised, prophesied, and prayed for, millennium dispensation.

My companion returned from the northward; and, in a day or two, we left the place. Our brethren encouraging us to be faithful, and not to forget them: and by the last of September, we arrived at home; I having had one meeting on our way, in which I spake about one hour, to a number of people. After which, my companion appeared to be somewhat dissatisfied; telling me "I spake in such a mystical manner about the faith, that "I shot over all the people's heads. Not one, said he, "knew what thou wast talking about. I want, said he, "to tell the people, in plain words, that I have found "the only true church and people of God, and the coming of Christ; and to recommend to them to go and "see for themselves, as I have done, and confess and forsake their sins before it is too late."

I replied, that it was needless to tell people what I knew they would not believe; and perhaps be laughed at, and called an enthusiast.

He said—"It was more useless to speak in such a "mystical manner; and, as to being laughed at and "called a fool, it was what he expected. But that he "wished to remember what the apostle had said; that "we must become fools in the judment of the world, "that we may become wise in the things of God."

I answered, when I recommend any thing, I wish to do it in such a manner, that there may appear a beauty in it. Suppose, in order to recommend our church, I was to say, Those people, whom the wicked world calls Shaking Quakers, are the only true believers and people of God on earth; and unless you go and join them, you'll be damned. Though it might be true, according to the faith, yet would not people be apt to conclude I was a mad man, and pay no attention to what I preached? I don t wish to follow your example in recommending the people and their doctrines; for you often introduce your discourse about them in such a plain, blunt manner, that it is enough to give people an antipathy and disgust against them. As to becoming fools, we should not make ourſelves appear ſuch, by imprudently ſpeaking and acting; but endeavour to do all things in wiſdom.

He replied—" Thou mayeſt plaſter and poliſh as much " as thou likeſt; ſtill I think thou wilt be counted a fool " by many for embracing this faith, which I eſteem as " the greateſt wiſdom; but being counted ſuch, and " called by the deſpiſed name of a Shaker, is, I expect, " a great croſs to thee."

I ſaid, I care as little what the people of the world ſay or think about it, as thou doſt; knowing many will aſſert at one time one thing, and at another time another, that it is not worth minding what they ſay; and I truſt I ſhall be able to vindicate and juſtify the faith, church, and myſelf, in joining them; and wiſh to do it in ſuch a manner, as not to be looked upon to be more of a fool than I am.

October 24. Going a journey to Long-Iſland, I had a meeting at Peekſkill, to general ſatisfaction. I ſpake principally concerning the vanities of the world, the uncertainty of life, the conſequences and effects of ſin, and the value and neceſſity of religion. I repreſented religion as the fountain of all true peace and happineſs in this world, and of eternal ſelicity in a life to come.

I often felt ſuch deſires for the happineſs and ſalvation of mankind, and ſaw ſuch beauty in religion, that I had thoughts of dedicating all my time to travelling and preaching, as I had done ſome years before. Being as yet ignorant that I could only proceed in that way, as I received the gift, order, or direction, from the Elders; and that I could not do any good until I was appointed and ſent by them to preach.

Now, though I was well ſatisfied reſpecting the faith which I had embraced, and the ſociety of which I was a member, yet I ſaid but little about it, except to ſuch as appeared ſincere and diſentangled from other ſocieties. To ſuch I recommended the ſociety and the faith, in ſuch a manner, that I wondered they did not do as my neighbour, R. Hodgſon, had done, after I recommended the ſociety and their faith to him.

January 1, 1800. I began this year as I wiſhed to end it, in reading, meditation, and thankfulneſs to God for mercies and favours received; and with sincere and earnest desires, that I might this year be preserved from all sin, and live an upright, just life.

Being zealous to gain many over to the faith, I persuaded my wife's sister to take a journey with me to Neskauna, and see these people, and examine for herself. Accordingly, the 20th of the month, we left home, with my horse and chair, and after suffering with the cold, and tedious riding in the chair, in consequence of the snow being deeper to the northward than we expected, we arrived on the fourth day, late in the evening, at B. Youngs'.

Now, by this time there were ten or twelve young believers gathered to the church; three or four out of Albany, with Wm. Carter's family, he having bought a farm joining the church settlement. His wife and two daughters (who were so angry with me for informing Carter about these people, as heretofore mentioned) had now joined them; the others lived in a house the church provided for them. Most of the time we continued in Neskauna, we tarried with this family, and occasionally visiting the older believers and Elders, who all strove with me to persuade my sister to embrace the faith, and apparently endeavouring to conquer her with kindness. Indeed they were very kind to all who came to see them, if they believed they came seeking the way of life and salvation. Formerly, when I had been with the society, I assembled for worship with the elderly believers; but at this time with the young believers, who had meetings every evening. On the third day after our arrival, there came an elderly man (by name Seth Youngs) from Lebanon, who belonged to the backsliding order,* whom I had heard had the gift of speaking in unknown tongues, or in languages he did not understand: in the afternoon he spent some time talking to my sister, respecting the

* *Backsliding order.* By this phrase is meant those who have had faith and the privilege of hearing the gospel, but have turned from it, and afterwards have returned and acknowledged their error and confessed their sins. All such are placed in an order by themselves, having lost, as they say, their travel with those who remained faithful.

vanities of this life, the neceſſity and beauty of religion, and the happineſs to be derived from it. While he was thus ſpeaking, he broke out, with much earneſtneſs. in an unknown tongue, and ſpake about a quarter of an hour; which appeared to me aſtoniſhing, as I was ſatisfied from the appearance of the man, and previous converſation, that he was not a man of learning. Therefore I believed, and received it as immediate inſpiration, and concluded it was miraculous; and thought I ſhould have been very glad if it could have been taken down in writing, that I might have found out what language it was, and what he had ſpoken. It was ſaid to be Greek by one of the believers, (Seth Wells) who profeſſed to underſtand a little of the learned languages.

In the evening we had a meeting of all the young believers, and three Elders with us, and a number of ſpectators. He then ſpake again about half an hour, breaking out while one of the Elders was ſpeaking; at hearing which I was much affected, really believing it to be immediate inſpiration. It was ſaid (by the ſame perſon before mentioned) to be Hebrew, Greek, and Latin, ſpeaking part of the time one language, and then another. After meeting, all the family ſitting round the fire, as he was talking concerning the happineſs of a religious life, ſuddenly his head ſhook, as if by a ſevere electric ſhock; he then cloſed his eyes and ſung half an hour, in ſome language, ſaid to be Hebrew. As ſoon as he ended, he ſaid, "this was one of the ſongs of Zion;" and exclaimed, "how happy a ſoul feels that has a ſenſe "of the love of God."

The ſame evening he ſpake a few minutes in ſome Indian tongue, or it appeared ſuch by the geſticulations, &c. He told us that, "he could only ſpeak as he was "inſpired by the power of God, and then he had no will "or power to ſtop; and that it often came upon him "unexpected, and unthought of; and that he did not "underſtand what he ſaid, except when he had a ſenſe "of it given to him."

I was informed of an illiterate ſiſter at Lebanon, in the ſame order, that had the gift of interpretation of tongues; and that ſhe ſometimes could tranſlate, or explain languages thus ſpoken: and previouſly to that time, one of the young believers (namely, Seth Wells) who profeſſed to underſtand Latin, informed me, in company with ſeveral others, that he had heard this ſame man, at Lebanon, ſpeak half an hour in Latin, which much ſtrengthened his faith, and which he tranſlated into Engliſh; and that he had heard him ſpeak in French, a Frenchman being preſent at the ſame time. He further aſſerted that the forementioned ſiſter, who had the gift of interpretation of tongues, being preſent, interpreted the ſame; all of which he ſaid, "greatly confirmed him in the faith, as it was propheſied in the "ſcriptures, that *theſe ſigns ſhould follow them that believe.* "(Mark xvi. 17) *They ſhall ſpeak with new tongues.*— "Now," ſaid he, "all thoſe gifts that were propheſied of "in the ſcriptures, are in the church. Therefore all "thoſe who come to a knowledge thereof. and do not embrace and abide in the faith, will be left without excuſe."

I ſhall make ſome remarks on theſe gifts and operations, in their proper place; for having had the ſame myſelf, the reader will find me hereafter to be a more competent judge of them.

I ſhall now turn back, and relate a few words concerning this evening's meeting.

We all appeared to be exceedingly happy, dancing, clapping hands, and ſhouting with all the vigour, zeal, and earneſtneſs imaginable. This was the firſt of my joining them in their dance, as I felt a backwardneſs thereto; but as I was ſtanding ſtill looking on, one of the Elders whiſpered to me, and ſaid, "Thomas, labour." I thought I muſt be obedient, and keep in union, ſo I ſtept in among them, and laboured with them. Some ſpectators ſaid after meeting, "we were deluded and full of the devil." Others, that "it was as merry a frolick as ever they ſaw." Some ſerious perſons were much affected at ſeeing people proceed in this manner, under pretence of worſhipping God. A couple who were moſt diſpleaſed, who felt ſorrow, anger, and pity towards us, wept and ſaid, "O take us away from this horrid ſight;" notwithſtanding, they ſoon after joined the ſociety. I thought to be ſure it was a wonderful ſight to people who were preſent, ſeeing our worſhip. But this I declare, I was ſincere, and I believe all the young believers were. We did nothing from a principle of hypocriſy.

Next day I went with my ſiſter to the church, where an Elder and an Elder ſiſter ſpent two or three hours in talking to her, trying to convince and perſuade her to the faith. At laſt ſhe appeared to be much affected, on account, as ſhe conceived, of their condemning all other chriſtians, and ſaid, " you condemn all good people that are, or ever have been in the world; and there is no poſſibility of any being ſaved, unleſs they recieve your faith, and join your church." I replied, we do not condemn all others. I ſtill believe that Van Noſtrand, Benj. Abbot, and John Regan (with whom we were acquainted, and uſed to hear preach) were good men; and what I wrote in my journal reſpecting their piety, after I had read of their deaths, I ſtill believed.

She replied, " I'll warrant you will ſoon eraſe it." I ſaid, I never will.

One of the Elders ſaid, " We own all the work of " God that has ever been in the world, and in all peo- " ple. We believe all thoſe who have lived up to their " light and knowledge, have ſtood juſtified in the ſight " of God, and have been accepted by him, according to " the light they have had and improved," &c.

We left that houſe in order to return again to the young family. On the way ſhe appeared to be much exerciſed and tried in her mind. As we were walking, ſhe ſuddenly ſtopped, and appeared to be falling. I caught hold of her and held her up, when it appeared to me ſomething was the matter with her. In two or three minutes ſhe revived, and appeared for the ſame ſpace of time, to be ſomewhat delirious. After ſhe recovered, ſhe told me that a ſtrange feeling came over her mind, and that ſhe had been blind.

I told her it was for a ſign to her, to ſhow her that ſhe was in a ſtate of darkneſs while ſtanding in oppoſition to the gospel; and that I thought she was greatly favoured in having such a sign *

Next morning we bid all the young believers farewell. They with me, were sorry she would not open her mind before she left them; but on our way, we had about a mile to ride, before we passed the church, or the house in which the Elders resided; in which time, I improved every moment in representing the people in the most endearing manner I could, persuading her to join them, that they might feel a union with her in her absence, and by which she would gather a union with them, and receive great comfort and consolation. Finally she gave up, and consented to stop and see the Elders; and in a few minutes after we were in the house, she opened her mind to the Elder sister; after which she came out of the private room very cheerful, and said, "I now want to go back and see the young sisters;" which we did, and they gave her the right hand of fellowship, being much pleased that they now could call her sister.

The next morning we parted with them, and the 4th of February, arrived at home.

We now began to recommend our faith more strongly to our neighbours, representing these people as being christian-like and exemplary. We asserted, that their order, love, and union exceeded that of any christian society in the world. We frequently made use of the expression, "By their fruits ye shall know them;" and "by this shall all men know that ye are my disciples, if ye "love one another." Also, that there was that power of God among them that was to be found no where else.

Finally, my father, one of R. Hodgson's sons, and Abraham Hendrickson, a nephew of mine, who lived then in my family, and our neighbour Thomas Howe, were prevailed on by us, to go and see them, and examine for themselves. They set off in four or five days after I arrived at home, in company with my brother in the faith, R. Hodgson, in a sleigh, and returned in ten or twelve days; but to our disappointment, only one

* Afterwards, on mature deliberation, I was satisfied her illness was occasioned by much exercise of mind.

had joined them; viz. R. Hodgſon's ſon. My father, as ſoon as he ſaw me, ſaid, "Thomas, I have heard thee ſpeak about the power to be felt among theſe people, but I never felt leſs in my life; and when they talk, or preach, it is as dry as a bone." Continued he, "I told them that they conquered people with love and kindneſs."

As there were four of us now in the faith, we began to hold meetings once a week in private, except a few we ſometimes admitted by particular requeſt; and lively meetings we had. We danced, ſhouted, and clapped our hands with all the joy imaginable, to think we had lived to ſee, and partake of the long propheſied, and prayed for mellennium diſpenſation. I felt as light as a cork upon the floor. At one time I clapt my hands, and cried, "clap your hands all ye people that are ſo highly favoured; ſhout unto God with the voice of thankſgiving*—(Pſal. xlii i.) This was ſomewhat ſingular, as I had never heard any of them ſpeak intelligible words in the time of dancing; therefore I was fearful I had not a right gift, and mentioned it to one of the Elders ſometime afterwards, deſiring to know what he thought of it. He anſwered me, "I ſhall not condemn "ſuch a gift;" and told me of many wonderful gifts among the people at the firſt opening of the goſpel.

About the middle of March, came a couple of the brethren, (namely, Philip Bartley and Benj. S. Youngs) who were ſent by the miniſtration reſiding at Lebanon, to help build us up, and ſtrengthen us in the faith. By this time, Shakeriſm began to be noiſed all over the country; and after they had been with us a day or two, we gave public information for a meeting the ſucceeding Sabbath evening; to which many people came. Hodgſon's houſe, though large, was crowded, and many without; ſo that we had no room to dance. The old man, Philip Bartley, ſpake about an hour and a half on the increaſing work of God, from the fall of Adam, to the opening of the goſpel of the ſecond coming of Chriſt,

* I may juſt obſerve when one feels diſpoſed to clap his hands, all or moſt of the others inſtantly unite with him and do the ſame.

in order for man's final ſalvation and redemption: alſo, on the inconſiſtency of ſexual intercourſe, either married or unmarried, with the pure goſpel diſpenſation, and with the nature of a pure and holy being. He ſaid, "It "is certain that mankind, relative to the gratification of "their carnal minds in this reſpect, have ſunk below the "brute creation; as they have their times and ſeaſons, "but mankind have not" He alſo ſpake concerning the *bond woman born after the fleſh*, (mentioned by the apoſtle, Gall iv. 23) and the *ſon of the free woman by promiſe, which things* (he ſaid) "*were an allegory* of *the two* "*covenants*: one, of the covenant *which gendereth to bond*-"*age* in generation, and the other is free in regeneration; "or one of the fleſh, and the other of the ſpirit: that "thoſe who were under the covenant of the fleſh, were "in bondage, and not heirs with thoſe under the cove-"nant of the ſpirit. Therefore we, (ſaid he) who have "taken up our croſs againſt the fleſh, and obtained a "victory over it, are not children of the fleſh, or bond "woman, to live after the fleſh: for ſuch as *live after the* "*fleſh, ſhall die*; but they who *through the ſpirit, do mor*-"*tify the deeds of the body, ſhall live*—(Rom viii. 13) and "become children of the *free woman*, and of that Jeruſa-"lem (i.e. the church) of which the apoſtle ſpake—(Gall. "iv. 26) *which is from above* and is *free*; *which is the mother* "*of us all* in regeneration This mother can rejoice, "though ſhe bear not, nor travails not according to the "fleſh, and is deſolate as to having children after the "courſe of generation. Yet ſhe *hath many more children* "*than ſhe who hath an huſband*; i. e. according to the "covenant of the fleſh by generation," &c.

He alſo endeavoured to ſhow that ſexual intercourſe was pointed out to be impure and ſinful, even under the law, or Moſaic diſpenſation. In order to prove this, he quoted Lev. xii. 2—xv. 16, 17, 18, 30, 32. "Now (ſaid "he) why all this waſhing and purification? and why a "ſin offering, if no ſin was committed in the act? and "if no ſin, why did the prieſt make an atonement? "(ver. 8.) Alſo the impurity of it appears evident from "the injunction that was laid on the children of Iſrael, "in order for them to be prepared to behold the mani-

" festation of the Lord, which was, *Come not at your* " *wives.*"

He spake concerning the good and evil tree; and that " a tree may be *known by its fruit*—(Mat xii. 33.) " Also, that by the same rule we might know what ef- " feminacy and concupiscence proceeds from." He instanced much evil it had produced, and said, " that " wicked Cain was its first production. The apostle " James says expressly that '*wars* and fightings among " mankind, come from their lusts that war in their mem- " bers.—(James i. 4.) Yea, truly, according to the " apostle John, *The lust of the flesh is not of the Father, but* " *is of the world*—(ii 16.) Then all kinds of evil pro- " ceeds from this corrupt root. Therefore, the nature " of it cannot be good, and is not the same that Adam " possessed before his fall; but by his not abiding in the " state in which his creator placed him, he became *like* " *the beasts that perish*—(Ps. xlix. 20.) According to Jer- " emiah—(ii. 21) he was *planted* a *noble vine, wholly a* " *right seed*, but he became a *degenerate plant of a strange* " *vine;* and though his posterity *wash* themselves with " *nitre, and take much soap*, yet their *iniquity* in this respect, " is *marked before the Lord.*"

He spake of the seed of the woman, that was promised after the fall, that would destroy this corrupt nature; but that " it could not be fully or completely done, un- " til the last and final dispensation of God's grace com- " menced. Notwithstanding many, in preceding dispen- " sations, had some sight and sense of the evil of this na- " ture, and the root from whence all sin proceeded.— " The apostle (2 Thess. ii. 4) calls it the *man of sin, the* " *son of perdition*, and *mystery of iniquity;* and that he " stands opposed to God, and *exalteth himself above all that* " *is called God, or that is worshipped: so that he, as God,* " *sitteth in the temple of God.* Our bodies are the temple " of God—(1 Cor. iii. 16, 17—vi 19) and here it is " that the man of sin has sat, from the time that sin first " entered into man: and he has been the god, and great " delight of the sons and daughters of fallen Adam. " This they have loved, above all other things in the " world; and as it is a truth, that which a man loves "most, or sets his chief affection upon, that he worships; "and therefore, according to the text, this is the god "they have worshipped; and this is that, according to "the apostle, which withholdeth the complete salvation "of man, and *will let, or hinder it, until he be taken out of "the way*—(2 Thess. ii. 7.) The apostle also spake of a "time, when this man of sin should be revealed; when "the great mystery of iniquity should be opened; and "whom the Lord would then *destroy with the brightness of "his coming*—(8 ver.) The same apostle treating on "marriage, and showing how much preferable an un-"married life is to a married, says, those who marry *shall "have trouble in the flesh; but*, says he, *I spare you;* that "is, at that time he permitted it to be so. Then he speaks "of a future time, when *they that have wives* should *be as "though they had none*—(1 Cor. vii 28, 29.) And Christ "says, *in the resurrection they neither marry nor are given in "marriage; but are as the angels of God in heaven*—(Matt. "xxii. 30) and that he meant, that this resurrection is "(or may be) in this life, is evident from what he spake "touching the resurrection of the dead, *That God is not "the God of the dead, but of the living*"—(32d ver.)

The old man also discoursed concerning the resurrection; the substance of which was, "That the time had "commenced, and many were raised from the dead, and "had experienced that resurrection, of which we read in "many places in the scriptures; which is a resurrection "from a state buried in sin, to a state of righteousness and "life in Christ: according to his own words, *I am the "resurrection and the life: he that believeth in me, though he "were dead, yet shall he live*—(John xi. 25.) Also, ac-"cording to the apostle, *Even we who were dead in sins, "have* become *quickened together with Christ; and* he *hath "raised us up together, and made us sit together in heavenly "places in Christ Jesus*"—(Eph. ii 5, 6)

He also spake of the purity of the gospel of the second coming of Christ, and that "all should become pure as "the gospel itself is pure: like unto those of which we "read, who *were redeemed from among men; being the first "fruits unto God* and *the Lamb, and in their mouth was found "no guile;* for they were without fault before the throne

" of God. These, we read, *were not defiled with women*" —(Rev. xiv. 4, 5.)

He likewise spake of the impurity and iniquity of the gratification of the carnal mind, by way of onanism. He concluded by speaking on justification and sanctification, the purport of which was, "justification consists in " repenting, confessing, and forsaking all sin, of which we " have any knowledge as being such; and living in strict " obedience to the light and knowledge given to us, by " not defiling or violating our consciences in any respect. " Sanctification consists in being cleansed from, and hav- " ing power over all sin, in thought, word, and deed."

This was a long and, to many, a tedious discourse; and what made it the more tedious was, his not speaking loud enough to be distinctly heard. On the subject of what he called "the works of the flesh," he treated in so plain a manner, that many women wished themselves out of the house; but they could not well get out, in consequence of the crowd of people at the door and in the entry of the house. I considered that the subject he had principally discoursed on, could not be treated fully, so as to be understood by the unlearned, without making use of some indelicate expressions. After he had finished, B. S. Youngs spake about ten minutes, to general satisfaction.

Here it may be mentioned that a certain preacher, (whom hereafter I shall call our opponent) came rushing and crowding into the house with two of his friends, while the old man was speaking: as soon as our last speaker had finished, he desired permission to speak; saying, "I have not come to oppose, or to offer any thing contradictory to what has been delivered."— Then in a few minutes he entered on the subject of marriage, in direct opposition and contradiction to what the old man had said upon it. Many people took notice of his proceeding contrary to what he had proposed. He flourished away learnedly and fluently for about half an hour. I expected that neither of these brethren would make any reply to what he had said; and as I considered our credit relative to our faith, was in danger, as soon as he had ended, I stept upon one of the seats, to answer him. I first proposed for the consideration of the assembly, how he had proceeded contrary to his own first proposition, not to meddle in controversial points, and proceeded to state what we believed respecting marriage, and said, we do not deny the lawfulness of marriage in the manner as hath been represented, and we have been charged with tenets we do not own But while I was speaking, he cries out, "Come, friends and neighbours, let us be going." This I (and several others) considered as great impudence; and it was taking that on him which did not belong to him, as he had no right to come here and break up the meeting. It caused much confusion, some crying out, "the plain coat durst not stand his ground" Before he got out of hearing, I raised my voice, and said, it is well known that that man is not what he professes to be, and that he holds the truth in unrighteousness.

This was saying much; but I never heard that he, or any other one offered to contradict it.

I then desired the people to be still a few minutes, and I would endeavour to open the subject respecting marriage to their satisfaction, and desired that our meeting might break up in some order. They then were silent, and I proceeded and said * We do not condemn lawful marriage; but believe it best for all such as are of the world, who live in, and after the course of the world, to become married, and live according to the command and order of God in that state, and under that dispensation. According to the apostle, "it is better to marry than to burn, and those who marry do well; but those who marry not do better." Read chap. vii. of 1st Cor. there you will see our faith respecting marriage. We say no more than what Christ said: "He that is able to receive this saying," that it is not good to marry, "let him receive it." But he says, none can receive it, "save they to whom it is given—(Matt xix. 11) thus you see it is a divine gift.

When you come to have an understanding faith in the increasing work of God, through the various dispensa-

* I have given the foregoing, and following discourses at some length, that the reader may see the principle reasons and arguments these people advance for their faith respecting marriage.

tions, to the present, in order for man's complete salvation and redemption from all lascivious and evil desires, you may then receive this pure doctrine of being married "only in the Lord."

Christ mentions some in that day, who had become "eunuchs for the kingdom of heaven's sake." Why may there not then be some in this day?

Part of the prayer which Christ gave to his disciples, was, "Thy kingdom come, thy will be done on earth as in heaven." In heaven "they neither marry, nor are given in marriage:" so neither do those to whom this kingdom is come; or, in other words, who have come to it. The children of this world marry; and so long as they are the children of this world, belong to the kingdom of this world; under the dominion and power of this world; under the order and dispensation that God has heretofore given; and in short, as they have not come into this increasing work of God, they may become married. It has been asserted this evening, that we deny the ordinance, and lawfulness of marriage. I think I know the faith of my brethren; and I here speak their faith and my faith: that I verily believe the institution of marriage to have been an order of God; and I believe what I read, that God spake to Adam and Noah, and told them to go forth, increase, and multiply, as much as I believe circumcision and animal sacrifice was an order of God under that dispensation. But you are strangers to the typical meaning of these things, and to the increasing work of God.

Now I presume there is no one, in this audience, who believes that if a person, either man or woman, chooses, for some cause, to remain single, they commit a sin by not becoming married: at least, we know that the preachers of the different denominations, do not preach that it is an indispensable duty for all to become married. Many people think that the doctrine they have heard this evening, is entirely new; that none have ever preached it before the Shakers. But they are greatly mistaken; I had read much on the subject before I ever saw these people. The Essenians, an ancient sect among the Jews, held forth the same doctrine, for several hundred years before Chrift came. It is believed by fome, that with this fect Chrift united; for it is obferved, that although he often cenfured all the other fects of the Jews, yet he never fpake againft the Effenians. Jofephus fays,* that "they rejected marriage, and efteemed continence and victory over the paffions, as the greateft virtues." Many fucceeding the apoftles, held the fame doctrine; and I could mention feveral who have written decidedly on this point; and many eminent characters in the Catholic, and fome in the Proteftant churches, have recommended a fingle life as moft conducive to holinefs; witnefs William Law, and the late John Wefley, in particular.

It is believed by many, if there were to be a univerfal peace for a few centuries, mankind would increafe fo rapidly, that this terraqueous globe would not contain or fupport them: therefore, fome fay, that war is juftifiable and neceffary in order to thin mankind. But I think, that half had better become Shakers, than to murder half to get them out of the way. Therefore, our opponent need not be fo concerned about the world's coming to an end. He now is, I fuppofe, near forty years old, and has never yet been married; and who has ever faid that he is the more deluded, or a greater finner, on that account? He comes here haranguing about the command to increafe and multiply, and has never acted according to the command himfelf.

The great cry of many is, "If all were to become Shakers, the world would come to an end." Well then, all wars and fightings, all cruelty and injuftice, all fin and wickednefs, all the abominations of every kind that are in the earth, all of which have proceeded from the lufts of the flefh, would likewife come to an end; which I think would be a very good end.

The great objection to our faith is, "that the world would come to an end;" when at the fame time, they themfelves, who make the objection, alfo believe that it will come to an end, and that by fire. I think it had better come to an end by mankind forfaking generation,

* Wars of the Jews—b. ii. chap. vii.

and embracing regeneration, and thereby become ſaved from their ſins, than to be all burned in their ſins.

" If all were to become Shakers, the world would come to an end." This ſeems to be their great concern; but they are concerned nothing about it. The truth of the matter is, if all were to receive the pure doctrine that has been contended for this evening, there would be an end of the gratification of their carnal minds; this is it, as it hath been ſaid by our aged friend, " this is the God of " the world; this claims the uppermoſt ſeat in their af- " fections; this is their object of worſhip." They can part with any other thing eaſier than they can with this; yea, it is taking the very life of the natural man; and it is that life Chriſt ſpake of, which we muſt loſe by a daily croſs, in order to find life eternal—(Luke ix 23, 24.) When a man comes to take up a full and daily croſs againſt this nature, he will be brought under ſuch trials and mortifications that one, who had been an inſtrument in bringing him to this, might have cauſe to aſk him, as the men did Micah when he had loſt his gods, " What aileth thee;" and he might with propriety anſwer as Micah did, " Ye have taken away my gods which I made, and what have I more" (of the things of this world that I can take comfort in;) " and what is that ye ſay unto me, what aileth thee?—(Judges xviii. 23, 24) Some people ſay, they " like the Shakers very well, their manner of living, &c.; but I have a wife, and I would not like to forſake her; I love my wife too well to join the Shakers I would join the Shakers, if they would let me live with my wife," &c. Thus they ſpeak the very truth and language of their carnal hearts. Yea, truly, it is with ſuch as it was with one of thoſe that Chriſt mentions, who were bidden to a great ſupper; ſeveral made excuſes, but the one that had married a wife made none, but peremptorily ſaid, " I have married a wife, and therefore I cannot come."—(Matt xiv. 2)

Many people ſay, " curſed is he who parteth man and wife;" and they think this is a text of ſcripture; but there is no ſuch text in the book Chriſt ſays, " What God hath joined together let no man put aſunder"—(Matt. xix. 6.) And what were they when joined together? Why, "one flesh," i. e. one in the flesh. The apostle speaking concerning our bodies being the members of Christ, he quotes these words of Christ, and saith, "What, know ye not that he who is joined to an harlot is one body? for two (saith Christ) shall be one flesh." So then, he that is joined to a wife, is the same flesh with her in carnal affections, as he who is joined to an harlot; yea, in their carnal gratification, their feeling, and sensation are the same. "But," saith the apostle, "he that is joined to the Lord is one spirit"—(1 Cor. vi. 16, 17) here is a wide difference. Also, "the unmarried care for the things of the Lord, that they may be holy in body and spirit. But those that are married care for the things of this world," how they may please one another—(1 Cor. vii. 33, 34.) The apostle says further, "that every one should know how to possess his vessel in sanctification and honor; not in the lust of concupiscence"—(1 Thess. iv. 4, 5.) Nevertheless, "What God hath joined together let no man put asunder." Nay, we do not wish to have any man separated from his wife, who is of the world and lives according to the course of nature, but to abide with her (as long as he remains under a back dispensation law) and be kind to her, according to those natural affections he possesses, as a natural man. Further, we would have no man separated from his wife, who is "under the law of a carnal commandment"—(Heb. vii 16) but only such as are "after the power of an endless life"—(ib. 18 ver.) We read, "There is verily a disannulling of the commandment going before, for the weakness and unprofitableness thereof; for the law made nothing perfect, but the bringing in of a better hope did; by which we draw nigh to God"—(ib. 18, 19 verses.)

Christ, in answer to the Pharisees, whether it was lawful for a man to put away his wife for every cause, spake to them as under the law; which is evident by what he said to his disciples afterwards in answer to what they said to him, i. e "if the case of the man be so with his wife," (as he had told the Pharisees) "it is not good to marry:" he answered them, "all men cannot receive this saying, save they to whom it is given;" and then he proceeds to inform them respecting eunuchs, that some were born so and some were made so of men: "and there be eunuchs which have made themselves such" (by taking up their cross) "for the kingdom of heaven's sake:" and then he adds, "he that is able to receive it, let him receive it"—(Matt. xix.)

But again, concerning the world's coming to an end. This need not be our concern; but our greatest concern should be, to live according to the commands of Christ, to take up our cross against all sin, and follow him "in the regeneration"—(Matt. xix. 28) and travel back again into that innocent state that Adam stood in before the fall; and leave the world to God, who "is able of these stones to raise up children unto Abraham"—(Matt. iii. 9.) The sin and fall of Adam consisted in his yielding obedience to that which was of the earth, earthly. But I have not time at present to enter on this subject. I say, our principal concern should be, to take up our cross against all sin, and every thing in our knowledge contrary to the nature of a pure and holy God. That this nature, of which our friend has spoken, is sinful and contrary to purity, is evident from many other passages of scripture besides those he has quoted. The apostle Paul says, "Make no provision for the flesh to fulfil the lust thereof"—(Rom. xiii. 14.) Does not marriage make provision? Is it not the dictates of the carnal nature that causes men to seek wives, and women to seek husbands? Like as we read of some, "who when they have begun to wax wanton against Christ, they will marry"—(1 Tim. v. 11) What, not marry before they wax wanton against Christ? What do you think of this, my attentive hearers? The apostle says, "Walk in the spirit, and ye shall not fulfil the lusts of the flesh; for the flesh lusteth against the spirit, and the spirit against the flesh; and these are contrary the one to the other; so that ye cannot do the things that ye would"—(Gall. v. 16, 17.) Many people wish to do the things that are right, and to become holy, but they cannot until they come at the root of sin and destroy it, according to the apostle in another place. They that wish to be Christ's, must "crucify the flesh, with its affections and lusts"—(ib. 24 ver.)

"For they that are after the flesh, do mind the things of the flesh; but they that are after the spirit, the things of the spirit"—(Rom. viii. 5) "For to be carnally minded is death"—(ib. 6.) Because the carnal mind is enmity against God; for it is not subject to the law of God, neither indeed can it be: so then they that are in the flesh cannot please God—(ib. 8 "If ye live after the flesh, ye shall die: but if ye, through the spirit, do mortify the deeds of the body, ye shall live"—(ib. 13) The apostle James also says, "When lust is conceived, it bringeth forth sin; and sin, when it is finished, bringeth forth death"—(i. 15.) How many thousands have experienced this to their sorrow! The apostle Paul gives us an account of several characters that shall not inherit the kingdom of God; one of whom is the *effeminate*—(1 Cor. vi. 9) delicacy debars me from giving any explanation, or making any comment on this word. A certain author,* in his reflections on this text, says, "It is absurd to hope for heavenly happiness without being weaned from our lusts, and reformed from our gross sins." The apostle Peter says, "Dearly beloved, I beseech you as strangers and pilgrims, abstain from fleshly lusts, which war against the soul"—(ii. 11.) I might quote several other passages from the scriptures, that speak of the lusts of the flesh and the carnal mind; all which means the fallen, corrupt nature of man, which stands opposed to the salvation of the soul. In truth, every one might know its impurity from their own experience and the evil impulses of their thoughts; also from the sensations of shame which they feel attending its gratification.—According to the apostle, "It is a shame even to speak of those things which are done of them in secret"—(Eph. v. 12.)

A certain author† expresses himself on this subject thus: "O the extreme filthiness of fleshly lusts, which not only effeminates the mind, but enervates the body; which not only distaineth the soul, but disguiseth the per-

* J. Brown. † Fra. Quarles.

ſon: it is uſhered with fury and wantonneſs; it is accompanied with filthineſs and uncleanneſs, and it is followed with grief and repentance."

We agree with the church of England in part of her ninth article, "That the deſires of the fleſh are not ſubject to the law of God:" alſo, "that concupiſcence and luſt hath in it the nature of ſin:" and likewiſe we agree with part of the liturgy of the ſame church, where it is required of all perſons, before baptiſm, to promiſe, "To renounce the devil and all his works, the vain pomps and vanities of this wicked world, and all the carnal deſires and inclination of the fleſh," ſo as "not to follow nor be led by them." We alſo fully agree with the prayer that follows:

"O merciful God! grant that the old Adam" in us "may be ſo buried, that the new man may be raiſed up" in us "Grant that all carnal affections may die" in us, "and that all things belonging to the ſpirit may live and grow in" us. "Grant that we may have power and ſtrength to have victory, and to triumph againſt the devil, the world, and the fleſh." Thus we believe as that church expreſſeth concerning concupiſcence, &c; our faith requires us to renounce the ſame; alſo, in like manner we pray.

But we are condemned for believing as others profeſs to believe, and for renouncing what others only promiſe to renounce, and for praying and forſaking what others pray for only, but never forſake.

A certain commentator, in his reflections on the fifteenth chapter of Leviticus, ſays, "How ſhameful and infectious are the ſcandalous outbreakings of original and inward corruptions, and particularly thoſe which are any way connected with fleſhly luſt." Alſo on 2d Samuel, eleventh chap. he ſays, "The luſts of the fleſh are the moſt powerful and deceitful ſins, and the laſt to be ſubdued." Yea, many have had a ſight and ſenſe of the root and ſeat of ſin, but to fully deſtroy it in themſelves but few have been able. Many more ſuch like quotations I might make from ſeveral other authors, but as it is late in the evening I muſt draw to a concluſion.

Now as an unmarried or ſingle life, ſtands juſtified by Jeſus Chriſt, St. Paul, and many other characters, celebrated for their learning and piety, why then ſo much noiſe about the Shakers? Why ſtigmatize them with all the opprobrious language that apparent malice can invent? Why poor deluded creatures, on this account? Why ſhould they be drove out of the place or neighborhood? Is it becauſe they preach up a holy, ſinleſs life, and aſſert, with St. Paul, "That he who is married cares for the things of this world, how he may pleaſe his wife and bring up his children, and has much worldly concern and trouble in the fleſh; but that thoſe who remain unmarried care for the things of the Lord, are concerned to lay up a treaſure in heaven, and to know how they may pleaſe the Lord, and become holy in body and ſpirit?" When you are at home, read for yourſelves theſe paſſages of ſcripture that have been quoted: alſo, when you read and meditate thereon, may the ſpirit of truth be with you to lead you into all truth, and may it abide with you henceforth and for ever. Amen.

The aſſembly now diſperſed in decent order. Several of the neighbours blamed the conduct of our opponent; obſerving he had no right to diſturb the meeting; and by leaving the houſe with ſuch abruptneſs, he evidently diſcovered his inability to confront the arguments I was bringing againſt him. Many of the audience charged us both with angry ſenſations Herein they judged us wrong; for as with me, ſo I believe it was with him, we were only actuated by motives of zeal. But I adopted it as a rule of caution on ſimilar occaſions, to keep a meek, humble ſpirit, and not to proceed in any religious exerciſes with any confidence in my own natural acquired abilities, but to become of a child-like ſpirit, which is the ſpirit of the goſpel; placing all confidence and dependence on God, for the guidance and aſſiſtance of his holy ſpirit; and wiſhed to remember what Chriſt ſaid, "Without me ye can do nothing"—(John xv. 15.)—That is, nothing that will be of any profit to the ſoul's ſalvation. Alſo the apoſtle ſaith, "Let nothing be done through ſtrife or vain glory, but in lowlineſs of mind"—(Phil. ii. 3.)

Next day I talked with the old man concerning his preaching; I told him I did not think his explanations of our Saviour's discourse with the Sadducees, right; but that I believed in an allusion to the express words of Christ, that he also exceedingly erred. The whole address of the Sadducees to our Saviour, was concerning the state of the dead; for we are expressly told that they did not believe in a resurrection, and denied the existence of angels or spirits—(Acts xxiii. 8.) They believed no part of the scriptures to be canonical, except the five books of Moses. Therefore they told him what Moses had written, " If a man's brother die, and leave his wife and leave no children, that his brother should take his wife, and raise up seed unto his brother; and that seven brethren had, in this way, one woman to wife, and dying left no children, last of all the woman died also " Now they ask the question, " In the resurrection, therefore, when they shall rise, whose wife shall she be of the seven?" —(Mark xii. 19, 23) Jesus told them that they erred, i. e. in thinking that they married in the next world as in this. For they that shall be accounted worthy to obtain that world, and the resurrection from the dead, neither marry nor are given in marriage. Mind, it is "*that world*"—a future state of existence, of which he is speaking of, which is as clearly evident as that two and two are four. If Christ meant, as you and the other brethren believe, i. e. " a resurrection from a state of death in sin, to a life of righteousness,'' the reply he made to the Sadducees, was no answer to their question; for that had no reference at all to this present life, it was wholly respecting those who had died a natural death. Christ also told them, " neither can they die any more"—(Luke xx. 35, 36) He also referred them to what they had read in those books which they believed; that God was the God of Abraham, the God of Isaac, and the God of Jacob—(Exod iii. 6) Then said he, " God is not the God of the dead, but of the living." For if Abraham, Isaac, and Jacob, were in a state of non-existence, God could not, with propriety, be called their God. I also objected to his having asserted, " that the account of the marriage in Cana of Galilee, recorded in the seventh chapter of St. John's goſpel, was not a natural marriage, but a ſpiritual marriage and union between Chriſt and his apoſtles." Which I told him I was very ſorry to hear him aſſert, for a greater perverſion of ſcripture I never heard; and if I could not ſupport my opinion or faith, without wreſting the ſcriptures in ſuch a manner, I would give it up; for a plainer deſcription of natural marriage could not have been written; and that there is not, in all the account, any intimations to the contrary.

He did not appear diſpoſed to controvert the point with me; but only ſaid, "Firſt Mother underſtood it ſo;" thinking, as I ſuppoſed, the opinion or belief of ſo great an authority would have ſome influence on me. But I thought as little of her underſtanding about it as I did of his; and this was the firſt inſtance that leſſened her in my eſteem, particularly when I found, from further evidence, that it was really her belief.*

They ſtaid with us four or five days; in which time, by confeſſion of ſins, there were three more added to our number, viz. my nephew, Abraham Hendrickſon, mentioned before, and a black man and his wife

The two brethren met with us every evening in our ſmall meetings, and gave us much good advice. They both appeared to me to be honeſt, well-meaning, loving, and kind men. I had conſiderable converſation, principally with the old man, concerning the faith. What appeared to be moſt on his thoughts, and which he ſeemed to delight to expatiate on, were the deep things of the faith. The following is a ſummary of his diſcourſes with me at this time:

He ſaid—"The ſoul was of divine origin; but ſin "had ſeparated the ſoul from God, and that being re- "moved, we may have a communion with angels, and "with departed ſpirits." Further, "that he and ſome "others, had often heard their ſinging, and had ſeen the

* Some time after, I mentioned this aſſertion to Elder John Meacham. He did not tell me what his belief was concerning it, but only ſaid, "If it was made known to me by immediate reve- "lation, that it was a ſpiritual marriage and union as Bartley has "aſſerted, I would not mention it." Becauſe, as I underſtood him, the account on record was ſo plain to the contrary.

" order and worſhip of the ſpiritual world. But man-
" kind have become ſo loſt from God, and ſunk in na-
" ture's darkneſs, that they have no true idea of the ſpir-
" itual world But when the ſoul, or ſenſitive part of
" man becomes awakened, to ſee and have a ſenſe of its
" loſs, and feel the weight of ſin, it is brought into bit-
" terneſs and anguiſh; and as it cloſes in with the goſ-
" pel, knowing a travail therein, and a reſurrection out
" of that loſs, then their ſpiritual eyes and ears become
" opened, that were cloſed by ſin, and then is capable of
" communion with the ſpiritual world; which world is
" not ſo far diſtant above or beyond the ſky, as the car-
" nal and ignorant imagine. For, as they have never
" partaken of the nature of it, they know nothing about
" it, nor where it is. In truth, the kingdom of heaven
" is where God is. As to his omnipreſence, he is every
" where; but as to his particular reſidence, he is with
" his Saints, or it is by them that he is felt and known;
" and thoſe in the body, in their travail, are one in ſpirit
" with thoſe departed. We are united to thoſe in the
" ſame order, who have left the body; they are abſent
" in body, but preſent in ſpirit. We are one in ſpirit,
" according to our meaſure, with all the heavenly hoſt.

" In conſequence of a reſurrection, reſtoration, or com-
" plete ſalvation and redemption from all ſin, we be-
" come united to God, and conſequently to holy ſpirits.
" For whether abſent in body, or preſent in ſpirit, we
" are in one kingdom, and all in one travail: travailing
" nearer to God, and becoming more and more like
" him, though we never become equal to him in wiſdom
" and purity, as he is infinite in all his divine attributes.
" We may arrive at a ſtate of equality with the ſera-
" phim, the higheſt order of angels, in wiſdom and pu-
" rity, and they may then be as far beyond us as at pre-
" ſent. As there will be a continual and eternal travail
" from the time we firſt received the goſpel, all in and
" according to our order, in this world and the world of
" ſpirits. Indeed, with open viſion do ſome of us, in
" this life, behold the angelic company of the ſpiritual
" world, and join the ſong of the New-Jeruſalem.

"The vail of the flesh being rent, the spiritual eyes "become opened. Some of us have seen the worship of "the spiritual world, in the same order with the church. "It is the redeemed and sanctified saints, that constitute "the pure church of Christ There are millions of spir- "its with and around such a church. As the spirit of "God dwelleth with holy souls, or such as are in obedi- "ence to the gospel, so do holy spirits Wicked spirits "dwell with and around wicked people, or such as are "in a state of disobedience to the gospel."

He treated concerning the gospel being offered and preached to the world of spirits; and the possibility of their not receiving it, in consequence of their being clothed with the same darkness, or being in the same dark state as when in the body.

"After the death of the body, (said he) all find "themselves, as to their understanding and state of their "minds, the same as before. Those, before their depar- "ture hence, who have received the gospel, confessed "their sins, and begun the work of salvation, do, after "the death of the body, find themselves in the same state "of attainment therein as before; and travail on in spir- "it in the same. Like unto a workman lying down "and leaving his work in the evening, and in the morn- "ing finding it where and as he left it; he then begins "and carries on the same until finished. But the nature "of the soul is such, that it admits (as I intimated be- "fore) of an eternal improvement Its work of an in- "crease in purity and knowledge will never be finished. "There is not so great a difference from our state in this "world, and first entrance into eternity, as people gen- "erally imagine Though the wicked may be more un- "happy, being separated from all sensual delights, until "they confess their sins and receive the gospel. Such, "who have confessed their sins and received the gospel "in this world, may become more happy, being then "separated from a body which was a clog and hin- "drance, and travail on with greater rejoicing. Fur- "ther, as all, on their entrance into the world of spirits, "are, as to their state and improvement of mind, the "same as they were here, therefore an infant is an infant

"ſpirit in the world of ſpirits; and they increaſe in un-
"derſtanding, and come to a conſcious ſenſe of good and
"evil.

"No creature's probationary ſtate ends, either in this world or the world of ſpirits, until he attains a ſtate, by obedience to the goſpel, from which there will be no more going out or relapſing. But the greateſt part of mankind have run into many errors, by confining repentance and all the ſalvation from ſin, to this life, that can be obtained; in conſequence of which, many have concluded that the heathen, who never heard the goſpel in this world, muſt be unavoidably and irretrieveably loſt. In ſhort, all ſuch as have not heard, or had the offer of the goſpel in this world, will have the offer of it in the world of ſpirits; where the goſpel will finally make a complete conqueſt.

"Thus I have converſed with you on ſubjects concerning the ſpiritual world, which knowledge we have obtained by putting away all ſin, and having our ſpiritual eyes opened. But ſuch, who are loſt in ſin, will not believe this our teſtimony, though it is according to the teſtimony of thoſe whom they profeſs to believe. Do we not read in the ſcriptures of ſeveral (though they were in an inferior diſpenſation) who had communion with angels and departed ſpirits, and that they ſaw into the ſpiritual world, and to whom the heavens were opened?"

Theſe two brethren having given us much encouragement, we now continued to hold our meetings publicly twice a week, and many people attended them, not only of our neighbours, but from different parts of the country; principally, I expected, on account of the novelty of our dancing. Some intimated they believed our intentions were a burleſque on all religion; but others could not believe we were capable of ſuch hypocriſy. I was generally engaged before, or after our dancing, in ſpeaking to the people. Sometimes I had a hope and reaſon to think, many came to hear; and I truſt, from me they generally heard the truth, as my preaching was but little on the controverted points of religion, but on thoſe ſubjects wherein all profeſſors of religion are agreed, viz.

to "fear God and keep his commandments;" or, according to our fundamental principle, repent of, confess, and forsake all sin, and live a holy, just life.

I said but little about the people with whom I professed faith; for I thought that R. Hodgson, who often had something to say, praised them more than was necessary. I often said he did not preach the gospel, but the Shakers; representing what an orderly, exemplary, holy people they were, and advising the people to go and see them.

About this time I began to have operations of shaking, trembling, and stamping, similar to some of my brethren and sisters at Niskeuna; and likewise a gift, as it is called, of speaking languages, or unknown tongues. At one time I had a gift to sing; but no one understood what I sung, nor myself neither. These things I did not do as a sham, nor with intentions to make others think I was under the influence of divine power; but I really and sincerely believed I was influenced by the power of God; and these operations and gifts were in a great measure involuntary. I shall reserve my observations on these operations and gifts, for a future place in this work

I often heard them say, that "these gifts and operations were to shew the power of God; and likewise for signs, *not to them that believe, but to them that believe not*"—(1 Cor. xiv 22) They told me that some had had gifts of mortification, to bark like a dog, and crow like a cock, make a noise like a squirrel, and mew like a cat. Also, that many have had gifts to rejoice by laughing, &c. Something like this I was an eye-witness to, shortly after the two brethren left us.

In one of our meetings, while dancing, I was seized with an operation of trembling and stamping, (which generally continued two or three minutes, in which time my eyes would be closed, and when the operation was over I always found myself several feet from the place where I was dancing;) one of the sisters, a young woman, seeing me coming towards a child that lay on the floor, instantly jumped and caught it up, for fear that I should stamp on it. This being seen by R. Hodgson, who was singing for us, he held his handkerchief to his mouth, till at laſt being unable to contain himſelf, burſt our into laughter and left the room; all except two or three left the room, alſo laughing: when my operation ended, I found our meeting was broken up I was ſurprized, and wondered what was the matter, till one preſent informed me of the cauſe. Afterwards I told them I was glad there were no ſpectators preſent; becauſe they might have concluded our dancing and operations were in reality (as ſome had intimated) a burleſque on all religion. Our brother, R. Hodgſon, felt ſomewhat condemned for his conduct, particularly as he began the laughing; but that condemnation ceaſed, when he was told by the Elders he had a gift to laugh. For my part I had no faith in ſuch gifts. But my faith in theſe operations was ſo great, that I believed if there had been a dozen children on the floor I ſhould not have hurt one of them; for I doubted not but the power by which I was actuated would have kept me clear of them.

While I am on the ſubject of gifts and operations, I will relate another inſtance, which I received an account of ſoon after the above tranſaction But firſt I may obſerve, that in the early time of the church, there were many more of theſe ſtrange gifts and operations. One was, of having the arm extended and following the way the hand pointed. Elder Ebenezer Cooley related, that the power of God, at a certain time, ſtretched out his hand which he was conſtrained to follow, and which led him to a certain houſe where reſided a man who that day had broken three of his ribs, and that his hand led him into the houſe and to the place where the man lay, and finally ſtopt on the broken ribs; the man immediately felt an healing power, and was reſtored whole in a few minutes.

I do not mention theſe things to diſparage or to detract; but in order to give the whole truth without diſguiſe, that the reader may be able to judge for himſelf.

Now many of our neighbours were inquiſitive concerning the riſe of theſe people, and whence they ſprang; and of what characters thoſe were who began this work. As there was no way to obtain a correct account, many reports were in circulation. One that paſſed the moſt currently was, that the first was a woman that cam from England to America with Burgoyne's army.— This story, which was absolutely false, our opponent wa very assiduous in reporting in the neighbourhood; an many other reports as false. But what appeared to re tard the progress of our faith in the minds of some was the assertion of a certain person who had been amon these people soon after they came to America, and ha left them, living now in a neighbourhood contiguous t us; that many of the Shakers, when he was among them were in the practice of dancing naked, men and wome together; which when mentioned to me I denied, an declared it to be an absolute falsehood.

But the principal objection that people far and nea made against us was, dancing, and singing jig tunes, an hornpipes, particularly on the Sabbath, under pretenc of worshipping God. They said we had neither precep nor example in all the scriptures, nor neither could w produce any thing reasonable for it. Therefore I care fully examined the scriptures to find proofs in favour o it. These I committed to writing, and treated the sub ject at large Shortly after I had written, I read th same to a large assembly.

In order to do these people justice, I wish to give thei reasons for their faith and practice, as far as the limits o this work will permit. I shall therefore give an abridg ment of said writing, consisting of the scripture quota tions and their most weighty reasons

True and acceptable worship, in every dispensation has been only such as was performed according to th revelation and gift of God; which has ever been op posed and reprobated by a wicked spirit in fallen man which gave Paul cause to say to his opposers, and so sa we, "In the way that ye call heresy, so worship we th God of our fathers." All who are conversant with th sacred writings, know that dancing was practised by th people of God in ancient times; and in this way the returned thanks for mercies and blessings received; whic the heathens and people of the world learned and stol from the people of God,* and corrupted the same in their nocturnal recreations, and vain, ungodly mirth, as the Babylonians and Belshazzar did in their impious feast, with the golden and silver vessels taken out of the temple of the Lord. It has been objected by many, that dancing, under pretence of worshipping God, is a solemn mockery. This objection, however, will cease, if we consider the frequent practice of this kind of worship in ancient times, as will appear on examining the following texts of scripture. Exodus xv. 20—xxxii. 19. Judges xi. 34—xxi. 21. 1 Sam. xviii. 6—xxi. 11. 2 Sam. vi. 14, 16. 1 Chron. xv. 29. Psalm xxx. 11—cxlix. 3—cl. 4. Eccl. iii. 4. From these texts it is evident, that dancing was not only practised as worship, but that it was approved of God, and used more particularly on all festive occasions, as being the natural impulse of joy.

It is likewise objected, that the novelty of this thing evinces its impropriety, as it has not been practised in the Christian world. Here it may be observed, (as before) that dancing is the effusion of joy, which (though the church has long been without, and many in a mourning state) at length in this glorious dispensation of the second coming of Christ, according to the prophesy of Jeremiah xxxi. 4, emanates through the hearts of his people, and causes them to leap for joy. Therefore, it can be no objection, since the cause which it produces is as novel as the effects produced. No novelty can be deemed an impropriety, so long as it is the natural effect of a proper cause. Sacred dancing would not appear in so debased a light, had it not been perverted by the wicked generally for the purpose of nocturnal recreation; and by its pernicious consequences has become odious in the sight of every friend of morality.

If singing had, for many hundred years past, been only practised by the vulgar and profane part of mankind,

* This is a palpable absurdity, which I cannot refrain from contradicting, though often repeated by these people. When I wrote I was in their faith, receiving as truth every thing they said; but there is nothing, either in ancient or modern history, to corroborate such an assertion.

it would now appear full as ſingular and ſtrange to hear a Chriſtian ſociety ſing hymns as part of divine worſhip, as to ſee the Shakers dance.

Muſical inſtruments have, in like manner, been perverted and turned from their ancient uſe; and ſhould we now uſe them in dancing, inſtead of ſinging, it would be looked upon by many as an abomination in the ſight of God. Yet we believe there will be a time, when they will be reſtored to the people of God, and to their proper and primitive uſe in the worſhip of God.

Therefore we ſay of theſe things ſimilar to Dr. Watts, on ſinging or poeſy. See preface to his Lyric Poems. "It is to be lamented that poeſy, whoſe original is divine, ſhould be enſlaved to vice and profaneneſs; that an art inſpired from heaven, ſhould have ſo far loſt the memory of its birth-place, as to be engaged in the intereſts of hell. How unhappily is it perverted from its moſt glorious deſign! How baſely has it been driven away from its proper ſtation in the temple of God, and abuſed to much diſhonour! The iniquity of men has conſtrained it to ſerve their vileſt purpoſes, while the ſons of piety mourn the ſacrilege and the ſhame."

If ever any people had cauſe to uſe ſuch lively acts, expreſſive of their joy in God, certainly thoſe in this day have, who have received and experienced the greateſt bleſſing that ever deſcended to the children of men, even that which hath been long propheſied of, long deſired and prayed for, by the ſincere in every age of the world.

David rejoiced in the dance, becauſe he had received the ark from among the Philiſtines. Theſe people rejoice becauſe they have received that of which the ark was only typical. The children of Iſrael rejoiced in the dance, becauſe they had experienced a final deliverance from Egyptian bondage.

Theſe people rejoice in the dance becauſe they have experienced a deliverance from a more potent and powerful enemy, even him who hath reigned and ruled in the hearts of all the children of men ever ſince the fall of Adam. And becauſe they have experienced a redemption from under the bondage of the reigning power of ſin and Satan, and behold every ſpiritual enemy deſtroyed by the power of God, and behold their ſins, as the children of Iſrael did the red ſea, ſeparated from them.

Chriſt informs us, that in the return of the prodigal ſon, "there was muſic and dancing"—Luke xv. We have all been prodigal children. We have all ſtrayed away from our heavenly Father, and ſpent our ſubſtance, or uſed the talents he gave us, in ſin and riotous living: and when we become ſenſible of our poverty and loſs, and return, will there be leſs joy than at the return of the prodigal in the parable? And we believe this parable is figurative or typical of the return of mankind in the millennium. The Jews have ſtrayed from the goſpel, and the Gentiles ſimilar unto them—like unto the prodigal. The goſpel, their portion, their inheritance, their living, the gift of the Father, has been, according to the diſpenſation of it, offered and beſtowed on many; but not long after the apoſtles as ſome of them foretold, they travelled into a far country, and waſted all in ſin and riotous living, and there commenced a famine in the land, and they joined themſelves unto the ſpirit of the god of this world; whereby they have ſerved their ſwiniſh, beaſtly nature, and they fain would have ſupported their religion with ſome little ſubſtance like unto huſks: but no man gave even that little unto them, as the leaſt ſubſtance of religion is received by rightly applying unto God. Now by becoming ſenſible of their loſs, and applying unto Chriſt in this his ſecond coming, and confeſſing their ſins, ſaying, Father we have ſinned againſt heaven and in thy ſight, and now ſee we are not worthy to be called thy ſons, nor neither to be called by honorable titles, as has been with the greateſt impropriety applied to many of us,* but deſire to receive the goſpel as humble ſervants. Now, by Chriſt and his people, they will be received joyfully: they will be clothed with the robe of righteouſneſs, and a ſignet put on them that they are of the Father's children, and their feet ſhod with the

* Your Grace, Your Holineſs, Your Lordſhip, Your Worſhip, My Lord, Reverend, &c.

preparation of the gospel of peace—Ephesians vi. 15. Here the fatted calf is killed; here is given the nourishing richness of the gospel; and to crown all, to make poor returning prodigals happy, here is music and dancing.

Then such, with us, will have abundant cause to say with the Psalmist, "Thou hast turned my mourning into dancing; thou hast put off my sackcloth, and girded me with gladness"—Ps. xxx. 11. Jeremiah, speaking of this time, says, "They shall go forth in the dances of them that make merry—xxxi. 4. Then shall the virgin rejoice in the dance, both young men and old together"—ib. 13 ver. It is very singular to see these people sometimes in time of worship clap their hands and shout; but it is what was prophesied of, "Ye shall go out with joy, and be led forth with peace; and all the trees of the field (meaning people in the gospel field) shall clap their hands"—Isa. lv. 12. O clap your hands all ye people, (that are so highly favoured) shout unto God with the voice of triumph"—Ps. xlvii. 1. "Sing with gladness, and shout among the chief of the nation: publish ye, praise ye, and say, O Lord save thy people"—Jer. xxxi. 1. "Sing, O daughter of Zion; shout, be glad and rejoice with all thy heart"—Zeph. iii. 14.

We read in the fourteenth chapter and sixth verse of Matthew, of vain, ungodly dancing, and the consequences attending. The wicked, instead of rejoicing, should mourn on their birth days, and at all times, until they know their sins forgiven, and a reconciled God. Dancing, musical instruments, and singing, is not adapted to their state, and which in truth does not belong to them, but to the people of God. The wicked should rather go to the house of mourning, than to their houses of levity and ungodly mirth. Poor lost creatures, in a state of separation and alienation from God, and every thing good and lovely, sunk in the mire of their iniquities, polluted, according to Isa. i. 6. Have not such creatures much more cause to mourn, than to sing and dance? All that we do should be done to the honour and glory of God. We should praise him in and with every thing we enjoy. Every faculty of the body ſhould be dedicated to his praiſe. Our tongues were made to bleſs the Lord; our voices were given to ſing his praiſe; and the Pſalmiſt calls on every thing that hath breath to praiſe the Lord. cl. 6.

Now why ſhould this worſhip I have been advocating, be thought ſo ſtrange and unlikely to be of God, when, as I have clearly ſhown, it has been performed by the people of God formerly? Theſe people are led to worſhip God in a way different from all the dead traditional forms of fallen Chiſtendom, and to be a wonder to the world. We read the prophet Iſaiah went naked and barefoot as a ſign and a wonder—xx. 3. And we are called to worſhip him in a way not of our own chooſing. Therefore let all deſpiſers, like the wife of David, beware that they are not deſpiſing and oppoſing the work of God, "Leſt that come upon them which is ſpoken of in the prophets. Behold, ye deſpiſers, and wonder and periſh" —Acts xiii. 41.

Sometime in July, 1800, two Elders from Lebanon, namely, John Meacham and Hezekiah Rowley, made us a viſit. They met with us in our evening meetings, exhorting us to be faithful, to live an exemplary life, that our neighbours might ſee a reality in the religion we profeſſed. At this time I was ſo ſtrong in the faith, that one day as we were converſing concerning extraordinary gifts, I told the Elders I believed if I continued faithful, I ſhould be ſo endued with power in ſpeaking languages, I ſhould be able to ſpeak and preach to people in the different tongues, ſo that any nation or tribe of Indians could underſtand me, and ſhould be inſtrumental in gathering thouſands to the church. To which Elder Meacham replied, "Thomas, we don't like that "expreſſion of gathering to the church, but to the goſ-"pel."

We gave notice to our neighbours of the Elders being here, and of a meeting the ſucceeding Sabbath. By this time I had cleared out, and ſeated off the upper part of Hodgſon's houſe, which made a large, commodious meeting-room, eaſy of acceſs. On the Sabbath, according to appointment, came a large concourſe of people.

Elder Hezekiah ſpake about half an hour; which diſcourſe I ſhall give, as it contains their fundamental principle, and that doctrine which they generally preach. I thought he delivered this diſcourſe with more life and feeling than I had ever heard from any of them before.

## A DISCOURSE

### *DELIVERED BY H. ROWLEY.*

" There are many people aſſembled here at this time. " We are willing, and indeed glad to ſee them, and " wiſh that they all came with deſires to ſeek the truth; " but whatever your motives are in coming, we wiſh " you to behave in a ſober, civil manner.

" Now whatever you think of us, we come here in " goſpel love, and deſire and ſeek for nothing elſe but " the happineſs of our ſellow creatures; knowing that " people are in a loſt ſtate as to their ſalvation, and that " the world lieth in wickedneſs—(1 John v. 19.) " And we teſtify none can ever be happy, or find accept- " ance with God, who live in ſin, and after the courſe of " this world; and all we ſeek, all we deſire, and all that " we want of people, and all that we preach unto them, " is to forſake their ſins, become reconciled unto God, " and to live a holy life. We teſtify it is ſin that ſepa- " rates the ſoul from God. It was ſin that caſt Adam " and Eve out of paradiſe, drove them from the preſ- " ence of God, and the whole creation is groaning in " pain and bondage from that time to this—(Rom. viii. " 22.) It is the ſame now with every creature, as with " our firſt parents. It is ſin that keeps them out of the " garden of the Lord; it is ſin that keeps them from a " union and communion with God; and people may " labour and try ten thouſand ways to ſeek God, and " find peace to their ſouls, and to regain that paradiſiac- " al, or happy ſtate, and fellowſhip with God, from " whence all are fallen or loſt; and there is no other " way but in renouncing that which cauſed the fall, and " travailing back again out of ſin. Adam and Eve, by " the inſtigation of the ſerpent, opened the way into ſin;

"and the second Adam, Christ, has opened, and is the "way out of sin, and the way into that paradisiacal state, "and all that communion and fellowship with God, that "our first parents stood in before they sinned. People "exclaim against us as being deluded, and deceivers: "but there is no delusion but sin; and *all who live in sin,* "*are deceived.* The deceitful pleasures of sin, deceived "our first parents. Sin from that time to this, has de- "ceived, blinded, and hardened the hearts of all man- "kind; whereby they have lost a sense of, and relish for "the things of God; become spiritually dead, and as it "were, *plucked up by the roots*—(Jude xii) Now since "sin has been of such terrible consequences, being the "cause of all the wars, miseries, troubles, and afflictions "that are, and have ever been in the world, it is our la- "bour, and travail to die to sin, taking up a full cross "against the world, flesh, and devil, travailing in the "regeneration and redemption, not only from the fruit "of sin, but the very nature and inward power thereof: "in which travail, many of us in this day and dispensa- "tion of the mercy of God, have obtained a victory over "sin, and an evil nature; and I am a living witness for "God, and can testify to the efficacy of his power and "grace. That for this twenty years past, I have com- "mitted no sin, have not done any thing by night nor "day, in the dark, nor in the light, that I am ashamed "to be seen doing, by God, men, or angels. Now I "don't speak as boasting, far from it; but in humility, "and only to bear testimony to that power of God, "which through obedience to it, has worked in me both "to will and to do his pleasure—(Phil ii. 13): and if "you all had faith in the gospel, which is the power of "God, and were obedient thereto, it would work in you "mightily to the *pulling down strong holds of sin*—(2 Cor. "x. 4.) But the generality of people appear to be so "bound under the power of their carnal nature, and in "such a state of darkness, alienation, and separation "from God, that it is hard work, like digging in the "earth for a treasure, to open the gospel to them, or to "come at their hearts; and such gross darkness covers "the minds of the people (Isa. lx. 2) that while I am "speaking, it is like pressing against a wall, or beating "against a rock. I wish that people could see, feel, and "sense their loss, and what a distance they are from God. "You all desire to be happy; you wish to die in peace, "and go to heaven; but to which state there is but one "door to enter, which is by confessing, and forsaking all "sin. Jesus Christ, out of pity and compassion to the "poor lost children of men, came to open a door for "their salvation, and to save them from their sins (not "in their sins) Many profess to be christians, and fol-"lowers of Christ, and at the same time live in sin, liv-"ing after the *lusts of the flesh, the lusts of the eye, and* "*pride of life.* What hope can such have? If any, it "is the hope of the hypocrite, which *shall perish*—(Job "viii. 13.) Oh the darkness of the minds of most peo-"ple, deluded and deceived by the deceitfulness of sin, "under captivity to their hearts' lusts, and evil nature; "and yet pretend to judge the people of God, and as-"sert those are deluded and deceived, who deny them-"selves, take up their cross, and follow Christ. What "astonishing inconsistencies!

"There is but one way to the kingdom of heaven, "but one door to enter, *one faith, one Lord, and one baptism* "(Eph. iv. 5) though people have got many ways, and "*have sought out many inventions*—(Eccl. vii. 29): some "flattering themselves they are in the right way in such "a church, and others in such a church; but Christ is "*the way, the truth, and the life*—(John xiv. 6) not the "many ways Christ is not divided. Such who are "led by the spirit of Christ, are of one faith, one heart, "and one mind; and are united together in love Now "Christ has left us two plain rules to judge who are the "people of God: *by their fruits ye shall know them*—"(Matt vii 20) also, *by this shall all men know that ye are* "*my disciples, if ye love one another*—(John xiii 35) It is "*not every one that saith unto me, Lord, Lord, shall enter into* "*the kingdom of heaven; but he that doth the will of my* "*father which is in heaven*—(Matt vii. 21) *for this is the* "*love of God, that ye keep his commandments*—(1 John v 3) "*and he that committeth sin, is of the devil*—(ib iii. 8.) "Therefore, it matters not what people may pretend to, "or what profession they may make, or society they may "belong to, if they live in sin. For whosoever professes "to know God, *and keepeth not his commandments, is a liar, "and the truth is not in him*—(1 John ii. 4.) I wish people "ple would seriously consider these things, and compare "their lives and conduct with the scriptures, and live up "to the light and knowledge God has given them; "whereby they would come to see more and more clear "respecting those things which concern their salvation, "and then would be better able to judge who are the "people of God and followers of Christ, and who are "not; what is of God, and what is not; and thus become able to judge righteous judgment."

Now there were none that I heard of, who made any general objections to this discourse; but many denied the truth of his assertion respecting "not having committed any sin, or done any thing for twenty years, by day or by night, in the light or in the dark, that he would be ashamed to be seen doing by God, men, or angels."

My father, who was at this meeting, being in company with some neighbours a few days afterwards, and they speaking about it, said, "Whether Hezekiah spoke the truth or not, I cannot say; but this I can say as confidently as he did, that it is the very state we all should come to, or the life we should all live: i. e. to do nothing we would be ashamed of, and indeed think no thoughts we would be ashamed should be known. But such is the depravity of mankind that if all their secret sins, their wicked thoughts and actions were exposed, many would endeavour to find some cave or place to for ever hide themselves from human sight.

We should always remember that we are at all times in the sight of God, and should make it a rule to always act as in his presence, and not to do any evil in his sight, which we would be ashamed to do in the sight of our fellow creatures. If people always lived as in the presence of God, or really did believe, and always kept in mind, that God is at all times present, and knows all our thoughts, and sees all our actions, they would be more reserved and careful in their conduct, and would endeavour to rectify their thoughts."

Next day the Elders visited a few of the first characters in our neighbourhood, called Quakers, who had said they came creeping here and leading silly people captive —(2 Tim. iii 6) and were ashamed to visit any, except those few they had caught in their net. The Elders informed them of their motives in coming here, and that they had no intentions of causing any uneasiness or disturbance in the neighbourhood, but that they came from a conscientious sense of duty, &c. They likewise visited my father's family, where they were kindly and respectfully treated; and with whom they had considerable conversation concerning their faith. They staid with us four or five days; and before they left us, they appointed our brother, R. Hodgson, as head, or to take the lead of us principally in our meetings. Likewise, if any of us were dissatisfied about any thing, or committed any sin, to open our minds to him. I told the Elders I did not fully agree with them in their choice, and thought our brother Abraham Hendrickson was the most proper person. They made no reply; but only told me to be *obedient*. This was the first time I heard of obedience to the Elders. As they were about leaving us, (all we who professed faith being together) Elder John said, "Now we wish you all to be faithful, and keep out of "all sin; live in love and union with one another; be "kind, tender, and obedient to one another. We don't "wish you to put your dependence on us, to think we "can save you or do any thing for you, any further than "to give you advice; for we are but poor dependent "creatures. We desire and recommend you to look to "the *word* of God in your *own hearts*. So we bid you "all farewell."

I thought they appeared to have a great deal of care and concern for us, and that they dealt by us as tender parents do by their children, and I thought they gave us much good advice.

Our opponent made it his business to go about the neighbourhood, warning and cautioning people to guard against the increasing delusion of Shakerism. Therefore, a few days after the Elders left us, I wrote him the following letter:

CORNWALL, July, 1800.

*FRIEND,*

As thou avoidest personal conversation with me, I therefore give thee a few words in this way. Thou sayest, thou art much concerned about the spirit of Shakerism, which is a spirit of delusion which has crept into this place; and repeatedly behind my back charging me with being the cause. Running from house to house like a mad man, crying "delusion, delusion! wolves in sheep's clothing!" and repeatedly asserting about us and the church we belong to, absolute falsehoods, through ignorance, I presume: talking about a people thou hast never seen, and with whom thou hast never conversed. All the knowledge thou hast of them, and their doctrine, is from flying and false reports; such as this, that the first Shaker was a woman who came from England with Burgoyne's army. This story, which I can prove to be an absolute falsehood, I expect thou hast told in almost every house in Cornwall. What a simple, unwise man thou art, to undertake to give an account of a professing Christian society from reports and stories fabricated by drunkards and people of ill fame.

Thou knowest how many false and scandalous stories were reported about the Quakers, when they first arose, by people like thyself; who, in their ignorance, could cry delusion.—Thou knowest the song sung by the biggotted and nominal priests and professors about the Quakers, particularly in New-England and *Boston*, when they first appeared there: and thou hast pretty well got the old persecuting tone, "delusion, delusion! deceivers, antichrists, ah! wizzards and witches too!" What, think the Elders have learned us witchcraft, hocus-pocus, &c. already? It is no wonder thou art afraid to come to our meetings, or talk with those of us who are able to talk with thee; for surely thou shouldest act as thou advisest others, "keep away for fear of being caught." Pray be as wise as one formerly was, who told those (like thee) who were zealous in crying delusion, to "refrain from these men, and let them alone; for if this work be of men, it will come to nought; but if it be of God, ye cannot overthrow it"—Acts v. 38, 39.

Now it is wisdom not to pass judgment before hearing and examination, and not to detract from any person's or people's character by uncertain information.—Any ignorant person can cry error and delusion, but it requires a wise man to prove who are in an error and deluded, and who are not. Wishing that thou mayest act with more wisdom for the future, I for the present bid thee adieu.

THOS. BROWN.

Several persons said they believed my motives in joining with these people, and vindicating them and their faith, were pecuniary. About this time being in company with a few of the friends, one of them said, "Thomas, I expect thou art on some religious speculation, for thou art a man of too much sense and understanding, to be duped by those Elders, and believe in, and vindicate such an inconsistent system of faith; therefore I expect thou art some way to be paid for thy apparent zeal, or hast some pecuniary motive in what thou doest.

I replied—If what thou sayest be true, I must be a most consummate hypocrite. But I tell thee, I am sincere, believing in my heart that it is the way of God, and trust I shall continue to be sincere, until I see I am in an error; and then I hope as an honest man, I shall not be ashamed to recant. And if thou like a wise man, shouldest inform thyself respecting our faith, before thou judgest and condemnest, it would not appear such an inconsistent system as thou dost now imagine it to be; particularly, as to your fundamental principle of the light of Christ in all men, and to be influenced as that light directs, wherein we agree.*

One said, "As your society has never published their faith and practice, that the world might know what they

* So I then thought, as I had not yet heard them preach, either in public or private, any doctrine contrary thereto. See pages, 43 and 51.

believe, and have never contradicted those reports, if false, that have been in circulation about them, therefore you should not blame people for representing their doctrines and practices, according to such information as they can procure. For instance, I have been credibly informed that the first Shaker was a bad woman, who came out of Burgoyne's army, and settled at Niskeuna, and that she drank spirituous liquors to excess, and in her time, they used to dance naked. Now am I blamable for telling those stories again, since they are not publicly contradicted by them. If they are innocent, and these things are false, why do they not do it? and if they are the only people of God, and have got the gospel necessary for mankind to believe, in order to their salvation, why do they not come out into the world and preach it boldly. If they have the light, why do they not shew the light; not put it under a bed or bushel, at Lebanon, or in the woods or wilderness, at Niskeuna. They never would have shewn themselves here; this neighbourhood would never have been favoured with the gospel of the second coming of Christ, as you call it, if thou hadst not had a curiosity to go and see them."

I replied—It would be almost an endless work, to answer all the objections, and foolish fabricated stories. It is now, as it was formerly respecting Christ; the unbelievers in that day, had many ifs and objections, because he came and acted not according to their carnal imaginations, of what was right; and it has always been much the same towards the people of God, whenever such have arisen: and if these people were to come out into the world, and travel about, and preach their faith boldly, as thou sayest, the objection then would be as hath already been made in this place;—viz. "If they were the people of God they would not come here and make disturbance." But their business and concern is to pay attention to the divine gift, and proceed as they are thereby influenced; and when acting under this direction, they go where they are sent, and preach their faith boldly, and that with authority.

Some time in August, 1800, I was again among my brethren at Niskeuna, and staid with them three days; in which time I received an account of a miracle ſaid to have been wrought among the young believers a few weeks before. According to the account, "four of them having had the intermitting or remitting fever ſo long, that they were reduced to ſuch a low ſtate, no proſpect of their recovery remained, when one of the ſiſters came from the church order to ſee them. She firſt ſpake to the one who was ſuppoſed to be the moſt debilitated. She told him to open his eyes. As he could not ſpeak audibly, he whiſpered, "that he could not." She ſaid—"I have come to ſee you in the gift of God, and you muſt have faith." He then, as he told me, "received ſtrength to open his eyes." She then ſaid, "ſit up." He replied, "I cannot." As he told me afterwards, "at that time he had no more ſtrength than an infant. She ſaid again, "I have come to ſee you in the gift of God; have faith, only believe, and all things are poſſible." He immediately received faith, and ſtrength to ſit up. She then ſaid, "all of you may receive faith, ariſe, and labour." They aroſe accordingly and laboured or danced near half an hour, to a tune ſung by B. Youngs' wife (who firſt gave me the account) from which time they began to recover, and in a few days were perfectly well."

This miracle was wrought to ſtrengthen the young believers' faith; and was told me, to ſtrengthen mine. I ſhall not take notice, or mention any thing elſe that I heard or ſaw at this time, but return to Cornwall.

Soon after I returned home, I wrote the following letter to my wife's ſiſter who was now with the brethren and ſiſters at Niſkeuna.

Now I chooſe to inſert a few letters written when I was in union with theſe people, 1ſt. becauſe they are expreſſive of their faith; and 2d. becauſe they have preſerved ſuch letters, written by ſome while in the faith, and have ſometimes ſhown them for their own vindication, when attacked, upon the change of ſentiment in their authors, ſaying, "read this letter, and you will ſee what his faith was, and what he has turned from." Thus making ſuch letters a criterion by which to judge and condemn. But I ſhall ſave them the trouble, by producing thoſe which are the moſt expreſſive of my faith, when written; as undoubtedly ſome paſſages in this publication will be quoted by ſome in converſation with them; and I keep nothing back which they ſay backſliders (as they call them) are aſhamed of, becauſe ſuch things condemn them for leaving the church.

CORNWALL, *Sept.* 6, 1800.

*DEAR SISTER,*

Conſidering the privilege thou haſt with the believers, I am in hopes thou wilt become ſtrong in the faith; which will be ſuch a ſatisfaction to me, that I ſhall think myſelf amply paid for all my concern and labour in gaining thee to the only true living goſpel on earth. Thou haſt thy reaſonings and doubts ſometimes. I have reaſoned and doubted before thee. But let us remember that thouſands reaſoned when Chriſt was on earth, whether or not he was the promiſed ſaviour. They died in that day; they die in this, reaſoning and diſbelieving in him. Thou in thy day art greatly favoured. I hope to ſee thee eſtabliſhed on the ſure foundation, the rock of ages, which all the turbulent agitations of a carnal nature within, and the world without cannot ever overthrow. What ſhall I ſay? What can I ſay with more propriety than, "glory to God in the higheſt, peace on earth, and good will towards men"—Luke ii. 14. All I deſire is, that I may live as becometh the goſpel, and die triumphant in the faith. May it be the ſame with thee, and that proſperity may attend thee in the one living and true faith, is the wiſh of they affectionate brother.

T. B.

About the middle of September, a couple of Elders came to ſee us again; namely, Ebenezer Cooley, who was the Father (ſo called) and firſt Elder to the young believers, having the care of them next to, and receiving his gift to act from the firſt in the miniſtration, and accompanied by one whom we called Elder Stephen. At this time I was not at home, conſequently, as it will appear, I loſt the benefit to be derived from the Elders at this time; for Elder E. left orders with our leader R. H.

for me not to labour, or dance, only to assemble with them, and I might still occasionally speak to the people.

Now why I must be debarred from any privilege, or the performance of any part of our worship, by my unavoidably being absent while the Elders were here, appeared unaccountable to me. I told Hodgson it was perfect nonsense, as I did not intentionally stay away, but improved every minute to come home before the Elders went away; but it was impossible, as I was becalmed on the passage.

He replied—"It is the gift for thee not to labour, and any reason or satisfaction why it is not, I cannot give thee."

But on a little consideration, I saw the reason, which was they had had a greater, or an additional privilege; and if any of them had done any thing wrong, they had had an opportunity to open the same; and as I had not had that opportunity and privilege, the Elders thought it best for me not to labour with them until I had; as they believe dancing is a part of worship the most sacred; "In which," they say, "none may enter with any sin "covered, as it is expressly contrary to the gift of God; "and would be an offering like unto Nadab and Abi- "hu—(Lev. x. 1.) For the Lord will be sanctified "in them that approach him—(ib. ver 3.) And the of- "fering or sacrifice of the wicked, or of such as have "any sin covered, *is an abomination to the Lord*"—(Prov. xv. 8.) Also this exercise of dancing or labour is particularly called the works of God; as I have often heard the Elders, or the one who has the lead of the meeting, after speaking a few words, conclude by one or the other of the following sentences: "All who feel justified—Or "such as have not violated their consciences—Or those "who have no sin covered, may prepare* to labour in "the works of God, or go forth in the works of God"

And there is so much said and preached on the direful consequences of presuming to join in this part of worship, with any sin unconfessed, or if they are in any re-

* What is understood by *prepare*, is for the brethren to take off their coats, and form into order.

ſpect irreconciled to the Elders, or to the gifts they have had for them, or irreconciled to any of the brethren, that many would not dare to join in the dance, believing if they did, ſome judgment would fall on them.—And they believe the Elders ſee through an through them, and ſin is not long hid from them.

The following inſtance which was told me among many others, may clearly evince the truth of this aſſertion: "One of the young ſiſters committed ſin in meet-" ing, by looking at a young man, a ſpectator, (Whoſo-" ever looketh, &c.)—(Matt. v. 28) At this time " James Whittaker being in a room in the upper part of " the meeting houſe,* and having a ſenſe of what was " done, came down into the meeting room while they " were dancing, and ſaid, *God is of purer eyes than to be-" hold iniquity There is ſin committed and coverd among " you, and your worſhip will not be owned until it is put away.* " The young woman was convicted, knowing herſelf " guilty, fell on her knees and confeſſed ſhe had ſinned; " after which, he told them *they might proceed.*" If this is not exactly true, it is exactly as they told me. I may further obſerve that it is their belief that their dancing for worſhip, is ſo ſacred, reverential, and awfully ſolemn, that no perſon dare, or can join in it, who has not confeſſed his ſins; and the few who through wantonneſs have attempted it, have always failed in proceeding, by inſtantly being taken with ſome violent pain, or contortion of the body, one inſtance excepted; as I have been informed, " a perſon who, from motives of ſport, joined them in the dance; but after they had finiſhed, he was unable to ſtop, but continued dancing near two hours."

Now I began to conclude that the Elders ſtood as ſole leaders, teachers, and directors; and that acquieſcence and obedience to them was what in all things was required. But then I knew not how to reconcile this out-

* It may be proper to obſerve that the upper part of their meeting houſes are partitioned into rooms, finiſhed principally for the reſidence of the miniſtration.

ward popiſh leading and preaching to what they had heretofore preached. But more of this a few pages hence.

January, 1801. Elder John, and Hezekiah came again to ſee us, and ſtayed five days. Many people attended our meetings, particularly while the Elders were with us at this time.

Our greateſt opponent appeared again in one of our meetings; at the concluſion of which, he broached the ſubject of marriage. He addreſſed himſelf principally to the Elders, who entered into ſome controverſial converſation with him upon the ſubject, though they wiſhed to be brief at preſent, as the meeting had been lengthy.

Now I took particular notice of one ſentence he had aſſerted in ſupport of marriage, and was determined to contradict it before the meeting broke up; ſo I took the opportunity of a moment's ſilence between him and the Elders, and ſaid, It has been aſſerted in this meeting, that all, and the moſt pious men and women in every age of the world, have approved of marriage. I aſſert the contrary, that all have not, and that the moſt pious in every age of the world, and ſeveral whole churches have recommended and approved of the doctrine of virginity, or abſtaining from marriage. As to the truth of my aſſertion, I leave it with thoſe to judge, who are acquainted with eccleſiaſtical hiſtory.

My friend R. Hodgſon, when I began to ſpeak, gave me a pull to ſtop me, and after meeting blamed me for ſpeaking, and ſaid, I ſpake out of order, and interrupted the Elders. But Elder H. ſaid, we have nothing againſt Thomas for ſpeaking, ſo R. H. was ſilent.

Now in this aſſertion in contradiction to our opponent, I went too far in ſaying the moſt pious in every age of the world; for I do not recollect reading of any who recommended virginity, or an unmarried life, before the coming of Chriſt, except the Eſſenes, or Eſſenians in Jewiſh antiquity.

Our opponent aſked the Elders if they were willing to appoint an hour for him and a few ſelect friends to meet with them, to have ſome converſation on particular points of their faith; to which the Elders agreed, and appointed 3 o'clock the next day. He next requested of them, that I should not be present. They told him, "that request could not be granted; for they could not, with any propriety, hinder me, especially in my own house." He then desired that I should not be allowed to speak, or have any active part in the debate. They answered, "we cannot comply with this request neither, as we have no authority to forbid his speaking; but we are willing to propose to him to be silent, from thy request; to which we think it is likely he will agree." Afterwards they told me (smiling) of our opponent's singular requests. I said, not to be present and have the satisfaction of hearing the conference, I will not agree to. A pretty story, indeed. It is to be a public conference; all or as many of the neighbours as have a mind may come, but I must not be allowed to be among them. Did ever any body hear of such a request? But as to his third request, I will satisfy him, and promise not to speak; knowing, that if I do not grant him this, there will be no conference at all; he will never appear against you, if I am permitted to defend you and combat him. Let the poor creature and his select friends have the conversation, and make the best they can of it. But now you see how unreasonable he is. He proposes to bring with him a few select friends to assist him, to which you assent; but you are not allowed to have one. I believe his select friends will be few, as there are not many Friends in this place who have union with his zeal against us, or conduct towards us; as it favours too much of that old persecuting spirit, which most people wish might die away.

At the hour appointed, he came with only one Friend and a neighbour, who made little or no profession. Few of the neighbours attended as hearers, as there was but little notice given of the meeting. Our opponent began and continued in a lengthy discourse, in the manner of his public preaching, consisting of warnings and cautions to the Elders of the dreadful consequences of preaching and propagating false and erroneous doctrines; and of the day that was coming when, said he, "You would be weighed in the Lord's balance and found wanting."

After he had concluded, one of the Elders ſpake and ſaid, "It is far from our intention knowingly to preach "or propagate error; but we wiſh well to the ſouls of "all our fellow creatures; and our greateſt deſire and "labour is to bring creatures out of darkneſs into light," &c. He next broached his old ſubject of marriage, and their preaching againſt that divine ordinance; which, he ſaid, "was labouring to murder ſouls unborn, depopulate and bring the world of mankind to an end. Which if all mankind was to embrace your ſyſtem, as you wiſh, in an hundred or an hundred and ten years, there would not be a human creature on earth; and how you can preach ſuch doctrine as this, without knowingly preaching error, and your deſiring to bring mankind out of darkneſs into light in preaching a doctrine contrary to all natural and revealed light, is a myſtery."

One of the Elders proceeded to anſwer him, and acknowledged it had been an ordinance owned of God under former diſpenſations, as circumciſion and ſacrifices were; ſpake ſomething of the increaſing work of God, in which many things were done away which were ſuffered under former diſpenſations, and on account of the darkneſs and hardneſs of their hearts—Matt. xix. 8. And as to the world coming to an end, "we read (ſaid they) "it is to come to an end; and how is it to end, but by "creatures travailing back to the place they fell from, "and becoming redeemed from that nature which "brought (under the fall) all mankind into the world, "and all ſin and miſery with it?"

Our opponent's companion, the neighbour before mentioned, ſpake a few words on the ſubject, and in about an hour the conference ended; and on both ſides they came off, as they thought, victorious. But I think an impartial hearer was the beſt judge.

Now I ſhould have given theſe dialogues in full, but they were ſo inſipid, and want ſo much dreſſing to make them fit to be ſeen, I have thus paſſed over them

One of the Elders aſked me afterwards, if I did not think our opponent had been well anſwered and confuted I anſwered, neither of you have any thing to boaſt. But you are more excuſable than he, as he is reputed to be a ſcholar; I was therefore ſurprized to hear his weak arguments and reaſonings. About this time he indirectly oppoſed us in his meeting. My father being preſent, aroſe and contradicted him.

As ſoon as I could get a convenient opportunity to converſe with the Elders, I inquired of them the reaſon and propriety of Elder E. Cooley's breaking open a letter I had ſent to a young believer. They ſaid but very little as an apology; but afterwards I found it was the order of the church, and practice of the Elders, to intercept and break open all letters ſent to any of the believers or members of the church; principally to ſee if they contain any thing contrary to the faith Though I believe they commonly deliver letters after they have read them, as directed, let them contain what they may I may further obſerve, that no faithful or obedient member writes and ſends a letter without firſt conſulting the Elders. If they concur therewith and approve of what is written, it is ſent; if not, it is deſtroyed, or an alteration made according to the minds of the Elders In ſhort, they do nothing but in the gift or by firſt ſeeking advice from the Elders.

I next queried with them reſpecting the propriety of the gift that had been left for me, not to join in the labouring part of our meetings, in conſequence of my abſence, as heretofore mentioned. One of them ſaid, if you would be obedient to every gift that is for you, you would find ſtrength and a bleſſing to attend you. I told them though it appeared ſtrange to me when I firſt heard that I muſt not labour, neverthele ſs I had been obedient, except a few times when many people were preſent, that none might have cauſe to think or ſay I was weak in the faith, or did not approve of dancing. One of them ſaid, "We are ſatisfied in your labouring a few times from that motive; and we do not charge you with any evil, or blame you for being unavoidably abſent, by no means; but we look upon labour in meetings to be a moſt weighty and ſolemn work of God It is the order of the people of God, for none to proceed therein but ſuch as are clean, and particularly under the protection and gift of God.—

" But, Thomas, if you do not ſee fit to be reconciled and " obedient to the way and order of the people of God, " you muſt go your own way."

I replied, that is juſt like the ſpirit and people of the world; if one does not pleaſe them, or think and act much as they wiſh, if they have not power, the next thing is, you may go your own way—go about your buſineſs. But I am willing to drop all that is paſt, as I do not wiſh any unneceſſary controverſy; and if I have been in the wrong by being diſſatisfied about any thing, I hope you will forgive me, and think no more of it. One replied, " We ſhall not hold any thing againſt you."

They had hours of converſation with me, endeavouring to ſtrengthen and eſtabliſh me firm in the faith. Particularly on the ſubject of the increaſing work of God, from one diſpenſation to another; of which Elder Hezekiah wiſhed me to have a thorough underſtanding— An abridgment of his diſcourſe on this ſubject at this time, which is, as I have heard from ſome others at various other times, I think beſt to give here.

" When Adam, by tranſgreſſion, became loſt and ſunk " far from God, and without hope, the firſt work of God, " in order for his reſtoration, was by promiſe—(Gen. iii. " 15.) Therefore his righteouſneſs, and that of the faith- " ful antediluvians, principally conſiſted in believing in " the promiſe. The covenant God made with Abra- " ham, was an additional promiſe, and with the ſign of " circumciſion was a further increaſe of the work of God " in this diſpenſation; and which ſign was typical of the " deſtruction of that nature of the fleſh which, according " to the firſt promiſe, the ſeed of the woman was to " bruiſe or deſtroy. From Adam to Moſes was the firſt " and patriarchal diſpenſation. How far, under that diſ- " penſation, they were ſaved from ſin, is ſignified by E- " zekiel's viſion of the holy waters, as being only up to " the ancles—(chap xlvii 3.) The ſecond diſpenſation " and further increaſe of the work of God, was the Mo- " ſaic, or law given to Moſes; which abounded with or- " dinances and ſacrifices typical of the firſt and ſecond " coming of Chriſt; and ſalvation attained under that " diſpenſation is ſignified by Ezekiel, as *waters to the knees*.

" The miniſtration of John the Baptiſt, was an increaſ-
" ing work and end of the Moſaic diſpenſation ; a fore-
" runner and preparatory to the third diſpenſation, and
" firſt coming of Chriſt : and the ſalvation attained in
" that diſpenſation, was as *waters to the loins*. And in
" that as in antecedent diſpenſations, another day is ſpo-
" ken of, called the ſecond coming of Chriſt, which is
" the fourth and laſt diſpenſation ; in which is a greater
" diſplay of the work of God than has ever been hereto-
" fore, even complete ſalvation ; repreſented by Ezekiel
" as *a river that could not be paſſed over ; for the waters were*
" *riſen, waters to ſwim in*.

" Former diſpenſations conſiſted principally in out-
" ward purifications and ſacrifices, which did not redeem
" from ſin, or make the comers thereunto perfect ; nev-
" ertheleſs, they who were obedient to that of God made
" known by patriarchs and prophets, found juſtification,
" and were accepted of God, according to the light and
" power afforded. But this diſpenſation being as a river
" which cannot be paſſed over, except we become ſtript of
" all ſin, and walk or depend on nothing but the goſpel and
" power of God : and that has ever been required of
" creatures as they come to further light, (and it is rea-
" ſonable it ſhould be ſo) which never was required in
" former or darker diſpenſations. In the firſt coming of
" Chriſt, they were required to confeſs and forſake their
" ſins, and travail in the new birth or regeneration, which
" was not preached or required under the law. And
" there was more required under the law; and a further
" ſalvation was obtained, that was not required and ob-
" tained under the diſpenſation preceding Nevertheleſs,
" all will be benefitted, reſtored, redeemed, and ſaved
" from all ſin, by the ſalvation brought to light by the
" goſpel."

Thus I have only given the ſubſtance of his diſcourſe at this time, as one on the ſame ſubject has been inſerted in the former part of this work.*

A few weeks before the Elders came to ſee us at this time, I happened in company with a man who appeared

* See page 33.

to be candid and honeſt, and bore that character in general; and, as we were in ſome converſation reſpecting the Shakers, he informed me that he had ſeen a number of them, both men and women, dance naked; and told me when and where he ſaw them. Though I had often heard the ſame before, yet I had given no credit to it, as I had never heard any one aſſert the truth thereof from perſonal knowledge; therefore I could with propriety deny the aſſertions. But now, I had heard the account ſo correct and authentic, that I knew not what to think, or how to reconcile it with what the old believers in the church had told me. I now opened the matter to the Elders, informing them what I had heard, and that I was almoſt inclined to believe the truth of it. I therefore ſaid, now let me aſk you one queſtion, to which I hope you will give me a direct anſwer. Have the people, or any of them, ever danced naked? Before you anſwer me, I added, if they have, you need not be afraid it will hurt my faith to let me know it. I promiſe you it ſhall not: and I aſk you this queſtion principally, that if they never have, I may confidently contradict it when I hear it aſſerted.

Elder Hezekiah anſwered me: "I never ſaw any ſuch "conduct, neither do I believe there ever has been any "ſuch conduct." And he intimated that he did not wiſh me to give people the lie; the perſon I had mentioned might have ſeen ſuch conduct, which, if he did muſt have been by ſome out of order, or that the church had no union with.

Now the reader will recollect, I received much the ſame anſwer to the ſame queſtion before, as well as at ſeveral other times. I had heard this report declared to be falſe by ſeveral old believers, but afterwards (as will be ſeen) I came to a further and full knowledge reſpecting ſaid conduct.

The next thing I ſhall take notice of is, the Elders requeſting me to confeſs my ſins again, to which I agreed; as it is cuſtomary for believers to confeſs their ſins more than once, as ſome might not think of all the firſt time. Indeed, they are to confeſs until they have opened every evil in thought, word, or deed, of which they have ever been guilty. They say, "as believers attain a travail in "the gospel, they come to have more of a feeling sense "of their loss while in sin, and the odious nature of it, "and so confess with a more penitent disposition." I proposed reading a piece which I had written a few weeks before, including, by way of examination and queries, a catalogue of the sins of mankind. Those queries or questions, which in any respect concerned me, I told them I would remark, and such queries as did not concern me, I told them I would read without making any observations. This they did not appear fully to unite with, as there was no gift or order in the church to make use of any written form; but finally they left me to do as I thought best. And as I wished to make a full and complete confession, therefore I made use of what I had written; and by reading these queries, and how far each concerned me, much evil was brought to my mind, which otherwise I could not possibly have thought of; and in consequence of which, I more fully confessed my sins than I had done either time before. And all that I thought of, and all that I believed to be evil that ever I had done in thought, word, or deed, I fully and faithfully confessed; and concluded by saying, all the sins I have confessed, and those which I at this time have not recollected, I utterly detest and am heartily sorry for, and pray that God may forgive me, and that the people of God may feel the spirit of forgiveness towards me; and hope I may, for the time to come, utterly forsake all I have confessed, and endeavour, to the utmost of my ability and power, to live a just and holy life. To which, in brokenness of heart and with tears in my eyes, did I sincerely say, amen.

Elder Hezekiah said—"Thomas, I believe you have "confessed all you have thought of, and likewise believe "you have been sincere in so doing; and I hope you "will, as you have said. utterly forsake all you have con-"fessed, and become a faithful man of God in the gos-"pel."

My wife (though a member of the society of the poeple called Quakers) was now, by much preaching and persuasion, prevailed on to join us; though she had but little faith in our gifts and dancing; but as ſhe was with us, ſhe endeavoured to comply and unite as much as ſhe conſcientiouſly could.

I invited the Elders to viſit my father and his family; and with them they had conſiderable converſation on ſeveral points of faith But I ſhall only take notice of Elder Hezekiah's diſcourſe reſpecting backſliders. But previous, I had beſt go back a little

Three or four weeks before the Elders came to ſee us at this time, our opponent had got a pamphlet, entitled, "Reaſons offered for leaving the Shakers, by Reuben Rathbone," part of which he read to ſeveral; and came, when I was from home, and read it to Hodgſon, and to his and to my wife. My father alſo borrowed it of him and read it. The conſequence of which was, he entirely loſt what little faith he had. He now informed the Elders he had read ſaid book, and that, if the author had written the truth, they were a deceived, deluded people.

Elder Hezekiah ſaid—"We were acquainted with the "author, and knew his life and conduct while he was a-"mong us. For a time he was a faithful man; but by "not keeping low and humble, and ſuffering himſelf to "be lead away by a ſenſe and feeling contrary to the "goſpel; and alſo, being naturally of an aſpiring diſpo-"ſition, he was reaching after office and authority in the "church; which he, nor no one, can obtain in their own "will and time; as it is obtained only by ſuch as keep "humble, according to the words of Chriſt, *The leaſt a-"mong you ſhall be greateſt*—(Luke ix. 48) and that ſuch "ſhould riſe in the order and gift of God;* but by his "not keeping in the gift of God he fell, and great we "believe has been his fall. Likewiſe, by his thus giving "way to his aſpiring mind, he ſo loſt his ſtrength and "power before he left us, as to be overcome in the fleſh. "It is clearly to be ſeen, that it was the fleſh that cauſed "him to leave us; for he took a female away with him, "whom he had lived with contrary to his faith, and ſoon

* My father little knew what they meant by the gift of God.

" after he left us he married her.* All who leave us, " or the way of God, are under the necessity of speaking " against us, and patching up some reason to justify " themselves for so doing. But all those who forsake

* As this story has been often told, and undoubtedly as they will continue to tell the same on occasions like the above, therefore I think it would not be right if I did not let the man here speak for himself Page 26, he says:

" I have understood that it has been intimated, while I lived in the church and professed to be strong in faith, that I lived in unlawful connection with a woman, who is since my wife Now this appears to be mean and ill usage, and beneath the church of Christ, even if it was true You may remember, doubtless, some of you, what I spake to you a few days before I came away I told you, if any of you had any thing against me, or knew any wickedness of me, to tell me of it before I came away, so that I might confess it; and not serve me as you did others as soon as they were gone, try to rake up every thing you could against them. Now why was you not so kind, if you knew these things, as to tell me of it while I was with you? for I presume you knew as much about it then as you do now However, I will tell you the simple truth, as I expect to answer it to God From the time I first professed Christianity (which was a year or two before I heard of the people called Shakers) to this day, I never have had any unlawful connection with any woman, and from the time I first knew the Shakers to this time, I never defiled myself with what is called among you effeminacy, neither did I ever know, by any certain knowledge, while I lived with you, that there was any females in the church or any where else, except it was at the time when there was a gift for men and women to strip naked and go in the water together, I was sometimes a spectator, and perhaps might *observe* the difference. As to the woman who is now my wife, I never knew whether she was male or female till after I was legally married to her. As to my making any agreement with her to come away from the church, I never did only a few minutes before I came away, then I spoke with her and gave her the offer of my friendship and protection, if God spared my life, if it was her choice to follow me"

As to what Elder Hezekiah told my father and me, of his being of an aspiring disposition, and reaching after office and authority in the church, he says, page 21.

" I came to a resolution, and accordingly carried my resolution into effect, and gave up my place as Elder Brother, June 30, 1799, and desired all not to look to me for any help or counsel as they had done, but to labour for myself only, and to be esteemed one of the least of all."

"the gospel and sin against the gift and light they have "received, come under the power of darkness; in con- "sequence of which, Judas-like, their hearts become so "darkened and their eyes blinded, that they lose a sense "of the gospel and way of God. Indeed, they can no "more speak the truth than Judas could. As he gave "way to an evil spirit, an evil spirit entered into him; "whereby he was so blinded and under the power of "darkness, that though he had been with Christ and had "seen his works, and knew he was the Son of God, yet "by that evil spirit and power of darkness he was con- "strained to deny Christ and betray him. After which "he was brought under such powerful conviction and "distress, that he confessed his guilt, and bore testimony "to the innocency of Christ, and in despair ended his "life. Like him, many in this day, who have turned "from and denied the way of God and Christ in this his "second coming, have pierced themselves through with "many sorrows; in consequence of which, some have "become delirious, and some have died in despair. Ju- "das knew that Christ was the Son of God; so do those "in this day who have been among us, who have tasted "the heavenly gift, and have experienced somewhat of "eternal life, return again to the world, flesh, and devil, "*wallowing, like the sow, in the mire*, living in the flesh; "and many of them in all manner of iniquity. Never- "theless, divers of them have been constrained to ac- "knowledge that they have forsaken the way of God, "(for their faith they cannot lose, though they often de- "ny it;) but they have become so bound by the flesh "and the power of darkness, that they are holden fast "and cannot get back. As the apostle says, *It is impos- "sible to renew them again to repentance.* Whereby they "have become the most lost, sunk, and miserable of all "God's creation; daily feeling a hell within them, to "which those in the world, who have not sinned against "so great light, are strangers."

They told my father if he would go with them to Lebanon, they would show him a letter R. Rathbone wrote and sent to his father Valentine, only two years before he left them. In that may be seen what his faith was, and how he bore teſtimony to that which he has ſince turned from; alſo his travail and experience in the goſpel; all in direct contradiction to his book, which my father had read. They, with me, adviſed and perſuaded him to go with them to Lebanon and ſee for himſelf, whether what he had read, and the reports that were ſpread abroad reſpecting theſe people, were true or not. Finally he conſented to go; and rode with the Elders in their ſleigh.

By this time I began more clearly to ſee into the real doctrine and diſcipline, or government of the church; and how and in what manner Chriſt, according to their faith, had made his appearance. A few days after the Elders left us, ſeveral of the believers being together and converſing concerning the Elders, their preaching, the counſel they gave us, &c. I told them I had not been rightly informed by the Elders and brethren reſpecting a material point of their faith. For I had been taught to underſtand and believe, that the ſecond appearing of Chriſt had now commenced by immediate revelation of his ſpirit and power individually, according to each one's underſtanding, faith, and obedience. In this reſpect it was an increaſing work, a greater maniſeſtation or revelation of the ſpirit and power of God in the hearts of believers, than had ever been before; whereby they were cemented in union, and empowered to act with rectitude of conduct, according to the prophetic words of the ſcriptures, "Behold the days come, ſaith the Lord, that I will make a new covenant with the houſe of Iſrael; not according to the covenant I made with their fathers." N. B. That was an outward covenant, an outward miniſtration, an outward leading. "But this ſhall be the covenant that I will make with the houſe of Iſrael; after thoſe days, ſaith the Lord, I will put my law in their inward parts, and write it in their hearts; and they ſhall teach no more every man his neighbour, and every man his brother, ſaying, know the Lord;" (no more go to the prieſt and prophet) "for they ſhall all know me from the leaſt of them unto the greateſt"—Jer. xxx. 31. This, I ſaid, I had reaſon to conclude was the faith of the church from what the Elders told me the ſecond time I went to ſee them, i. e. "for all to live up to the light "God has given," &c. And, as Elder John told us ſome time paſt, "we deſire and recommend you to look "to the word of God in your own hearts, and not to us." And I have hitherto thought, that the Elders ſtood in the church for, and that their buſineſs was, to excite or perſuade, and adviſe believers (i. e believers in an inward law and word of God) to be obedient thereto, and to examine whether their order and example was conſiſtent with the ſpirit of Chriſt and ſcriptures of truth.

Brother Hodgſon replied, "the deſcription thou haſt given, is juſt as I have always underſtood it."

I ſaid—Thou with me, haſt been very much miſtaken; and thoſe of us who continue in this deſcribed faith, will not be owned by the church. I perceive they have heretofore fed us with milk, but we will ſoon have ſome meat; and I think they have flung out ſome pretty tough pieces already; but they have covered them in ſuch a manner with milk, that you have not ſeen them, nor chewed them; but I have got hold of ſome pieces, and find them exceedingly tough indeed. I was aſked what the faith of the church was, and wherein they differed from the deſcription I had given.

I anſwered—Diametrically oppoſite. But as I have found the firſt link of the chain, I can the eaſier find the others; therefore, I'll begin with the firſt, and proceed on. As the ſpirit and power of God, was manifeſted in that body born of the virgin Mary; ſo, and in a greater meaſure, has that ſame power, called Chriſt, appeared the ſecond time in a prepared body. Firſt in her whom they ſtyle the firſt mother of the church, viz. Ann Lee, according to what we have heard the brethren aſſert: "That ſhe received the greateſt gift of God in her day;" and that they believe ſhe is the perſon propheſied of by the prophets, particularly by David: "Hearken, O daughter, and conſider, and incline thine ear; forget alſo thine own people, and thy father's houſe; ſo ſhall the king greatly deſire thy beauty: for he is thy Lord; and worſhip thou him. And the daughters of Tyre ſhall be there with a gift; even the rich among the people ſhall entreat thy favour. The king's daughter is all glorious within: her cloathing is of wrought gold. She shall be brought unto the king in raiment of needlework: the virgins her companions that follow her, shall be brought unto thee With gladness and rejoicing shall they be brought: they shall enter into the king's palace. Instead of thy father's shall be thy children, whom thou mayest make princes in all the earth." St. John also speaks, they say, of the same person. "There appeared a great wonder in heaven; a woman clothed with the sun, and the moon under her feet, and upon her head a crown of twelve stars,"* &c to the end of the chapter. And this is what St. John was told to come and see, under the character of the bride, the Lamb's wife,† with many other passages of scripture prefigurative of this person. Also by her obedience and suffering, similar unto Christ, she opened the door for admittance into the gospel of complete and finished salvation, and became the mother of all in the new creation. While she lived, obedience to her was taught as the only way to obtain salvation. It is the same now; the present mother of the church is Lucy Wright. She communicates the divine gift to Abiathar Babbot, and he to Elder Ebenezer Cooley, and he to Elders John and Hezekiah, and they to us. Previously to our hearing the Elders preach, and having faith, they were men of God, and believing in, and receiving the word they preached, we were total strangers to the gospel, and had never received any light, talent, or measure of the spirit of Christ in our hearts (according to the doctrine of the Quakers, and Methodists, and some others) that would ever save us from sin. As under the Mosaic dispensation, God spake to Moses, and Moses delivered the words he received to the people, or to the Elders and priests, and they to the people; so is the order of God in this church.

Hodgson's wife exclaimed—"No popery. I am not going to be led by popes. If it be true what you say, it is just as it is in the popish church; confessing of sins, obedience to the clergy, and they to the pope; I see no difference, it is just so now."

* Rev. xii. 1. † xix. 7, and xxi.

I replied, True, our brethren say "the Romish church "have got the order of God, which has been handed "down by tradition from the apostles; but the power "they have lost." As to confessing and forgiving sins, after Peter had confessed Christ to be the son of the living God, Christ told him, "Flesh and blood hath not revealed this unto thee, but my Father which is in heaven. On this rock," i. e. on that revelation or spirit of God by which Peter spake, "I will build my church," &c.: "and I will give unto thee the keys of the kingdom of heaven:" i. e. unto Peter and all his successors, (not successors by generation, but by regeneration) or who retained or possessed that revelation which Peter possessed: "and whatsoever thou shalt bind on earth," i. e. being under the influence of that same revelation or spirit of God in man, leading and directing him, "shall be bound in heaven: and whatsover thou shalt loose on earth," (by the same spirit still) "shall be loosed in heaven."—(Matt. chap. xvi.) We read of the same authority given unto the apostles in chap. xx. of St. John's gospel, after they had received the Holy Ghost. Therefore, by the Holy Ghost, "Whose soever sins ye remit, they are remitted unto them; and whose soever sins ye retain, they are retained." As this church profess to have the same revelation restored, that was given unto the apostles, and that in an increased degree; by which, in her ministration, she is invested with the same authority: and I tell you further, all judgment is in the church. The ministration will judge us, and all men living, either in this world, or world of spirits; i. e. they will judge and condemn the principle of evil in all men, and the soul in its adherence to it.

Hark what the apostle says, and which I have often heard the old brethren quote: "Do ye not know, that the saints shall judge the world:" and in the next verse he goes further yet, for he says, "Know ye not that we shall judge angels? how much more things that pertain to this life." And I'll tell you the faith of the church further, for I have got hold of the chain, and can follow on link after link, not only as it extends thro' this world, but far into the other. God never will be known, or ſeen in time nor eternity any farther or more, than in his ſaints and angels; for he ever has, doth ſtill, and ever will manifeſt himſelf through, or by ſome medium. The whole creation is to us, as far as we behold it, a manifeſtation of God. According to Pſalms, "The heavens declare the glory of God, and the firmament ſheweth his handy work." As to his purity and ſpirituality, the man Chriſt, or in him, was a greater manifeſtation and revelation of God, than had ever been before. As this is the ſecond coming of Chriſt, it is an increaſing work, and a greater manifeſtation or revelation of God to the deſtruction of ſin, particularly in the miniſtration reſiding at Lebanon, than ever there has been in any church ſince the creation of the world.

One ſaid—"I fear you have got hold of the wrong chain." I replied—I believe I have got hold of the right one, and you will know hereafter, if you continue in the faith. The doctrines of the church will be taught you, as you become able to receive them.

As to confeſſing ſins to the Elders, they having the ſpirit of God, by that ſpirit they forgive ſins; i. e if they feel the ſpirit of forgiveneſs towards us, and union with us, they bind us on earth, or receive us as members of the church, or (according to our faith and obedience) own us in union; we then become owned in heaven.—Thoſe who by continued diſobedience, are caſt out by the Elders, they feeling no union with them, or further gift for them, are caſt out in heaven. In ſhort, the ſpirit of God in all reſpects, accords in the ſaints in this world, and world of ſpirits: they are all of one ſpirit, and all in union.

One ſaid—"If all you ſay, be true, reſpecting the faith of the people, I have done with them."

I replied—What, "done with them," becauſe I tell you they profeſs to have the revelation of God, and in what manner they have received and poſſeſs that revelation Why, if this be true, it is the very point that ſhould ſtrengthen us in the faith; for what are a people the better for their profeſſion, if they have not the ſpirit of Chriſt? What is a church, deſtitute of the ſpirit of Chriſt? Is it not anti-chriſt? But to return to the doctrine reſpecting the miniſtration, and obedience to it. Though this has not been plainly preached to us, yet we might have ſeen it was their faith, by the way they have talked round about, and ſome words they have dropped ; for, according to a common ſaying, " a word to the wiſe, is ſufficient." If I had been wiſe, I might have ſeen ſometime ago, that this was the doctrine, and faith of the church ; but they hindered me from coming to ſuch a concluſion, by repeatedly ſaying—" We muſt act our " own faith : we muſt do what we believe and feel to " be right ; and not do any thing we believe to be wrong, " or that we feel convicted for. We muſt look to the word " of God in our own hearts, and not to them ; for they " were poor fallable creatures." But I expect the cauſe of their not preaching their real faith, was fearing we would not be able to receive it ; according to what we have often heard, of " Feeding firſt with milk, and afterwards with meat."

A. Hendrickſon, a zealous believer, ſaid—" I do not believe the Elders have ever been deceitful with us. I believe they will never preach any doctrine contrary to what they have preached."

I replied—I hope they never will, and wiſh I may never diſcover deceit in any reſpect ; if I do, I ſurely ſhall loſe my faith. But as to the doctrine, I am much miſtaken if I have not heard ſomething contrary to what they firſt preached already. If what I have ſaid reſpecting the faith be true, I aſſert it is diametrically oppoſite to what they taught at firſt. I heard nothing about a miniſtration and obedience, except a few words from B. Youngs ; and he repreſented it as leaving all to the dictates of the ſpirit of God in our own hearts. I believe we ſhall find the order and government of the church to be abſolute eccleſiaſtical monarchy. We ſhall be led on until we have to give up every thing, and are ſtripped as naked as we were born : that is, we muſt come to have an implicit faith in the miniſtration, to be obedient to the Elders in all things that can be mentioned or thought of, whether appearing right to us or not.— We muſt lie open to their teaching, and become as paſſive as clay in the hand of the potter. As I heard one of the brethren (namely, S. Wells) ſay, not long ſince: "The goſpel is juſt like a tunnel; the farther in, the narrower it grows." As you have often heard, that it is a ſtraight and narrow way; yea, you will find it narrower than you have any conception of at preſent. Your very life will be taken from you, according to the words of Chriſt: "He that loſeth his life, ſhall find it." The ſoul and body of ſin, muſt become ſeparated aſunder—(Heb iv. 12.) This is their faith; and all brought about by obedience to the word preached Alſo, no ſoul has any word of God, outward or inward, talent or light, that will finally ſave it. Without the Elders, we are totally helpleſs, and can do nothing as to our ſalvation. No creature can be ſaved from ſin, (though he ſtrive, pray, and labour to live near God,) but by having faith in the ſecond coming of Chriſt, revealed through the miniſtration, as I have already explained. Alſo having faith that they are men of God, having the revelation of God, and in faith receiving the word they preach, and being obedient to the ſame, is the only way to be ſaved; and without this faith and obedience, there is no ſalvation for any creature under heaven.

One aſked me—"What then has become of all thoſe who have died before the opening of this goſpel?"

I anſwered—As I conceive the faith of the church to be, all who have lived up to their light and knowledge, or according to the light of the day and diſpenſation in which they lived, have found juſtification, and died in a meaſure of peace. But as to a travail in regeneration, they have fallen as aſleep. According to a text which I have often heard them quote: "That we which are alive, and remain unto the coming of the Lord, ſhall not prevent them which are aſleep—(1 Theſſ iv. 15) They with us, may receive the power of the goſpel of Chriſt's ſecond coming, enter in the work of regeneration, and experience a reſurrection to eternal life: but firſt they muſt confeſs their ſins.

I was aſked—"To whom?" I anſwered—To the miniſtration, who receive the goſpel of the ſecond coming of Chriſt in this world, and knew firſt for themſelves, ſalvation from all ſin, and a reſurrection to life eternal, and have entered the heavens. Yea, I have been told by some of the elderly brethren, that many spirits confessed their sins to the first ministration, viz. Ann Lee and James Whittaker, before they departed this life—Now I will tell you a story verbatim as it was told me by an old believer: "Some time in the last American "war, the mother of the church Ann Lee, was, on ac-"count of her faith, imprisoned in a fort at Albany. "At that time, a certain captain, going to the north-"ward with a company of men, to assist General Gates "against Burgoyne,* visited the mother in her place of "confinement, and had conversation with her, and final-"ly received so much faith, that he promised her as soon "as he could get released from the army, he would come "and confess his sins, and join her people: but he was "killed in the battle. Fourteen days after, he came in "spirit, and confessed his sins to her;† so he was fa-"voured to make good his promise." And I have likewise been told that many thousands confessed to James Whittaker before he died

Now the Elders have preached to me, that, "there "is but one way for all souls to enter, and that is by "confessing their sins: this is the first step; and thou-"sands, who have professed to be christians, have been "so far mistaken, that they have never taken one step; "they lived and died with their sins covered Confes-"sion is the door; and the first step into the door of the "kingdom of heaven: and whosoever *climbeth up some* "*other way, the same is a thief and a robber*"—(John x. 1.)

In order to have a right understanding respecting this doctrine, and the faith in general, you should know, that the work of salvation, by the first coming of Christ, was not completed. The new, or spiritual creation, in order

* This account was not given me quite correct The officer was Colonel Brown, of Pittsfield; shot at Stone-Arabia, near Johnstown, under the command of General Schuyler.

† A short time after, two of the brethren were deputied by the mother, to go to Pittsfield and inform Col. Brown's family that he had returned in spirit, and confessed his sins, and was in the faith and travail with the church.

for the great work of regeneration, was not finiſhed, no more than the natural creation was finiſhed when the firſt Adam was created: while Adam ſtood alone, there could be no generation; but after Eve was formed, natural creation, in order for generation, was completed. Chriſt is the ſecond Adam, and ſpiritual Father in a new creation. People think they are going to be regenerated, made whole, and finally ſaved, without the ſecond Eve, the ſpiritual Mother, and before ſpiritual creation is finiſhed, which muſt be in order for regeneration.— Now as Adam, without Eve, could not increaſe in generation, ſo neither could the ſecond Adam, without the ſecond Eve, increaſe in finiſhed regeneration. Our great divines, with all their learning, have never been able to make this diſcovery, though the apoſtle gives a broad hint of it, "Neither is the man without the woman, nor the woman without the man" N. B. In the Lord—1 Cor. xi 11—that is, in the work of redemption. Thus you ſee, according to the faith, the work of God, in order for the ſalvation and complete redemption of fallen men, was not finiſhed in the firſt coming of Chriſt; which diſpenſation was but as waters to the loins. According to Elder Meacham's conciſe ſtatement, this is called the third diſpenſation; the myſtery and work of God is not yet finiſhed, though "Chriſt received power and authority to adminiſter the power of the reſurrection, and eternal judgment to all the children of men:" but it is only meant thereby as a beginning of the work of God in this diſpenſation; for it is ſaid ſhortly after, "They who were obedient to that form of doctrine, &c. were in the travail of the reſurrection and redemption of the body" But if I can underſtand Elder Meacham's diſcourſe, before recited, they did not attain a full and complete redemption; only were in the travail of it, and attained according to the power of that diſpenſation. According to the apoſtle, "Even we ourſelves groan within ourſelves, waiting for the adoption, to wit, the redemption of our body"—Rom. viii. 23. They were in that day and diſpenſation, as firſt fruits of the ſpirit in the work of redemption. According to the apoſtle James, i. 18, "Of his own will begat he us with the word of truth, that we ſhould be as a kind of firſt fruits of his creatures" The fullneſs of time was not then come; the myſtery of God, in man's ſalvation, was not finiſhed; before it was to be, a falling away from the power in which the church then ſtood, was ſpoken of. But now the time is come, in which I tell you plainly, that I believe it is their faith that Ann Lee is the ſecond Eve and firſt Mother of all in regeneration; and, as ſuch, is the ſubject of ſcripture propheſies, as I have already mentioned. Thus the work of God is finiſhed. As it is expreſſed in the conciſe ſtatement, "It will be a deciſive work, to the "final ſalvation or damnation of all the children of men; "which, according to the propheſies rightly calculated "and truly underſtood, began in the year of our Saviour "1747."

Now according to the diſcourſe of Elder Meacham, in which he refers us to Daniel and the Revelations, reference muſt be had to the prophetic numbers of the time, times and an half—Dan. xii. 7—and of two thouſand three hundred days—Dan viii. 14—one thouſand two hundred and ninety days, and one thouſand three hundred and thirty-five days—ib. xii. 11, 12: and the forty-two months and one thouſand two hundred and ſixty days, mentioned by St. John in the Revelations, xi. 2, 3. To rightly calculate theſe prophetic numbers, as the church profeſs to underſtand them, I expect they muſt be calculated in the following manner; but firſt a few preparatory words are neceſſary: the time, times and an half, by Daniel, muſt be underſtood as equivalent to forty-two months, by St John. Time, times and an half, are three prophetic years and an half, and three prophetic years and an half, are twelve hundred and ſixty days; which days, in this and the other numbers, muſt be underſtood to be years; which is conſonant to all the commentators I have ſeen. Thus far premiſed, I proceed to a brief calculation of theſe numbers anſwering to the faith of our brethren reſpecting them.

The prophetic numbers muſt be conſidered as refering or pointing to three periods of time. Firſt, to a preparatory period; second, to a time at which this work actually commenced; and thirdly, to the time the church was brought into its present order.

I can the easier perform this difficult task by referring to the concise statement, or discourse of Elder Meacham, where it is said, "The falling away began soon after the "apostles, and gradually increased until about the year "457, at which time the power of the church of Christ "was scattered and lost." Which I think very probable, (as it was shortly after Constantine openly professed Christianity; then the church was no longer persecuted, but was protected and favoured by the civil power: this proved the fatal means of corrupting the doctrines and relaxing the discipline of the church; many became Christians, or pretended to be of the religion, only because it was the religion of the empire,*) as from this time, according to St. John, Rev. xi. 3, the "two witnesses have prophesied in sackcloth," and they so were to continue forty and two months, i. e the man and the woman, for the first and second coming of Christ; or those who have been faithful in this time to testify against sin. According to St. John, in the fifth verse of the thirteenth chapter, "Power was given by the dragon unto the beast to continue forty and two months, and to slay the witnesses—Rev. vi. 9: agreeing with Daniel, seventh chap. and twenty-fifth verse, "Unto the beast shall be given a time, time and dividing of time." Daniel heard a question asked, "How long shall it be to the end of these wonders?" (that is, the wonders of the sinful reign of the beast) and the answer was, "a time, times and an half;" at the expiration of which time, he "shall accomplish or end in scattering the power of the holy people" —Dan. xii. 6, 7. Now as I have said before, a time, times and an half, and likewise forty-two months, are three years and an half; now three years and an half are twelve hundred and sixty days, and those days are twelve hundred and sixty prophetic years. Computing these years from 457, they will lead us down to the year of Christ 1717, which is the first period of time, when the

* See Mosheim's Eccl. History.

way began to be prepared for the second coming of Christ, similar to John the Baptist preparing the way to Christ in his first coming.*

The prophetic numbers of the second period of time, when this work actually commenced, are given by Daniel in the eighth and twelfth chapters. In the eighth chapter he gives the same account of the reign of the beast, as before, under the character of the ram and he-goat. Also he heard one saint ask another saint, "How long shall be the vision concerning the daily sacrifice, and the transgression of desolation to give both the sanctuary and host to be trodden under foot?" and the answer was, "Unto two thousand and three hundred days, then shall the sanctuary be cleansed." The two thousand and three hundred days, which are as I have said two thousand and three hundred prophetic years, are to be reckoned from the time the prophesy was given,† which ends at the commencement of the year 1747; when, according to the concise statement, this work began.

The angel informs Daniel, (12th chap 11th ver.) that "From the time the daily sacrifice" (i. e. of obedience to God) "shall be taken away, and the abomination" (the spirit of anti-christ) "that maketh desolate set up, there shall be a thousand two hundred and ninety days." Which calculating from 457, when "the abomination that maketh desolate was set up," the time ends at the year 1747, the same as the number two thousand three hundred. There is still another period of time, spoken of by St. John, when "the mystery of God should be finished"—Rev. x. 7; and according to Daniel, "Blessed is he that waiteth and cometh" to this time, that is, to the end of thirteen hundred and thirty-five days or years. Which calculating from 457 as before, brings us to 1792; when they say the church was brought into such order, and that salvation attained, which the world can form no idea of; and at which time all prophesy

* What these preparations were will be seen hereafter.

† According to Bishop Usher's chronology, about the year 553 before Christ.

ends, except ſuch as will be more and more amply fulfilled as the work increaſes; one of which is, Daniel vii. 26, 27, "But the judgment ſhall ſit, and they," that is, the ſaints, "ſhall take away his dominion," i. e. the dominion of the beaſt, "to conſume and deſtroy it unto the end And the kingdom and dominion, and the greatneſs of the kingdom under the whole heaven, ſhall be given to the people of the ſaints of the Moſt High, whoſe kingdom is an everlaſting kingdom, and all dominions ſhall ſerve and obey him."

Much more might be ſaid on this ſubject, as alluſions to this day are to be found in many parts of ſcripture. But I ſhall conclude nearly in the words of Daniel, vii. 28, "Hitherto" (that is, all dominions ſerving and obeying) "is the end of the matter. As for me" Thomas, "my cogitations," in often pouring over the propheſies reſpecting this day, have "much troubled me, but I" have often "kept the matter" and muſed it "in my heart."

I have been told by ſeveral of the brethren, that before they heard of theſe people they were convinced that the time ſpecified in theſe prophetic numbers, was paſt; therefore the millennium muſt have commenced among ſome people ſome where on earth; and when they found theſe people, and heard their teſtimony, they rejoiced, and joined them.

Now all the ſons and daughters of Adam will have to come to this laſt and final diſplay of God's grace, and confeſs their ſins, either in this world, or to the miniſtration in the world of ſpirits; and then commences their travail and final ſalvation, and not before. For before the opening of this goſpel, and ſounding of the ſeventh trumpet—Rev. xi. 15, none were ever admitted into heaven. "No man," ſaith Chriſt, "hath aſcended up to heaven but he that came down from heaven"—John iii. 13. and the apoſtle tells us expreſsly, "David is not aſcended into the heavens"—Acts ii 34. Daniel was told to wait the thirteen hundred and thirty-five days in which time he ſhould reſt, and at the end of the days he ſhould ſtand in his lot; and the leaſt in this work and diſpenſation is greater than John or any one you can mention in inferior or back dispensations. Also as souls in this world, or world of spirits, come to this finished work of God, then their resurrection commences, and they travail or increase in wisdom, holiness, and purity eternally. Those who have the gospel offered to them, (for all will have the offer of it either in time or eternity) and do not receive it, (no matter how great their reputation as Christians has been) will, as they continue to reject it, travail from God into such a state of misery and darkness, called hell, that finally they will be conquered, give up and become poor humble souls, and thankfully accept of the least drop or crumb to alleviate their misery. Then the mercy of God, in the order of God through his ministers, will reach them; and then by confessing their sins, and receiving the gifts of God, they will arise out of that miserable lost state, and travail, as I have said of others. Thus every stiff knee will have to bow, and every tongue will have to confess—Rom. xiv. 11; and when death and hell have given up all their dead—Rev. xx. 13; when all souls have bowed to and acknowledged the gospel, bowed to the conquering power of Christ, then even the fallen angels, if any there be, will become so humbled that the mercy of God will reach them, and his goodness save them in the manner before described.

A Reply—"You seem to express a doubt of there being any fallen angels."

I answered—By examining of the doctrines advanced by our brethren, concerning the evil nature in man, I am inclined to think, that those who have a thorough knowledge of the faith, do not believe there is any devil or fallen spirit, except the *evil nature in man, and his fallen spirit* from its original rectitude.

What I conceive to be their belief concerning fallen angels, I will endeavour briefly to explain.

The body of Adam was of the earth, earthy—(1 Cor. xv. 47); his soul was from God. He was created male and female—(Gen. i. 27) the female was separated, or taken out of the body of Adam. She also, of course, was of the earth, earthy, and was likewise endued with a rational soul. Adam was commanded to yield obedience to God, and no one thing beneath him. Eve was commanded to yield obedience to Adam, and to God through him. To Adam was given the *dominion over all creatures, and over all the earth*; and the woman was given unto him as an help to subdue, and keep all things in subjection under them: but she neglected her duty, and debased her noble soul, by yielding obedience to her *nature*, which was of the earth; and Adam did the same by yielding to her: in consequence of which, they both became fallen creatures, fallen from that angelic state in which they were created. Instead of their continuing under the order and government of the spirit and pure law of God, they came under the order and law by which the brute creation are governed; which order and law for them was good, as every thing was good according to its kind—(Gen. i. 24) and while remaining in the state that God had placed them. But when our first parents debased the dignity of their rational souls, by becoming governed by the same *earthly nature*, by which the brute creation were governed, then to Adam and Eve this nature was evil. Therefore, this debasement of their rational, immortal, and angelic souls, was the cause of shame. It is also the same that causes shame in all their posterity. Thus you see according to this doctrine, that which was the sin of our first parents, has been the sin of all mankind ever since. Instead of keeping in the spirit and light of the spirit, they fell into nature and nature's darkness: and this is what our brethren call the man of sin, which has become set up in the temple of God, captivating and ruling every faculty of his soul. Though, as I said before, all things in the world are good in the order in which God placed them; but when man becomes governed by them, they become evil, or the soul sins in yielding to any thing beneath God; indeed, this is according to the doctrine of many others. They say "We are to love God supremely, and not to place our affections on any creaturely enjoyments. We are to be led by the spirit of God, and not by the things, and spirit of the world." Thus, if what I have stated be true, we need not go far to find what the serpent, and sin of Adam was; for whenever we become influenced by our earthly, carnal natures, or things of this world, we yield to the voice of the same serpent, and commit the same sin I have often said I knew of no devil but what was in man, that is, his earthly, carnal nature, and I knew of no temptation but what proceeded from our natures, or the things of this world.

I may just observe that our brethren believe that Adam and Eve were created in a probationary state, and capable of much greater attainments; and if they had continued in obedience to the command of their creator, they would have obtained a complete victory and power over all things earthly, and they would have become established in the spiritual order of God. The gospel is to redeem us from all earthly things; and by obedience to it, we shall obtain the same victory, power, and establishment, that they might have obtained Thus this nature which has become evil in man, is, in my opinion, what our brethren understand by the words, *devil* or *serpent;* and the rational, angelic spirit of man being debased and fallen, is what they understand by *fallen angels*.

One asked me, if I believed all the doctrines of which I had treated?

I answered, I cannot say I believe them all. And as to the truth thereof, as professed or believed by them, I leave it; as the ways of God are deep, and mysterious, and far above our comprehension.

Concerning the faith and government of the church, it appears not to be, in several respects, as I at first was taught, or understood it, as heretofore mentioned. I then conceived it to be republican; but I cannot describe my conclusion respecting it, more full and clear, than in the words I heard the second time I went to see them; by which you may judge if I had not reason to understand it in this light. One of the brethren who had been of the faith many years, said, (and I have heard others to the same purport,) "We are not bound "up by written articles, and discipline, like other soci-"eties, formed by their predecessors, and if one believes "in, or adopts sentiments contrary to their established "doctrine, he is soon silenced or excommunicated; but "we admit of liberty of conscience: all have the privi-

"lege to believe, and ſpeak what appears to them right: "no one is excommunicated for his ſentiments The "goſpel among us, don't bind creatures: it opens a "door of liberty, and we have union with all our breth- "ren and ſiſters, whatever their ſentiments may be, ſo "long as they keep out of ſin. We wiſh and profeſs to "be in a travail individually, and as a body of people "into an increaſing light and underſtanding, and our "conduct improved accordingly. We are willing to be "taught by the leaſt brother among us: and individu- "ally or as a body, as we come to ſee we are wrong in "any thing, either faith or practice, to put it away, and "mend.

"We don't look back to firſt mother's day, to the "miniſters or Elders who opened the way of life and "ſalvation, as a rule for us to walk by, though we "own them as *pillars* and *foundation ſtones* But they "did only begin the building, that is, the work of God, "and we who come after muſt go on with the work "they began, and know an increaſe, and travail in the "way of God."

Thus you ſee in all diſcourſes like this, which we have often heard, a miniſtration and obedience to the Elders, as the only way to obtain ſalvation, was kept out of our ſight I have heard ſome of the brethren and ſiſters ſay, that "the church was in much the ſame order as the Free Maſons were, only they were *travailing downwards*, but the church was *travailing upwards*;" and that as no man could gain a complete knowledge of Free Maſonry, without being initiated into a true and perfect lodge, in due manner and form, through the ſeveral degrees, "ſo no one can obtain a real knowledge of the doctrine and order of the church, only by travail in *obedience* to the gift of God."

One ſaid—"Well, what are you going to do? are you going to give up your faith?"

I anſwered—Nay, not for the world; and I hope you will not neither. I know there can be much ſaid in ſupport of their miniſtration doctrine, but I ſhall let the truth of it, and ſome other points of faith, reſt in a great meaſure, on the conduct of the miniſtration, or Elders, and people. According to their criterion, they often give us, I shall judge whether they are men of God or not, that is, " By their fruits." I think I have hitherto had reason to believe that they are the people they profess to be, not only by their life and example, but what has had great weight with me, to cause me to believe the time has commenced, of which they testify, is their holding to the doctrine of virginity, which doctrine appears to me to be more pure than professed by any other sect. I have read that St. Clemens, bishop of Rome, (who lived in the times of the apostles) relates that Christ being asked when his kingdom would come, answered— " When two things shall become one, and that which is outward, be as that which is inward ; the male with the female, and neither male nor female ," and these words were, in the next century, quoted by Clemens of Alexandria. The same author also relates another answer given by Christ to much the same question, put by Salome, to which he was answered thus—" When ye shall have put off the garment of shame and ignominy, and when two shall become one, the male and female united, and neither man nor woman," i. e. the male and female united in spirit, or in the Lord, and neither man nor woman in a carnal sense These passages are also quoted by Wm. Law in vindication of this doctrine. They have had a tendency since I read them, to strengthen me in the faith, that our brethren and sisters are the people of whom Christ spake, and that his kingdom has come. I mention these things, that they may also strengthen your faith.

Thus we often spent hours in conversing about our Elders, the church and believers, and their wonderful *gifts*, *miracles*, *faith*, and *doctrines*. My friend Hodgson was by this time, strong in the faith ; though for the first six months after he joined, I often went to see him (living then about half a mile from him) to solve his doubts which were principally concerning the truth of our testimony respecting marriage, and to strengthen him in the faith, as, apparently at times, he was ready to give up. Thus I acted then with all the believers at Cornwall, for I verily believed that this was the only way of God on earth: and I thought the loss of one sheep out of the fold, would be inexpressibly great; and that the gaining of one to it, would be as a star in my crown—(Daniel xii. 3) But alas! if it be the only way of life and salvation, though I have preached it to others, I myself have become a "castaway;" though in every respect, according to my light and knowledge, I have acted the honest, sincere part.

1801. By this time I had partly written, according to the information I had received, an account of the rise of the church, with an explanation and vindication of their doctrines, faith, and practice; part of which was on dancing, an abridgment of which I have heretofore inserted. I had thoughts of continuing this work, but beginning to see that some points of the faith were not as I had at first understood them, and that whatever I did, must not be in my gift, but in the gift, or according to the minds of the Elders; and that there was no gift from the ministration to write and publish respecting their faith and practice: thesore I wrote no more, except a few letters.

In about four weeks my father returned from Lebanon, and we were glad to hear that he had received a measure of faith, and had opened his mind. Poor old man, he appeared to be happy to think that he had lived to see the long prophesied of, and prayed for millennium.

He intimated to me, that while he was at Lebanon, something extraordinary had happened to him; but gave no particular account of it. I thought it was probable that he had been advised to say nothing about it, as I was when my feet were frozen, on a visit to them, for fear it might be construed into a judgdemt, or have a tendency to discourage others from visiting them, or receiving their faith. Be that as it might, I had afterwards reason to think that while he was there, he was seized with a fit of the palsy, which might have been caused by much exercise of mind.

Many more people now came to our meetings, for they thought it strange and unaccountable that a man of his learning and understanding, and who had been a steady member of the society of Friends near thirty years, should now unite with these people, and join in the dance. Some time previous, he had often appeared in the ministry in the Friends' meetings: he now often spake in our meetings; mostly recommending religion, and exhorting the people to live according to the principles of it.

A few days after he came home, he told us that the heretofore mentioned letter written by R. Rathbone, (which the Elders promised to shew him, if he would go to Lebanon) had much strengthened him in the faith; because he saw such instability in the man, in writing so contradictory only two years afterwards: the cause of which he believed was, that he had departed from the truth, and a sense of the gospel. While he was at Lebanon, he took a copy of said letter, and now gave it to me.

The pamphlet I had not yet read, but from what I had heard of it, and now reading the letter, it appeared to me respecting the author as I have mentioned it did to my father For I had not then a sufficient knowledge and understanding of the faith to assign a reason, how a man could be so confident in support of the faith and first Elders, and only two years afterwards represent it all to be error; and that Ann Lee and the first Elders were very intemperate, and either deceivers or deceived.

As I have not room for the insertion of this letter at full length, I shall only give the heads of it.

As to his confidence of the truth of the faith, he says, "That it is the only way of everlasting life; and that if "it was a scheme, (as his father Valentine had called it) "it was contrived by infinite wisdom before the founda-"tion of the world. and revealed by the Lord Jesus "Christ for the redemption of fallen man; and that it is "that mystery which the angels desire to look into."— That he had an experience of more than sixteen years, and had received a continual confirmation and establishment in his faith; that his soul was "joined to the foun-

" dation of God which was laid in Christ Jesus, being " made a partaker of his grace and the operation of his " power."

Concerning the first Elders, he says, " It is in vain for " you to tell me any thing about Mother, Father Wil- " liam and Father James, who first ministered the gospel " to us, by exclaiming against them with railing accusa- " tions. As an eye and ear witness I can testify of their " faithfulness in the gospel of Christ, and of their afflic- " tion, long-suffering, and patience, and of their unfeign- " ed love to the souls of mankind; and who, while they " were here in the body, shewed the greatest and most " infallible evidences to us that believed of their relation " to the kingdom of God."

He speaks of his father (who was a Baptist preacher) thus: " Notwithstanding your great pretensions, you are " yet in your sins, and in the gall of bitterness and bond " of iniquity. That part of the work which Christ came " to do in this world, was, *to set a man at variance against* " *his father*: you have rejected the gospel and despised " the offers of salvation; the truth of which you will " know by sorrowful experience."

He concluded by pointing out the following passages of scripture for his father's perusal—Matt. xii. 31, 32—Heb x. 26—1 John iii 10

1801. Sometime in March I took another journey to Niskeuna, in company with our zealous brother, Abraham Hendrickson, where we tarried with the brethren and sisters seven or eight days. I had considerable conversation with several of them respecting the faith and the doctrines of the church. From hence we went to Lebanon, thirty-eight miles S. E. of Niskeuna. The first day we travelled about 16 miles, taking our way through Stephentown, to see and tarry the night with D Train and his family, who were six or seven in number, all in the faith. In the evening we had a meeting, a few spectators being present; and a zealous, lively meeting it was. We danced near an hour; several turned round like tops. And to crown all, I had a gift to speak in some other language; but the greatest misfortune was, neither I nor any other one understood what I said.—

After we had finished our exercise, I spake near an hour to the spectators, on the vanity and uncertainty of all terrestrial things; the necessity and beauty of religion; the peace and satisfaction derived from it; and of our living to answer the ends of our creation, which was not to live in sin and pleasure, but to become redeemed and saved from sin, and to live to the honor and glory of God.

This family was kind to us; and in the morning we left them, and in the evening arrived at Lebanon much fatigued. Here I saw a neat settlement of (as I was informed) about four hundred of our brethren and sisters. We put up with the family in which our Elders resided, called Elder Ebenezer's family, containing about thirty men and women; the men living in several rooms in one part of the house, and the women the same in the other, as is customary in all their different houses and families. Each family assemble morning and evening for worship, in a suitable room in their own dwelling-houses.

Next day I made a short confession of some things I had done (which I did not think were right) since I opened my mind before. It is a practice, and it is required of all in the faith, if they commit any sin or do any thing which they are conscious is wrong, to open the same to the Elders, or Elder, the first opportunity; for they believe there is no possibility of gaining a victory over sin, or travailing in the gospel, so long as we knowingly keep one sin covered, according to Proverbs xxviii. 13.

The same day in the afternoon, our first Elder Ebenezer came in our room to see us; and after asking a few questions respecting the believers at Cornwall, and of our journey, spake to us in a solemn manner, as follows:

"We are glad you have come to see us, and hope you
"may be rewarded for your time and labour, which you
"will be if you have sincere desires after the gospel;
"and I hope you have come to a determined resolution
"to forsake all sin and live a just and holy life. This is
"what we desire of all souls, because we wish the happi-
"ness of all; well knowing there is no real happiness or

"peace of mind to be obtained in living after the course "of this world *For the wages of sin is death, but the gift "of God is eternal life.* Through the mercy of God we "know a salvation from our sins, and experience that "peace which the world cannot give, and we desire that "all may come to know the same.

"The world of mankind, professors as well as non-"professors, are in such a state of darkness, that we are "glad to find one soul seeking the way of life and salva-"tion; knowing all that do so, and confess and forsake "their sins, will find mercy.

"The people of the world have many erroneous ideas "about us; and so they had respecting Christ in his first "coming, and many think we are a deluded people; "but we have seen wherein we were lost and deluded, "since we have found the gospel, and that it was by "the deceitfulness of sin. *Sin blinds the mind and hardens "the heart* Now here is the sole cause of delusion.— "And as mankind have travailed into sin, they have trav-"ailed from God into darkness, and consequently into "ignorance of God and all good. But it is the gospel "that gives light, and shows unto mankind their lost "state and condition; and as we are obedient to it, it "leads us out of darkness into light. Many in the world "think they are serving God in preaching, praying, sing-"ing and in private devotion; and think they are in the "way to heaven when they daily live in the commission "of sin, and the generality of professors acknowledge it. "But Christ came to save people from their sins; the "way of Christ and to the kingdom of heaven is by sal-"vation, and salvation is to be saved from sin.

"Now we who are of this faith, having confessed our "sins, taken up a full cross against the world, flesh, and "all evil, and forsaken all sin; not travailing farther "and deeper into sin by daily commission, and living af-"ter the course of this world, marrying and giving in "marriage, and travailing in the works of generation; "but, as I said, taking up our cross according to the "doctrine and example of Christ, and travailing in re-"generation, which is being born again, for *Except a "man be born again he cannot see the kingdom of heaven;*

" therefore, regeneration and redemption from ſin, is the
" way and the only way to the kingdom of heaven, and
" the only way of peace and comfort in this world ; and
" we experience, according to Chriſt's words, *an hundred*
" *fold* even in this life, and have a comfortable hope of
" life everlaſting in the world to come.

" As the ſalvation of the ſoul and laying up a treaſ-
" ure in heaven is of the greateſt importance, I wiſh that
" you may ſeriouſly conſider thereof, and become deter-
" mined to forſake all evil, and once for all take hold of
" the way of life and ſalvation, and count all things in
" this world but as droſs in compariſon with it."

As ſoon as he had concluded, he aroſe to leave us ; I immediately replied to what he had ſaid—I believe thou haſt ſpoken the truth.

While I was here I ſpent moſt of my time in reading a hiſtory of the Martyrs, which I found in this family. But I have ſince ſeen that in ſo doing I did not act like a good believer ; for ſuch an one would not paſs his time, while he is with his Elders, in reading accounts of reputed good men in former days. I eſteemed it a privilege to have a book. But good believers in the faith eſteem it a much greater privilege to hear their Elders and be attentive to what they teach.

The third day I had been here I began to feel uneaſy, and to have a ſtrong deſire to be travelling homewards. The Elders wiſhed us to ſtay three or four days longer, but in the afternoon I felt ſo uneaſy and ſuch a ſtrong impreſſion to be going, that I could not read nor ſit ſtill, but walked the floor. I told my companion how I felt. He ſaid, " You had beſt open it to the Elders." I accordingly went to Elder Hezekiah, who was at work in his ſhop, and told him I felt very uneaſy, and had a ſtrong impreſſion in my mind to be going ; but that I knew not what the cauſe of it was. I had been labouring to put it off my mind and make myſelf eaſy, but could not. I hope you will not think this deſire to go proceeds from any diſlike I have taken to any one, or any thing in the family. Nay, your kindneſs is ſuch, and company ſo agreeable, it would be a pleaſure for me to ſtay a month if I could feel eaſy.

He left his work and went and informed his Elder of what I had told him. In a few minutes he came in our room and said, "If you can be content to tarry till morn- "ing, as the day is far spent, we shall be willing that "you should then go."

After a few minutes silence, I replied, As the time mentioned is short, the weight seems to be taken off my mind, and I think I shall feel easy till then.

In the morning, after breakfast, we parted with this kind family, and walked on about two miles, and then stopped and took dinner with our brethren in what is called the backsliding order. I conversed principally with the man who had such extraordinary gifts in speaking different languages, as I have before related. He said, "It is my gift and labour now to travail into a "deeper work of God in my soul; for without charity "or an inward work of God, all those outward gifts will "profit nothing, according to the apostle, 1 Corinthians, "xiii. chap."

Next day we arrived at Kenderhook-landing, about twenty-five miles from Lebanon, just in time to secure a passage.

There were a number of passengers on board the vessel, and much idle, vain conversation; but we kept ourselves very still and quiet, having but little conversation with any of them. In two days we arrived at home.

I was now, as to my faith, in the meridian; and soon after I returned home I wrote a lengthy letter to my brother-in-law, John Everitt, of Long-Island, a serious professor in the Presbyterian church, with whom I had had some conversation respecting the faith, and obtained permission of Elder Ebenezer to send it. In this letter I spake of the great strength of my faith—of the glorious halcyon days, which had been the subject of prophesy and prayer. I observed that Christ was revealed and made known to us; that he had descended in as conspicuous a manner as he ascended; that such as were dead in sin he had raised to life eternal. I treated concerning the man of sin; and asserted that all other churches were churches of anti-christ. I expressed a strong wish that he might come into the glorious light in which we were, and obtain a full power over sin. I urged him to come and behold "Jerusalem a quiet habitation;" and that he would be constrained to call "her walls salvation, and her gates praise;" and bid him adieu, until we met and saw eye to eye in the millennium.

My father, after he had read this letter, said, "Thomas, thou mayest yet find thyself mistaken; thou art too "confident; I could not write or say what thou hast. "*Let not him that girdeth on his harness, boast himself as he "that putteth it off*"—1 Kings xx. 11.

I replied—If I do find myself mistaken, it must be occasioned by seeing, on a more intimate acquaintance with them, dissimulation and conduct that I have heretofore discovered from some others who make a great profession; which if I do, it will be a greater disappointment than ever I met with before; I therefore shall conclude Christianity and revelation is nothing but hypocrisy and priestcraft, and shall become a deist.

My father said—"Thomas, I am sorry to hear thee "say so."

I replied—What must I think and conclude, when I look over professing Christendom, for many centuries back, to the present day? They have professed to "Do justly, love mercy, and walk humbly with God"—Mich. vi. 8. But the reverese is true, and Christendom is the model. Witness their contention and quarrelling about their religion; and their persecutions and murders one of another. But I need not be particular; thou knowest the lamentable history of the churches. Professing Christians (a few characters excepted) by giving their faith the lie, by their works have made more deists than a Lord Bolingbroke, Hobs, Hume, Tindal, Voltaire, Rousseau, Gibbon, Allen, Palmer, Paine, or all the deistical writers that have ever written. Now the church called Shakers make the greatest profession of any on earth, and many of them testify that they have power over all sin. Witness what Elder Hezekiah publicly said in this house; and they say that "the Christians of the "world shew their faith without their works, but we "show our faith by our works." But if we come to see we have been miſtaken or deceived in theſe people, I ſhall be more diſappointed than ever I have been; and it will be the greateſt deception of its kind I ever read of, and the greateſt cloak of religion that ever mortals put on. Will it not be diſcouraging, and almoſt ſufficient to make me conclude as I have ſaid.* And will not the poor deiſt, being made ſo by beholding the conduct of profeſſors, meet with the compaſſion and mercy of God, and not ſtand at his tribunal bar ſo culpable as the Chriſtian believer ſuppoſes he will?

My father replied—" There is ſome reaſon and truth in what thou haſt advanced; and the conduct of profeſſors has been a great trial to me; and I have ſaid none claims my ſympathy more than thoſe who are made deiſts by profeſſors' not proving the truth of their religion by its energy, on their lives. Notwithſtanding, if even theſe people prove to be like others, or worſe, I could not renounce the ſcriptural chriſtian religion; at leaſt, not until the deiſt could produce a ſyſtem more congenial to the good of ſociety in general, and happineſs of individuals. When we renounce (that which is believed to be) divine revelation, as a guide through life, to teach us our duty to God and man, (for its precepts are incomparable, as love to God, and our neighbour as ourſelves) and to adhere to natural reaſon as a guide, we know not where nor when to ſtop, as the next ſtep from deiſm is atheiſm: for we can reaſon away the exiſtence of a God, and particularly the immortality of the ſoul, as eaſy, and with as much propriety as we can revelation. Indeed, it appears to me, one unavoidably falls with the other; as we only know we are immortal by revelation; and we only know the mind and will of God as it is by revelation made known. Therefore, it will be the greateſt wiſdom to adhere to it, and to the light God gives us; and not to let the conduct of profeſſors ſway us one way or the other; and to keep on our watch, and endeavour to weed our own gardens, and be determined

* Contrary to what I ſaid, I ſtill firmly believe in the neceſſity of religion; the principles of which will, if properly adhered to, make men wiſer and better.

with Peter, Though all ſhould be offended, though all ſhould deny the maſter, and the efficacy of his goſpel, yet will I not—(Matt xxvi 33.) And if ſometimes the maſter pleaſes to withdraw his ſupporting hand from us, or by not keeping on our watch, or through the fallability of human nature we fall, may we make this good uſe of it, i. e to convince us of our weakneſs, without his ſupporting aid ; and a look of pity from him will bring us to repentance, and reſtore us to his favour"—Luke xxii. 61.

I obſerved—Father, thy advice is very good ; I ſhall endeavour to remember it.

1801. Sometime in April, two of the Elders came to ſee us again, but I was not at home, which was a diſappointment to me. I always endeavoured to be at home, if I knew when they were coming

I ſhall now relate a ſorrowful circumſtance (particularly to us in the faith) reſpecting my father.

The latter part of April he went to New-York, and returned 5th of May, in the afternoon, and did not go home that day, but ſtayed at my houſe, as he wiſhed to attend the evening meeting ; in which he ſpake about a quarter of an hour on the excellency of a truly religious life, and the peace of mind attending the practice of it. He alſo ſpake a few words on the exemplary life of our brethren and ſiſters, and recommended to the believers preſent, to endeavour to live that ſober, exemplary life which they appeared to live.

In the morning, a few minutes after he aroſe, apparently in health, R. Hodgſon came into the room to begin the meeting, as he was our leader ; and as my father was attempting to riſe to join them, he was ſtruck with an apoplectic fit, and for two or three hours he lay with but little appearance of life. It was near two months before he was able to ſit up ; and he was afterwards paralytic in his right ſide, and loſt the uſe of his right arm and leg ; and was never after able to ſpeak or write, thou he in a great meaſure retained his underſtanding.

Our opponent was glad to catch at any thing by which to condemn us. He came to my houſe, and ſaid—" That it was a judgment upon my father for embracing, and becoming an advocate for this new faith; and would have the reſt of us, and others take warning by it." He alſo ſaid—"It was a pity there was not ſome law made to ſuppreſs our meetings."

He drew up a written petition to have us baniſhed out of the place, as a public nuiſance, and went to Jeremiah Clark, judge of the court of common pleas, to get him to ſign it firſt; and then he intended to proceed through the neighbourhood, and procure as many ſigners as he could; but the judge would not, in the leaſt, countenance it, and told him his proceedings were illegal; and that we had as much right in the neighbourhod as he had; and there was no law by which we could be baniſhed. And to the credit of the judge, he abſolutely refuſed to countenance perſecution. Our opponent ſaid he did not intend it as perſecution. After controverting awhile, the judge told him it had the appearance of perſecution, and that he would not countenance, but diſcountenance the moſt diſtant appearance of it.

When I heard there was ſuch a petition in agitation, I went to ſee the judge, to know the truth of it; and the account, as I have ſtated, I received from him. In converſation with him on this ſubject, I told him I thought we ſhould be thankful to God and our country, that, though the ſpirit of perſecution remained yet in ſome, they cannot get their proceedings to baniſhment, impriſonment, and blood, ſanctioned by popes, kings, judges, and courts, as they could a century or two ago. Alſo, that I wiſhed that all judges and rulers, of every deſcription, might imitate him in ſuppreſſing perſecution; and that the ſpirit of it might become baniſhed to the bottomleſs pit, from whence it firſt originated, never more to be known on earth, ſo long as the earth abideth or the ſun ſhineth. I alſo told him, as the Friends were a people I eſteemed, I was ſorry that there was one among them who manifeſted a perſecuting ſpirit; and admitting we were in ever ſo great an error, it would be wrong to perſecute us, or any other people, for erroneous ſentiments! But alas! ſaid I, did I ever expect to hear of ſuch proceedings and ſpeeches, from a Quaker minifter. Several others in the neighbourhood difapproved of our opponent's conduct; and though they did not unite with us in our faith, yet would not have feen us injured or molefted on that account: and fome faid—"Now we fee the Quakers would perfecute, as others have done, if they only had the power." Which on my hearing, I replied, A few individuals might; but as a fociety of people, I did not believe they would, as perfecution was diametrically oppofite to their principles. I further faid that I had not a doubt but that the Friends in general, though they may believe we are in an error, would, neverthelefs, exceedingly difapprobate our opponent's conduct, if they knew it.

But our opponent had fome plaufible reafons and plea for his conduct.

"Oh, we do not mean to perfecute by any means; but thefe people pretend to a religion which is no religion. They pretend to worfhip God in dancing on firft days; which, to every judicious mind, muft appear mockery of every thing facred: and people of every defcription running there, as to a frolic, and likewife hearing their corrupt doctrines (particularly the delufive, pernicious harangues of that deluded, enthufiaftic Thomas Brown, jun.) whereby our neighbours, efpecially young people, are in great danger of being corrupted, and ruined by fuch pernicious, delufive tenets. We confcientioufly believe it juft and right, that fomething be done to put a ftop thereto, before any more fuch valuable members of fociety, as old Thomas Brown, are deluded, and ruined by judgments falling on them."

Similar to this (thought I) has been the cloak and language of all bigotted perfecutors in every age of the world.

I again wrote to our opponent (May 20, 1801) ftating that his treatment of us in afferting, that what befell my father, "was a judgment on him for leaving the Friends and joining the Shakers," was unbecoming and unchriftian-like, particularly in a man of his learning and public character; and that it was no prodigy for a perfon to be ftruck with death in the performance of religious duties. Alfo concerning its being "a pity there was no law to ſuppreſs our meetings;" and on ſome other expreſſions he had made, tending to perſecution. I then remonſtrated to him in the language of ſympathy againſt perſecution; referring him to former ſanguinary proceedings againſt the Quakers; and appealing to his inward light, if his conduct towards us, according to his power, was not equally inhuman and unjuſt: concluding, by deſiring him to explore the tenor of his conduct towards us, by examining his own heart, endeavouring to attend to that inward light in which he profeſſed to believe; and to cultivate that charity eſſentially neceſſary to form a chriſtian character.

After thus writing to him, I heard but little more of any proceedings againſt us. Whether my writing had the deſired effect, or whether he being now married, had his attention otherwiſe employed, I know not.

Shortly after I had written to him, I received the following anonymous letter from him, though not written by him; but by a phyſician who then reſided in the neighbourhood.

CORNWALL, *May*, 1801.

" *Mr. Thomas Brown*,

*SIR*,

Pleaſe to read, and well conſider the following ſubjects, the fundamental principles of your religion:

1ſt. Of ſinging—When Moſes ſang praiſes to the author of his deliverance, his ſong did not conſiſt in bare, empty tunes. He was a man that was better acquainted with his maker's will, than to ſuppoſe that an external ſound, varied ſo as to gratify the muſical ear, and continued a conſiderable length, could be an agreeable ſervice to a God that requires to be worſhipped in ſpirit and truth. We do not ſo much as hear of tunes in the ſongs of Moſes, or Deborah, or any of the rejoicing ſaints, before David's time. He ſeems to have been the firſt that inſtituted tunes. Alſo, we never hear of his uſing the tune, without expreſſing the moſt pathetic ſentences of praiſe in every meaſure of his tunes. It appears their ſinging did not conſiſt in ſinging, loo, loo, loo. When Jeſus Chriſt was diſpoſed to ſing, he ſung an hymn; and we are directed, if we are merry, to sing psalms. In all the scriptures, we hear nothing of singing tunes without words We must suppose Christ knew the true worship, and the true manner of performing it. Wherever we are exhorted to sing, it is to sing not tunes, but praise. It will be in vain to say, that the expressive part is performed by the spirit; for if the spirit performs part, let it do the whole, and the corporeal part be silent.

2d. Of dancing—It did not originate with the true worshippers of God It originated among Idolators. It was very common at Athens, in the days of Diogenes. It was practised among the Chinese, who never heard of Jew nor Christian, till of late years. It has been, and still is practised by every savage tribe that has yet been discovered. It is said in history, to have been practised in Sodom and Gomorrah. When it was used by the Israelites, it was not done by way of worship, but by way of rejoicing on certain occasions, or by way of diversion We read that David leaped and danced before the ark, accompanied with shouting, and the voice of the trumpet: this appears nothing more than an occasional rejoicing, and not so much as deemed a part of their stated worship It indeed appears to have been very uncommon for the male sect to have danced on any occasion; nor do I remember of any man's dancing, but David, except when they danced to the golden calf Aaron made. Miriam led out the Israelitish women with timbrels and with dances, after their passage through the Red Sea And we read in Judges that the Benjaminites were advised to lay in wait and see if the daughters of Shiloah would come out to dance after the feast of the Lord; and for every man to catch him a wife. So that we find no where in sacred history, of dancing, except on special occasions of some good turn of fortune. Jeremiah mentions the cessation of the timbrels, the harp, and the dance, at the captivity of the Jews by the Babylonians; but in the same manner, and same chapter, he mentions Jerusalem's being forsaken of her lovers and adulterers; and of their being deprived of the enjoyment of the vast multitude of vices they practised; which he does not distinguish from their dancing. And it appears that the heathen claim the origin of dancing to be among them ; and that it was introduced among them before the Trojan war ; and taught by Terpſichore* the daughter of Jupiter and Mnemoſyne ; and always believed that the ſame Terpſichore preſided over dancing, as a genius or goddeſs : which is as likely a ſtory as that the Supreme ever required it as worſhipping himſelf — I believe the truth of the matter is, that it originated among the heathen, and that the Iſraelites learnt it of the Egyptians, as we hear nothing of dancing among them before they came to Egypt ; but immediately after their migration, they began to dance : and that although it was made uſe of by ſome good perſons, yet it was practiſed generally as a vice.

Now concerning the coming of Chriſt—Can it be poſſible that any man in his ſenſes, can believe that he is come the ſecond time? When was the trump of God, and the voice of the archangel ſounded?—1 Theſſ. iv 16. When, or where has Chriſt deſcended in like manner as he aſcended, and in ſo conſpicuous a manner as that every eye could ſee him? Have thoſe who perſecuted him, particularly the Jews, ſeen his wounds, and all kindred of the earth wailed becauſe of him? Have the dead ſaints been raiſed, and thoſe alive changed? Where is the Lord Jeſus Chriſt revealed from heaven, with his mighty angels in flaming fire, taking vengeance on them that know not God?—2 Theſſ. i. 7, 8. If all theſe ſcripture queries are to be ſpiritualized, then what proof do you give us of the ſecond coming of Chriſt? Do your Elders preach in the power and demonſtration of the ſpirit, as one might reaſonably ſuppoſe they would, if they had experienced the power of the ſecond coming of Chriſt? But theſe are harder queſtions to anſwer, than to tell who thoſe are that wreſt, to their own deſtruction, what the apoſtle Paul has written of theſe things which are hard to be underſtood. If the twenty-fourth of Matthew, and the correſponding chapters in Mark and Luke are to be underſtood of the ſecond coming of

* One of the nine muſes, or one of the nine imaginary heathen deities ; to whom is attributed the invention of dancing and balls.

Chriſt, as you ſay, then your church does not anſwer the deſcription at all, particularly, as the light ſhineth out of the eaſt, even unto the weſt, ſo ſhall the coming of the Son of man be. Can it be poſſible that Ann Lee, and ſeven or eight men, coming from England to America, was this light ſpoken of, ſhining out of the eaſt? Did every eye ſee them? Why, Sir, I am ſurpriſed at a man of your learning and reading. It appears to me you have loſt your ſenſes, as to diſtinguiſhing truth from ſuch barefaced error.

And Chriſt tells us if any ſhall ſay, behold he is in the deſert, (at Niſkeuna) or ſecret chambers, believe it not. Where are thoſe who ſay, Lo here is Chriſt? Where are thoſe who forbid to marry? Where are thoſe who pretend to ſhew great ſigns and wonders, and if poſſible, deceive the very elect? Where are thoſe who pretend to receive an additional power? It may be the power of the beaſt and falſe prophet, with which they pretend to do miracles—Rev. xiii. Miracles they may do, and fulfil what is propheſied of them; but their miracles are as falſe as themſelves. If they can do miracles, it would be well for them to cure the palſy on your father, and then we will believe on them. This cure would be but a trifle in the hands of thoſe poſſeſſed of apoſtolic power; particularly, as he is a believer. Wiſhing you may come to ſee your errors, we conclude,

Your's, &c."

I was never more conſcious of my inability to give a reaſonable anſwer to any ſubject, than I was to thoſe contained in this letter: I therefore wrote no anſwer. By this time my wife had been viſited ſeveral times, by a few of the Friends, on account of her uniting with us; but ſhe was not willing to renounce what little faith ſhe had, in order to retain her memberſhip with that ſociety: ſhe therefore received the following certificate of diſownment:

*From Cornwall Monthly Meeting, held at Marlborough the 28th of fifth Month,* 1801.

Whereas Elizabeth Brown, wife of Thomas Brown, a member of this meeting, hath neglected the attendance of our meeting, and united with another society; and she having been laboured with, without the desired effect; and as we can have no unity with such conduct, we hereby disown her as a member amongst us, until she, from a sense of her error, shall condemn the same to the satisfaction of this meeting.

Signed in, and by order of the above said meeting, by
WILLIAM COCKE, } *Clerks*
PHEBE EARL, } *this day.*

Some time in June, our first Elder, Ebenezer, and his companion Stephen, came to see us again. Some of us had faith to believe that my father would be restored by them, and I did not know but it might be so, as I had heard much of miracles being performed at different times, by the Elders; and as they professed to apostolic gifts and power.

My friend Hodgson was dissatisfied with me for doing some necessary business on the Sabbath; asserting I had broken the commands of God. After controverting the point with him respecting the commands, and doing works of necessity on the first day of the week, I told him I was willing to leave the subject to the Elders while they were here, and abide their decision; to which he agreed. We met with them, and I opened the matter in dispute. Elder Ebenezer said, "it was the order of "the people of God, that were brought into order, not "to travel, buy, or sell, or do any thing that can be a-"voided, on that day; and to be careful not to give of-"fence to the world. But do not you differ about such "things; but each one look to himself, and not blame "and condemn one another; but leave each one to God, "and his own conscience. We sin as we violate our "conscience, and do that which we believe, or which is "made known to us, to be wrong."

So the matter ended. Brother Hodgson little knew yet, that, according to the faith, the particular, and essential commands of the gospel in this day, were what the Elders taught us to do, and to leave undone: and not altogether according to what is contained in the scriptures, which were commands to those under the dispensation in which they were written.

The Elders tarried three or four days with us. I had considerable conversation with them concerning the faith. Elder Ebenezer was more sociable with me at this time than ever after; but we were then humoured, and dealt by as children.

About a month after the Elders returned to Lebanon, we sent them the following letter:

CORNWALL, *July* 12, 1801.

*KIND FRIENDS*,

According to your request when last with us, we now write to you. We all retain the faith received, and endeavour to act consistent with the counsel you (in gospel love) have given us. Though we are sorry to write that we do not make a progress and travail according to the desire of our hearts; but we beseech you not to be discouraged with us. We feel thankful for your visits and labours of love among us. Thomas' father is in better health than when you parted with him. His being struck with such a disease, has been much of a trial to us; but we wish to be resigned to it.

We endeavour to live in love and union, and act consistent with our holy profession, according to your counsel; but the gospel is against nature. We hope you will not be discouraged with us. In love and esteem for you, we conclude, and subscribe ourselves your children in the gospel.

RALPH HODGSON,
THOS. BROWN,
ABM. HENDRICKSON,
ELIZABETH HODGSON,
JANE HODGSON,
ELIZABETH BROWN,
MACEE EVERITT, &c.

Our meetings were not ſo large as they had been, ſince the circumſtance of my father happened; and as there appeared now no proſpect of any further increaſe in number, in Cornwall; therefore, ſometime in September, the miniſtration at Lebanon ſent orders by Hodgſon (who was then there on a viſit) for all at Cornwall, who had faith, to move, as ſoon as they could conveniently, to Niſkeuna, and gather their union with the believers and people of God there.

Hodgſon, with his family, moved by water, ſometime in November. Two or three days after he had left us, a couple of the Elders came again to ſee us, but I was not at home. This makes ſeven times that they came upwards of an hundred miles to viſit us. They appeared to ſpare no labour, nor pains, to eſtabliſh us in the faith.

Shortly after the Elders left here, A. Hendrickſon and my wife's ſiſter went to Niſkeuna; and a couple, ſometime back, having forſaken us by giving up their faith, our number was now reduced ſo ſmall, we gave up our meetings.

January, 1802. I went to Niſkeuna to conſult the Elders what I had beſt to do. I tried to procure a houſe near the ſettlement of my brethren, but could not without building; and as my buſineſs was much unſettled in the world; and as there was no proſpect of my following any buſineſs at Niſkeuna, that would turn to much account, I had thoughts of removing to, or near Albany; at which place, I had a proſpect of a profitable employment. I opened this matter to the Elders, and they agreed it was beſt for me to remove to that place: obſerving at the ſame time, that "I and my family could "there attend meeting almoſt every Sabbath." I accordingly hired a houſe near a mile northward of the city, at a place called the Colonie; where I could almoſt every day have the ſatisfaction of ſeeing, and (as I hoped) at times, of entertaining my brethren, who would paſs, and repaſs by the houſe in travelling from Niſkeuna to Albany and Lebanon.

I returned to Cornwall; and March 24, 1802, I removed to the aforementioned place.

The remaining believers (except my father) removed to Nifkeuna; but before they did, I had to vifit them, and ufe many perfuafions to prevail on them to leave Cornwall; knowing if they remained behind, they would not be owned in the faith; neither did I think they would be able to keep their faith.

This fummer my father vifited the believers at Nifkeuna, and ftaid with them three weeks; and tarried about the fame time at my houfe; and then returned to Cornwall. About a year before he died, he attended the Friends' meeting feveral times; and in one of them ftood up and looked round on the affembly fmiling, and by a few figns, fignified (as the people generally underftood him) either his comfortable ftate of mind, or unity with that fociety. He was ftill a member of it, as the Friends did not difown him. He lived above four years after he became paralytic, and appeared to be refigned to his fituation. He died on the 6th of the feventh month, 1805, aged nearly-fixty-five years.

Soon after I moved to Albany, being with the Elders at Nifkeuna, and fpeaking concerning the people at Cornwall, one of them faid—"Thomas, the caufe why the "people did not receive the gofpel there more than they "did, is becaufe you have not been ftrictly obedient to "your faith, and kept in the gift and power of God in "preaching to them."

I replied—What! are you going to throw all the blame, and lofs of their fouls, on my deficiencies? I fee no propriety in this; for the Elders were there repeatedly, preaching in public to hundreds, and in private to feveral; exhorting and perfuading: therefore, I think they may bear at leaft half the blame; for, if none were gathered to the gofpel in confequence of my not preaching in the gift and power of God, what gift and power did you preach in? for you never gathered one foul; at leaft, not till I firft began with them, and brought them on by recommending the people, and perfuading them to go and fee you, &c.; except two, who have fince renounced the faith. The people at Cornwall, who look upon it all as a delufion, blame me for the whole; and the believers from that place have faid that I was the first cause of their becoming believers; and not only at Cornwall, but those who were gathered out of Albany. I was the first who made the stir, for which I had like to have got my head broke by Wm Carter's wife; and was severely threatened by her son Now this assertion appears to me the most unreasonable of any thing I have ever heard you advance. I do not speak as boasting, by no means; but only to show that if I had no influence, you had less.

(But thus speaking my mind so plainly to the Elders, was not behaving like a good believer; for such will conclude that whatever the Elders do, or say, must be right; at least, they will not contradict, and dispute it.)

He replied—"Thomas, we believe if you continue "faithful, you may be the means of bringing many more "souls to the gospel."

I now attended meeting every Sabbath when I was at home, (with part of my family;) and as I wished to spend as much time with them as I could spare, I would generally ride to Niskeuna on Saturdays afternoon. My brethren always appeared glad to see, and free to entertain me, particularly B. Youngs and his family.

I often wished it was so that I could live nearer them, and be more disentangled from the world; well knowing, that an intercourse with the world, retards the progress of vital religion. I often, when at meeting, spake to the spectators as I had done at Cornwall But after four or five months, a couple of the inferior Elders, who took the lead of the meeting, spake to me of a gift from their Elders, "who thought it best, as I was so much "connected with the world, to refrain from public preach-"ing"

I told them I was of their mind, and had come to a conclusion to speak no more in public, if I could avoid it; at least until such time as I could become more retired from the world, and composed as to temporal things.

One replied—"It was needless to come to any con-"clusion about it, one way or the other; but to conclude "and act just as the gift from the Elders was for me. And "such as wish to walk in the way of God, and become "united to this people, muſt totally forſake the world, "and help to build a partition wall; which wall we are "building between us and the world. And we believe "(ſaid he) the day will come, when the people of God "will have no dealings with the world," (i e when there are a ſufficient number ſettled and eſtabliſhed in different parts of the world, the churches then can ſupply one another with all neceſſary articles of conſumption )

By this time there were collected fifty or ſixty called young believers; ſome of which were gathered into family order, ſimilar to the church, having all things in common, or what is called united intereſts; wherein no one is to ſtudy his own temporal intereſt, excluſive of the good of the community. B Youngs had given to this family an hundred acres of land, and the church aſſiſted them to build a large commodious houſe; in the lower part of which, a partition opens and enlarges the meeting room, where the brethren and ſiſters aſſemble morning and evening, but at other times they are ſeparate, having ſeparate apartments.

With ſome of theſe young believers, there were ſtill operations of ſhaking, trembling, and ſhouting; ſometimes I had theſe operations myſelf. But theſe outward operations began to ceaſe, as they were now taught by the Elders to travail out of them into a deeper and more inward work in the ſoul. One evening, about this time, being at a family meeting, a certain zealous woman turned all the time the others were labouring, and when we kneeled (which we generally did at the concluſion of the meeting) ſhe prayed about fifteen minutes in an unknown tongue. As ſoon as we aroſe, ſhe was taken with the operation of turning again, and continued it about fifteen minutes. She then retired to her room, where ſhe was directly taken with the operation again. Being deſirous to ſee every thing that was going forward, I went into her room and took a ſeat. She continued whirling rapidly above half an hour. I thought ſhe would have died under the operation; for it appeared to me it was more than human nature could bear. She broke out ſeveral times apparently in an unknown tongue, and ſpake with great energy and emphaſis, uſing violent geſticulations, and ſhaking, to appearance, ſufficiently to diſlocate every bone in her body. It was believed ſhe was then thundering the goſpel to diſobedient, damned ſpirits. When the operation was over, ſhe ſat down. I then immediately entered into converſation with her, to ſee if her mind was not affected; but I could perceive no alteration in her. She told me what ſhe uttered in prayer, was on a ſheet of paper held before her by an angel. The man of the houſe told me, that a few evenings before while they were labouring, ſhe ſpake and ſaid, "ſhe ſaw an angel labouring by the ſide of him," and he believed it.

I ſhould not here paſs over mentioning that this woman, who had repeatedly ſuch extraordinary gifts, as turning, ſpeaking languages, ſeeing angels dance, hearing them ſing, ſeeing damned ſpirits in torment, and ſome who had and were receiving the goſpel, and their torment mitigating; alſo a variety of other wonderful viſions—at laſt departed from the faith and people. I have often heard the Elders and others in the faith ſay, "that "many of thoſe who have ſuch operations forſake the "way of God; of the truth of this, I know a number of inſtances. I had likewiſe been told, that "theſe opera-"tions were to ſtrengthen believers in the faith, though "they are no real profit to the ſoul in its travail out of "ſin." I therefore began to doubt the divine reality of them. Is it not, ſaid I, unaccountable or rather inconſiſtent, if theſe operations are by the power of God, that moſt of thoſe who are thus operated on ſhould loſe their faith and forſake the way of God. The reply and cauſe aſſigned was, "that the work with ſuch is outward; they "don't come to an inward work in the ſoul, and expe-"rience the ſubſtance of faith." Further, "ſome muſt "travail out of ſin as they have travailed in."

But a believer muſt not examine for himſelf the propriety or impropriety of things, nor dive into theſe and other myſteries and be ſo inquiſitive, if he wiſhes to retain his faith; for this was a principal cauſe of my loſing mine.

I ſhall here, according to the order of time, inſert a diary written while I felt as therein expreſſed. I had had ſimilar feelings ſome years before, and the light that now ſhone upon my mind did not tend to ſtrengthen my faith wherein it was deficient, viz. that there is no revelation except through the miniſtration, or that we can know nothing of God but through the Elders, by obedience to them; which by this time I was ſure was their faith. Moſt of the time in which this was written, I was on a paſſage from New-York to S. Amboy, and from thence to Albany; and much of the time alone and retired.

# A DIARY,

## *CONTAINING THOUGHTS AND REFLECTIONS ON SEVERAL SERIOUS SUBJECTS.*

1802. September 5th, firſt day of the week, (at N. York) Felt my mind much ſolemnized—read a few chapters of Pauls epiſtles. In the afternoon took a contemplative walk, and paſſed by four aſſembled congregations for worſhip, and ſtopped at each in the hearing of preaching long enough to collect each ſubject Ah! how much is preached about Jeſus Chriſt, his birth, holy life, miracles, ſufferings, death, reſurrection, aſcenſion, his divinity, of the Father, Son, and Holy Ghoſt; and at the ſame time how little is known, felt, and experienced of the work that Chriſt came to do. I doubt not but there are many who breathe after holineſs; who have good deſires, begotten by that ſpirit which viſiteth all. I felt ſolemn, and my mind drawing to God; and felt love towards all mankind. I returned to the veſſel; being alone, I read St. John's goſpel—bleſſed doctrine. My ſoul longed this afternoon, to experience more and more of what Chriſt taught. If there is any ſuch thing as the ſpirit of God, as the love of God operating on the human mind, I have felt it this day. Divine love begins to kindle in my ſoul: oh! what a bleſſed thing true religion is. In the evening I went to the Methodiſt meeting—I love to hear gospel truths when they come from honest, sincere souls of any sect—no matter to me what their outward profession may be—all who love God are brethren; and all who love God will love one another, and will be kind and tender towards all their fellow creatures Ah! if this love was universally to prevail, I am sure it would make a heaven on earth—it would cause us to bear with one another in our ideas and different sentiments—we should be careful to treat those who differ from us with kindness: all hard feelings, all cruelty, all fraud, injustice, and deceit, would be done away. In short, that excellent precept of Christ would be universally practised, "Whatsoever ye would that men should do unto you, do ye even so to them." After meeting, being alone, I read a few chapters—bowed to God in silent ejaculations. I believed I was a going to be visited again—I began to find him whom I had sought; my soul was filled with gratitude for his goodness and mercy to me a poor creature.

Second day, Sept. 6. I felt that the spirit of the world in transacting business, hurts or silences the life of God in the soul. I hope I may see the day I can live more retired, and retain this heavenly company without interruption. But I feel thankful for what I enjoy, while many I see this day appear to be destitute of the only good Read a few chapters this evening—bowed in thankfulness to him whom I desire in spirit to serve.

Third and fourth day of the week. I feel continually thankful that I am preserved from sin. There is a possibility of keeping a *conscience void of offence*; but it is only by the assistance of the grace of God. I feel humble and thankful for this grace. My soul sings redeeming love—Oh! the sweet sensations I feel—Is not this heaven?

Fifth day, Sept. 9. I am continually kept in remembrance of that good part which I have chosen, or rather which my Saviour has chosen for me; and which I trust will never be taken from me. Am I then elected to eternal life? I feel electing love, and that for me is all-sufficient. I feel the drawings of the Father—and that to me is satisfactory.

Sixth day. More yet, but tongue cannot tell what! Oh, ye deists! revelation is true—religion is a reality. The light and love of God surrounds me!

Seventh day. I sailed near and had a view of four ships of war; and my mind was almost involuntarily occupied with such reflections as these: When will mankind become wise? When will they cease from their wickedness and folly, and use such things no more in transporting themselves from one part of the world to the other, to destroy those whom Christ came to save? Oh how contrary war is to the peaceable, loving spirit of Christ! What an incomprehensible distance are millions of souls from God! How lost, how sunk in sin! My soul praises God for his mercy towards me—I want an eternity to praise him, and an eternity I shall have.

First day, or Sabbath, Sept. 12. Left New-York in the morning for Albany. My soul this morning blesses and praises God. Bless for ever, continue to "bless the Lord, Oh my soul;" and all my powers and faculties "magnify his holy name" I am satisfied and happy under a sense of the love of God, and the good spirit having revisited me. Renewedly convinced I am, that all endeavours after holiness, all preaching and teaching, is but little worth, setting aside this divine and heavenly gift. It is as the apostle said, "By grace we are saved." I feel poor and nothing of myself—I feel humble and altogether dependent. The Lord visited me with a sense of his love a few years ago—I never can forget the revelation of the love of God to my soul at that time.* O Lord, since thou hast been pleased to revisit me, if it be consistent with thy will and wisdom, continue the same; in thy inexhaustible treasure there is enough for ten thousand worlds. In this state I love and continually worship thee. I live according to thy first ordained purpose, to thy honour and glory. May I be enabled to die daily. "He that loseth his life," said the lip of truth, "shall find it" Lose what life but a carnal life, a carnal mind, that only delights in sin and in the things of this world—a life and spirit contrary to the gospel? And what

* See page 13.

ſhall he find but the life of God in his ſoul? My ſoul taſtes the ſweetneſs of the heavenly world—I feel as a watered garden. The well of living water ſpringeth up—I drink thereof, and thirſt not after the pleaſures of ſin and things of the world, that never did nor can give true peace How I find the words of Chriſt verified: "My peace I give unto you: not as the world giveth, give I unto you." "By this ſhall ye know," ſaid a beloved apoſtle, "that ye are the ſons of God, by the ſpirit of God witneſſing with your ſpirit." Why am I thus favoured, and ſo many left to delight in vanities, in phantoms of a moment? I know not; I leave it to the wiſdom of God, who I hope will bring all to himſelf to enjoy his divine beatitude in his good time. It is enough for me that I love and praiſe him. Nay, it is not this I, but that of God in me; that of God draws to God, and it draws me with it. Oh, may I never reſiſt it. Oh the ſweetneſs of divine love. What joys beyond expreſſion am I ſenſible of! (What an infinitely wide difference there is in being under the influence of, and led by, a good ſpirit, and being under the influence of, and led by, an evil ſpirit; one cauſes peace and conſolation, and the other perturbation and remorſe.) "If ye love me," ſaid the divine Saviour, "ye will keep my commandments." But what love is this? Why, the love of God in the ſoul, that which I this day feel; and as long as I retain it I ſhall commit no ſin. That which is divine and holy, cannot conſent to that which is in direct oppoſition to holineſs. Ah! this love of God that St. John writes about, this life of God in the ſoul—in it conſiſts all true and living faith, all believing, all prayer that is acceptable and effectual. "Whoſoever believeth that Jeſus is the Chriſt, is born of God." "He that believeth in the Son of God, hath the witneſs in himſelf." Now this is not that hiſtorical belief in Chriſt, which the majority in Chriſtendom have; if it is, they are all born of God, at the ſame time they live in ſin; when the ſame apoſtle tells us, "He that committeth ſin is of the devil; and whomſoever is born of God, doth not commit ſin." Few there are who appear to know what true faith is. It is love, life, and power of God in the ſoul—and it is that which gives power and victory over ſin. And it is only by the ſpirit of God in the ſoul that we believe in God. "He that believeth on me," ſaid Chriſt, "the works that I do ſhall he do alſo." "If a man love me, he will keep my words." What a wide difference there is in underſtanding all this literally, and knowing it experimentally, or by a divine work in the ſoul! There is much ſaid about faith by thoſe I profeſs faith with, but I fear there are not ſo many who know what true and ſaving faith is. It is only in the light we can ſee or have light. I feel Chriſt with me—I feel that "which paſſeth all underſtanding." My ſoul is filled with love divine; and ſo long as I have this love I ſhall keep his commandments.

This day I have felt the power and efficacy of faith. It is ſufficient proof to me that I have true and ſaving faith, when I "love God and keep his commandments" in ſpirit and practice. The ſpirit of it is, to "love the Lord my God with all my ſoul, mind, and ſtrength, and my neighbour," and all my fellow-creatures "as myſelf." Yea, this bleſſed experience is proof of itſelf from whence it comes, and what it is; excluſive of the ſcripture and every outward teſtimony, it carries its own evidence with it. He who is totally ignorant of all ſcripture, and who has never heard a word preached, if he experience what I now feel, his ſoul will be all alive, he will have a true and living faith in the Great Spirit; or at leaſt he will have the ſubſtance of faith; he will feel happy and know it is from above. Oh! bleſſed experience! If God was thus to pour out his ſpirit on all ſouls, what a heaven there would be on earth! This would be a millennium indeed! Soon would all wars ceaſe—ſoon would the words of the prophet reſpecting ſwords and ſpears be fulfilled. No nation or people would learn war, but all would learn peace. Then the language of every heart would be, "Peace on earth and good will towards men." O Lord, from the overflowing of my heart I cry, haſten the day: O heavenly Father, pour out of thy ſpirit on the children of men, that they may all know and love thee, as my ſoul now loveth. But

" thy will be done"—thy time is the beſt time. This is the power I muſt put my dependence in—this is that alone that will redeem.

But I fear, yea I feel confident, that there are many of my brethren, whoſe faith is too much in man, whoſe faith is in the Elders; that is, they believe the Elders have the revelation of God, and that obedience to them in an outward order will anſwer every purpoſe, and ſo look no further; i. e. they don't ſeek to feel the revelation or power of God in their own hearts. What would it ſignify, if an angel from heaven was to come to me with divine revelation, and only ſpeak to my outward ears? If there was no power nor virtue attended the word ſpoken, it woul be of little profit. And if a miniſter or Elder preaches to me in the ſame manner, it is but an outward teſtimony; like unto the " Letter" which " killeth, but it is the ſpirit which giveth life." Words without the ſpirit, are but like unto a body without life. " It is," ſaid Chriſt, " the ſpirit that quickeneth; the words I ſpeak unto you, they are ſpirit and they are life." Words or teaching, without this, profiteth nothing. And even if by my natural powers and efforts, I was obedient to an outward teſtimony or teaching, and kept from actual ſin, it would be all only the labour and work of the creature—I would ſtill be out of the covenant of grace. It is by grace I muſt work—it is by grace I am ſaved. And this grace, in a meaſure, is in all men. It is within the evil lies—and where the evil is, the remedy muſt be made uſe of, and applied. If one preaches to me profeſſing to have the revelation of God, I ſhould have ſome evidence of his being ſent, either internal or external; if I have no evidence, then my faith is in the creature. Chriſt came on earth with the word and revelation of God to man, and he ſhowed his credentials; he repeatedly gave proof not only by the miracles he wrought, but his word reached to the heart; and bleſſed be God it has reached mine—and this is the beſt of all evidence. Fully convinced I am, that the only way to arrive at true and ſaving knowledge of God, is by the revelation of his ſpirit to each ſoul. I do firmly believe, there is no other ſatisfactory evidence of my acceptance with God, and that my fins are forgiven, but by his fpirit; this is the teftimony of St. John. What I have felt of the love of God, the heavenly movings of the good fpirit on my heart, endowing me with power over all evil in thought, word, and deed, as I have experienced the week paft, and efpecially this day, is a greater evidence to me of acceptance with God, than the teftimony of all external things that can be mentioned. And fo long as I feel this inward peace, and love to God and holinefs, if all the deifts on earth were to tell me, It is all imagination and enthufiafm, I could not doubt its divine reality. But if they call this enthufiafm, *I hope to live and die an enthufiaft*; for I enjoy more real happinefs in one hour under the influence of it, than I ever did without it. And if I could be certain of living as long as I have, and that in perfect health, and I could have my choice either to have all my heart's defires of this world, and enjoy all the pleafures it could give—or to live in abject poverty, and enjoy this heavenly peace, I would not hefitate a moment in choofing the latter, in preference to the former. I believe what I write is the truth; I am fure it is fcripture. "A day in thy courts is better than a thoufand" elfewhere. "I had rather be a doorkeeper in the houfe of my God, than to dwell in the tents of wickednefs"—Pf. lxxxiv. 10. "Eye hath not feen, nor ear heard, neither have entered into the heart of man, to conceive the things which God hath prepared for them that love him. But God hath revealed them unto us by his fpirit"—1 Cor. ii. 9, 10. "If our hearts condemn us not, then have we confidence towards God"—1 John xxx. 20 "There is no condemnation to them who are in Chrift Jefus"—Rom. viii 1. Bleffed be God I feel none.

O, religion is a bleffed thing! I mean a fenfe of the love of God Deifm is diametrically oppofite. It is what I have been much troubled with, before I experienced what I now enjoy; after which I had not a doubt remaining of the truth of Chriftianity in its purity; and under my prefent feeling of the love and goodnefs of God, it is impoffible to doubt.

Further consideration this afternoon on internal light and obedience.

All mankind who live in sin, are under condemnation according to the light they have; all have a talent, or talents, to improve. What is this light but a seed of divine grace in the heart, "a manifestation of the spirit given to every man to profit withal?" Christ is "the true light, which lighteth every man that cometh into the world" This light is called by various names, all meaning one and the same—as monitor, reprover, talent, light, seed, word, gift, grace, and good spirit; and to which many of the thoughtful and serious part of mankind of all nations and sects, have borne testimony, either to the convicting, convincing, or efficacious power of it. I have a preacher every hour of my life wherever I am, either to my condemnation or consolation. The moment I have a thought of doing evil, that moment I feel within me, as plain as language can express, Do not do it. Or if I am thoughtlessly running into evil, I feel a check, and am instantly reminded. If I persevere on against its reproofs, I am brought under disagreeable feelings, and according to the enormity of the evil, I feel remorse and distress of mind. If I am obedient to its reproofs, I feel inward peace and serenity. If I, from time to time, continue obedient, and refrain from every thing it makes known to be evil, the light increases, from a spark it kindles into a flame; and glory to God, my soul is all on fire! "My heart," said David, "was hot within me; while I was musing, the fire burned." O may this heavenly flame, this heavenly fire never be extinguished! I believe it will eternally increase! Now by yielding obedience to this (which is called, and in the beginning is but as a) seed of divine grace sown in the heart, it will lead from all sin and bring salvation.—"The grace of God," said the apostle, "that bringeth salvation, hath appeared unto all men." This is the greatest and most blessed gift of God ever given to man; this is that which distinguisheth him from, and raiseth him above the brute creation. This is the true, the real, infallible revelation of God. O may I never more quench the spirit, never more act contrary to its warning and reproofs, but live in continual obedience.

This evening I thankfully recollected the time when I was powerfully convicted for sin, about eighteen years ago,* sailing then near where I am now. I being then alone, (it is good to be alone and retired sometimes) I began to seriously consider of my awful state and condition; living in sin and wickedness as I had done, conviction soon took hold of me. I was brought under as great distress of mind and penitential sorrow, I think as I could then bear. I lay on the deck, rolling and clinching my hands together, and crying in a flood of tears, Lord have mercy on me—forgive and preserve me for the time to come, &c. My grief and compunction for sin continued about a couple of hours, when I felt some hope and faith arise in my heart, and felt that peace of mind I never did before From that time began my reformation; I forsook those practices I was most addicted to, as frolicking, drunkenness, and swearing. And what caused all this? What was it that thus visited me, and gave me a sight of my condition and of the odiousness of sin, but that light or good spirit of which I have written? My soul bows in humbleness and thankfulness to God for all his mercies to me, once a poor sinner. He visited me when I was in the gall of bitterness and bond of iniquity. O may I be more watchful and faithful for the time to come than I have been! O may I for ever love and praise him. If so small a drop of the love of God, as I now feel, makes my soul so happy, what must the happiness of those be, who are totally cleansed from all sin, and have launched into the ocean? Ah! truly, "there is a river the streams whereof make glad the city of God"—Ps. xlvi. 4. What now are all the pleasures, honours, and glories of this world to me? Would all that this world could give, be any equivalent to the loss of this precious jewel? I pity the souls who are lost from God—who are taking their delight in the shadows of a moment—who think nor care any thing about

* See page 13.

their poor immortal ſouls—who are feeding and adorning their mortal bodies, and letting that precious jewel, the ſoul, ruſt and ſtarve. O how ſhort is life, how certain is death and eternity! In a little time we muſt bid an eternal adieu to all earthly things, and enter a naked ſpirit into the world of ſpirits! O my God, how ſolemn the thought! How terrible to the wicked! I feel my ſoul drawn out in love to all mankind!

I heartily wiſh that all my relatives, friends, and acquaintance, may experience with me, the redeeming love of Emmanuel; may become companions with me in this peace and joy. Then when our earthly toils and trials are ended, we ſhall become companions in a happy world of ſpirits. Oh! remember that time here is ſhort—that we muſt all die—be ſincere ſouls—forſake all evil—live as for eternity—prepare for a world to which we are all haſtening, and God will favour you with a ſenſe of his love; then you will know that it is the greateſt of all favours.

My ſoul this evening, is on the wings of love—I ſoar above all terreſtrial things. "Eye hath not ſeen, nor ear heard, nor hath it ever entered into the heart of a man," who has never experienced this, to form the leaſt conception of the love of God I now enjoy. Oh! ye chriſtians, what do ye loſe by living beneath your privilege? living in a luke-warm death-like ſtate. Remember that ye are not truly chriſtians, unleſs you have Chriſt in your hearts. Praiſe the Lord, O my ſoul, from this time for ever; and all within me magnify his holy name. Twelve o'clock this night, bowed in humility and heart felt gratitude to God, my father and preſerver; and retired to bodily reſt. I ſay bodily reſt, becauſe the ſoul in this ſtate need none. It is never weary nor tired, but wants an eternity to praiſe him. What a bleſſed Sabbath I have had. It is ſomething like the eternal Sabbath. Yea, aſſuredly, I have had a foretaſte of heavenly joys. I have feaſted on angels' food.

All that I have written, I have experienced in ſilence and retirement. My men wonder why I am ſo ſtill, and do not talk more. They little know my bleſſed company and communion; and it would be vain to talk to them of that which they cannot comprehend.

Second day, Sept 13 I felt a calmneſs, and peace of mind all the day; and moſt of the time my ſoul was delightfully engaged in ſecret prayer. Oh! who that knows the value of prayer, will neglect it? Not a dry, lifeleſs prayer of the head, or the tongue; but of the heart.

I had ardent deſires this evening for the continuation of what I have enjoyed. I had rather lie in a dungeon, loaded with chains, and have it, than dwell in a palace without it. But I can ſay, the will of the Lord be done. I ſhould be reſigned to his will and wiſdom, in all things; in death as well as in life

Third day. The night paſt; and forepart of this day, I experienced another ſtate, wherein I was clearly taught that I muſt be willing, and rejoice in ſuffering with, and for Chriſt, as well as to reign with him. Or, in order to reign with Chriſt, I muſt ſuffer with him: and that I muſt love the croſs while in the body, in order to obtain the crown.

While experiencing this ſuffering ſtate, I did not think of one paſſage of ſcripture, nor receive a mitigation of it from any quarter; but after, I could not help admiring its agreement with the apoſtolic doctrine. See Rom. viii. 17. 18 2 Tim. ii. 12. 2 Cor. i. 5. Phillip iii 10. 1 Peter iv. 13. Many are very deſirous of reigning with Chriſt, and rejoicing in his love; which, to be ſure, is a heavenly and deſirable ſtate; but few are willing to ſuffer with him, and bear his croſs. Theſe things cannot be truly underſtood, but by entering into, and feeling the work; and even this is a work of peace, and in which I have found his grace ſufficient for me, and his ſtrength made perfect in my weakneſs—(2 Cor. xii. 9.)

Fourth day. I ſpent much of the time in retirement and ſilence, waiting on God; and felt my ſoul much drawn out in ſecret prayer, that God would more and more diſcover to me the evil of my heart, and endue me with power to crucify the ſame. It is in the heart we want God, and there we muſt find him to its cleanſing and comfort; and blessed be God, there we may find him. Oh! my heavenly comforter! thou hast ever been near me, and I have ran hither and thither, seeking thee; and all for want of understanding these words of thy gospel: "The kingdom of God cometh not with observation; neither shall they say, lo here, or lo there; for behold the kingdom of God is within you."

Fully convinced I am, that there is no real, and permanent strength to be received from, or through any mortal on earth. Paul may plant, Apollos may water; but it is God that giveth the increase, life, light, and power. May I ever have a single eye to God alone. From this time forward, I renounce all dependance on all beneath the unchangeable God: all that is inferior to this inward divine principle; to which I believe, by a close and strict attention, watchfulness, prayer, and obedience, I may work, or it will work that work in me, and I live that life which will be acceptable to God. I believe what I have written is the truth; it is what I have seen and felt in the light that has shone on me, and love which has covered my mind.

Two or three months after I had written this account, I read it one evening to a number of my brethren; to which, one of them replied—"I believe you were favor-"ed with an extraordinary gift of God." I said—According to the faith, all good comes through the ministration; then how came this?

He answered—"By means of, and through the min-"istration" I replied—The Elders, to my knowledge, never administered any thing like it; if they had, I should have had that faith in them that you have; but I have not the least shadow of reason to believe as you do. I experienced the same before ever I saw them; but in a greater degree. For three days (in May, 1796) my soul was one continual song of gratitude and praise to God; and I felt no more of an inclination to sin, than to put my hands into the fire. But it is not in the power of language to describe what I felt: in short, it was part of the time extatic. I was in as much of a heaven as I could contain, and live in the body. Now I have no more reason to believe, that this last blessed experience was a gift of God through the miniſtration, than the former. And if this I have laſt mentioned, were a gift of God (which I am ſure it was, and it accords with the experiences of all good men in every age of the world) then it is clear there is a revelation of God one ſide of the miniſtration; and how can you acknowledge, or believe this account that I have read, to be a gift of God, when, under the influence of which, I write againſt the very foundation of your faith? i. e. reſpecting the miniſtration; and I believe if the Elders, or thoſe who have a thorough underſtanding of the faith, were to read this diary, they would not own it in the manner you do; for I conceive they do not believe in this which is called chriſtian experience, to be in reality the gift of God; or at leaſt, they do not believe that it is of any real advantage to the ſoul in its travail out of ſin. It certainly has a tendency to hinder increaſing in your faith; as it gives that ſoul ſatisfying evidence that nothing ever did, or can give, that can be mentioned or conceived. And as an experience ſome years ſince, that I have juſt mentioned, prevented me from embracing deiſm, ſo I have thought this laſt will prevent me from fully embracing Shakeriſm. The former, I verily believe, was in mercy given me, to ſee and feel the truth of the chriſtian religion in oppoſition to deiſm; which, on account of the conduct of profeſſing chriſtians, I was about that time ſettling into. And I have thought I was favoured with the latter, or a reviſitation, to let me ſee the truth of revelation one ſide of the miniſtration.

We had conſiderable converſation reſpecting the miniſtration doctrine. I told them at laſt, if the Elders were to tell me they had a ſpecial gift for me to go to Albany and walk acroſs the North River on the water, I would go, and exerciſe all the faith I poſſibly could; and if I could not walk on the water, I would walk in, until I could not touch bottom; I would then turn about and come out, and conclude there was no gift of God in it.

The one who ſpake before, a zealous believer, (and who has ſince ſtood as leader) ſaid—"I would do more." I aſked him what more. He anſwered—"I would "walk in as you have ſaid, and if I did not riſe I would "ſwim; and if I could not ſwim acroſs, I would drown "before I would come back againſt the gift of God."

I replied—I think I went full far enough in the gift; but you have gone beyond all bounds of reaſon.

A ſhort time after, I had converſation with our Elder brother S. Wells, concerning the beforementioned experience. After controverting ſometime, he againſt the divine reality, or beneficial effects of it, and I for it, he told me at laſt, there was no ſalvation in this experience; at moſt, it was but as a traveller, ſtopping at an inn to take refreſhment; at which time, he did not travel one ſtep. Shortly after, he came to my houſe, and he converſed with me about two hours on the inconſiſtency of my profeſſing to be united to the people of God, and, at the ſame time, united to the world; and on my being in partnerſhip (in a certain branch of buſineſs) with a man of the world. To which, the ſubſtance of my reply, was, that it was neceſſary in order to be able to pay ſome debts I owed, and to ſupport the character of an honeſt man; and if I moved to Niſkeuna, or near the church, I could not ſee any thing I could do, that would turn to much account.

Upon religious ſubjects, he endeavoured to convince me of the propriety and neceſſity of faith in, and obedience to the Elders, as the only way to obtain ſalvation from ſin. And I argued an obedience to the written goſpel, and the light that enlighteneth every man that cometh into the world. He adviſed me, if I could not ſee, and believe with the people, not to own them. To which, I replied—I wiſh to be more ſatisfied reſpecting them and their faith.

A few days after, I wrote him a letter on "a meaſure of the manifeſtation of the ſpirit which is given to every man to profit withal"—(Rom. xii 7.) He afterwards told me what I had written was not his faith; and that if I wiſhed to ſtand among the people of God, I muſt get a different faith from what I had.

It was repeatedly ſaid, one to another—"Thomas has not got a right line, or manner of faith." And when they mentioned theſe things to me, I teld them, I had the ſame principal faith, I had at firſt: I had not altered, or changed; and the faith I at firſt heard preached by the Elders and others, "That the rule for man to walk by, was that of God, manifeſted in man; and by that light which enlighteneth every man."

But now as the real faith of the church was preached in plain terms; and what we muſt come to, and abide by; and as a new ſcene began to be opened, by which I became tried and wounded in my faith, I ſhall therefore cloſe the firſt part of this work, and leave the reader to compare it with the ſecond, and judge for himſelf

END OF PART FIRST.

AN

# ACCOUNT, &c.

## PART II.

*A cautious inquiry and examination into the truth and propriety of the Doctrines and Practice of the people called Shakers, together with the ſubſtance of ſeveral diſcourſes with the Elders and others concerning their Faith and mode of Government; with the author's trials and exerciſes of mind, until he left them.*

I HAVE obſerved in the firſt part of this work, it was on account of the people called Shakers profeſſing to be in the millennium, and exhibiting the fruits of their faith, by appearing to live together in love and union, that induced me to unite with them, and become a member of their ſociety, wiſhing to prove whether they were the people they profeſſed to be or not. I ſhall now proceed to ſtate how, for the firſt time, my faith became hurt, reſpecting the revelation of the will of God to us through the Elders. I may firſt obſerve, that though many reports about theſe people, that were in circulation when I joined them, I ſoon found to be falſe; nevertheleſs, by this time, (latter part of 1802) I found ſome were true. One in particular, which I am ſorry to have cauſe to mention, and which I would paſs over, if by ſo doing, I could do juſtice to the work I have undertaken; which is to give an impartial account—neither intentionally to withhold or add any thing, for or againſt; but to adhere cloſely to my motto, "Not dare to tell a falſehood, or leave a truth untold."

The circumſtance I am about to relate, is reſpecting the practice among theſe people, formerly, of dancing naked; (the reader may recollect how this matter was denied when I queſtioned the old believers and Elders concerning the truth thereof;) which I now found to be true. Some time the latter part of this year, being in company with a kind friend, Derick Veeder, a young believer, I aſked him if he knew of there having been ſuch conduct among the people in firſt Mother's day.

He replied—"Yea, I knew it ſome time ago; and I "have been ſomewhat tried in my mind reſpecting it; "becauſe the Elders at firſt denied it, when they knew it "was the truth, and had danced naked themſelves."

I told him, that ſome time after I opened my mind, I inquired of the old believers and Elders about ſaid conduct, and they had denied it to me. I aſked him how he got along with his faith in the Elders after ſuch falſifications?

He replied—"I will talk to them about it." A ſhort time after I ſaw him again, he told me "he had done "ſo, and they had ſatisfied him reſpecting it."

I aſked him how?

He replied—"They told me every ſoul muſt look to "himſelf, and attend to his own wrongs; and whoever "had denied the truth of ſuch conduct, (or ſpoken in "any other reſpect falſe) muſt anſwer for it themſelves; "and ſuch would have to confeſs it." Further they ſaid, that "I ſhould not let that, or the failings or wrongs "of others, in any reſpect hurt my faith."

I replied, That come-off will not do for me, as the Elders place themſelves as leaders, and declare that the revelation of God muſt come through them to us; and according to their own doctrine, that pure revelation don't come through, nor dwell in, an impure, falſe veſſel: and as I have found they have falſified their word in one thing, it is likely they have, or may, in another. Therefore, I think it will be wiſdom in me now to examine for myſelf more particularly than I have done; and alſo to take care I am not deceived by others; and I intend to open this matter to the Elders the firſt opportunity.

Soon after, I was with Elder John Meacham, who was now at Nifkeuna. After fome converfation on indifferent matters, he faid :

"Thomas, how can you expect to hold any relation
" to the people of God, in a travail, and be united to the
" world in trade "

We had confiderable converfation on divers matters. He preached to me refignation to the gift, and obedience to what I was taught by my Elders. I told him, at laft, I defired to open a matter wherein my faith was hurt, and wherein I thought I had reafon to be diffatisfied ; and that is, faid I, refpecting Elder Hezekiah and alfo feveral of the old believers having denied that they had ever danced naked I told him how I had queftioned Elder Hezekiah, (who was now at Lebanon) he being prefent at the time, concerning the truth or fallacy of faid conduct, and the anfwer he gave me. Now, faid I, Elder John, I know you have all danced naked, men and women together. When we find a man has told an untruth in his dealings, we cannot place that confidence in him afterwards, which we fhould have done, had we found him to be a man of truth ; how much lefs in matters relating to our falvation. Therefore, how can you then expect me to have that faith in the Elders and obedience that is required I tell you, my kind friend, before I can, this matter muft be cleared up, if there is a poffibility of doing it.

He replied—" Thomas, you are miftaken. Elder H.
" never told you fo ; if he did, he told you an untruth ;
" and I do not know what I fhould think of him—I
" could not have fellowfhip with him in it, or have any
" union with him."

I faid, I will admit of no miftake—I am certain he anfwered me as I have ftated he did ; to which I could be qualified, if I was going to leave the world; and it has been not only him, but feveral old believers, who have denied that they ever danced naked. Mary Hocknell, in particular, denied it entirely, in the prefence and hearing of D. Wood and widow Bennet, (old believers) R. Hodgfon and myfelf. Now, I know they have all danced naked ; and this was denied when I firft endeavoured to gain information of the rise, faith, and practice of the church. Don't deny it, Elder John; it is a well known fact, that that conduct was hidden from us and denied: and the world, particularly backsliders, were called liars, for fear it would hinder the young believers from coming forward in the faith. Further, it is not only my assertion, but I can prove it by a number of believers.

He replied—"We don't wish any fending and proving "about it. It will be best for you and Elder Hezekiah "to be face to face."

I said, that is what I desire. Now I would not have you to understand me, that my faith is hurt by the apparent impropriety of such conduct; as I can dispense therewith, as it was done in the infancy of the church, and under the lead of first Mother; but what hurts my faith is, discovering positive falsehood in those who make so great a profession of truth.

He said—"If Elder Hezekiah, or any of the old be-"lievers, have said or done wrong, they will have to an-"swer for their wrongs themselves Therefore, you "should not let wrongs and failings in others hurt your "faith; but confess and forsake your own wrongs, and "labour for yourself, (as every one should do) to be-"come an honest, upright, holy man, and not look at "the failings of others, which will be no food to your "soul."

I replied—What deficiences and wrongs I see in the young believers, or my equals in the faith, or if any of them had told me falsehood, I should think nothing of it touching the faith; but the ministration or Elders preach, and not only so, but profess truth, honesty, purity, and holiness; as Elder H. publicly declared at Cornwall, that he had "done nothing in the day or night, in "the light or in darkness, that he would be ashamed to "be seen doing by God, men, or angels" You likewise profess and testify, that it is only by obedience to the counsel of our Elders, that we can obtain salvation; and that there is no other revelation of the Divine will, but by this medium; and we are taught to follow you as you follow Christ—and to look up to you, as standing in Christ's stead for example.

I told him my faith was likewise tried in another point; which was, respecting sins confessed being told by the Elders to others; when he knew I had often heard them say, "that they went no further; what was opened to them they did not divulge, but, if possible, buried all in oblivion." But now, said I, I know to the contrary; and that they were not only carried upwards through the line of the ministration, but likewise some things downwards, among young believers. In short, I found that I had not been rightly informed respecting several things; and in confessing sins, I considered the Elders had violated their promise.

We had two or three hours of conversation (it being one Sabbath afternoon) on several subjects; but I must study brevity, and pass over many things that were done and said.

1803. In a few months after this conference, (some time in February) I was at Lebanon; and the first conference I had was with Elder Hezekiah, respecting my charge of falsehood. I stated the question I put to him, and the cause why, exactly as heretofore related.* Now, said I, Elder Hezekiah, I know the old believers, or church brethren and sisters, have danced naked repeatedly, under an idea, or with intention, to mortify the fleshly nature, and you have danced so with them.

He replied—"Yea, once; and I did not tell you there "never had been such conduct; but that I did not know "of nor believe there was any such conduct now."

I said, it would have been needless to ask such a question as that answer would have implied; because I knew there was no such conduct among the people now—and I had not heard any one charging the people with it in the present day. The question I asked was in the past tense, Have the people or any of them ever, &c.; and the way you now state it, would have been no answer to the question I asked. The truth is, Elder Hezekiah, thou didst deny there ever having been such conduct, as several of the old believers did, for fear it would hurt

* See page 108.

our faith. He did not contradict me the second time, neither did he appear forward to controvert the point farther with me—but said:

"Since I have been called to be an Elder and minister I have been sorry I ever saw such conduct among "the people; for I have been often asked the question by "young believers, and people of the world; and often "I have known not what answer to give, as it would "not do to tell them we had danced naked, admitting "it to have been a real gift of God; it would have been "so out of their sight, they could not see it nor receive "it as such. Some times when I have evaded such questions, I have been asked more particularly and I have "often been exceedingly tried."

I replied—You did not appear to be tried when I asked you the question very pointedly, but answered me very readily; and I never shall believe you did right. But I do not want to say any thing more now to hurt thy feelings about it. And I can make some allowance, as I expect thou and others meant good, viz. in consequence of a concern for my faith. Therefore, I'll drop it, that a door may be opened to proceed on other subjects, perhaps of more consequence.

But I was not fully satisfied* nor reconciled, and began to think I had received false information respecting several other matters besides what I have mentioned; therefore I could not place that confidence in them which they desired, and as I have heretofore intimated, if I discovered any conduct contrary to what they professed,† I should more doubt the truth of some points of their faith, particularly that of obedience to the ministration, and their being in a superior dispensation. I also con-

* How could I be satisfied when Elder John said, he could have no union with Elder Hezekiah in his denying the truth of such conduct—then how could I have union with him and several others I have mentioned? Indeed how could I have union with Elder John, when I verily believed he knew that Elder Hezekiah had denied it? I began to think of Romish pious frauds.

† See page 29, fourth line.

sidered, that according to their own criterion, I must "judge of a tree by its fruit; a good tree cannot bring forth evil fruit."

About this time I began to look more closely and examine for myself, whether what they advanced was the truth or not; and not take for granted every thing they asserted for truth, without examination.*

I tarried at Lebanon this time three days; and most of the time each day the Elders spent with me, labouring to convince and establish me in the foundation, faith, and doctrine of the church. The substance of which conversations I think best to give, as their faith and doctrines were by this time plainly opened; and I shall likewise bring in occasionally the substance conversed, (on those subjects here treated) with a few others in the faith at different times, mostly preceding. Here will be seen the reasons they advance in support of their faith, with my objections against those points wherein I could not believe as they did: and in giving their reasons for their faith, I think it is a fair way of representing it; and by giving my arguments against those points controverted, their faith and doctrines becomes more clearly understood.

Next day I met with the Elders in a retired room, set apart particularly to converse in, or in which they generally laboured with the believers; Elder John first spake and said:

"Thomas, it is now some years since you first heard "the gospel, and received a measure of faith; and those "who received faith about the time you did, by their "obedience, have travailed far before you; while, we "are sorry to say, you are tarrying behind. It is time "you now come to a final conclusion; whether to forsake the world or not; and take up your cross, and "become obedient to the gospel; give up, and renounce

* "We are justly chargeable with criminal sloth and misimprovement of the talents, with which our Creator has intrusted us, if we take all things for granted which others assert, and believe and practise all things which they dictate, without due examination." *Dr. Watts' Improvement of the Mind.*

"your own way, will, and wiſdom, and become as a "child, and believe, receive, and go forth in obedience "to what you are taught."

Elder Hezekiah obſerved—"Chriſt ſays we muſt 'be-"come as children, for of ſuch is the kingdom of God.' "You muſt become humble and willing to be taught by "a child. We are but children in the world's wiſdom "and learning, to what you are; but you muſt become "humble, and willing to count all but as droſs and "dung, that you may win Chriſt. If you were to take "hold, and really come into the work of the goſpel of "the ſecond coming of Chriſt, you might be of great "ſervice in helping others, and might be the means of "gathering many ſouls in the way of God; but other-"wiſe, thoſe abililties and talents, which you have, will "be buried and loſt, and be of no ſervice to yourſelf nor "others. As Elder John has ſaid, you muſt become "ſimple as a child, and conclude you know nothing as "you ſhould know, and believe and receive what you "are taught.

"When I firſt received the goſpel, I found, as I was "obedient to my Elders, that I knew nothing right be-"fore; and as I was obedient to what I was taught, I "received the gifts and power of God. I now know, as "we all do, who have been obedient, that this is the only "way of life and ſalvation; and you never will come into "this work of God, until you renounce a caviling ſpirit; "and looking for faults, and catching at things that "don't concern you. You muſt look at your own faults, "and weed your own garden, as every ſoul muſt an-"ſwer for their own ſins. No longer now, the fathers "have eaten ſour grapes, and the children's teeth are "ſet on edge. Admitting you were to ſee your Elders "do, or ſpeak wrong, you ſhould not judge, or find "fault with them; nor have hard feelings towards "them, on that account; as you cannot help them out "of their wrong. Chaſtiſement and counſel would come "contrary to the order of God: you could not reach "us. If we were to do wrong, we muſt be brought out "by thoſe above us, not by thoſe below us, i. e. by our "Elders; we would have to confeſs to them, and bear

"their chastisement: and we have to travail in obedi-
"ence to what they teach us; as we have our Elders,
"and are taught by them, as you and other young be-
"lievers are by us; and in our going forth in obedience
"to what they teach us, we receive from them the gifts
"of God, and become able to administer to others, as
"they are able to receive. I only mention these things
"to show the order of God in his church. God is now
"revealed and manifested in the second coming of
"Christ, the final and last display of God's grace to a
"lost world Not by immediate revelation to each soul;
"but by, and through his ministers, whom he hath ap-
"pointed; and we find that under every dispensation of
"God's grace to a lost world, he has always made use
"of instruments by patriarchs and prophets; and so
"long as people were obedient to the mind and will of
"God manifested through, and by them, prosperity and
"a blessing attended them; but when they were disobe-
"dient, they became an easy prey to their enemies.—
"Witness the consequence of their disobedience at vari-
"ous times to Moses. Now we desire nothing of you,
"but your salvation; and that you may become a man
"of God in the gospel, and come forward in the gift
"and order of God; and then you will be able to help
"those who come after you, and to judge both in your-
"self and others, what is wrong and right."

I replied—As to forsaking the world, or more properly the evil that is in the world, and taking up my cross against all sin, and becoming obedient to the gospel, as Elder John has said, I agree; and have come to a final resolution some time ago, according to the strength and grace afforded. But respecting the gospel, obedience thereto, and the way I am to receive power, we may not agree, as I clearly perceive what is required; and that is, an implicit faith in my Elders, non-resistance, and passive obedience. I presume you will allow that I have cause, and should be exceeding cautious to whom I resign myself up, and by whom I suffer myself to be led, knowing how full the world has been of confident pretenders to revelation; and likewise, how many ecclesiastical leaders there have been, and how mankind have been deceived and impoſed upon by many of them; though I do not ſpeak this as if I believed that it is your intention to impoſe on, or deceive any one. There is a poſſibility of your being miſtaken, and deceived in ſome things yourſelves reſpecting your faith, as many other confident profeſſors of revelation have been before you. Therefore, it is actually neceſſary that I ſhould have good and ſufficient evidence that you are ſent of God, before I can, with any manner of propriety, reſign myſelf, body and ſpirit, I mean all I have and poſſeſs, to you. You ſay "proof will come in conſequence of obedience;" but I muſt have faith firſt, before I can go forth in obedience with any heart. You ſay that "faith is the gift of God" Now here is an eſſential, immediate revelation, entirely on one ſide of the miniſtration, unleſs you adminiſter the gift of faith; if you could, all would be ſettled at once; the controverſy would be decided; but you have not power to do it; if you had, many would have faith, and would begin to conclude the mellennium was commenced ſure enough.

Elder Hezekiah ſaid—"Thomas, you ſay you want "proof, and how am I to know? How is any creature "to know according to your faith, the truth of the chriſ-"tian religion, until he prove it by experiencing the "power and virtue of it? How is any one to know "there is any efficacy in that which convicteth for ſins? "which you call the ſeed of divine grace in all men, which "you believe will work the ſalvation of all, as creatures "are obedient to it. Now how can any one know what "it will do for them, but by obedience to its firſt con-"victions for ſin. You may ſay, as you are always "ready to give an anſwer and raiſe objections, that it is "proof of itſelf, or that it carries its own proof with it; "and it is likely you will tell what it has done for thou-"ſands of men who have been obedient to it, turning "them from ſinners to ſaints, as you believe they were. "Now we ſay it is by obedience to what you are taught "by your Elders, that you are to know whether they "teach you by the gift of God, or not. But firſt you "want proof that we have the gift or revelation of God. "You have already had proof in conſequence of your

" receiving a meaſure of faith; and by what little you
" have been obedient, you have felt a meaſure of the
" power and gift of God. Chriſt has left a rule for
" you and all to know who he ſends and who not; i. e.
" *By their fruits ye ſhall,* or may *know them. and by this*
" *shall all men know that ye are my diſciples, if ye love one*
" *another.*

" Now you have been repeatedly from one family to
" another, and you have ſeen ſuch good fruits, ſuch love
" and union, as you never ſaw before; which you have
" often acknowledged. A bad tree cannot bring forth
" good fruit; and if the miniſtration were falſe and de-
" ceivers, or deceived themſelves, how could it be poſſi-
" ble that their miniſtry ſhould be attended with ſuch
" good effects? Here are thouſands of living witneſſes
" in this day, who have obtained that ſalvation from ſin,
" and borne that fruit that none ever did before, as a
" body of people. You will alſo grant, that the church
" of Chriſt ſhould be all as one, of one heart, and one
" mind; well, they are ſo. I ſuppoſe you have read
" an account of all the denominations of people on
" earth. You appear to be acquainted with the world;
" then ſearch it all over, look abroad, and examine all
" who profeſs religion, and you cannot find a people, as
" a body, who take up ſuch a croſs againſt the world,
" the fleſh, and the devil, and all ſin, as theſe people do;
" and who live in ſuch harmony, love, peace, and union.
" Likewiſe, behold their outward order, decency, and
" cleanlineſs on their farms, in their houſes, manufacto-
" ries, and in every reſpect that can be mentioned; and
" ſhow, if you can, any thing on earth to equal it You
" may find private families who live in a good degree
" of love and order; but I ſpeak of ſo large a ſociety of
" people. The church is not brought forward in this
" way, by wiſe men in this world's wiſdom; but un-
" learned, ſimple men, like the fiſhermen and apoſtles of
" old God has not choſen the wiſe of this world, but
" ſuch as I have mentioned, to confound the wiſdom of
" the world, and the worldly wiſe; and I have an in-
" ſtance of it before me.

" You are confounded when you think on these things, " and are not able to assign a satisfactory cause how all " this can be, when you throw away a revelation, and " hand of God in it Also, the order of the church in " the present day, and the victory it has obtained over " all sin, is a living proof that first Mother and Elders " had the revelation of God; for is it at all likely that " such a people, and order, would ever have arose from " the work they began, unless they had had God on " their side? Christ has told you, and I tell you, that " *an evil tree cannot bring forth good fruit.* The people of " the world, what little they know of us, say *The Shakers* " *are a sober, honest, industrious people*; and this is saying " a great deal These words contain much more than " they are aware of But you know a thousand times " more about the people of God, than the world does; " and unless you are obedient, that knowledge will be " your condemnation. You want proof. You have " proof upon proof, and you will be left without excuse.

" Now I have spoken principally of the church, or " those who have travailed many years, and are brought " into the order of the gospel. But only look at the " young believers in Niskeuna (now near an hundred) " and compare them with what they were a few years " ago, or before they received the gospel. Several of " them you then knew, living in sin, following the van- " ity and evil customs of the world. How do they live " now? You know, and I need not tell you. They " have become thus changed by their obedience, and by " what they have been taught; which was, to take up " their daily cross against all sin; to live an upright, " just, and holy life; to love and fear God; and live in " love and union one with another. If you had ever " heard the Elders preach, teach, or give any counsel " that was evil, or appeared to have that tendency, then " you might have some reason to doubt, and dispute " their having the gift of God; but I cannot see with " what propriety you can before.

" Now you mentioned in the latter part of your last " discourse, that faith is the gift of God, as we believe. " *No man can come unto me* (said Christ) *unless the Father*

" *draw him.* We do not deny immediate revelation, fo " far as of the convicting power of God; but believe " the fpirit of God is in the world at work with many " fouls, preparing their minds for the reception of the " gofpel, as God can only be known in Zion to their " complete falvation. We believe all are more or lefs " convicted of fin, as Paul was when driving from Jeru- " falem to Damafcus, to perfecute the faints. He was " powerfully convicted; fo that he cried out, *Lord, what* " *wilt thou have me to do.* He was then directed to a " man of God who would tell him what he fhould do.— " (Acts vii. 6)

" Now if mankind felt no conviction for fin, and God " had not raifed up witneffes, more or lefs, in every age " of the world, to teftify againft it, mankind would have " become fo loft and funk in a ftate of fin and wicked- " nefs, that this world would have been turned into, or " become a complete hell. But the mercy of God has " made ufe of thefe, and other means, to bind, and re- " ftrain poor, fallen, depraved man, until the fullnefs of " time fhonld come for their redemption. For there is " nothing in man one fide of the order and gift of God " in Zion, that will finally redeem and fave him from " all fin. For it is only in Zion that complete redemp- " tion can be obtained: therefore cries the Pfalmift— " *Oh that the falvation of Ifrael were come out of Zion* — " The prophet alfo fays—*From Zion fhall go forth the* " *law; and the word of the Lord from Jerufalem.* We " read that many will inquire the way to Zion, faying— " *Come let us go up to Zion.* And the Lord fays *he will* " *place falvation in Zion.* And *the Lord is great in Zion;* " *whofe fire againft fin is in Zion The Lord dwelleth in* " *Zion. God is known in the palaces of Zion* Now what " is Zion but the church of God? and why fo much faid " about Zion, as afking the way going up; the Lord " great in Zion, if all mankind have Zion and the word " of God in their own hearts? Why fo many outward " witneffes fent of God to preach the way of life and fal- " vation; to open the blind eyes; to bring people out " of darknefs into light? If all mankind have a light " within them fufficient, why does the apoftle fpeak in this

" manner?—*How ſhall they believe in him of whom they have* " *not heard? And how ſhall they hear without a preacher?* " *And how ſhall they preach except they be ſent? So that faith* " *cometh by hearing, and hearing by the word of God.* Not " the inward word it is clear; but by the outward word " preached. I aſk again, why does the apoſtles ſay ſo " much about obedience, and being taught by them, if " there be a ſufficient teacher in every man; and obedi- " ence thereto will anſwer every purpoſe neceſſary to our " ſalvation? And why does the apoſtle recommend the " believers in that day to *follow them, as they follow Chriſt,* " if following an inward guide be all-ſufficient? You have " read the ſcriptures over and over, and you profeſs to " believe in them. I am aſtoniſhed to think how you, " or any other man of common underſtanding, can hold " forth doctrine or ſentiments, ſo contrary to the whole " tenor of the ſcriptures; and likewiſe contrary to reaſon " and common ſenſe I can impute it to nothing but " their darkneſs and blindneſs."

I replied—I hope you will bear with me (if I am ready to give an anſwer, and make objections, as thou ſayeſt;) for, to know the truth is my only motive; and it is often, if not always the caſe, that greater truth and light appear in conſequence of objections being raiſed, than would have been otherwiſe diſcovered; and not only ſo, but the reaſons and evidences for belief, are more pungent and clear. Our ideas are grounded on the evidences exhibited to the mind; and we are influenced as theſe evidences appear more or leſs powerful.

Now that which appears unreaſonable and inconſiſtent to me, I think I had beſt to open; and then I wiſh to have the privilege to give my reaſons why it appears ſo. But if I were to keep my faith locked up in my own breaſt, and by my ſilence, give aſſent to all you advance in ſupport of your faith, and in my heart think different, I ſhould act the part of an hypocrite; though if I were obedient in outward things, I might paſs for a good believer. And I know ſome that do, who have the ſame faith that I have, reſpecting the ſubjects upon which we have converſed. One in particular, who (I believe) will never give up this doctrine of being taught by the ſpirit of God in his own heart, as he muſt do to have a right manner of faith; which, when he is convinced of, he will return to the Quakers, from whence he came—Though I do not charge him (as I ſaid of myſelf) with acting the part of an hypocrite. He is a man of few words; therefore, not diſpoſed to controverſy. But he had no idea of the faith being as it is, when he joined you, any more than I had. He was taken with a good outward appearance, as I was; but now I have come to a further knowledge, I wiſh to have the privilege to examine the faith, and count well the coſt before I further enliſt; which I could not, when I firſt came among you, and for ſometime after, as I knew not the faith. It was not then opened to young believers. You preached ſuch doctrines as we could receive; according to a common expreſſion among you, of "feeding with milk, and coming to creatures where they are." As I have heard your zealous preacher, I. Bates, ſay—"Catch them any how, ſo as we can but catch them."

When I was a boy, I heard about people pinning their faith upon the prieſt's ſleeve, and wondered what it meant; but now I rather wonder how people can be ſo duped as to do it. But I tell you before I can pin my faith, or have an implicit faith, non-reſiſtance, and paſſive obedience, I muſt be convinced of the truth of your faith; and if I have been caught in the true goſpel net, I do not wiſh to get out. If I know my own heart, truth in love, is my conſtant aim; and I am not ſo prejudiced in favour of any thing which I hold, but that I would willingly be convinced; and when I am convinced, I ſhall be willing to retract.

Now the difference between us, in an eſſential point, is, you believe we are to be ſaved by hearing the outward declarative goſpel, and an obedience thereto, as preached by you; and I believe I ſhall be ſaved by an internal goſpel, or by the ſpirit of God in my own heart, which the outward declarative goſpel of Chriſt bears witneſs to; as being a "light which enlighteneth every man that cometh into the world;" and that the ſpirit of God ſtriveth with all men You aſk "how am I to know the efficacy of this light, that I believe ſhineth on the hearts of all, but by obedience thereto?" I grant that obedience to its convictions and reproofs, is the most effectual, and soul satisfying way of knowing. But even in the sinner's breast, it carries its own proof with it, as you have truly said He feels convicted and condemned, and at times, powerfully and irresistibly; whereby he knows in his own heart, what is wrong; and he is made to see and feel himself a sinner, even such as never heard the declarative gospel. Indeed betimes, as such have felt their own wills slain, or have united in their minds with this holy leaven, they have felt peace arise they have an internal conviction of its truth. Now if a man feel pain or ease in body, does not he know it? Is it not proof itself? We have many instances on record of those who never heard the outward gospel, bearing testimony to this truth. In Romans ii. 15, we read, "The Gentiles show the work of the law written in their hearts; their consciences also bearing witness, and their thoughts the mean while, accusing or else excusing one another." The apostle John testifies, that "Christ enlighteneth every man that cometh into the world." Now who will dare to assert it is not a saving light. "A manifestation of the spirit is given to every man to profit withal"—1 Cor. xii. 7. But, according to your faith, it will not profit to salvation. Then what is it given for? Only to condemn them?. But the same apostle contradicts this assertion, in plain words, and tells us what the light and spirit (which is all grace) will do—"The grace of God that bringeth salvation, hath appeared," to whom "to all men, teaching," &c —Titus ii. 7. Here the apostle tells us this grace appeareth to all; and that it bringeth salvation, and is a saving grace; but you say it is not. Under the Mosaic covenant, when God took the children of Israel, by the hand of Moses, and led them out of Egypt, the people had to go to the priests and prophets to know the mind and will of God; which was the order of God under that dispensation, which you are repeatedly referring to, as proof of the ministration doctrine in this day. But it appears you have totally forgotten the new covenant; at least, I never heard you mention it—"But this shall be the covenant I will make with the houſe of Iſrael after thoſe days ſaith the Lord;" not according to the former covenant, but "I will put my law in their inward parts (or minds) and write it on their hearts: and they ſhall no more teach every man his neighbour, and every man his brother, ſaying, Know the Lord." Here it is plainly diſtinguiſhed from the former covenant, when they had to know the Lord, and be taught by the prieſts and prophets—"For they ſhall all know me from the leaſt of them unto the greateſt of them, ſaith the Lord"—Jer xxxi. 32, 33, 34. Not from the leaſt believer to the greateſt Elder, as I heard one of the brethren ſay; but all ranks and conditions of men. Now, according to your faith and order, we are yet under the ſame as the Moſaic covenant. We muſt go to the prieſt to know the mind and will of God, and be taught by them Every one of us muſt be taught by our neighbour or brother. The apoſtle to the Hebrews, ſays—"That covenant was not faultleſs; and that it was ready to vaniſh away." Chriſt told the Phariſees that *the kingdom of God was within them;* which could, conſidering their ſtate, have been no more than as a ſeed of the nature of the kingdom. And he alſo ſays that "The kingdom of heaven is like a grain of muſtard ſeed;" "but when it is grown, it is the greateſt among herbs."

Reply.—"We believe all you have mentioned of an "inward law, light, and ſeed, was received by the word "preached; and thoſe who believed in, and made a good "uſe of what they heard, were benefited thereby; but "*the word preached, did not profit all that heard it, in conſe-*"*quence of unbelief*—(Heb. iv. 8) We believe the nat-"ural conſciences of all are at times, viſited by the ſpir-"it of God, excluſively of the word preached, which "convinceth and condemneth for ſin; and thoſe who "have not the opportunity and privilege of hearing the "word preached, nevertheleſs, if they live up to that "light which God gives them by his ſpirit, ſuch will "find juſtification, but not ſanctification. "*No man* "(ſaid Chriſt) *can come to me, except the Father draw him.*" "You and many feel the drawings of the Father to the "Son, or to Zion the church of God, where Chriſt the

" Son is revealed. Here they may hear the word that " is power and life; and by obedience, they may find " salvation, redemption, and sanctification. You and all " must come for salvation, where Christ reveals and " manifests himself, as the apostle Paul, after he was " convicted, went to a man of God, as he was directed; " to one who had Christ in him; to one united to the " church, the members of which, are one body. Here " Paul was taught what he must do in order to be sav- " ed; and so as all become convicted, they should pray " as he did, *Lord, what wilt thou have me to do*, and re- " frain from those things for which they feel condemn- " ed; and patiently wait, and the Lord in his good " time, will show them what they should do to be sav- " ed. For the gospel will be preached or offered unto " every creature. It will find all souls that God ever " made; and it will find all in their sins unconfessed.— " When souls hear the gospel, if they are not then obe- " dient, their condemnation will be the greater.

" Before Paul was convicted, he was zealously engag- " ed in persecuting the disciples of Christ; and he tells " us he verily thought he ought to do many things " against Jesus: and we read of some who would kill " his followers, and at the same time think they did " God's service; then where was the inward light that " teacheth all men? The truth is, Paul had none till he re- " ceived it from those who were in possession of it, and of " the only means of salvation; but he was influenced " by his own carnal, wicked nature, as all mankind are, " who have not heard and received the gospel As a " proof of this, we need only take a view of the past and " present state of the world (taking the heathen nations " into consideration) and we clearly see they are all " in a lost state. *They are all gone aside; they are altogether " become filthy; there are none that doeth good; no, not one.* " They appear to have but little idea of any other good, " than what will answer the gratification of their carnal " natures. If hitherto a divine principle or power had " been in man, equal to or greater than the power of " evil, as you hold, then righteousness would have pre- " vailed as universally as unrighteousness has done; but

" the past and present state of the world, is a convincing
" proof to the contrary. Also, when we take a view of the
" professors of Christianity, and behold how they have been
" divided, and how they have differed about their religion,
" and how they have been deceived in many respects;
" in short, when we look at the lost state of mankind uni-
" versally, there appears to be a great want, and we see
" the insufficiency of this inward light, which you hold
" forth as a light teaching all men, &c. This is the
" fundamental doctrine of the Quakers; they have
" preached it up as a salvation principle, and have en-
" deavoured to prove the efficacy of it. The Metho-
" dists also believe much the same, or that all have a
" sufficient call, and that the spirit of God strives with
" every creature sufficient to save from all sin, if they do
" not resist; or that all may have grace sufficient if they
" seek for it. Now what has this principle done for ei-
" ther of them? We should always judge of a doctrine
" from the lives of its professors. If this had been an
" effectual saving principle as they profess, or if grace
" be given sufficient to save from sin, one might rea-
" sonably conclude that the Methodists who so firmly be-
" lieve it, would become saved from sin, and the Qua-
" kers would have travailed in the increase.

" The first Quakers preached and wrote as their faith,
" that *this inward light would finally increase, until all the*
" *kingdoms of the earth should become the kingdoms of Christ:*
" but time has proved the contrary; as instead of in-
" creasing and proving more and more the efficacy of
" this inward principle, they have degenerated, as you
" acknowledge—and as they themselves confess. They
" have become much like the rest of the world; and
" some times, in their preaching, they lament their own
" degeneracy, and have concluded by saying, But, friends,
" we trust there is a remnant among us yet. What sig-
" nifies their remnant? There was a remnant of faith-
" ful, sincere souls, among the Jews at the time they
" crucified Christ; and there may be a remnant of sin-
" cere souls in every society and in every nation. But
" does this look like the way in which all the kingdoms
" of the earth are to become the kingdoms of Christ,

" when they have now so far proved the insufficiency of " this inward light, that they are reduced to a remnant? " If the garment has been worn out in about an hundred " years, surely the remnant cannot last long. They may " exclaim, Alas! our light is on the decline, and going " out. Yea, and it will go out, as will all other lights, " insufficient for salvation, among every sect, as stars at " the rising of the sun.

" The truth is, God has provided a remedy for all " souls; the plaster is as large as the sore. The effec-" tual saving principle of good was given to the man " Christ; and by his obedience he overcame all evil, had " power given sufficient to foil Satan in all his attempts " against him; and that power he received from the Fa-" ther, he gives to the church, sufficient to administer " salvation to all the world: and in God's time, as I " said before, all will have the offer of the gospel suffi-" cient to save from all sin. But that this gospel can " only be obtained by the word preached, is abundantly " proved by the words of the apostle to the Romans (x. " 13, 17)—*How shall they hear without a preacher?* &c. " So then *faith cometh by hearing, and hearing by the word* " *of God.*"

To which I replied—I have often heard this text quoted by the Elders and believers, both in public and private conversation, and construed in the same manner you have now done. But the apostle, in the previous verses of the same chapter, gives a plain definition what the word of God is, and where it is. " Say not in thine heart, who shall ascend into heaven, or who shall descend into the deep;" that is the same as saying who shall or need go to any particular place on earth to find Christ, or to any priest to inquire where Christ is. If I was asked by a sincere inquirer, Where shall I find Christ to save me from my sins? which would be the best preaching or direction, to say, Where thou already feels his spirit, for this is it that causes thee to feel the burden of thy sins and need of him, and where he has began the work, there he must be found to finish it, and that is in thine own heart. How? By prayer and obedience to the light he giveth. Or to say, Lo, here; or lo, there;

directing him to man. Where we have found help, there we should direct others; and all that have found help, have found it by the spirit of God Therefore, to the same spirit all should be directed; and where is this spirit but within, operating upon the human heart?—"The word (said the apostle) is nigh thee, even in thy mouth, and in thy heart; that is, the word of faith which we preach." We preach unto you faith in, and obedience to, the inward word, the spirit of God—"Christ in you the hope of glory"—Col. i. 27. If it was not for this internal word, a measure of the spirit of Christ in us, from which faith proceeds, we never could have any more faith and hope than brute beasts; as there could be nothing as a ground from whence any good could proceed; for in nature there must ever be a first cause, to produce a consequent event, or action. I believe, that the great first cause hath imparted a measure of his spirit to every intelligent creature; which, in process of time, will be so improved and increased, that all the people of the earth will be gathered into the kingdom of Christ, according to the beforementioned words of the prophet. It is believed by many, that those words refer more particularly to the millennium, when all will know the Lord. "By the law being written on the heart," it is signified, that there will not be any necessity of an outward teaching. This prophesy of a new covenant is so pointed against your Mosaic order, that I believe I never should have heard it quoted, if I had not brought it forward for consideration. As to the Quakers and Methodists having proved the insufficiency of grace, spirit, or light, in order to salvation, it is not so; but, directly the reverse; they have not, it is true, proved its sufficiency as they might have done, and as I hope yet will be done. Further, is the degeneracy of the Quakers, any proof of the insufficiency of the grace and light for which I contend? Nay, the principle itself is eternal and unchangeable, like the Fountain from which it proceeds.

There is, in man, a principle of honesty, which is considered to be divine; yet many are to be found who do not act in conformity to it; but this is not considered as a proof that there is no ſuch principle. Whatever proof may be brought of the inſufficiency of the principle for which I contend, may be applied, at leaſt, with equal propriety to the Shakers; for more of them have degenerated, or left the ſociety. in twenty years, than of the former in forty years; notwithſtanding the great diſproportion of the Shakers in number, when compared with the Quakers and Methodiſts. I have heard it ſaid among you, that as many have fallen from the faith and have left your ſociety, from firſt to laſt, as there are now in the faith. But you will ſay they departed from the principle or power of the goſpel. The ſame may be ſaid of the Quakers and Methodiſts who have degenerated; but the principle and power of the goſpel remains the ſame in thoſe who have continued under its influence. In ſhort, after you have ſtood as many years as the Quakers have, it is more than probable that the remnant may be applied to your ſociety with as much fitneſs, as it is now to that of the Quakers.

Now let us inquire of the apoſtle concerning the univerſality of the principle for which I contend. Paul—have all got the word in their hearts? We want to know in particular, how it is with thoſe who never heard the outward goſpel Now, hark! let us hear the anſwer! "Yea, verily, their ſound went into all the earth, and their words unto the ends of the world; teaching them to deny ungodlineſs." "If ye continue in the faith grounded and ſettled, and be not moved away from the hope of the goſpel, which ye have heard, and which was preached to every creature which is under heaven; whereof I Paul am made a miniſter"—Col i. 23 Now we have been told of the univerſality of the goſpel; but that we may know for certainty which goſpel he means, whether the external, preached by man, or the internal, preached by the omnipreſent God, in whom we live, move, and have our being—we will aſk him.

Paul, by what goſpel waſt thou made a miniſter?—Didſt thou go to thoſe who were miniſters before thee, to be taught by them?

"I certify you, brethren, that the goſpel which was preached of me, is not after man; for I neither received it of man, neither was I taught it, but by the revelation of Jesus Christ; for, when it pleased God to call me by his grace, to reveal his Son in me, I conferred not with flesh and blood. Neither went I up to Jerusalem to them which were apostles before me; but I went into Arabia, and returned again to Damascus. Then after three years I went up to Jerusalem to see Peter. But other apostles, or ministers, I saw none, save James. Now the things which I have told you, behold before God I lie not"—Gall. i. 11, 12, 15 to 20.

This answer is full and clear: therefore, I may thus argue, and deduce the following conclusions. As the gospel has been preached to every creature under heaven, and all have heard the sound thereof, and as by this gospel Paul was made a minister, and as he expressly tells us, that "the gospel that made him so was not of man, neither was he taught of man, but by the revelation of Christ;" then the gospel preached to every creature, is not of man, neither are they taught it by man, but by the revelation of Christ Therefore, as the first is true, so also the last; and the result of this doctrine is undeniable according to my premises, that Christ has revealed himself, has given himself as a light, seed, &c. in all; and that it is not only received by the word preached. But again, as I presume none will deny, that that gospel of which Paul was a minister, was by obedience, salvation to him; therefore, without any more proof—by obedience, salvation to all. But I may just mention further, that every creature under heaven had not heard the outward gospel. When the apostle wrote, they had not heard a word of it either in China or America. Nay, one half of the world, from that day to this, are utter strangers to the outward coming of Christ, his sufferings and death, to atone for their sins Nevertheless, I verily believe they are all partakers of a measure of his spirit.

Now that the apostle, on his conviction, was directed to a man of God (as the believers word it) to tell him what he should do, I have repeatedly heard mentioned among you: and it is the principal instance I have ever heard you bring forward to prove the truth of the minſtration doctrine. But it is certainly directly oppoſite to your faith in this reſpect; and I think if I were as ſtrong in the faith as any of you, I would never mention this conviction and converſion of the apoſtle, as a proof of the truth of my faith in a miniſtration.

I was in company, not long ſince, with a believer, (B. Youngs) whom I had often heard before, mention about the apoſtle Paul being directed to a man of God, as a proof of the neceſſity of being taught by the Elders. I told him I hoped he would never mention it again; for he could not mention an inſtance in all the ſcriptures, ſo oppoſite to your faith in this reſpect. For Paul did not receive the goſpel of man, neither was he taught it by man. And he tells us he went not up to thoſe who were apoſtles before him.

He then replied—"Paul was ordained an apoſtle to "the Gentiles; therefore, it was not conſiſtent with his "call to go to, or receive the goſpel of thoſe who were "apoſtles before him."

To which I replied—Why you confute your own poſition. What a weak ſubterfuge! Why then have you mentioned ſo many times this conviction and converſion of this apoſtle, to prove your miniſtration doctrine? Do you think it will anſwer well enough to mention about the apoſtle being directed, &c. to thoſe who never read the ſcriptures, or who are ſo little acquainted with them as not to be able to recollect the context, or any further account than what you mention? To which he made no reply. But I am much more ſurprized at the Elders and teachers, in drawing ſuch inferences from that paſſage. Muſt we receive and believe every thing you aſſert for truth, and not think and examine for ourſelves, when we ſee ſuch glaring inconſiſtencies?

As to the apoſtle, after his conviction, being directed to go into the city, (not to a man of God, as it is always worded by believers,) and it ſhould be told him what he ſhould do—Acts ix 6. What does this amount to. but that he was directed to go where he might become united to thoſe very people whom he was going to perſecute, and to build up that church of which before he was going to make havock? When he became united thereto by Ananias, and the ſpirit of perſecution was totally given up, the ſcales of darkneſs fell from his eyes, and he received the Holy Ghoſt. Now if he received and was taught the goſpel by Ananias, (which we have no account that he was) then his telling the Gallatians he neither received it of man, nor was taught it by man, is a plain contradiction. But I have ſaid enough on this ſubject. The plain account, as it ſtands on record, is a ſufficient confutation of your concluſions, deduced therefrom, and your miniſtration faith.

Reply—"But did not the apoſtle, by the inſtrumentality of Ananias, receive his ſight and the gift of the "Holy Ghoſt? But, to paſs over this, and leave the "apoſtle Paul—What think you of Cornelius being in a "viſion, and an angel appearing to him informing him, "that his *prayer and alms* were *come up for a memorial before God*, but were not yet anſwered? He was not yet "ſhown the way of life and ſalvation, but in order thereto, he was told to *ſend men to Joppa, and call for one Simon, whoſe ſirname is Peter;* and that he would tell him "what he ought to do. When Peter came, as he was "preaching to Cornelius and thoſe who were preſent, *the Holy Ghoſt fell on all them that heard the word.** Now why "was he told to ſend for Peter? Why preach the goſpel at all, if the goſpel within is all-ſufficient?"

I replied—There appears ſomething in this a little like your faith. But I have never denied that God has made uſe of inſtruments to carry on his work. It is our duty, and Chriſtianity teaches us, to be of help to one another in ſpirituals, as well as temporals. But you believe that ſalvation can be obtained in no other way than by outward teaching; and that man has no ſaving light or gift of God given him previous to hearing with the outward ear, and receiving Chriſt, or the divine gift, by means of, and through inſtruments choſen for that purpoſe.—But if you were to adminiſter thoſe gifts, or ſuch a bleſſing attended your miniſtry as the preaching of Chriſt and his apoſtles, we might believe you were in the ſame ſtanding, and had the ſame life and power. But ſeeing

* Acts x. 44.

in others, and feeling in myſelf, the want thereof, has cauſed my faith to be hurt reſpecting the miniſtration. It is an obſervation that ſerious people in general make, that "if you were in a ſuperior diſpenſation, as you profeſs, you would be able to preach with more life and power than you do" The preaching I hear almoſt every Sabbath day, in the meeting-houſe at Niſkeuna, is as dry as a bone The people ſit and hear with as little impreſſion made on them, as if they were hearing indifferent matters. They feel no power or efficacy in the word preached; their hearts remain unreached, and yet they will be damned for not believing the teſtmony of a lifeleſs miniſtry.

Elder Hezekiah replied—"We are not to preach away "our power!"

I ſaid, Moſt aſtoniſhing! and yet you profeſs to be in, and under a ſuperior diſpenſation to all that have ever been before. Chriſt and his apoſtles, who were in an inferior diſpenſation to you, preached in the power and demonſtration of the ſpirit. As to your not preaching away your power—Is this Chriſt-like? did he not adminiſter power? A woman only touched the hem of his garment, and he felt that virtue had gone out of him. And did not Peter adminiſter power to Cornelius and others? The Holy Ghoſt fell on all that heard the word. But you are not to preach away your power; and yet you ſay it is through the miniſtration all muſt receive power. Who can underſtand you? Oh, "it is by obedience! Go forth in obedience to what you teach—the obedient ſhall eat the good of the land."

Again—was not the power of the Holy Ghoſt adminiſtered by the apoſtles previous to obedience? ſo that faith and obedience were the effect of power received The Holy Ghoſt fell on all them that heard the word. If ſuch a power and bleſſing attended your word, I ſhould have the evidence I ſtand in need of; without which, (admitting you have a divine gift or revelation) all you ſay, is to me but hearſay, and my obedience will proceed only from faith in man. Without a divine, internal conviction of the truth of what you teach, I can never come under condemnation for not believing and obeying.

You teach, or counſel me, "to renounce my buſineſs—to move to Niſkeuna—gather among the believers, and go to work, or be obedient to all things as you direct:" and I know what will follow, ſtep after ſtep—firſt, I muſt put away all my books, and read no more, that I may learn nothing but what I learn from you. The next ſtep, I muſt give up my intereſt, come into one of thoſe families who have all things in common, my wife perhaps in one family, and I into another, and my children I know not where; and, it may be, I may ſeldom or never ſee her or them any more. So I muſt go on to prove what obedience will do for me; and after ſome time, if I cannot feel ſatisfied and believe with you, I muſt return impoveriſhed in temporals, (as others have done) and begin the world again, and ſeek God for myſelf. And alas! I may alſo loſe my wife and children, (as ſome others have) for they, by that time, may become ſo prejudiced in favour of the faith and people, in conſequence of your kindneſs, that they will not return with me, and I could not take them away by force, againſt their faith and wiſh to abide with you, as that would be cruel, and like perſecution (which above all things I deteſt.) Thus I ſhould be left in a lamentable plight! Therefore I think I had beſt "look before I leap."

I have talked with thoſe who have been obedient to the Elders many years; but I cannot get much more out of them, than that they keep their faith, and feel peace. I know peace ariſes from various cauſes. If a ſervant is conſcious of obedience to his maſter, and his maſter is pleaſed, and commends him for his work of obedience, he, as to his duty to his maſter, feels peace. Thoſe who have travailed in obedience to their Elders, feel peace of mind, according to their faith. So the Mahometan enjoys peace of mind in obedience to his faith; and ſo do thoſe of every other faith. But the eſſential thing is, have they love towards God? and do they love their neighbour, i. e. all their fellow-creatures, as themſelves? I read, "on theſe hang all the law and the prophets"—Matt xxii. 27. This is the ſum and ſubſtance of the goſpel—"This do and we ſhall live"—Luke x. 28.

Now as far as I have experienced the efficacy of an inward divine principle, I have had an internal evidence of the truth of it, and know what the love of God is. In conversation with a believer on this subject, not long sice, he said, "I don't feel now as I have done in times past. But this," said he, "is a different work; the work of God is not the same in every dispensation." Now for me to give up that, the truth of which I have an internal evidence, for an outward testimony, the truth of which to me is uncertain, and of which I have no internal evidence, I think I should be very unwise.

As to what you have heretofore mentioned of the sobriety, order, and good fruit which the people bring forth, and my not being able to assign a satisfactory cause how all this can be, when I throw away a revelation and hand of God in it, I have considered lately, that Christ tells us we must not judge by outward appearance; and he says of the Pharisees, that "they indeed appear beautiful, and outwardly they appeared righteous unto men" —Matt. xxiii. 27, 28.

Also we learn, not only from sacred. but other history, of people that have been exceeding precise and circumspect in all their outward appearance, whereby thousands have been for a time deceived in them, as I could abundantly show. Besides, I do not know whether those in church order, bear such very good fruit at all times. I know they are much on their guard when strangers or young believers are present, (though that is seldom the case) But admitting that they are at all times as they profess to be; then, can no other reason, than what you have advanced, be assigned why they are so? Are they not shut out from the world, and all its temptations, and bound by their faith to the Elders? They are not admitted to go among, or converse with any other people. The greatest part of them, for many years, have not been a mile from their dwellings, or spoken a word to any one but their brethren and sisters in their own order. They live as complete monastic lives, as ever any did in the Romish church, who were entirely secluded from the rest of mankind, having no intercourse with their nearest relations, nor any but such who were confined, generally for life, within the ſame walls. Like unto them, they have not the leaſt concern about procuring the neceſſaries of life: they riſe up and go regularly to their work appointed them; and the Deacons tranſact all buſineſs with the people of the world for them, as ſelling and buying. Therefore, are they not excluded from all temporal concerns, temptations, and trials, that other Chriſtians paſs through? Suppoſe they had to provide for, and take care of themſelves, and were expoſed to all the temptations and innumerable trials that other Chriſtians are, and then, as a body of people, I doubt whether they would bear better fruit, according to the number, than ſome other ſocieties do. We know not ſo well whether a thing is good, till it is tried.

A reply by Elder Hezekiah—" The people of God " have their temptations, tribulations, trials, and croſſes, " to which you and the Chriſtians of the world are utter " ſtrangers, and ever will ſo remain, till you and they " come to travail in the way and work of God."

I ſaid, I have ſometimes thought, that they take up ſome croſſes, and have trials of their own making, or which the Elders make for them; and which will never be of any real profit to the ſoul. And if you were well read, you could ſee the almoſt innumerable croſſes, that many devotees have taken up—only look at the Monks of the church of Rome: what auſterity! what mortifications! what croſſes to nature! and what penance did they voluntarily chooſe and undergo! Penance was a doctrine they preached—and without penance there was no admittance into the kingdom of heaven; and, herein as in many things, you and they agree. And now I wiſh to correct a miſtake that is among you, viz. that no people ever took up ſuch croſſes, and denied their own wills, &c. as you do in this day. Now, as you told me, ſo I tell you—you are utter ſtrangers to the croſſes that many have taken up, and have lived and died under.

He replied—" Their's were outward croſſes and tri- " als—our's are inward, againſt a carnal nature; labor- " ing to become reinſtated in the image and likeneſs of " God, which was loſt by tranſgreſſion. Though we " have outward croſſes to come into the outward order

" of God, and separate ourselves from the world, and the " evil thereof, to *touch not, taste not, handle not*,* the un- " clean thing: and, are we not called to come out of " the world, which is Babylon, and be separated from " them? and as God is a God of order, should there not " be an order of God in the church? and should not all " who come into it, take up their cross, and conform to " that order?

" And not only so, but each one to experience the or- " der of God in their own souls; and in order to this, " each one must take up the real and greatest cross of " all, which you will find to be so when you come to " travail into a death to a fallen nature—come to expe- " rience an inward fire and burning, a *baptism of fire* with " which John said Christ would baptize. This will cause " trial and tribulation to the old man: he is not put off, " with all his evil deeds, in a moment, by the *love of* " *God shed abroad in the soul*, as the Methodists and some " others imagine, which they call justification; and per- " haps in a moment, sanctification. As to this love of " God, which you and Christians of the world profess to " experience, we know what it is, and what it will do for " them; and they might know too, as it does not save " them from their sins, but leaves them as it finds them. " Then they have their dark times, and fall into sin " again. Why this is so, they know not. But the true " cause is, they have never confessed their sins. *The* " *strong man armed, keepeth his palace or place in the heart;* " *and his goods are in peace*, or safe. But cast out his goods, " i. e. his sins, *and a stronger will enter*—(Luke xi. 21.) " Thus their sins, the *strong man's*, *the devil's goods*, re- " main in their hearts; they have never confessed their " sins, cast them out, or put them away, and the devil " has a right where his goods are. Therefore, if they " rise a little, Satan having power over them, soon pulls " them down. Even that love and joy, that they at " times feel, will lead them into the flesh; or at least, " under the influence of that love, they can gratify their " lusts. Though the apostle said, *She* (and consequent-

* 2 Col. ii. 21.

" ly he) *that liveth in pleaſure, is dead while ſhe liveth*—
" (1 Tim. v. 6.) Yet they can enjoy this ſenſual, car-
" nal pleaſure, and at the ſame time believe they have
" the love of God. What aſtoniſhing darkneſs of mind!
" how eſtranged from the real and true love of God!
" Yea, they are totally dead to God, and all ſenſe of di-
" vine life, even in their higheſt imagination of feeling
" the love of God. They believe themſelves regenerat-
" ed and born of God; and ſome profeſs ſanctification—
" and at the ſame time gratify a beaſtly, carnal nature.
" Yea, they act contrary to their own faith; and do that,
" in many reſpects, which they believe to be ſin: when
" the apoſtle tells them, *He that committeth ſin is of the de-*
" *vil; and whoſoever is born of God, doth not commit ſin*—
" 1 John iii. 8, 9. But we feel thankful that the Lord
" has ſhown us the fallacy of all their religion, and all
" the religion in the world; and called us to become
" partakers of a goſpel that redeemeth us from our
" ſins.

" But becauſe we don't talk ſo much about the love
" of God, great flows of raviſhing enjoyments, and cry-
" ing out, *I know that my Redeemer liveth:* but when we
" tell you, we feel peace under a conſcientious ſenſe of
" duty towards God, and one another; feeling a calm-
" neſs and ſerenity in our minds—yea, that peace that
" the world cannot give nor take away; and that we
" feel love towards all our brethren and ſiſters, and to
" the ſouls of all mankind; and feel and find our union
" to the goſpel and way of God; and feel thankful to
" God for all his favours and bleſſings to us, and that
" we feel a comfortable hope of an happy immortality,
" all this don't ſatisfy you! When we tell you that the
" goſpel leadeth us in a ſteady perſeverence, and that we
" find a continual, gradual, ſolid, weighty increaſe, or
" flooding without ebbings; and that the righteouſneſs
" of the obedient runs even with their lives; and that we
" experience a continual growth in grace, receiving more
" and more power over ſin and an evil nature—travail-
" ing until we become entirely redeemed from the leaſt
" and laſt remains of ſin, and finally gain a ſtate from
" which there will be no more going out—all this don't

" satisfy you; we know not, then, what will. We be-
" lieve you are sincere, and your soul is after the gospel
" and way of God; and we are willing to labour with
" you, and to spare no pains to gain you to the gospel,
" as long as we can feel a gift of God for you."

I replied—I acknowledge your good will—I have faith in your sincerity; I believe your intentions are good. But it appears to me you err in your judgment; for, in your last discourse, you have expressed yourself similar to what I have often heard among believers before; and you have joined hand with the deist, and struck at the very root and essence of scriptural Christian experience. Now however much Christians have differed in opinion respecting various points of their faith, in this experience the sincere of every denomination have unanimously agreed; and the testimony of many of them contradicts your assertion. For all that you have testified of an experience, travail, and salvation, others have testified the same.

Elder John Meacham said—" I tell you, Thomas,
" there never has been one soul, from the falling away
" of the apostolic church, that stept one step in regene-
" ration, redemption, sanctification, or the new birth —
" I tell you again, there never has been one soul, from
" first to last, that ever found complete redemption, sanc-
" tification, regeneration, or the new birth, i. e. not until
" the opening of this gospel."

I replied—Then they were liars, for many testified and declared they had.

He said—" Nay, I would not call them liars."

I replied—If that word is too hard, I may say, they were all greatly deluded and deceived.

He answered—" Yea."

I said—Now let us come to a fair statement. It is said there are about three thousand now in this faith; suppose that all these were to assert as you do—now I ask which will be the most reasonable to believe, these three thousand, or thirty thousand who have testified to the truth of which you deny of them, many of whom have sealed their testimony with their blood?

He replied—" Why, according to your carnal way of " reaſoning, it is moſt reaſonable to believe the greateſt " number."

I proceeded, and ſaid—When you convince me, that that which ſupported the Martyrs in the flames, with ſuch calmneſs, ſerenity, and joy, was nothing but imagination, or enthuſiaſm, I honeſtly tell you, that you muſt not think I ſhall then be a believer. Nay, I ſhall believe nothing at all in divine revelation, and ſhall totally give up the chriſtian religion as profeſſed by you and all others; as it is this very experience of the love and peace of God to my ſoul, that has hitherto preſerved me from deiſm; which, if I had never known, I ſhould have been a deiſt long ago. I wonder that ſuch as never really experienced the comforts of religion, are not all deiſts, on their beholding the various fluctuating opinions of the profeſſors thereof; and hearing how they have, and do ſtigmatize one another with error; and how they have quarrelled about their religion. That for many centuries paſt, there has been completely a (anti-chriſtian) religious war, though latterly they don't ſhed ſo much blood about it. But it is ſtill among many, and none more than among you—you are no chriſtian, or he is no chriſtian; you, or they are deluded; they are falſe prophets; wolves in ſheep's clothing; anti-chriſt, deceivers, impoſtures, poor dark creatures, blind ſouls, full of error; and the other party retorting the ſame. It appears as if they were weary in perſecuting, and fighting, and now ſit like a parcel of dogs growling at one another; and you (like the moſt angry dog of all) declare they have been, and are all deluded and deceived. My God! when people look at theſe things in this light, what muſt they think? What muſt the informed part of the heathen conclude, reſpecting the religion of the chriſtian world? We have heard, a chriſtian among many of them, is the moſt odious character Some of them have refuſed miſſionaries that have been ſent among them, and have ſaid, " how can you expect us to embrace your religion, when you differ ſo much about it yourſelves." Alſo the Jews beholding the differences, and conduct of profeſſed chriſtians, what little reaſon have they to believe * When any of the professing christian sects, endeavour to convince the Jews, heathen, or deist, of the truth of the christian religion, they may all with propriety say, Agree among yourselves first about your religion and revelation, and in what way and manner you receive it, before we believe, agree, and join with you; for you have ever been in a fermentation, contest and quarrel about your revelation and book; from which you draw all your religion, and all your disputes. Oh ye professing christians of every name, ye may cease sending missionaries to convert the heathen, until you all agree to give them one and the same account of the religion you profess; otherwise you will set them at variance concerning the way to heaven, and make them as bad as yourselves.

It is said by believers, "that in order for a man readily to receive the faith, he must first run out with all other sects, and come empty." I don't know but what I shall run out with you also, for you are altogether enough to distract a man. I firmly believe that before another century after this passes away, there will be a revolution in religion; but I must stop, as this is departing from our subject. Please to excuse me; for what I have said, has proceeded from a mind sorrowfully affected, and overburdened with the conduct of professors. I am now willing to return.

A reply.—"If the professors of christianity could "agree among themselves, while living after a beastly "nature, they would only imitate a number of beasts in "a field, whom in fighting become weary, and in conse-"quence thereof, feed together in peace; but they "would remain beasts still; and so long as the former feed "on a beastly nature, we cannot agree with them.— "And they never can agree among themselves so long "as they live in sin, nor until they renounce their union "with the flesh, the fallen nature; and that spirit which "governs them; and that can only be done by confess-

* See Dr Levi's letters to Dr. Priestly; this being an argument with the Jews against christianity's being the peaceable kingdom of the Messiah, as foretold by the prophets.

" ing and forsaking their sins, and coming into a king-
" dom where the spirit of Christ reigns and rules, and
" become governed thereby. Some people say we have
" no charity; but we have charity for their souls, but
" not for sin, nor for those who live in sin. The chris-
" tians of the world talk of charity, but they do not
" know what true charity is. They have a charity like
" unto a crow that can light upon carrion.

" But now to return to what you have been speaking
" concerning experiences of some. We believe as we
" have told you before, that many of those you have had
" reference to, have had a measure of the light and spir-
" it of God; and as they were obedient to that light
" and manifestation, which God favoured them with,
" they found the blessing of God. We believe it
" was a measure of the spirit of God, that supported
" many of the martyrs in their sufferings. And we be-
" lieve that you, and thousands, have felt the spirit of
" God; and do not wish you to disbelieve therein; but
" to come forward in the increasing work of God.

" The early believers in Christ, attained a good de-
" gree of salvation and redemption, while they had the
" revelation of God; but when there was a falling away
" (of which the apostle spake) and they lost the saving
" gift of God, there commenced a night of darkness,
" called by many, a night of apostacy.

" Now in this vacant time, you produce many to prove
" contrary to Elder John's assertion, of none having ob-
" tained redemption, sanctification, &c But I think it
" can be proved from such of them, of which we have
" an account, that from the early part of the falling
" away, to the opening of this gospel, as professed by
" us, that Elder John's assertion is the truth. For after
" the falling away, they testified, in direct contradiction
" to your assertion, That freedom from sin is not attain-
" able on this side of the grave. It is a doctrine all the
" Protestant churches have held, Quakers and Method-
" ists excepted. They have all cried out, more or less,
" *Lord, have mercy upon us, miserable sinners.* If misera-
" ble sinners, how then can they be saints, or sanctified!
" And hark, how they sing:

"Our ſins, alas! how ſtrong they be,
"And like a violent ſea,
"They break our duty, Lord, to thee,
"And hurry us away.
"The waves of trouble, how they riſe!
"How loud the tempeſt roars!
"But death ſhall land our weary ſouls
"Safe on the heavenly ſhores. *Watts.*

"Here death is to do the work. Death is to com-"plete their ſalvation; for they believe (truly) tha "nothing ſinful, or unholy, can enter heaven; and the "have no idea of a work and travail hereafter. Th "Methodiſts believe in freedom from ſin; yet hear how "whole congregations of them will, year after year, re-"peatedly ſing:

"A poor blind child, I wander here,
"If haply I may feel thee near,
"Oh, dark! dark! dark! I ſtill may ſay,
"Amidſt the blaze of goſpel day.

"Again:

"Barren although my ſoul remains,
"And no one bud of grace appear;
"No fruit of all my toils and pains;
"But ſin, and only ſin is here!
"Although my gifts and comforts loſt,
"My blooming hopes cut off I ſee,
"Yet will I in my Saviour truſt,
"And glory that he died for me.

"How can a ſoul that has not one bud of grace, glo-"ry that Chriſt died for him? And how was it poſſibl "they could be redeemed, &c. when they lived after th "courſe of the world in the fleſh? which you yourſel "believe to be the root of all evil. Some of them cu "off all the branches, but the root ſtill remained alive "and they had not a ſight of it, nor power to come a "it, to deſtroy it. We believe there have been man

" who have experienced a comfortable ſenſe of the love " of God, and which has continued with them for a " time, for their encouragement and ſupport; and in " which time, all evil was bound in them; and while " they were carried along thus, like à child in the arms " of a parent, they were not learning to walk themſelves. " I mean, they were not bearing the croſs, and dying to " an evil nature. Therefore, it is true what has been " told you, that they did not travail one ſtep in the real " work of redemption, no more than a child, who is " carried along in the arms of the parent, is learning to " walk.

" All ſuch have found, however great their experi- " ences of the love of God have been, when that was " withdrawn, they have felt again ſin all alive in them; " and thus they have been favoured time after time, be- " cauſe they had not the proper means to become ſaved " from ſin. But ſuch as come to, and have the privi- " lege of hearing of a greater light, an effectual revela- " tion, even the ſecond coming of Chriſt, to bring a full, " complete, and finiſhed ſalvation; I ſay, if ſuch ſtop " ſhort, or do not come forward, they will be left with- " out excuſe, and inſtead of being favoured as above, " they will loſe the light they had, and come under " greater condemnation. Juſt like unto the Jews who " would not receive Chriſt a greater light, becauſe he " came not according to their carnal imaginations.— " Therefore, that light which they had, and in obedi- " ence to which they ſtood juſtified, until a greater came, " and in their not receiving of it, they were rejected from " all light; as all leſſer lights are extinguiſhed (as to " our being lighted by them) on the approach of a " greater."

I replied—Admitting what you have ſaid, to be true, that none could attain a ſalvation ſufficient to make them fit ſubjects for the kingdom of heaven, before the ſecond coming of Chriſt, then the next moſt important point of all, is to prove, or make appear that this is his ſecond coming, and that greater light of which you ſpeak, or what is called the mellennium (which thouſands have been, and are ſtill looking and praying for.) If you can do this, all controversy about doctrine and order, would be settled at once. If Christ is in, and with you, and it is the word of God you speak, that is enough. I should have an implicit faith, and be passively obedient immediately. On this hangs, as it were, all the law and the prophets. All that you have said, all that you have quoted out of the law, prophets, and gospel, this is all that I and many others, want proof of. This may be called your major proposition. If your major proposition is false, your ministration doctrine, and several other points of your faith, are of course. Your telling me that you know, it is little to the purpose. Many before you have said, with as much confidence and assurance, as you do, "*We know.*" Many of every denomination, are as firm in their faith, as you are; and one sect can produce as much scripture and reason, as the other.

To this Elder Hezekiah replied:

"I think it is likely many in Christ's first coming, reasoned much as you do. The devil, or evil nature in man, will turn every way to evade the true coming of Christ. We know that this is the second coming of Christ, by the light in which we see, wherein all others are mistaken"

Now being much exercised, tried, and worn out in my mind, I only replied—If it be really the second coming of Christ, the Lord grant that I may be enlightened to receive it; and I hope you will have patience, and bear with me

The third day after I came here, one of the Elders asked me, if I wished to see Elder Ebenezer. I told him I was willing to see him, if he desired it. I accordingly was directed to his room, entered, and took a seat. Now the reader should be informed, that the Elders I had been conversing with, received their gifts, or order, from Elder Ebenezer: (and he receiving, according to their line of order, his directions from Abiathar Babbot, who stood next to the Mother of the church.—Each one acting in their gift, or according to the orders, as they received them from their Elders above them.—The Mother, according to their faith, receiving her gift, or commission, from God; and likewise acting in the gift she received from the ministration, at her election.)

Therefore the ſubſtance of our controverſy, and wherein I was deficient in my faith, was carried by the Elders who labored with me, up to Elder Ebenezer; and by him, the ſubſtance, or what he thought neceſſary, to his Elder. Therefore the miniſtration above thoſe Elders who converſed with me, knew all that was paſt; particularly, my lack of a right manner of faith, in being taught. Having thus premiſed, I proceed.

After I had been a few minutes in his room, and ſome indifferent converſation had paſſed, he began upon the old controverted ſubject, of faith in a miniſtration; and that God had always ſpoken by inſtruments; and by obedience to ſuch, in this day, ſalvation was obtained. I ſoon quoted that of the apoſtle (Titus ii. 11)—The grace of God that bringeth ſalvation, hath appeared unto all men, teaching them, &c.

He replied—" I don't read it ſo."

I aſked him—If he would pleaſe to let me know how he read it.

He anſwered—" The grace of God that bringeth ſal-" vation unto all men, hath now appeared."

I replied—I do not recollect to have ſeen, among all the different readings and expoſitors, that have come to my hand, of any of them reading, or conſtruing of this text, in the way thou doſt. And as thou art not acquainted with Hebrew, Greek, nor Latin, would it be reaſonable for me to believe thy reading, in contradiction to all others?*

He ſaw I would diſpute with him alſo: (and I thought I had reaſon to be thankful that I was not under a deſpotick, eccleſiaſtical government, in which I ſhould not dare to ſpeak my mind, for fear of an Inquiſition;) and he not being diſpoſed to controvert with me, it not being his gift, or place ſo to do; he aroſe and walked towards the door and back again, which appeared to me, I thought

* My recollection at that time, appears to have been deficient. *In contradiction to all others*—Herein I was wrong, (and I hope I ſhall ever be willing to acknowledge my errors) See margin of J. Brown's Bible, and explanatory notes on that text. M. Henry's expoſition. And in the margin of J. Guyſe's Bible; and ſeveral others.

as a ſignal to retire; I therefore, ſoon aroſe, walked towards the door, and he beginning again to ſpeak, I ſtopt a few minutes.

He ſaid—"We deſire nothing of you, but your good, "and we know this is the way of God, and you will find "it ſo, one day or other; and I hope you may not to "your loſs."

When he appeared to have done ſpeaking, I withdrew; and the remaining part of the day, I ſpent with one of the former Elders. We converſed on ſeveral other ſubjects, which I think beſt, at preſent, to omit, and only take notice of the following. In the evening, by their requeſt, I met Elder John Meachem, Hezekiah Rowley, and one whom we called Elder Stephen. The ſubject of the propriety, and neceſſity of obedience to the miniſtration for ſalvation, was again renewed. Elder John told me "If ever I came to be eſtabliſhed in the faith, "and become a good believer, I would be aſhamed of "my diſputations with them;" and ſaid—"Thomas, we "believe the day will come, when creatures will not dare "to contradict, and ſtand againſt the gift of God, as "you do."

I replied—If ever I ſee the propriety of your doctrines, and become eſtabliſhed therein, I ſhall be willing to confeſs my errors; and hope, and expect you will forgive me, and paſs by it, as if it had never been. But ſaid I, you and others have deceived me.

Elder John interrupting me, ſaid—"Not ſo much as "you are deceiving yourſelf, in not believing what is "preached to you, and being obedient thereto. You "are, and ever have been deceived by your own wiſ-"dom, ſelf-will, and evil nature."

I replied—I am not deceived, or miſtaken in contending for the doctrine you preached to me at firſt; and herein I mean you have deceived me, as you now preach a contrary doctrine. When I firſt came to Niſkeuna to ſee you, it was with honeſt intentions, and I expected you were what you appeared to be. I deſired to know what you believed, and wherein you differed from others— I firſt converſed particularly with Benjamin Youngs, on many points of your faith, and you won't deny that he knew the faith of the church; and his abilities are ſuch, I am ſure he was able to give an account of it. The account I afterwards received from the Elders, and old believers, agreed with what he firſt gave me. I then heard nothing of a miniſtration doctrine, and obedience, as the only means, and way of ſalvation, any further than to keep up an outward order in the church. But the doctrine then was, "Each one has the privilege to "act his own faith. Do that which you are conſcious "is right, and refrain from what you are conſcious is "wrong. A *meaſure of the ſpirit of God, is given to all*; "and diſobedience thereto, is the cauſe of condemnation. "And the ſpirit of God that ſtriveth with, and teacheth "all, is every man's rule to walk by, and to whom all "ſhould be obedient. Don't place your dependance on "us, but look to the word of God in your own hearts." This was the doctrine you preached then.* Now let any man with a grain of ſenſe judge, if you don't preach a doctrine diametrically oppoſite. This is the doctrine I have been contending for, and you endeavouring to invalidate, and to ſubſtitute another in its room. You may depend on it, if my father had continued in health, he never would have continued in the faith, after he found this change; for the ſame doctrine was preached to him. Now you had better have told us plainly, what the real faith was, at firſt You would have appeared more like honeſt men; or, at leaſt, if you thought there was ſome things we could not receive, ſaid but little about them, and not have advanced any doctrine contrary to any point of your faith; then I, nor any others, could not have charged you with advancing contradictory tenets. You would alſo have ſaved yourſelf the trouble of all this labour with me; as I was as able to hear, and bear, your real faith then, as well as now. Indeed, a principal cauſe of my faith being hurt, is your thus telling two ſtories; for you, (I don't only mean you who are here preſent; but others in the faith, with whom I then converſed) did then preach, as I have ſtated.

* That is, they accommodate themſelves to the ſentiments of thoſe they converſe with.

At first we were treated like children, and had many pretty pleasing stories told us—As, "act your own faith; "the gospel don't bind creatures." But now, as I have been told, "the gospel is like a tunnel; the farther we "travail in, the narrower it grows." If squeezing into the narrow part of a tunnel, is not binding a creature, I know not what is.

Elder Hezekiah observed—"Christ says the way of "life, or to the kingdom of heaven, is a narrow way. It "is a way you never can pass, until you become stripped "and cleansed from all sin. Every thing you have re-"ceived from the world, or spirit of it, must be left be-"hind. There is nothing but a pure and holy spirit, "can pass the narrow passage to heaven; there is no "more room than just enough for it.—(Rev. xxii. 14.) "But I believe you are very fearful of having an evil "nature squeezed out of you. I think it's likely it is the "cross that is in the way; and it is this that causes all "this disputation about the doctrines of the gospel."

I replied—I have no such thoughts, or fear of the cross. It is but a short time I have to stay in this world; and I know there is nothing here, worth setting my affections on; and if I do, death will soon strip me of it all. I feel willing to do, or suffer any thing, to serve God, and secure a happy immortality with him. To lay up a treasure in heaven, is my principal aim, labour, and desire. If it had not have been thus with me, I should never have troubled you, I should never have taken up my cross, to be called by the despised name of a Shaker. What do you think I came among you for? I believed you were a good people; you appeared to be so: and, "I chose rather to suffer affliction with the people of God, than to enjoy the pleasures of sin, for a season;" esteeming the reproach, and love of Christ, greater riches than all the treasures of this world. Now this is a short, comprehensive, honest statement, from the bottom of my heart. You must think of it, as you like; I have spoken the truth.

He replied—"We believe your soul, and desires, are "after God, and that which is good; if we did not be-"lieve so, we should spend no time, nor labours with "you; and it is the light and spirit of God, wherewith

" he has measurably enlightened every man that cometh
" into the world, that has caused you to seek him, and
" take up your cross to be called a Shaker, and come
" among the people of God.

" You say we preach to you a doctrine contrary to
" what we did at first. Herein you are mistaken, or
" have misunderstood us. We bear the same testimony
" now, as at first. We tell you now not to violate your
" conscience; and to act up to, and in obedience to the
" light you have; and that disobedience thereto, is the
" cause of condemnation. We subscribe to all this. If
" a person was totally destitute of the spirit of God, we
" might as well preach to a rock, as to such an one; as
" the gospel could take no hold of him, as he would
" have nothing in him of the nature of the gospel. But
" did we, or any among us, who have a knowledge of
" the faith, ever tell you that this light, measure of the
" spirit, &c. would finally redeem, sanctify, or save from
" all sin?"

I answered—I cannot say that you, (or any others) ever did so express yourselves.

He replied—" Well then, wherein have we deceived
" you, or preached a contradictory doctrine? We have
" told you concerning the operation of the spirit, the
" love of God that sincere souls have experienced, and
" what this experience did for them, or how far it saved
" them: in all which, there is nothing contradictory to
" what we preached to you at first. But you say, *why*
" *did we not preach our real faith* We did so, as far as
" we thought it necessary, and you able to receive it.—
" And you say we treated you as a child *in the gospel;*
" *we fed you with milk.* We did so; and can you blame
" us for so doing? Are you dissatisfied because we dealt
" by you and others, as tender parents by their children?
" Then blame, and be dissatisfied with Christ, and his
" apostle Paul, without mentioning any others, whose
" examples we have followed—*I have yet many things to*
" *say unto you,* (said Christ) *but ye cannot bear them now.*—
" How gradually did he lead them, step by step: how
" he bore with their ideas and expectations of his becom-
" ing an earthly king; and their expectations of an out-

" ward kingdom. He did not tell them plainly, along " at firſt, that he was to be crucified; and when he did " tell them, it was ſo contrary to Peter's expectation, " that he ſaid, *it ſhould not be*—(Matt. xvi. 22.) He " told them many things which they did not rightly un- " derſtand; nor could they, until they came to travail " in that ſtate in which he was, and received of his ſpir- " it.

" We ſay of you, as the apoſtle did to thoſe to whom " he wrote—*We had many things to ſay, and hard to be ut- " tered; ſeeing ye were dull of hearing. You were ſuch as " needed milk, and not ſtrong meat; and now when ye ought " to be a teacher, ye have need that one teach you the firſt " principles of the oracles of God. And we could not then " ſpeak unto you, as unto ſpiritual, but as unto carnal; eveu " as unto babes in Chriſt. We fed you with milk, and not " with meat*, (i. e. we did not tell you how the real, and " true revelation of God, muſt come, in order for your ſal- " vation,) *for ye were not then able to bear it; neither yet now " are ye able. Unto the weak, we had to become weak, that " we might gain the weak.* We were willing to be *made " all things, to all men, that we might by all means ſave ſome.*

" Thus what you have been diſſatisfied about, you " have now in ſcripture language; and we could not " have framed words more pertinent, to juſtify us. We " could abundantly ſhow, from almoſt the beginning of " the ſcriptures to the end, that the work of God has " been opened to the minds of mankind, by little and " little, or gradually. That which you taught your " children once, it would be needleſs, or fooliſh, to teach " them now; and that which you teach them now, it " would have been needleſs to have taught them when " younger, as they could not then have comprehended " it.* You ſay it has been ſaid, the goſpel don't bind

* As I have quoted ſome authors in this work corroborating with my thoughts and aſſertions, (when I was with theſe people;) and as it is not my intention, in ſo doing, to gain the reader on my ſide; but to endeavour, impartially to give the arguments on both ſides their due weight; I therefore, quote the following, which I alſo, at this time, recollected corroborating, in ſome meaſure, with their arguments and reaſons, on the above ſubject: " The

" creatures: neither does it, against their free consent, " or faith. Binding signifies compulsion: but no one is " compelled. And as to each one's acting their own " faith, so they may; and if it is your faith, or if you do " not choose to be obedient, and come in the order of " the gospel, you will not be bound and compelled; you " can have your choice, and do as you please; take to " the world, or the way of God. But if each one is to " act their own faith, in the manner you have understood " us, and in the sense you mean, i. e every one suffered " to have their own will and way, and exercise their own " private judgment, what order would there be in the " church?

" Thus I think we have said enough to your objec- " tion, or charge against us, in preaching a different " doctrine, or one contradictory to what we did at first, " to give any reasonable man satisfaction. Wherein you " are not satisfied, we hope you will not, by reasoning, " discourage others, nor Elizabeth; as she has a simple " faith, and if you was satisfied, and would take hold of " the gospel, there would be no difficulty with her; and " I have not a doubt but you would have your children " with you; and what a comfort it would be to you, to " have your family walking in the way of God with " you; when many others have, with sorrow, to reflect, " that their families have left them, and are living in the " world in sin, and exposed to all the trials, and troubles " thereof. What a pity it is, that while you are doubt-

ancient christians," says Dr Mosheim, " are supposed by many, to have had a secret doctrine; and if by this, be meant, that they did not teach all in the same manner, or reveal all at once, and to all indiscriminately, the sublime mysteries of religion, there is nothing in this, that may not be fully justified It would have been improper to propose to those, who were yet to be converted to christianity, the more difficult doctrines of the gospel, which surpass the comprehension of imperfect mortals. Such were, therefore, first instructed in those points which are more obvious and plain, until they become capable of higher, and more difficult attainments in religious knowledge Nay, more; even those who were already admitted into the society of christians, were, in point of instruction, differently dealt with, according to their respective capacities." *Eccl. Hist. vol. I. page* 117.

"ing and disputing the way of God, and standing back, "you are hindering others from coming forward. We "hope you will seriously consider of these things."

I replied—I confess there is some propriety, and reason in all you have said; and I do not feel disposed at present, to raise any further objections. I believe you have been sincere, and desired my good, from first to last; and I shall endeavour to remember, and seriously consider of all you have said; and thank you for your concern, and labours with me.

One of the Elders told my wife, next morning, that they believed I was satisfied; but I was not. The reasons they had advanced against what I had asserted, of their having deceived me, might have fully satisfied me, if I had not considered, that, we wilfully deceive, when our expressions are not true in the sense in which we believe the hearer to apprehend them.—*Paley's Philosophy.*

Besides these discourses with the Elders, I had one evening considerable conversation with two of the old believers. They gave me an account of the first Elders, viz Ann Lee, Wm. Lee, and James Whittaker; and of the travels, labours, and sufferings they passed through, to open, and plant the gospel. Also, of several extraordinary gifts, and operations, that had been in the church.

During the time we tarried, the family were very kind to us; and at our departure, I thanked them for all favours we had received.

After I returned home, I continued to attend meetings, and visit among the believers as I had done; and often heard them converse together concerning the faith, the work of God in this day, and the lost, dark state of the world; and it appeared to me that they often spake the truth, and sometimes error.

Now as it was contrary to the gift, to open our minds to one another in any respect, wherein we were dissatisfied; or to talk contrary to the faith, I therefore endeavoured to keep silent; but neverthess, was often drawn into conversation; and as I could not talk one way, and in my heart, believe another, therefore, my dissenting from them, caused often much conversation pro and con, though on the account of which, I felt no hardness against them; and I believe that they did not feel any against me. Though there were several points, on which we conversed, and amicably agreed.

About once a month, the Elders came from Lebanon to see the believers at Niskeuna, to encourage, bring in order, build up, and establish them in the faith. Therefore, I often heard them in our meetings; but had not much private conversation with them, until sometime in December (same year) when I spent with them nearly two days; in which time, they endeavoured to convince me of the propriety, and reality of the faith.

As there were several subjects which we conversed on, the last time I was at Lebanon, which, in the former discourses, I omitted, I shall now insert them, with the substance of our conversations at this time.

*What follows contains the result of nearly all the conversations, which I have had with the Elders, and several believers, respecting those doctrines and practices, with which I did not unite. I have thus connected our discourses into one body* (on account of brevity, and) *in order to have them clearly understood. Those discourses which contain the words of several persons, begin with* " A Reply." *But any discourse that has been entirely spoken by any one Elder, has the name of that Elder at the beginning.*

Elder Hezekiah said—" Thomas, we are sorry to find, " that after all our labours with you, you have not yet " a right manner of faith; knowing that none ever stood " long among us, where you are; and it is impossible " for you to abide, unless you get hold, and believe in " the present revelation of God. You may believe firm- " ly in a revelation past, i. e. to the prophets, apostles, " and others, but such a faith will profit you nothing; " you must have faith in a living ministration; and by " obedience, you will find that our teaching gives pow- " er; you will find that the words that we speak unto " you, are spirit and life Now only see how you, and " others act the part of the Jews. They would not be-

" lieve in a present revelation of God in their day, and " receive the words spoken by Christ and his apostles; " but they repeatedly refer to their dead ones; to Mo- " ses, and the prophets, and to what they had written. " They were willing to own a past revelation, which " would do them no good. (Oh the subtilty of Satan!) " But says Christ, *if ye had believed Moses, ye would have* " *believed me; for he wrote of me* * So we say of you " and others, if ye believed in Christ and his apostles, " ye would believe in us; for they wrote of us, i. e. the " work of God in this day. But *if ye were the children* " *of Christ*, and followers of him, and did as his apostles " taught, *ye would do the works of Christ;* but now ye " seek to destroy the teaching of those who have taught " you the truth, which we have received of the Father. " And I suppose you would think it too hard, if we were " to say to you, as Christ did to those who pleaded for a " past revelation—*Ye are of your Father the devil; and* " *the lust of your Father, ye will do* † But we don't wish " to be hard, but deal tenderly with all souls, especially " as long as we can feel a gift for them, and mercy of " God towards them.

" Christ told Peter, after he confessed faith in, and ac- " knowledged the true revelation of God—" *Thou art* " *Peter; and upon this rock, I will build my church,*" &c. " i. e. upon that spirit, or revelation in Peter, by which " he spake: *and I will give unto thee the keys of the king-* " *dom of heaven: and whatsoever thou shall bind on earth,* " *shall be bound in heaven; and whatsoever ye shall loose on* " *earth, shall be loosed in heaven*—(Matt. xvi. 18, 19.)— " He also told his disciples, " *Whose soever sins ye remit,* " *they are remitted; and whose soever sins ye retain, they are* " *retained*—(John xx 23.) It appears Peter had the " greatest gift, and was the first who had the lead; and " it is clear that the same order was in the apostolick " church, that is among us; and the same obedience " was required. The apostle says—" Remember them " that have the rule over you." " Also, " Obey them " that have the rule over you, and submit yourselves."

* John v. 46. † John 8 to 44.

"By the power and authority that the apostles received "of Christ, they ordained bishops to preside over the "several churches. To those bishops, the people were "exhorted by the apostles to be obedient. *Remember "them,* says Paul, *that have the rule over you* Also, *Obey "them that have the rule over you, and submit yourselves.*— "There is still something of the same order in almost "every church, though they are destitute of the power. "Most of them have bishops; and are not the ministers "of those churches, much ruled by them? and are not "the members of each church taught, and much gov-"erned by their preachers? Many of them, if they "have no minister, their meeting houses are shut up, "their worship is stopped; as if they could receive "teaching and salvation, no other way; and most of "them believe that it is by the word preached: then "why do they blame us for the same order? The truth "is, because it is in greater perfection, and that in the "life and power. According to the life and power their "preachers possess, so is that of the people. Their "preachers cannot administer more than they have in "possession, which is not sufficient to save them or their "people from sin. The truth is, the saving gift and "revelation of God, become lost in the degeneracy of "the apostolick church; but the outward order was still "retained, which has been handed down by tradition in "the Romish church, to this day; from which, all oth-"er churches have got more or less of this same order. "They have received it from the corrupt church of "Rome, and not by revelation."

I replied—I have repeatedly heard the Elders and believers say, that the Romish church had the order of God in several respects; particularly in confessing sins, and church government; and because it has so near a likeness to our church in this respect, you conclude that it received this order from the apostles, and the form has been continued to this day.

This is also what the Roman Catholicks have always endeavoured to support. They say that the intention and appointment of Christ, was, that his followers should be subject to St. Peter and his successors; and it must be confessed that much is to be found in the writings of several of the apostolick successors, i. e. St. Clemens,* Ignatius,† Polycarp,‡ Cyprian,§ and others, concerning the succession of Bishops from the apostles: and also, enforcing and exhorting the people to obedience to them; particularly in those of Ignatius. If these are the genuine writings of those to whom they are ascribed, they are decidedly in your favour. But I may observe, that those writings, particularly those of Ignatius, are much disputed by the learned. It is believed by many, that they were evidently adopted, if not purposely contrived, to exalt the clergy, and secure to them all power, reverence, and subjection. But the papists plead for their authenticity, with zeal and vehemence.

According to all the ecclesiastical history (written by protestants) that I have seen, the government of the apostolick church in the first, and part of the second century, was strictly republican; and it was not until sometime in the fourth century, that a government like unto yours, became fully established.

The power and authority of the bishops had, from the earliest time, been gradually increasing; but when Constantine, the Roman Emperor, embraced (as it is said) the christian religion (I think it was more like anti-christian) their power and authority became greatly augmented. The bishop of Rome, now became the first in order, and was held superior to all the other bishops. In the fifth century, he was called God's vicegerent, and claimed a spiritual dominion over the minds and sentiments of men. But to be short, in the eleventh century, their power appears to have risen to its utmost height. They now were called Masters of the world, and Fathers of all in the church.

Now if the protestant historians are correct, you are mistaken respecting your order of government being handed down from the apostles, by a succession of bishops in

* Bishop of Rome, A. D. 70. † Bishop of Antioch, A. D. 105.
‡ Bishop of Smyrna, A. D. 140. § Bishop of Carthage, A. D. 250.

the church of Rome; for it appears that your order was not in the apostolick age of the church, but arose in that of its degeneracy. A certain author, speaking of the power of the Popes in the eleventh century, says, "But happily that power is now on the decline."

On this I would observe, that if this power is declining in the east, it is rising in the west: and it seems that some people in every age, must be oppressed and chastised with a monarchical government, either civil or ecclesiastical; and mankind deprived of those natural and unalienable rights which God has given to them. We have only to look into history, to see its direful consequences.

To this one of the believers said—"I hope you do not "compare our harmless and innocent Elders, and their "power, to those you have been mentioning, and the "power they possessed."

I said—Nay, I do not, in their present state. What I have said, has only been to show the danger of investing individuals with power, either in church or state; and the bad use they have hitherto made of it. And if the ministration of our church had as much power over mankind as those had to which I have referred, I doubt their long remaining the humble people they now appear to be.—I would not dare talk to them with the freedom I have done. I have reason for what I say, from their own words; for Elder John told me last conference at Lebanon, That he believed the day would come when creatures would not dare to dispute, and stand against the gift of God, as I did Again, as I have often heard, The time will come when the word of God will not be bound, but will come so against creatures, that they will not dare to resist. Yes, I suppose it will come as it did not long since, when one of the believers was saying something in his defence, before Elder Ebenezer; the latter stamped his foot, spoke sharply, and told him to hold his tongue, he should not speak a word; and I have heard of several similar instances of commanding with much authority; and the simple believer trembles at the word when so spoken. I think I see the seeds of that power which I have heretofore described. Our first leaders now profess to be as high in power as the popes professed to be in the fifth century, i. e. of being God's vicegerents, and fathers of all the church. I again repeat my fears, that you will degenerate as other churches have done.

A reply, (by Elder Hezekiah)—"Nay, that we, and "our successors, never will; for God has began a work "which he will carry on to his own glory, and the salvation of all who have faith therein."

I said—There is a possibility of your being mistaken. I know there have been many, and they men of great parts and talents, who have been as confident of their being right respecting the millennium, as you are; but time has proved they were mistaken. Witness Emmanuel Swedenborgh and his followers: they express themselves in much the same language of assurance and thankfulness as you do.

The following are a few of their expressions, from an address to the brethren, entitled, "To those that are called of Jesus Christ according to the new dispensation, which he hath been pleased to open in these latter days, by his servant Emmanuel Swedenborgh:"

"Ye have cause to be abundantly thankful to the Lord; for, that in these last days, when darkness had covered the earth, and gross darkness the people, he hath been pleased to raise up unto you a great, and marvellous light The words of the prophet are now also fulfilled. There shall be a shaking," &c. "And he will destroy in this mountain, the face of the covering, cast over all people; and the vail that is spread over all nations. Blessed are ye; for many prophets and righteous men have desired to see the things which ye see, and have not seen them; and to hear those things which ye hear, and have not heard them" But to be short—"They are confident that living waters are gone out from Jerusalem, and that the Lord is indeed come in the clouds of heaven (in his witnesses) with power and great glory."

They talk of the vail being rent, and of those of this new dispensation, the second coming of Christ, penetrating into the holy of holies, entering into paradise, experiencing the light and joy of the heavenly society, of the light of the moon having become as the light of the ſun, having a view of the inviſible world, converſing with angels and departed ſpirits, (as ſome in our church profeſs) and a deal about the glories of the ſecond coming of Chriſt, and new diſpenſation.

I may obſerve, it was likewiſe maintained by Swedenborgh and his followers, that all thoſe paſſages in the ſcriptures, generally believed to ſignify the deſtruction of the world by fire, and the end of the world, does not mean the deſtruction of the world, but the deſtruction, or end of the profeſſing chriſtian churches of every deſcription; and that the laſt judgment actually commenced in the year 1757 (only ten years difference from the time our church ſay it commenced) from which time, is dated the ſecond coming of Chriſt.

If I was now among them, inſtead of being among you, I ſhould hear much the ſame arguments that I now hear, to convince me that they are in the laſt diſpenſation, and only true church.

I may juſt obſerve, that Emmanuel Swedenborgh was a Sweediſh nobleman, and a man of extenſive learning. He had but few equals. Many of his followers were men of education; but withal, I think they were, and are ſtill miſtaken reſpecting the millennium.

And witneſs the Avignon ſociety in France; their revelations, viſions, prophecies, and confidence of the near approach of the millennium (when, according to your faith, it had commenced above thirty years before.)—Alſo, the late Richard Brothers. He appears to have not the leaſt doubt of divine revelations to him, of the ſpirit of God carrying him away in viſions, and of his ſeeing wonderful things.

There were many who believed in him; and ſeveral men of talents wrote in vindication of his revelations—The principal one was N Braſley Halhed, member of parliament, a man of liberal education, and who appears to have been ſincere. You cannot expreſs your faith in your Elders, with more confidence than he did in R. Brothers, and his revelations.

I only mention theſe inſtances as ſpecimens, out of many that might be collected, to ſhow how men have been miſtaken reſpecting this great point, as well as to many other respects. And I think the safest way is for us to conclude, that we are poor, fallible, erring mortals. It appears to me, that the scriptures represent that in the millennium, Christ's coming will be attended with such evidence, as not to admit of a doubt.

To this, Elder Hezekiah replied—"I don't see that "all you have said of the faith of others respecting the "second coming of Christ, and their being mistaken, op-"erates at all against us, or the work of God in this "day; but rather the reverse, as thereby we see how "strong many have been in the faith respecting the sec-"ond coming of Christ. And faith brings things near, "and there may have been many, who had some light "and sense respecting it; but they being, as it were, in "the twilight, they could not see clearly; and were mis-"taken as to the real nature, and work thereof; and the "manner, way, and time of its commencing.

"There were many mistaken respecting Christ's first "coming, before and after; but that is no reason, or "proof that Jesus was not the real Christ promised."

I said—I acknowledge there is some truth and propriety in what you have said; but notwithstanding, I have such reasons for not fully believing, that I doubt my ever being able to get over them.

I shall now proceed to state several other particulars in the practice of the church of Rome, after its degeneracy, and show that in all these particulars, our church corresponds with that.

1. Several of the popes and inferior clergy, particularly the monks of the Romish church, and several other characters, in order to be honoured and esteemed, and to make people believe they had a correspendence and near union with God, and likewise to induce others to believe in divine revelations, which they pretended were made to them, have lived retired and recluse lives, and were seldom seen by any except their colleagues; and people were taught and impressed with the idea of its being a great honour and privilege to be admitted into their company, or to hear them speak; and when so favoured, they approached with signs of reverence and humility, even by kneeling in their presence.

Now to apply this to our church—The Mother lives a recluse life: she seldom converses with any, but those of the highest order, or next in authority to her. It is true there have been instances of her visiting and conversing with young believers; but when she does, they are taught to esteem it a great privilege. Thus this woman, and the first Elder, or Father of the church, are as much reverenced as ever the popes, or any others were. The inferior Elders also have a respect shewn them, according to the order in which they stand, and the company of Elder Ebenezer, is considered as a privilege, inferior only to that of the Mother. The Elders also suffer kneeling before them; and that this is wrong, appears from Rev. xxii. where St. John was forbidden to do it.

2. You are like the Romish church also in the doctrine of infallibility; and like it, hold forth the tenets of implicit faith in, passive obedience to, and non-resistance of the Elders. "As men," you say, "they are fallible, but the gifts of God are infallible; (they being received by succession from first Mother, who received them from God*) and by obedience you will find an infallibility attend them." This is precisely in substance, the language of the popes. "As men," say they, "we are fallible;† but that power and spirit, we have received by succession from St. Peter, are infallible; and we are subject to the judgment of no man."

You hold that we must have an implicit faith, i. e. what you term a simple faith; believe, because the Elders say so, without any examination. Passive obedience, i. e lay like clay in the hands of the potter; be obedient to what we are taught, whether it appears right to us or not;‡

* They believe also that these gifts have been continued and increased to the ministration by subsequent revelations.

† See Gother's two-fold character of Popery, page 36. R. Manning's shortest way to end disputes, page 23 to 68; wherein he endeavours to substantiate the infallibility of the church.

‡ It was taught in the Romish church that an opinion or precept may be followed with a good conscience, when inculcated by

and as I have been often told, " as you go forth in obedience, you will come to see what has been taught you, was right; though at first, you did not see it so. And non-resistance, i. e. do not stand against, resist, or be irreconciled *to what the Elders teach.*"

3. The clergy in the church of Rome claimed divine right and submission—the same do our Elders; and the people were taught implicit obedience, and heard the constant warning of the deadly crime of resisting the authority of their bishops;* we hear the same.

4. Private judgment is not allowed in the church of Rome: it is virtually denied, that religion is a personal thing between God and a man's own conscience; for the members of it are not permitted to examine and judge, nor even think for themselves†—their belief is taught and enforced—it is not the result of investigation. The case is the same in this church. Private judgment, the Papists say, has been the cause of all the heresy, or different and contradictory opinions and practices in religion.‡—Much the same does our church believe. I would just observe, that you both require an implicit faith and passive obedience; but in order to have a rational and well-grounded faith, either in that church or this, it is necessary to have sufficient evidence presented to the mind to produce that faith. Now whatever arguments the Papists may produce in support of their faith, many of which

a doctor of any considerable eminence, even though it be contrary to the judgment of him that follows it. *Mosheim, vol. iv. p.* 230.

* See Haweis' Church Hist. vol. i. p. 220.

† Even those of them who are the most liberal and moderate in their sentiments, say, " All obscure and disputable points, should be referred to the judgment of those whom God hath appointed pastors and teachers in the church; never presuming to contend, controul, teach, or talk of their own sense or fancy, in deep questions of divinity, but expecting the sense of these from the lips of the priests, who shall keep knowledge, and from whose mouth they shall require the law Mal. ii. 7 "

*Gother's Two-fold Character of Popery—page* 29.

‡ See R. Manning's Shortest way to end Disputes.

are much ſtronger than you produce, yet how can I believe that they are the true church of Chriſt, when it is well known that that church has been a perſecuting church, and tortured thouſands to death for hereſy, i. e. becauſe they did not relinquiſh their reaſon and underſtanding in matters of religion, and exerciſe an implicit faith and paſſive obedience? So how can I believe that our church is the only true church, when I have diſcovered ſeveral things in it contrary to truth and right?—one principal thing to which I allude is, equivocation and deception, which ſhall be the ſubject of my next compariſon.

5. Forgeries were eſteemed lawful in the Romiſh church, or by the popes and clergy, on account of their tendency, as they believed, to promote the glory of God, and to advance the proſperity of the church:* and they even conſidered fraud as pious, when employed for that end.†

I have cauſe to believe there is much of a ſimilarity among you, in this reſpect, to that of the church of Rome. I have heard ſome of the believers quote a paſſage of the apoſtle wrong, and underſtand it in a ſenſe which it is clear, from the context, the apoſtle did not mean, i. e. Be deceivers, and yet true—2 Cor. vi. 8.—In converſation, on this ſubject, with one of the Elders the laſt time I was at Lebanon, he quoted this text in the ſame manner; and likewiſe referred me to ſeveral inſtances, recorded in the old Bible, of deception being uſed by the people of God in that day. He intimated a propriety in deceiving the evil ſpirit and nature in man, in order to ſave the ſoul.

I told him at laſt, that I had read ſo much of deceit and pious frauds in the church of Rome, that I had imbibed a ſettled antipathy againſt them; and if this be the way and work of God, as you ſay, it appears to me that God would carry on his work without our uſing deception to forward it. I have often heard, that "We ſhould

* Moſheim's Eccl. Hiſtory, vol. iv. p. 305, cent. 9th.

† Haweis' Hiſt. vol. ii. p. 290.

preach strong faith, (particularly in conversation with the people of the world) even if we have it not; as by preaching strong faith, or vindicating the faith according to the best of our ability, has a tendency to strengthen us in the faith; also, such who are weak in the faith, should not manifest their weakness to any one but to the Elders." Though we need not manifest our weakness, or our doubts of the truth of the faith, which I have not yet done, to any out of the society, but I consider, that to hold forth and vindicate points of faith that we do not in our hearts really believe, is deceit and hypocrisy. It is a fact, that there are many things we believe, of the truth of which we are not certain. But there are some things, the truth of which we are certain; one of which is, that we should speak the *truth* on all occasions, without any ambiguity or equivocation. Give me the *honest man*, the *candid man*, the man of *truth*: in such a man, according to the knowledge he may possess, I can at all times place the utmost confidence; him I believe to be truly a religious man and a man of God; for God stiles himself to be "the God of truth."

6. The popes and clergy of the church of Rome also endeavoured to keep the common people in ignorance, by suppressing books* and learning; and debarred them of even the scriptures,† that they might have no means of learning or gaining information contrary to what they were taught by the clergy. Indeed, it has been a maxim with many, that the best way to keep people in obedience, is to keep them in ignorance.

They believed a Christian was in the way of salvation, when he submitted to their doctrines, and yielded unlimited obedience to the orders of the church.‡

*See Priestly's Corruptions of Christianity, vol. ii. page 118 and 195.

† See Gother's Papists Misrepresented and Represented, p. 29, 30, 31.

‡ "The clergy, ignorant themselves and the patrons of ignorance had no desire the people should be instructed The grosser the darkness that enveloped their superstitious minds, the easier dupes they were to their sacerdotal directors."

*Haweis' Church Hist. vol. ii. p.* 415.

Now I aſk, do not the leaders of this church walk exactly in the ſame ſteps, as the Romiſh clergy have done, in this reſpect? Though the Elders (and others in the faith) tell people, as they told me, (when I firſt came among you) that they do not ſuppreſs learning and books; yet I have found that you do ſuppreſs almoſt all books. By the order, or, as it is called, gift of the Elders, moſt books are forbidden to be read. I never, in public or private, once heard even the reading of the ſcriptures recommended; and thoſe who have read, or do read them, they muſt underſtand (as in the Romiſh church) every paſſage conſiſtent with what they are taught by the Elders. I know of ſeveral who, ſoon after they joined the church, have been counſelled by their Elders to diſpoſe of their books, and have accordingly done it. Elder Ebenezer, being at my houſe once, on his ſeeing a number of books, he ſaid:

" Ah, Thomas muſt put away his books, if he intends " to become a good believer."

Converſing once with the Elders, at Cornwall, about books, they then endeavoured to perſuade me, that there was no profit in reading. I ſaid, I think I had better ſpend my leiſure hours in reading than ſleeping, or doing nothing; and aſked them what I ſhould read. Elder Meacham anſwered, " Almanacks and Spelling-books," i. e. as I underſtood him, nothing at all.

I have heard ſeveral of the believers ſay reſpecting reading—

" There is no neceſſity for believers to read—it is not " of any advantage. All authors have been in the dark; " as they have written in a back diſpenſation. Even the " ſcriptures are no more than an old almanack. There " is no ſalvation in any back diſpenſation book—no goſ- " pel in them. We muſt come into the increaſing work " of God—be obedient to what we are taught by our " Elders, that's enough. Herein conſiſts our ſalvation, " and all information neceſſary for us to know. No oc- " caſion or neceſſity to give our children learning, except " to read and write a little—and even that they can do " without, if they abide among the people of God; as " they need not concern themſelves about buſineſs where-

" in reading and writing is necessary; as all things they
" stand in need of will be provided for them by the Dea-
" cons, who have the care of temporal concerns. And
" if they leave the way and people of God, and go to
" the world, let them abide by the consequences of their
" obstinacy and folly, in departing from the way of God.
" As in so doing, they go to the flesh and the devil—let
" them take what the flesh and the devil will give them.
" For if they receive any benefit from the people of God
" as learning or property, they will then consume it
" upon their lusts, and in the service of Satan; and like-
" wise thereby be more enabled to serve him."

So I must put away my books and leave off reading, and pattern after my brethren and sisters, to be in union: two-thirds of whom, from year to year, (especially those in church order) don't take a book in their hands, not even the scriptures. Though they have time to read, particularly in the winter, as they leave off work about sun-set, wash themselves, and retire into their rooms; there they sit until nine or ten o'clock, except about a quarter of an hour at supper, and about the same time at family meeting—they arise at four o'clock in the morning, and soon assemble for worship—they breakfast about day-light, and do no work until near sun-rise, in which time, morning and evening, they have at least five hours leisure—often nodding and sleeping. I have told them, I thought they had better spend their time in reading to one another some edifying books. "Nay, there is no gift for so doing"—they can do nothing without a gift. Keep in the gift, is all the cry.

" Besides, we are not to spend our time in reading,
" because it will have a tendency to draw the mind from
" an attention to, and consideration on, what the Elders
" teach; and we should spend our leisure hours in si-
" lence, meditating on the gift of God received through
" them. This is the law and commandment—and we
" must therein delight, and meditate thereon by day and
" by night, as David of old did on that gift of God, or
" law and commandment, given to him by Moses."

Not long since, I asked, in Seth Wells' family of young believers, for a certain book they had, (as I wished to ſpend part of my time in reading while I was there)—"Oh," I was anſwered, "the Elders are here now—we "don't want books, we muſt pay attention to what they "teach."

Thus it is evident, that learning and reading is not approved of, but is ſuppreſſed; and it appears that the miniſtration believe, as ſome other rulers both in church and ſtate have believed, "That the eaſieſt way, or beſt method to keep people in obedience, is to keep them in ignorance."

In ſhort, by reading they might gain much information, and then they might doubt the truth of many things taught them by their Elders; ſome of them would then begin to controvert, and ſay things were not ſo and ſo, as they had been taught. To this one of the believers obſerved:

"Well, if this be the conſequence of reading, which I "think it is likely it would be, for it is believed by the "brethren in general, that reading is of no profit, but "only tends to cauſe objections and diſputations in the "church, (and many of us believe, if you had not your "head ſo full of book-knowledge, you would now have "been a good believer) then is not the miniſtration wiſe "in not encouraging reading?"

I anſwered—I grant they are; I give them the credit of being as wiſe as many of the popes and clergy of the church of Rome were, who ſuppreſſed all books written by (ſuch as they called) heretics; and who debarred the people from reading or gaining any information contrary to what they taught them.

7. Our church is alſo like the Romiſh in its belief reſpecting ſuch as depart from the faith, or doctrines, as profeſſed by it. Like the Roman Catholics, you believe all are heretics,* in a greater or leſs degree, who depart from, and hold forth doctrines contrary to ſuch as have been received and believed by the church. With this difference they believe ſuch will be eternally loſt; but

* "No perſon," ſays Dr. Campbell, "who in the ſpirit of candour adheres to that which, to the beſt of his judgment, is right, though in his opinion he ſhould be miſtaken, is, in the ſcriptural ſenſe, either ſchiſmatic or heretic."

you believe there will be a time when the mercy of God will reach them, though they will be the laſt of all the human race that will be reſtored.

According to the power this church poſſeſſes, its conduct towards backſliders, is like unto the Romiſh church towards thoſe they called hereticks, as I could ſhow by a number of inſtances of unkindneſs and inhumanity towards them; with which I ſhall never have union. If they, by means of temptation or error in judgment, have departed from the only true church, they are objects of pity and compaſſion, and we ſhould endeavour to reſtore them by manifeſting a ſpirit of love and kindneſs; and not drive them further off by harſh treatment, and calling them backſliders, liars, deceivers, impoſtors, reprobates, poor loſt miſerable wretches; darker than ever before; ſunk below all God's creation, eternal damnation will be their portion.* My friends, this is not that mild language that becometh our profeſſion of love and mildneſs, and having the peaceable, humble ſpirit of Chriſt; but is juſt like the ſpirit and conduct of ſome of the ungodly, perſecuting popes, prieſts, and inquiſitors of the Romiſh church, to thoſe they called hereticks. In ſhort, they only had the keys of the kingdom; they only could open, and none others could ſhut; and when they ſhut, none others could open; all were taught obedience to the popes and clergy; revelation and obedience was all the cry; the people were debarred from all means of information; they dared not open their minds, one to another, againſt any thingthey were taught; without the pope, or one ſide of that line of order in the church, the people could not judge, nor know any thing; they were ſo under the power of bigotry, that they had no fellowſhip, love, nor charity, for any out of the pales of that which they denomitated the catholick church. I am ſorry I have cauſe to ſay that in all theſe reſpects, our

* Elder Ebenezer Cooley is the only one I ever heard ſay, that "Eternal damnation would be the portion of thoſe who forſook "the way of God" Therefore, as I always underſtood that the real faith of the church was that ſuch would not be eternally loſt, I concluded he only expreſſed himſelf thus, to affright or terrify believers againſt turning off; for which purpoſe, to expreſs himſelf contrary to his own faith, I did not approve.

church is too much like them. Bigotry has been the cause of all the persecutions for religious sentiments, that has ever been in the world. I have thought that there is nothing wanting but a sufficient number and power, to make my comparisions complete; I hope I am mistaken. I may also observe, that the doctrine of several political, as well as ecclesiastical rulers, was also similar to yours. They affirmed, that "God, in whom is the disposal of all lives, and all properties, has given to some, as his representatives, a right of ruling over others; that he hath appointed the hereditary right of fathers over families, of patriarchs over tribes, and of kings over nations: and they treated much concerning the divinely inherent right of monarchs, implicit submission, passive obedience, non-resistance. Also, that our God is one God; and the substitute of his power should resemble himself; that their power ought to be absolute, unquestioned, and undivided; that monarchs over his chosen people, were of his special appointment; and that their persons were rendered sacred by unction, or the pouring of hallowed oil upon them. "Many miscarriages and woful defaults (say they) are recorded of Saul, as a man; yet as a king, he was held perfect in the eyes of his people. What an unhesitating obedience, what a speechless submission do they pay to all his commands! Though he massacred their whole priesthood to a man in one day, yet no murmur was heard; no one dared to speak a word, and much less to lift a finger against the Lord's anointed."

Thus these champions for monarchy, both in church and state, have founded their whole pile of argument and oratory on the divine appointment of the kingly government of the Jews. To this the Elders and believers have repeatedly referred. And in fact, I believe a monarchical government is in many respects the best; that is, if the monarch is really a good man, and his successors continue to remain so: but this is the great bar in the way, this knocks it all in the head; for make a man a monarch, you make him a tyrant, a despot, an imperious, proud, lofty being, who soon gets so high above his fellow mortals, that he apparently forgets that he himself is mortal, and looks down with contempt on those beneath him, as not worthy of his compassion, and only fit to be his servants and slaves. All men are tyrants by nature; all prone to domineer over, to covet and grasp at the rights of others, so strong is their propensity to usurpation. Therefore dangerous it is to trust one of them with power, as such who have been intrusted, have generally proved traitors; and deputed power has almost perpetually been seized upon as property. "Monarchy (says a certain writer) has ever been found to rush headlong into tyranny."

America began to groan under the rod of a foreign power; she petitioned for certain privileges and rights, for which no power had a right to debar them; they were not granted; she then declared herself independent. This was a bold step against the lofty power of his Britanic majesty. She contended for liberty, and to be released from a foreign, and in some respects, a despotick power. If providence had not favoured her cause, she must have been crushed in the attempt. She gained what she contended for. She saw the rock on which nations had split, the rod under which nations, from time immemorial, had groaned. She saw the consequences of a monarchical government; that it had, as I said before, been ever prone to rush headlong into tyranny. She therefore adopted a republican government, under which, hitherto, prosperity and blessings hath attended. The power next to God, is in the people; they choose their rulers; those chosen have a constitutional power, with which they are obliged to act consistently, and to study the good of those who have chosen them to their several offices, and the good of the country at large. If all men are tyrants by nature, and if there is a propensity to usurpation in all, that nature and propensity is curbed by the people. They cannot become tyrants, usurp, nor grasp at the rights of the people; they cannot swerve far to the right hand nor to the left, as they have the publick eye upon them watching and criticising on their conduct. Therefore they are compelled, and not only so, but encouraged to do right (I mean in a publick capacity) as if they do, they may by the favour of the people be elected again. All this is exceedingly mortifying to royal elevation, and what a monarch cannot bear.

Thus America contains a free people.* They sit every man under his own vine, and under his own fig-tree, and there is none as yet, to make them afraid—(Mic. iv. 4.) They have got no one to bow before, to adore and fear but God; and every one has the liberty and privilege to adore and fear him in the way which they believe to be right, or consistent with the dictates of their consciences. I may with propriety exclaim, Hail! America, what a highly favoured people under the blessing of God, all in consequence of a republican government. May they be wise and virtuous enough to retain it. Now when we look around the world, and see how nations have been, and still are kept in ignorance, oppressed and imposed upon by tyrants, our hearts should flow with gratitude for those unmerited favours we enjoy; and I feel thankful that I can thus freely converse with you, and when I am at home, sit in my house in peace, reading or writing without fearing the frowns of a tyrannical monarch, or popish inquisition. The uninformed mind is insensible of these privileges. They do not know what an excellent government they are under; and how greatly they are favoured beyond other nations of their fellow mortals. Thus this new world, like Adam's paradise, is now a bright example to the old, who have for ages groaned under a despotick, and what is worse than all, a tyrannical, imperious, ecclesiastical government. But all may now see the effects of freedom and liberty. But astonishing to tell, that under this benign government, in this land of freedom, where the sun of liberty first arose, and enlightened all with the bene-

* When we have considered that America contains millions of people who are in the enjoyment of freedom, and the rights of man in the fullest extent, our bosoms glow with heart-felt satisfaction; but when on the other hand, we have considered that this highly privileged and free people hold thousands, only because they are of a dark colour, in a state of absolute, degraded, painful, and miserable slavery, how sorrowfully the scene is reversed—how poignant is the reflection.

fits and advantages thereof, and among a people whom the Lord hath redeemed from bondage, there are above three thousands, and that number increasing, who are under the most absolute, ecclesiastical monarchy that ever was on earth; and like Issachar, who is called the ass, they willingly couch under it, because they think that the rest is good, and the government is pleasant; so they bow their shoulders to bear, and become servants thereto—(Gen xlix. 14, 15.) "Tell it not in Gath, publish it not in the streets of Askelon"—(2 Sam. i. 20) lest the uncircumcised, the enemies to a republican government rejoice. If your government is right, and the only true government that was ever appointed and owned of God, then all America is wrong, and we are only shouting praise to, and exalting a Babel of our own building.

A reply.—"We know they are all wrong, and you "too, as you see and judge every thing respecting our "faith and conduct, in a wrong light. You now think "you have made it appear that the first Elders are "walking in the same steps, and that their conduct is "like unto those ungodly rulers you have mentioned; "but you have not been able to make the comparison "complete, as after all you have said, there is a wide "difference between them and the leaders, or first Elders "in this church; as in the latter, you behold humility "and plainness in dress and living; in the former, pride, "vanity, pomp, and splendour; in the latter, love and "tenderness; in the former, hatred and cruelty; our "Elders live the life of the gospel; those monarchs and "popes you have mentioned, lived in sin, and in every "respect, contrary to the gospel. Then surely our Elders are far from being like them. But though they "live the life of the gospel, nevertheless you intimate "*they are of the same spirit, and fear that they will become fully* "*so in spirit and practice, as they increase in number and power.* "Herein your fears are totally groundless, and has no "foundation in truth. And as to what you have said "respecting the first Elders living a recluse life, &c it is "surprising that any man of sense should mention this "as an objection against us. When I believe there is "not a family at Niskeuna but what Mother has been to

" ſhe; and ſhe does aſſociate, and converſe with the be-
" lievers as far as is neceſſary and profitable; and all
" are benefited by the light and example of the firſt El-
" ders. Beſides, ſhould there not be an order in the
" church; and ſhould not all conform to, and keep in
" their own order, according to their ſeveral gifts and
" qualifications, as is the caſe in other ſocieties, accord-
" ing to their order; and indeed, with every thing in nat-
" ural creation?

" In anſwer to your objection, reſpecting kneeling be-
" fore the Elders, I may obſerve, that it is not a com-
" mon practice; and what few inſtances there has been
" of kneeling before them, were by ſuch who have had
" a long privilege, and had been taught the way of God;
" and who, nevertheleſs, have afterwards acted counter
" to the gift and counſel they had received, and had vi-
" olated their own conſciences by committing ſin; and
" ſuch kneeled before the Elders only as expreſſive of
" their humility, repentance, and ſorrow; and not from
" a motive of worſhipping, or adoring them. Beſides,
" they do not kneel before them as humbling themſelves
" before men, conſidered as man; but before the gift
" and power of God, or ſpirit of Chriſt, which they be-
" lieve dwelleth in the ſaints.

" That paſſage of the revelations you have quoted, is
" nothing to the purpoſe. You know that the Elders
" believe themſelves to be but men, and poor, depend-
" ant creatures; and that they would not receive any
" ſuch adoration; and if it was offered, they would like-
" wiſe ſay, *See thou do it not; we are thy fellow ſervants,*
" *and thy brethren; worſhip God.* There have been but few
" inſtances of believers kneeling before them; and then
" only from the cauſe and motive I have mentioned —
" And according to your own account (as I have under-
" ſtood) you did the ſame, as you kneeled in the preſence
" of him to whom you firſt opened your mind; and he
" kneeled with you. I preſume you did not ſo do, as
" paying any adoration, or particular reſpect to him;
" but in humility to God; and as you have ſaid, that
" you might confeſs in a right ſpirit, and others have

" done the ſame: this being the cauſe and motive, you, " or any reaſonable perſon, ought not to mention this as " an objection againſt our faith.

" You alſo object againſt us, becauſe we do not at- " tend to human learning, books, and reading. Inſtead " of theſe, we wiſh to attend to the goſpel that will ſave " us from our ſins. A ſoul never can learn the way of " life and ſalvation by human learning Books and " reading will never bring us nearer to the kingdom of " heaven. Reading will never give us power over ſin, " nor ſave us from our ſins. Salvation from ſin, ſhould " be the great concern and buſineſs of our lives: this " ſhould claim our greateſt attention; and not books, " which would only have a tendency to lead the mind " away from the ſimplicity of the goſpel. It is certain " that the true and ſaving knowledge of God, cannot be " obtained by books and reading. As proof of this, the " moſt learned have ever differed in their ſentiments on " the ſubject of religion; and many of them have re- " nounced the chriſtian religion, and all divine revela- " tion. Others have denied the exiſtence of a God, and " the immortality of the ſoul. And ſome have read till " they believed nothing at all (i. e. become ſceptics.)— " Truly, according to the apoſtle, many have *ever been* " *learning, and never have been able to come to the knowledge* " *of the truth*—(2 Tim. iii. 7.) *The world, by* this human " *wiſdom, knows not God*—(1 Cor. i. 21.) The things " of God are *hidden from the wiſe and prudent* in human " learning, and revealed unto babes—(Matt. xi. 25) i. e. " ſuch as are ſimple, and willing to be taught according " to the order of God.

" We believe that human learning, if kept in its proper " bounds, may be ſerviceable in tranſacting the concerns " of this life; and on this account, a few books on the " arts and ſciences, may be uſeful to thoſe whom they " may concern. We have no objection againſt geo- " graphical, and ſome hiſtorical books; but reſpecting our " ſalvation, nothing is neceſſary, but to keep in the gift, " and in obedience to what we are taught.

" Reſpecting thoſe monarchs and popes you have men- " tioned, we believe they received their power from the

" prince of this world; and have acted according to the " spirit by which they were governed. Therefore, be- " cause unholy men, under the influence of an evil spirit, " have imitated, or been found, in some respects, in the " outward order of God, and preached some doctrines " that were true, is it any proof we are wrong, because " we are, in some respects, in the same faith and prac- " tice? Does it furnish any reasons, that we should lie " under the censure of walking in their steps, and pat- " terning after them? You might as well say the Pa- " pists believe that God ought to be worshipped, and be- " cause we believe the same, therefore we are like them.

" You say you believe a monarchical government is " the best, if the monarch is a good man, and his suc- " cessors so continue to remain You believe the present " leaders of the church are good men. They seek the " good, peace, and happiness of the people in every re- " spect. Therefore, you have no reason to believe but " what their successors will so continue to remain.

" We hold to no man (or woman) ruling as man; " but the spirit of Christ in man. We hold to no other " government but the government of Christ, or by his " spirit, which is in love, tenderness, and compassion to- " wards all souls If ever the ministration, therefore, " deviate from this principle; if ever they become ty- " rannical and cruel, then may all the world exclaim " against them; as it is only the spirit of Christ by " which we now profess to be ruled and governed. We " totally renounce, and bear testimony against the least " appearance of that domineering, usurping, cruel spirit " and power that those monarchs and popes possessed; " and if that power, as you say, is sitting in the east, " which we hope it is, you have no cause to say, it is " rising in the west, meaning among us, as here is not " the least appearance of that spirit. It is, therefore, " unjust in you, to compare us with the popes of Rome, " though we may be like them in some points of faith " and practice (and so is every church.) It is unfeeling, " it is unkind in you, so to blacken us with the spirit of " anti-christ, which you believe they were governed by, " after all the love, forbearance, tenderness, and kind-

" ness, which you have seen among the people, and re-
" ceived from them yourself. I hardly know what to
" think of you. I would wish to have charity for you,
" and hope your heart is better than your tongue, which
" the apostle calls an unruly member, and hard to be
" brought into subjection.

" There never was a people on earth under so kind
" and tender a church government as we are; and we
" are confident it never will be applicable in the spirit
" of it, to your description of monarchy.

" Concerning America, we have nothing against its
" government. We believe providence was on the side
" of America in the revolution; but why it was so, the
" people did not know. In their constitution they al-
" lowed liberty for all to act according to their own faith
" in religious matters; all which, in the providence of
" God, was to make way and room for the first opening
" and establishment of the gospel. Thus, according to
" St. John, the earth, i. e. the earthly government, or a
" government of the spirit of this world, helped the wo-
" man and her seed, that is, the people of God. The
" earth opened her mouth and swallowed up, or took
" away the power of persecution—(Rev. xii.) Now here-
" in we see the wisdom of God in causing our first El-
" ders to leave England, at present a place of confusion,
" noise, and war, and to come to a land of peace. You
" say, *America is an highly favoured people.* Yea, they are
" as the Jews were, when Christ came among them; and
" it is a pity any should be as unwise as they were in re-
" fusing the gospel of his first appearance.

" You say, Many don't know the privileges they might
" enjoy. Yea, truly, they do not. They might, by be-
" ing so highly favoured, as in having the true and liv-
" ing gospel planted among them, whereby they might
" become saved from their sins, and be made a happy
" people.

" You say, 'Hail America! what an highly favoured
" people!' Yea, they are so. But not altogether in con-
" sequence of a republican government—but in conse-

"quence of the reign and kingdom of Chriſt being ſet "up among them, if they were wiſe enough to receive "this goſpel and come into this kingdom of peace.

"Then truly you ſay, 'when we look around the world "and ſee how nations have been and ſtill are kept in ig-"norance, oppreſſed and impoſed on by tyrants and an-"ti-chriſtian teachers, you feel thankful,' &c. But we "can ſay we feel thankful for the favours and privileges "of the goſpel we enjoy; and that we can go forth in "obedience thereto, without fearing the wrath of the "anti-chriſtian powers of this world. 'The uninformed "are inſenſible of the privileges' we enjoy, and know not "'what an excellent government is ſet up among them;' "even that government in which, according to prophe-"ſy, the Prince of Peace was to have the government "on his ſhoulders; and we find him a true and a wonder-"ful counſellor—(Iſa. ix. 6, 7) They do not know "what a 'highly favoured part of the world they live in; "and what a bleſſing and privilege they might enjoy. "Thus part of this 'New World is become like Adam's "Paradiſe.' Thus your language only wants a little al-"teration, a little ſifting and ſhifting, and it would be "the truth; many of your premiſes are true, but your "inferences are falſe: your tongue only wants a regula-"tor—if it was regulated by the goſpel, your inferences "would be as true as your premiſes.

"After you have given a ſhort deſcription of the Amer-"ican government, and the privileges and effects of free-"dom and liberty, you cry out, 'but aſtoniſhing to tell, "that under this benign government, in this land of free-"dom, there are above three thouſand who are under the "moſt abſolute monarchical government that ever was "on earth' Here you appear to be totally blind, as to "ſeeing the difference of the ſpirit of this government "and all former ones; for you ſeem to infer that it is "the ſame ſpirit, though you cautiouſly avoid adding "tyranical and cruel, which you have applied to former "monarchical governments, both in church and ſtate. "As from the knowledge you have of the people of God "under this government, your conſcience won't ſuffer "you to make that addition. We know that this is the

"government of the Prince of Peace, whose yoke is ea-
"sy, and his burden is light—(Matt. xi. 30.) And it is
"that which gives real freedom and liberty to the sub-
"jects of it; even a freedom from sin and bondage to
"Satan; and we have come into the glorious liberty of
"the children of God—(Rom. viii. 21.) For where the
"spirit of the Lord is there is liberty—(2 Cor. iii. 17.)
"And we mean to stand fast in the liberty wherewith
"Christ hath made us free—(Gal. v. 1.) And you may
"*tell it in Gath*, and *publish it in the streets of Askelon*, and
"all the towns and streets in America, if you like, that
"the uncircumcised and unacquainted with true liberty
"and freedom may know where to find it.

"You say, 'if we are right, or if our government is the
"only true government that was ever owned of God,
"then America is wrong, and they have only contend-
"ed for, and now are exalting a Babel of their own
"building.' There is nor never was any government own-
"ed of God, but what was under the influence of his spirit.
"The very intent of government is to establish and se-
"cure peace and order, to secure the rights of all men,
"and preserve them from injury. This, fully and com-
"pletely, all civil governments have ever been defective
"in; and the reason is, because their origin is of that
"nature, that is injurious to the happiness of mankind, i. e.
"they have all been formed and contrived in the will and
"spirit of fallen man. As proof of this, under all govern-
"ments, whether monarchical, aristocratic, democratic,
"or republican, the majority of the people have never
"been satisfied; they have ever quarrelled among them-
"selves and with their rulers, which has generally ended
"in the usurpation of some arbitrary tyrant, assisted by
"a body of military mercenaries, to rule and oppress the
"people. Some say, that civil government should have
"nothing to do with the church. True; because all
"civil governments are so defective and sinful; and it is
"evident that not any of these governments are owned
"of God, as they have all, more or less, persecuted those
"who have had a measure of his spirit; and have stood
"in direct opposition to the increase of the government
"and kingdom of Christ. It was the very spirit of these

" governments, or the ruling power and spirit of this " world, that would not have Christ to reign over them; " therefore crucified and put him to death: and all these " earthly powers are prophesied against, and their origin " described as arising out of the earth—(Dan. vii 17) " ascending out of the bottomless pit, &c.—(Rev xi 7) " And according to the prophesies, there is to be a time " when they are all to be destroyed, and the govern- " ment committed into the hands of Christ, and fastened " as a nail in a sure place, never more to be removed " and changed—(Isa. xxii. 23) And there will be giv- " en unto him *dominion, and glory, and a kingdom, that all* " *people, nations, and languages, shall serve him; his domin-* " *ion is an everlasting dominion, which shall not pass away,* " *and his kingdom that shall not be destroyed*—(Dan. vii. 14.) " And under the government of Christ will fully be ac- " complished what hath been wanting and defective in " all others; peace and order will be established and se- " cured, and men will not only be restrained, but the dis- " position in them to injure one another will be destroy- " ed; the rights of all will be secured, not only their out- " ward, temporal rights, but their right to the gospel, " the free gift of the Son, which will save them with a " perfect salvation from every thing injurious to their " peace and happiness; and they will be preserved from " all injury, not only outward, but inward, from an evil " nature and spirit. This we experience among us; and " it is a government that the wisest politicians have nev- " er been able to form, because they wanted the power " over the evil nature in man. Nevertheless, it is neces- " sary, that while creatures are not under the government " of the spirit of Christ, they be under some government " according to the state they are in, and according to " their comprehensions and understanding; and though " we have nothing to do with earthly powers, govern- " ments, and politics, yet if we must speak our minds, " we prefer a republican government before any other; " as no one man, in a state of nature, under the power " of his own natural propensities, lusts, and desires, is fit " to govern others. Therefore, when the power of choos- " ing and refusing rulers is in the hands of the people, "and the rulers bound by some law, the evil nature in "man prone to covet, and grasp at property, to domineer, usurp, and tyranize over others, has not such an "opportunity to rise to such an height as it has done, or "would do if not so bound But nevertheless, it is all "one side of the order of God, as being destitute of the "spirit of Christ, and is a babel of their own building, "which will only last for a time, and finally end in confusion as it commenced, because it is all of the spirit "of this world, which never could be at peace: and as "all the governments and kingdoms of this world have "been set up and established in the spirit, nature, strength, "and will of man, and by war, and that often in the "greatest injustice; also, as that spirit is akin to, or of "the nature of Satan, therefore he has power over them; "and it is impossible for mankind to be content and live "in peace under any government, so long as they live "in sin and wickedness. This is the sole cause of all "the dispute, of all the difficulty that arises from every "quarter.

"Can any man, that has the least sense of the spirit of "Christ, believe, that the present republican government "(which you and others extol so much) is of God, or "has the spirit of God for its support and protection, "when we see and hear how it is supported by pride, "strife, wrangling, and contention, particularly at electioneering times? The public papers are often fraught "with all manner of scurrilous, abusive language, which "plainly shows the spirit ruling the people. When they "assemble at their elections, they often act as if they were "influenced by the spirit of the devil—and truly they "are influenced by their evil nature. Is this the way to "choose wise, honest, and judicious men to take the helm "of government? One might reasonably conclude that "a wise man would have nothing to do with it, or would "not serve when chosen at such an election. Is this the "way to obtain the approbation and smiles of Providence, and draw down a blessing on the rulers, government, and country? And are these the people that "*the Lord hath redeemed from bondage*, when they thus "show how they are ruled and governed by the spirit of

" Satan, and are in bondage to this tyrannical monarch ?
" When all manner of ſin reigns from north to ſouth,
" and from eaſt to weſt, religion and the fear of God is
" deſpiſed, or little thought of; and many ſins have now
" become faſhionable, particularly that abominable ſin
" of ſwearing and taking the name of God in vain—and
" the greater ſin, as they have no inate temptation there-
" to, and for which they have no excuſe; and it may be
" ſaid, becauſe of ſwearing the land mourneth—(Jer.
" xxiii. 10.) If they are an highly favoured people,
" they are ſo much the leſs excuſable; and above all,
" according to their faith, they live under the ſound of
" the goſpel, and with the advantages of as much litera-
" ry knowledge and information as any people on earth.
" They are not kept in ignorance as many nations are;
" they ſee and know the conſequences of ſin; they know
" the rock on which nations have ſplit; they know that
" ſin and wickedneſs has ever been the downfall and ru-
" in of nations. But alas! alas! they are walking in
" the ſame ſteps, and it is likely they will continue ſo to
" do, until they become, like other nations, ripe for ruin;
" when God will withdraw his mercy and protection,
" and then they will more fully experience the effects of
" ſin, either by inteſtine commotions, a civil war, or the
" ſcourge of ſome foreign tyrannical power, and then
" become a people who no longer can glory in a repub-
" lican government, freedom and liberty. For true it
" is, that *Righteouſneſs exalteth a nation, but ſin is a reproach*
" *to any people*—(Prov. xiv. 34.)

" Thus we ſee the ſtate of America; and if we look
" abroad among other nations, what a miſerable ſpecta-
" cle preſents itſelf! Nations fighting againſt nations,
" and what is more inconſiſtent and deplorable, profeſſ-
" ing Chriſtians againſt Chriſtians; but it is evident they
" are all anti-chriſtians, they are of their father, the
" devil—and the luſts of their father they will do; whoſe
" luſt or deſire is to devour and deſtroy like a hungry
" lion ſeeking for his prey. If we look into cities, there
" we ſee ſin, and all kinds of wickedneſs, contention, and
" confuſion If we go forth into the field, there we hear
" the clattering of the inſtruments of war—thouſands

"are killed on both ſides—the groans and ſcreams of "the dying are heard! Flight, purſuit, victory enſues; "then often raviſhing, murdering, plundering, burning, "hating, curſing, and injuring one another every way "that lies in their power! Look at the nature of man-"kind—ſee their awful depravity!"

My reply—If all your arguments were as forcible on every other point of your faith, as on moſt of thoſe you have laſt treated, I ſhould be a believer. I fully unite with what has been ſaid of the origin, nature, and ſpirit of civil government. I firmly believe with you, that no nation or people, under any government, can enjoy permanent and uninterrupted peace, while ſin or the principle of evil prevails. Admitting the world is in the loſt ſituation you have deſcribed, on account of the inſufficincy of the light for which I have contended, and all other means it has had to prevent it, then I want ſufficient evidence preſented to my mind that the true and ſaving light now ſhineth, and that you are enlightened above all people that are or ever were on earth. I may obſerve, you have hitherto pulled down all ſyſtems, both civil and religious, and I believe you have pulled down ſeveral falſe things; but I know it is eaſier to pull down than to build up. True wiſdom does not conſiſt ſo much in diſcovering error, as it does in finding, exhibiting, and demonſtrating the truth. If you could as clearly point out that the government which you are under to be of God, as you have that others are not, I ſhould have more faith. When this point reſpecting the millennium is ſufficiently ſubſtantiated, all controverſy and doubts (as I have ſaid before) about other points of your faith, will be ſettled of courſe. But hitherto, on this ſubject, you have given me little more than your bare aſſertion; it is true, you mention your good fruits, and utter ſome good ſentiments, and I have mentioned ſome fruit among you, and many ideas and notions of things, which I think are not good. Your ſeeing and being able to ſhow wherein all others are wrong, and have erred, is no proof that you are right in every reſpect. Others can ſee and point out wherein you alſo err; and I think one is almoſt as deep in the mud as the other is in the mire!—

You do not produce, nor neither do I see, that evidence with which the scriptures testify, that the second coming of Christ will be attended The texts you quote from the scriptures to prove it are very few, and those I do not think applicable, viz. " If they shall say unto you, behold he is in the desert ; go not forth ; behold he is in the secret chambers—believe it not. For as the lightning cometh out of the east, and shineth even unto the west, so shall also the coming of the Son of man be." This text I think is pointedly against you.

Another text I have often heard Elder Ebenezer quote when preaching : " For wheresoever the carcase is, there will the eagles be gathered together"—Matt. xxiv. 28. The carcase is the church, the body, and the eagles are the airy, wild people, who must be gathered to the church. Now let us read the text according to the plain, literal meaning of it. Where the dead carcase is, there will the eagles be gathered together to devour it. These predictions were literally fulfilled in the calamities which befel the Jewish nation, in about forty years after they crucified Christ. The Jewish nation was the carcase, and the Roman armies were the eagles.*

Elder Hezekiah observed—" All who have been faithful and have travailed in obedience, have proof sufficient within their own souls that this is the way of God, and that we are under his government. We experience the prophesies of the second coming of Christ within us. We feel no spirit or disposition to hurt or injure any creature, but love and tenderness towards all souls. We feel a kingdom of peace set up within us ; and you see there is an outward order and peace among us, such as was never seen on earth before, which is the product of that of which I have spoken, which is spiritual and unseen by the carnal eye, therefore you have no reason to doubt nor dispute the truth of this our testimony."

I replied—Your feeling no disposition to hurt or injure any creature, but love and tenderness towards all, is

* See Bishop Newton's Dissertations on the Prophesies, vol. ii. p. 181. Bishop Pearce on the Destruction of Jerusalem.

no proof that you are the only people of God on earth; as there have been and are many who can truly bare testimony of as much inward experience of peace as you do; and I myself can truly say, I feel not the least disposition to hurt or injure any creature, but love towards all souls, and would rather suffer wrong myself, than wrong or injure any one

I verily believe God is no sectarian, i. e. he does not favour those of one sect or name more than others, but his mercy is equal towards all his creatures; and such who sincerely seek him, he causes at times to flow into the soul an unction, which I cannot describe, but which fills or satisfies it completely.

I still believe, that by obedience and faithfulness to the light that God gives me, I may increase in that good work which I have already experienced, and finally gain a victory over all sin, and in the end have an admittance into those peaceable and heavenly mansions, where I shall hear no more of lo here, and lo there, no more of sects and parties, each one wishing and endeavouring to pull down others to build up themselves.

Elder John Meacham said—"Thomas, you never will "gain a victory over sin; but sin at times will have "power over you, unless you receive faith in the present "revelation of God in his people, and become obedient "to the gift of God, one side of which there is no salva-"tion from sin."

I replied—If all be true that you say, it appears to me it must be something more powerful to fully convince me of it, than a bare verbal testimony. It must be the power of God—I must have internal evidence. Before I became acquainted with these people, I thought (and which appeared to me agreeable to the scripture testimony) that in the millennium, Christ's coming would be attended with such demonstrative evidence, that none would have any doubt respecting it. Therefore I concluded, that all disputations and arguments about religion, that has hitherto so filled the Christian world, would then be at an end; for all would know the Lord for themselves. Also, that arguments and reasoning would no more be necessary to convince the people of the coming and ſhining of the Sun of Righteouſneſs, than they are now neceſſary to convince people of the riſing and ſhining of the natural ſun. But the truth is, I have heard more arguments and diſputations, ſince I firſt came to Niſkeuna, than ever I heard before. I have often ſat ſilent for hours hearing the Elders, or others in the faith, arguing with unbelievers, and they with them: and I have reaſon to believe the Elders have laboured much in the ſame manner with ſeveral other believers as well as with me. When I became ſo ſtrong in the faith as to vindicate your principles to the world, and ſhow that this was the millennium, there was no other way for me to do it but by arguments; in which I often failed of ſucceeding, and could not act the part of the apoſtle Paul diſputing with and confounding the Gentiles, (at Cornwall and other places) proving from the ſcriptures, that Jeſus is the Chriſt, manifeſted and had appeared the ſecond time in the people called Shakers. Thus, inſtead of all doubts and controverſy being at an end, it appears, if your faith increaſes, or this church becomes popular, there will be more in the world than ever before. If only the arguments and reaſoning that the Elders and ſeveral of the believers have had with me, endeavouring to convince me, and the controverſy we have had together, were all written, it would be a large volume Therefore, I think it time now to end. We have proceeded as far, and perhaps farther already, than has been profitable. But I can truly ſay, that my motive in plainly opening my mind to you, and making objections wherein I have been diſſatisfied, and rendering reaſons for thoſe ſeveral objections, has been for information, and that you might clear them up if poſſible to my ſatisfaction, and remove thoſe obſtacles to my increaſing in the faith, out of the way, ſome of which you have removed. And I believe your motive in bearing with me, and endeavouring to convince me, has proceeded from a concern (according to your faith) for my good; which I thankfully acknowledge. To which Elder John Meacham ſaid—

"Thomas, we are very willing to agree with you in "ending all diſputation."

Elder Hezekiah ſaid—"We hope you will not ſuffer "any hard feeling to ariſe in your heart againſt us."

I replied—Never, I hope, againſt you nor any other people, on account of difference in ſentiments. I ſhall ever reſpect you, and remember the time you ſpent with me, and your patiently and calmly bearing with all my contradictions and, I fear, ſometimes too harſh expreſſions againſt you and the faith; and whatever I have ſaid contrary to the ſpirit of meekneſs, I confeſs unto you I am ſorry for; and I hope your love and good will for me will not be leſſened.

Elder Hezekiah replied—"We ſhall hold nothing againſt you, Thomas; we feel nothing but good will "towards you."

I now was much affected, under a ſenſe of their love and kindneſs—and ſorry that I could not fully unite with them—and in tears I anſwered—I ſhall remember and conſider all you have ſpoken. If you are only in the right way, I pray that God may enlighten my underſtanding and lead me into it. We read, "The prayer of the righteous availeth much:" you profeſs to be ſo; and I hope you will pray for me, and that your prayers may prevail. I then left the room.

Now one principal reaſon of the Elders bearing ſo much with me in all that part of the controverſy I had with them, was becauſe it was the order for believers to open to the Elders all their doubts, and whatever they were diſſatisfied about, or wherein any one was irreconciled to the faith, or the Elders, in order that the Elders might ſolve the doubts and objections of believers, and ſatisfy them if poſſible. And I may obſerve, they bore with me more than they would have done, on account of my uniting with them in every point of faith and practice, not diſputed in this work.

A few days after I parted with the Elders, I being in company with a few believers, one of them ſaid—

"Soon after your laſt converſation with the Elders, I "being in company with them, I aſked them if you "was any more ſatisfied with and reconciled to the faith; "one of them anſwered me thus—It is eaſier to gain a "thouſand ignorant, unlearned perſons, than one who is

"learned and well read; but when ſuch an one is gain-
"ed, he is worth a thouſand of the former; and this,
"they ſaid, was one cauſe of their labouring ſo much
"with you."

I replied—I never profeſſed to be a learned man, nor did I ever conſider myſelf as ſuch. It is but little learning that I have. But can it be poſſible, that learning and reading is eſteemed ſo highly, that a learned and well read man is worth a thouſand unlearned, when I have heard ſo much ſpoken againſt learning and reading?

The anſwer—"The difficulty that attends human
"learning is, that it hinders creatures from receiving
"faith; as it is eaſier to gain a thouſand without it, than
"one with it, who can criticiſe and raiſe objections to ev-
"ery thing that's offered, be it ever ſo good. But if
"ſuch an one becomes effectually gained, and that wiſ-
"dom or learning becomes refined and brought into ſub-
"jection and obedience to the goſpel, then it becomes
"profitable in enabling ſuch, who poſſeſs it, to give a
"clear account of the faith, to convince unbelievers, and
"give anſwers to objections that may be raiſed againſt
"it; like unto the apoſtle Paul, who having more learn-
"ing than the other apoſtles, was more able to vindicate
"the cauſe of Chriſt, and prove that Jeſus was the prom-
"iſed Meſſiah; and on account of this ſervice in the
"church, the Elders meant one is worth a thouſand."

I replied—I believe it has been found to be the truth ever ſince the faith was firſt preached, that it is eaſier to gain a thouſand ignorant perſons, than one learned and well informed, as there has not been gained one of the latter to a thouſand of the former, or that have continued in the faith.

One ſaid—"We know it has been much as of old,
"*not many wiſe, not many mighty, not many noble are called,*
"or obedient to the call, becauſe of the croſs. But *God*
"*hath choſen the fooliſh things*, the weak, the unlearned in
"the world's wiſdom—(1 Cor. i. 26, 27) And it ap-
"pears as if the *goſpel was hid from the wiſe and prudent of*
"*this world, and revealed only unto babes;* and Chriſt thank-
"ed his Father becauſe it was ſo. Therefore, we ſhould

" be satisfied if there was not, nor never had been one " learned in this world's wisdom among us; and thank- " ful that we have not had that wisdom that might have " hindered us from receiving the gospel, which I would " not exchange for all the learning and knowledge in " the world.

" The Elders have understood that you had conclud- " ed to leave us, until you could more clearly see the " propriety of our faith and practice; but they told me, " that your faith and sincerity was such, that they be- " lieved you would soon return."

I replied—They have misunderstood me, or you have misunderstood them. I do not mean to leave the people yet. It is by becoming thoroughly acquainted with the faith, that I can see, or be able to judge of its propriety. If I leave the people, I shall have but a small privilege among them, and but little opportunity to become farther acquainted with their faith and practice; therefore I mean to abide with them until I am fully convinced whether this be the only way of God or not; and by waiting patiently, some evidence may be presented to my mind, sufficient to convince me

One said—" You cannot become convinced any other " way but by obedience, according to Christ's words— " *If any man will do his will, he shall know of the doctrine,* " *whether it be of God*"—(John vii. 17.)

Now on my considering what time the Elders had spent, and of their labours with me in all our past conversations; and knowing how subject many professed christians are to get warm in controversy, and suffer a spirit to arise contrary to what they profess; but not having hitherto seen the least symptoms of the like in the Elders, and others with whom I had conversed; but they having always appeared to bear with me, and patiently hear what I had to say; and having manifested throughout, a meek, mild, and quiet spirit; and in considering of their love, tenderness, and good will towards me, from the first, to this time; I felt a love for them, and was much reconciled to them. I considered there were many things I believed in common with them; some of which, I believed to be excellent principles; as confeſſing and forſaking every thing which they believed to be ſin, and living in love and unity. I believed as Elder Hezekiah had told me, that the order, love, and unity of the Shakers, exceeded that of any people, or ſociety with which we are acquainted. In ſhort, I believed that there were more good principles and practices among them, than any other ſect.

With reſpect to thoſe points in which I could not fully believe, particularly reſpecting the millennium, I admitted a poſſibility of my being miſtaken, as thouſands had been in oppoſing that which, at laſt, proved to be right. I alſo conſidered that though they might be like the Papiſt in ſeveral points of doctrine, yet that, perhaps I had done wrong in judging that their ſpirit was the ſame, according to their power. I reflected upon what Elder Hezekiah had ſaid, viz. That I ſaw, and judged things reſpecting them, in a wrong light; and that it was unkind to compare their ſpirit to that of the perſecuting church of Rome.

I now took the ſubject of obedience to the miniſtration into conſideration, and the arguments which the Elders had advanced on that ſubject. I alſo recollected what I had read in ſeveral authors in ſupport of obedience to the church. I now thought ſo favourable of the Elders, that I concluded to be more obedient. And alſo to act according to the advice of a certain celebrated commentator, viz. "Thoſe that join themſelves to Chriſt, will join themſelves to his miniſters, and follow them."*

Accordingly, the Sabbath after my laſt converſation with the Elders, I went to meeting, with an intention to inform our Elder Brother Seth Wells after meeting, that I was reconciled. Indeed, I felt ſo much ſo, that at this meeting I attempted to join them in the dance, which I had not done for ſeveral months before; but Seth Wells caught hold of me, and prevented me, and ſpeaking with a low voice, he ſaid, he wiſhed me not to join them in labour.

I replied—Why did you not tell me before?

* Matthew Henry, on Acts xiii. 43.

It being before a publick congregation, and many spectators being present, I much disliked his conduct. I thought he might have told me when he saw me taking off my coat, which I had seldom done before, but now I was for keeping in union.

In the afternoon I met with them in their private meeting, as usual:* before it began, I did not open my reconciliation, Seth having given me such a repulse, and Elder Ebenezer, who was at this meeting, gave me a greater. He spake as follows, in a sharp, authoritative manner; lashing, and whipping me, and two or three more, over the backs of others, though I was the principal one intended:

"I desire you would keep in the gift, and not give "heed to any doctrines contrary to the faith ye have re"ceived. There are some among us, who would bring "heresy and schism into the church. Guard against their "poisoned discourses, and hear not those who say that "Christ can be prayed unto, and found in the desert, "secret chambers, and closets of your own hearts;† *for* "*as the lightning shineth out of the east unto the west, so is* "*the coming of Christ*. and *where the carcase is, there the* "*eagles are to be gathered together*. Confess your sins, and "cast the filthiness out of your hearts, where Christ is "not, nor never will be until you do; and receive him "in the way that he doth now, and ever hath revealed "himself. He can only be known to your salvation by "receiving him in the word preached; *for how can you* "*hear without a preacher? and how can any preach, except* "*they be sent?* It is in Zion where God is to be known, "and revealed to you, by and through his ministration; "and salvation by that gift and word of God, we preach "unto you: and what we preach unto you is, to con-

* In the forenoon they assembled in their public meeting-house; but in the afternoon, in one of their dwelling-houses, where spectators, or those who are not members of the society, are but seldom admitted.

† When he expressed thus, I thought of the words of Christ—"When thou prayest enter into thy closet, and pray to thy Father which is in secret," &c.—Matt. vi 6. Therefore, it appeared to me Elder Ebenezer pointedly contradicted Christ.

" fess and forsake your sins. Don't think that you can " assemble here with your sins covered. I can see " through and through you. I can call you by name, " and expose the sins you have not confessed.

" We know that we have the word of God; and we " know that this is the way of God; and we can say un- " to you, '*thus saith the Lord;*' and cavilers and disput- " ers can never overthrow it. There are some among " you, who believe we are a sincere people, as many in " other societies are. But we want no such believers " among us, who believe no more than this. There is " one among you, who says, others before us have been " as confident and certain respecting revelations to them, " and of the second coming of Christ, as we are; but " time has proved they were mistaken, and so we may " be. This is the reasoning of the serpent, who wishes " to bring you under doubts, and destroy your faith.— " Away with it, for it will prove poison to your souls. " It is Satan working against the gift of God. Be on " your guard, keep in the gift, and there you are safe. " For Satan's reasonings are subtle; filled with error, " heresy, and poison. He will bring forth much truth, " and you are not able to judge the truth from the er- " ror, as by subtle reasoning, one will appear as plausi- " ble as the other; and when such speak truth, it is of " no profit, being one side of the gift of God. There- " fore, keep in the gift; for without us, you can judge " nothing; one side of the counsel of the ministration, " you are all in darkness. (I do not wish to hurt the " feelings of any one in the faith: I am only speaking " occasionally.) There are some who will tell you of " their great experience of the love of God; but he that " saith he loveth God, *and keepeth not his commandments, is* " *a liar, and the truth is not in him; and he that committeth* " *sin, is of the devil; for whosoever is born of God, doth not* " *commit sin.*

" Some talk about being taught by the spirit of God, " and will tell you about the great experiences and at- " tainments of christians of other societies; but Christ is " *the way*, not the many ways. There is but one way " of life and salvation; but one gospel, and only salva-

"tion by that gospel. Therefore, all talk about this "one and the other one, in that way or the other, being "taught by the spirit of God unto salvation, is fruitless "and vain And there is Thomas Brown, he expects "to be saved one side of the gospel and counsel of the "ministration, but he is deceived; and all will find themselves in the end deceived, who adhere to, and believe "him. Such as live in sin, and are disobedient to what "they are taught, however wise they may be, or great "profession they may make, are in a poor, lost, dark "state. And such as have had a privilege among the "people of God, and afterwards forsake the way of God, "eternal damnation will be their portion. Such as go "to the world, and to backsliders, to inquire about the "people of God, are one side of the gospel, and out of "the gift. We have no union with such conduct. It "is deceit, it is hypocrisy.*

"I have not spoken from any outward information, "but from the present gift of God. We wish all to keep "and abide in the way they have been taught; in which "you will find peace and rest to your souls; and not "become liable to be tost about with every wind of doctrine. We wish you to keep in love and union, one "with another; as you can no farther love God, and "be in union with him, than you love, and are in union "with the brethren. As much as you love the brethren, so much you love God; and your love and union "is your strength. We wish you to have no hard feelings towards any one; but each one to examine his own "heart, and mind his own concerns, and keep in the gift: "and all who have not any sin covered, and feel their "union to the way of God, may prepare for labour."

Now, as the other Elders and myself, had amicably concluded to have no more controversy, (and in the morning of this day all was peace and quietness, and I felt, as I have said, much reconciled;) but now the old controverted subjects are again brought up, which was much contrary to my expectation. Elder Ebenezer had often before spoken so pointedly as to designate me as

* I had conversed with several backsliders, and he had heard of it.

the principal object aimed at; and I thought it extremely uncandid, and unjuſt, to addreſs an individual in a publick aſſembly, where there is no poſſibility of his making a replication, without a breach of decorum; but as he had now mentioned my name, that none preſent might be miſtaken whom he had implicated as a dangerous perſon; and my mind being exceedingly tried by ſuch a ſudden oppoſition to the ſtate it was in juſt before; therefore, as ſoon as the believers ſtopped dancing, I ſpake a few words, ſignifying I had been miſrepreſented.

Thus publickly ſpeaking of a perſon, they call publick chaſtiſement.

After meeting, I requeſted to ſee Elder Ebenezer, which requeſt was not granted. He ſent me word he was not well. The next day I ſent word to him again, that I wiſhed to have a little converſation with him, if agreeable; but there was ſome excuſe, and I have never had an opportunity to ſpeak with him ſince.

I told ſome believers how I had felt reconciled, (but I told the Elders nothing about it,) and that I knew if I had informed Seth, or Ebenezer of it before meetings, they would not have treated me thus; but now ſaid I, where is the ſenſe of feeling which they profeſs to have? It appears they know nothing about any one, until they are outwardly informed.

I was anſwered—"The Elders may ſometimes err. "You ſhould not think hard of Seth, and Elder Ebene- "zer, for what they have done; they wiſh you well."

There were ſome believers who were diſſatisfied with thoſe proceedings towards me, and who examined for themſelves what they ſaw and heard, and had but little faith: with them I often freely converſed concerning the faith, the Elders, and their gifts; (for this was the topic of converſation at all times.) Shortly after this laſt mentioned meeting, being with one of them, and thus converſing, about 12 o'clock at night we retired into a garret, and went to bed, and ſtill continuing our converſation; when about 2 o'clock, I heard a ſinging drawing on from a diſtance. As my companion was then talking, I ſaid—Hark! We lay ſilent; when we both heard a ſinging exactly like that which the brethren often ſung, which they called a ſolemn ſong, apparently paſſed over us, near the roof of the houſe, which we heard about two minutes. It gradually ceaſed, by apparently going from us, as it came on in drawing nearer to us.—My bed-fellow aſked me what I thought of it? I told him I knew not what to think of it.

He ſaid—"Perhaps one of the brethren have come "near the houſe, and ſung, to make us believe we heard "the angels ſing, in order to ſtrengthen our faith."

I replied—I cannot believe any of them would be guilty of ſuch wicked deception; beſides, we clearly heard the ſinging over the houſe; and you don't conſider what a ſnow has fallen the day and evening paſt, it is now at leaſt four feet deep; ſo that no one can walk, or ride, until the roads are trodden; and it is not likely any body has been out this very cold night.

He ſaid—"The ſinging might have been only in our "imaginations."

I replied—If ſo, it is extraordinary that both of our imaginations ſhould be thus affected at the ſame time.—If only one of us had heard it, I ſhould not have thought ſtrange of it, as I could have aſſigned a natural cauſe for it.

He obſerved—"The church brethren ſay, they often "hear departed ſpirits, or angels ſing; and it may be, "it was the ſame, in order to ſtrengthen our faith."

I ſaid—Ah! it may be this, and it may be that, and it is all—may be. I muſt have more ſubſtantial evidence to ſtrengthen my faith, than—may be's. I alſo may reaſonably conclude, that, angels or ſpirits have more wiſdom, than to ſing for us only a tune which conveys not any information, and placing a puzzling-cap on my head, when it is loaded with them already.

A ſhort time after, I being five or ſix days with a family of believers (for I ſtill ſpent much of my time with them) at eleven o'clock one night, they all having retired to reſt, and I laying awake in a dry, well finiſhed room; and in which was a ſtove and fire, there fell a large drop of water on my temples: on examination, I could not diſcover where the water came from. I told the believers of it in the morning.

One ſaid—" Ah! it is ſome warning for you, reſpect-
" ing your unbelief."

I then aſſigned ſome inconcluſive reaſons how the drop might have become formed in the room, and its falling.

One replied—" Ah! that is the way you render a
" natural reaſon for the cauſe of every thing; and ſo rea-
" ſon away your faith, and yourſelf out of the goſpel."

1804. Fourteenth of March I took another journey to Lebanon, and my family with me.

Next day after we arrived, it being Sabbath day, I wiſhed to have a ſight of thoſe in the higher order; and accordingly I and my wife went to the meeting-houſe where they aſſembled. They were in much outward order, particularly in their labour, (which is different from that among young believers; but in time will be the ſame with them, as they improve or travail as they term it, into church order.) Their leader ſpake a few minutes on obedience to, and keeping in the gift.

When we returned from meeting, Elder Hezekiah aſked my wife " if ſhe had ever been to ſo good a meet-
" ing before."

She anſwered—" Yea, many I think much better."

But this is much contrary to the faith, to give other profeſſors, and their meetings, the preference.

The next day, ſecond of the week, I was requeſted by the Elders to retire with them into a private room; and after ſome indifferent converſation, one of them ſaid—

" Thomas, the gift from Elder Ebenezer, is for you
" to confeſs all your ſins again."

I replied—That I can ſhortly, and eaſily do. But then as I muſt do it as a religious act, I wiſh to feel and ſee it my duty, that I may do it ſincerely; and not as a mere matter of form, and only ſpeak with my tongue, and not with my heart.

Elder Hezekiah ſaid—" You ſhould immediately cloſe
" in with, and take right hold of the gift that is for you.
" This is your duty; and in giving up your own will
" and feelings to the gift of God, will be the moſt ac-
" ceptable ſacrifice you can offer."

I replied—I hope I may have a little time to consider of it.

He answered—" Yea, you may. We wish you to begin anew, and take up your cross in earnest, and be " obedient to the gospel, and become a man of God; " and not loiter behind as a babe, while others are travailing before, and out of sight of you. When, by this " time, if you had been obedient, you might have been " as far advanced as any of the young believers, or more " so, as you was the first that received a measure of faith " in this opening; and you might have been a help to " many other souls."

I asked him why they did not labour with, and endeavour to strengthen my wife in the faith?

He answered—" If you would become satisfied, and " obedient, there will be no difficulty with her, nor your " children. We believe they would make good believers; but if you shut yourself out, you will ruin your " own soul, and lead them in the way of ruin with you: " all which, one day you will bitterly repent."

They now left me in what may be properly termed the confessional room, as it was a small out-house, where they convened occasionally, and where the Elders laboured with the believers; and where the latter opened their minds. Some of the believers called it the potter's house, i. e. where the Elders fashioned and moulded the believers anew.

In the evening Elder Hezekiah came to see me again, and asked me " whether I had concluded to be obedient " to the gift."

I answered—I have confessed my sins several times already; and it appears to me to be an idle work, to tell you of what you know already; and foolish things that I have done in my childhood, and time of my youthful vanity and ignorance, which are of no consequence to any creature on earth, and are not worth a fool's hearing. At a time when I was powerfully convicted for sin, and felt myself a poor, lost soul, I begged of God to have mercy on me. He filled my soul with his love. I felt my ſins forgiven. I then wanted a thouſand tongues to praiſe him. And I this day verily believe they are forgiven.

He replied—"Why then, did you ever confeſs them "to us?

I ſaid—You appeared to be a more religious, and exemplary ſociety, than any other I knew of; and I thought it no evil to tell what I had done. But I fear it will be evil to continue telling an evil, idle, fooliſh ſtory over and over again. I care nothing about my ſins. They don't trouble me, and I am ſure they need not concern you; and I wiſh to do as I read in the good book—"Forget the things that are behind, and preſs forward to the good things before."

Elder Hezekiah ſaid—"You muſt chooſe your own "way, if you will not walk in the way of God. And "if you are not obedient to the gift in confeſſing your "ſins, you will be held in union with the people of God "no longer, and all doors will be ſhut againſt you, both "here and at Niſkeuna."

I replied—Nay, not all doors—you are miſtaken. There are ſome believers you never can perſuade to ſhut their doors againſt me; you may threaten them as you pleaſe, it will be all in vain. But I do not wiſh to do any thing to offend any one, or cauſe any believers to ſhut their doors againſt me. I wiſh to be in love with them, and if they were all to ſhut their doors againſt me, if I had ten thouſand I would open all to them; and if any of them were hungry, I would feed them; if thirſty, I would give them drink; thoſe of them who are ſtrangers to me, as well as thoſe I am acquainted with, I would take in and entertain them as well as I could; if they were naked, I would clothe them; if they were ſick, I would nurſe them; if they were in priſon, I would viſit them—Matt. xxv. Thus would I return good for evil. And the many believers that have been to my houſe, from time to time, have reaſon to believe that thus would I do unto them; not ſhut my doors againſt them, and uſe them or any others unkind, becauſe they believe not as I do. Never, never; O, God forbid that I ſhould be of ſuch a ſpirit. Oh! Elder Hezekiah, how much your laſt ſentence ſavours of perſecution! Can i: be poſſible you mean what you ſay? You may depenc on it, I cannot forget it very ſoon. Turn me out o your houſes, and ſhut your doors againſt me becauſe ] can't believe as you do, or becauſe I conſcientiouſly can not do what you deſire of me. So the Boſtonians, thoſe pretended Chriſtians, ſhut their doors againſt the Qua kers, who had to wander in the woods until ſome were almoſt ſtarved to death. What for? why becauſe they conſcientiouſly could not conform to what thoſe pretend ed Chriſtians required of them, or do any thing to whicl they felt an inward reluctance; and becauſe they con ſcientiouſly believed that no religious performances were acceptable to God unleſs done as moved thereto by hi ſpirit, or at leaſt unleſs they felt a free and willing mind.

Elder Hezekiah ſaid—" You ſhould not let your minc " run on in ſuch a manner, but labour to get hold of the " gift that is for you."

I was now brought under a trial; for I muſt either be obedient to the gift, or be ſhut out, which I was loth to be, as I wiſhed to have a further privilege among them to prove whether they were the only people of God o not; as yet I was not fully ſatisfied, thinking it migh be poſſible that they were what they profeſſed to be and I thought it would be wrong for me to leave them unleſs I was fully convinced that this was *not* the only way of ſalvation. Beſides, after a long and agreeable acquaintance and cloſe friendſhip, which had ſubſiſted and been uninterrupted between me and many individu als of the ſociety, the thought of having thoſe whom loved and eſteemed ſhut their doors againſt me, wa more than I could bear. It cauſed a grief, and gave me feelings that were truly poignant and diſtreſſing.— This was the principal cauſe why I was ſo loth to leave the ſociety.

I ſhall now proceed with my narration. In the even ing, being concerned and troubled in mind, I ate no ſup per, neither did I eat any thing for near three days af ter; during moſt of which time I continued alone in the aforementioned room.

The ſecond day of my retirement, third day of the week, Elder Hezekiah viſited me two or three times, counſelling, interceding, and perſuading me to be obedient unto the gift; and told me it was the wicked, carnal nature in me that cauſed me to ſtand againſt the gift of God, and hindered me from obedience thereto. I ſaid, I know not what to think of you; when I firſt came among you and confeſſed my ſins, you told me then—"If at any time hereafter I felt deſirous to open my "mind, I would have the privilege ſo to do; and it was "then as I felt and ſaw to be my duty. It was then "told me to act up to, and according to the light I had "from God. It was then the ſecret operations of the "ſpirit and word of God in my heart you recommended me to. It was then, the goſpel don't bind creatures, but gives liberty to act our faith, feelings, and "mind, in matters that are not ſinful. It was then, according to the light given us, and that no more is required of creatures than what is made known to them "to be their duty."

Now it is not my faith, but your faith; now it is not as I feel, but as you feel for me; now it is no more acting according to my light, but your light; no more now looking to the ſpirit and word in my heart, as you once told us at Cornwall, but the outward declarative word you ſpeak. No longer now do you ſay, "The goſpel don't bind creatures;" for I am bound to do what I cannot ſee or feel it my duty to do, or elſe I muſt be caſt off and all doors ſhut againſt me. I have no liberty now to act my faith, but I muſt act your faith, or elſe abide by the dread deciſion of *anathema maranatha*. Once I was told, it was only the continued commiſſion of ſin and violation of conſcience that ſhut any out of union; but now I am to be ſhut out for not violating my conſcience and doing that which I fear will be ſin. And I am now required to do what is not made known to me to be my duty—all diametrically oppoſite to the doctrine preached at firſt. But I forgot that I propoſed to drop all controverſy, with which you agreed—excuſe me for thus opening a door for it again..

He replied—"We have anſwered all theſe ſeeming "contradictions ſufficiently heretofore, and you do wrong "to let your mind run on things that don't concern your "preſent calling. We wiſh you to be wiſe and labour "in your mind, to be united to the preſent gift."

I told him, I believed I would go home; and that probably I might feel willing to open my mind ſometime hereafter.

I was anſwered—"Now is your accepted time, and "now is the day for you to come into the way of ſalva-"tion. If you are not obedient to the preſent gift of "God, you may never have the offer and privilege of "the goſpel again; and you will ſink below the wick-"edeſt and moſt loſt creature on earth, who never had "the offer of the goſpel. I think it is likely you will "come to nothing, and be a poor creature, like many "others who have turned their backs on the way of God. "And you will not be able totally to looſe your faith; "the impreſſion it has made on your mind will abide, "and it will be your torment as it hath been to others, "who have turned off—and it will be your and their "torment in hell! What a pity, when you might be-"come a bright man in the goſpel. I have known ſome "who have loſt their ſenſes, who have wandered about "day and night, and did not know where they were, or "what they were doing. I have alſo known ſome, and "heard of many, that have come to an unhappy end."

He told me a ſtory of a certain man who had left the people, and at laſt was drowned in a certain lake. Conſiderable more was ſaid about the danger and conſequences of ſtanding againſt the gift of God; and the loſt, dreadful ſtate of thoſe who left the way of God; which I have heard the Elders and others in the faith talk of, from time to time, enough to drive or ſcare ſome people into the faith and obedience, or make them diſtracted, which has been the caſe with ſome poor, diſobedient creatures. Many wonderful, lamentable ſtories I have heard about poor backſliders; but I believe that the Lord will have more mercy on them, than his profeſſed people.

I told him, it would be a droll ſtory for me to tell the world that I was turned off, diſowned, and all doors ſhut againſt me becauſe I would not confeſs my ſins the fourth time.

He anſwered—" Tell them the true cauſe, that you " would not take up your croſs and be obedient to the " order of God among his people—tell them this!"

I replied—Yea, I will tell them this, and more. For if I undertake to tell the world any thing about it I will not tell them half a ſtory, but give them a true and full account of all matters that have tranſpired from firſt to laſt, and they may judge for themſelves whether you are the people of God or not. And if I leave you, it is not unlikely but that I may write the wonderful religious life I have had among you; and if I was to do ſo, I expect I ſhould be treated by you as you have treated ſeveral others who have left you, i. e. you would call me an impoſtor, liar, &c.

He replied—" I ſuppoſe you will endeavour to juſtify " yourſelf in condemning the way and people of God."

I anſwered—Nay, that ſhall never be my motive, either to juſtify myſelf or condemn any; but if I was to do any thing in that way, I think I would endeavour to give a true ſtatement, without any colouring on one ſide or the other, and leave all to draw their own concluſions, or judge as they think right.

He replied—" The world in their loſt dark ſtate, are " not able to judge of the way and people of God. But " if you ever write any thing againſt the church, you " will finally ſhut yourſelf out in this world, and you " will have hard getting back in the world of ſpirits; " you will have to paſs through inexpreſſible ſufferings " before you will be reſtored."

I ſaid—What ſignifies talking about what I have no thoughts or intentions of doing; as I deſire to abide with you, if you be the people of God. And as to the other world, the Lord only knows how it will be with us. We poor creatures can't judge truly about this world, that we ſee and are acquainted with, much leſs a world we never ſaw. We do not know how our ſouls came into our bodies, nor what they are, much leſs whither they go. But I believe there is a good and merciful God, who will take care of, and have mercy on his poor creature man. But if he has no more mercy on us than we have on one another, it is a pity that ever we were born. But I ever wish to act according to those ever worthy to be remembered lines of the poet,

"*That mercy I to others show,*
"*That mercy show to me.*"

We had but little more conversation, as I felt so exercised and tried in my mind I was not disposed to talk, but desired silence and retirement. The fourth day of the week my trouble and concern of mind was much greater. I walked the floor most of the time, weeping (and wetting my handkerchief with tears, and repeatedly drying it by the stove) and praying to God that he would be pleased to enlighten my mind, and give me a sense of my duty, and show me whether this was the only way of life and salvation. Walking the floor, weeping, and often wringing my hands and repeating short ejaculatory prayers, as, O Lord, if these by thy people, suffer me not to leave them. O Lord, if this be the only way of life and salvation, open thou mine eyes to see it; be pleased to give me a sense of it. O Lord, if I am in darkness, disperse the darkness: break in, O Lord, break in with thy light and life in my soul; "in thy light I shall see light; O send out thy light and thy truth, let them lead me." O Lord, have mercy on me; "Look thou upon me, and be merciful unto me; order my steps aright, O Lord, and let not any iniquity have dominion over me." I am cast down, and my heart is almost broken; but, O God, thou hast promised, "a broken and contrite heart thou wilt not despise." Hear my prayer, O Lord, and be pleased to teach me what I must do. But I could receive no other answer but this, which several times feelingly ran through my mind, "I have already shewed unto thee the way, walk thou in it," i. e. what I had experienced before, and once since I saw these people, as my mind immediately received that impression.

In the afternoon, Elder Hezekiah came in, and after ſitting ſilent awhile, (ſeeming loth to ſpeak, ſeeing the ſtate I was in) he ſaid—

"Thomas, Elder Ebenezer deſires me to inform you, "of a ſpecial gift* he has for you; which is, if you do "do not confeſs your ſins in obedience to the gift of "God, all the ſins that ever you have heretofore com- "mitted and have confeſſed, will be retained."

Ah, thinks I, ye are all Job's comforters. Break my heart quite! kill me outright! or if ye have the gift, power, and light of God, and I can receive it no other way but from you, then adminiſter light, life, and power—give me ſome divine conſolation; bring ſome balm to heal a wounded ſoul; let the miniſtration unite together, and be as one man, and act the part of the good Samaritan; if ye cannot, then pray to God for me—and if ye are truly righteous, your prayers may avail; light will break into my ſoul, and all theſe trials will be ended. What ſignifies telling me about my ſins being retained, to frighten and afflict. My ſins retained, becauſe I cannot ſee or feel it to be my duty to tell them over again to you!

I deſired to be alone, that I might pour out my ſoul in prayer to God. I was invited to meals, and preſſed to eat—but I had no appetite; I thought my tears were my meat and drink day and night, while they continually ſay unto me, where is your God?—Pſ. xlii. 3.

Early in the evening, my mind having been ſo exerciſed and tried, I experienced what theſe people call a death-ſleep, (though not aſleep, and moſt of the time my eyes were open;) I continued in this ſituation about two hours; part of the time I did not know whether I was in the body or out; and it is only ſuch as have been among theſe people, and have experienced the ſame, that can read me and know what miſery I endured.† I thought

* A ſpecial gift is immediate revelation to, and from the Mother of the church.

† Some time after, I mentioned this death-ſleep to ſome of the believers. I was told that it was the beſt ſtate that I had ever ex-

that no one, God excepted, would ever know the trials, exercifes, and fufferings of mind which I had paffed through, from time to time, among thefe people—and what can it all be for? I was ready to wifh I had never feen them.

Next day in the afternoon, Elder Hezekiah came to fee me again, and affectingly faid—

"Thomas, we are forry for you and pity you, and the "whole family† are forry for you; it is like a houfe of "mourning. But we cannot alter the gift of God; it "is impoffible—it is unalterable. If you go from this "place without being obedient to the gift, and we own "you and have union with you, Mother won't own nor "have union with us; all will be fhut out who have un-"ion with you. Therefore, we cannot help you, nor do "any thing for you, but labour with you to be obedient "as long as a gift of God is felt for you. If you would "be obedient, we fhould all rejoice, and all the young "believers at Nifkeuna would be glad and rejoice on "your account. What fhall we do for you, or fay to "you? I would be willing to fuffer or undergo any "thing for your good. We are forry beyond expreffion, "that you fhould be loft; your foul is as precious, in the "fight of God, as ours are. We defire, we wifh, we "long for you to become a man of God and brother "with us in the gofpel. We are willing to forgive and "forget every thing hat has been paft; we would hold "nothing againft you, and have no other feelings to-"wards you but love and good will."

This and more was faid by feveral of the young believers, who vifited me in apparent love and tendernefs. I told them, words from without were all in vain, and that I was paft converfation.

perienced; as I was then dying to an evil nature. I alfo learnt, that but few of late years had experienced the like.

Some time afterwards in confidering of it, I was fatisfied that it was a fpecies of delirium, and that it was caufed by anxiety of mind.

† This family confifted of about thirty men and women, and, at this time, eight or ten young believers from Nifkeuna.

The ſame afternoon, Elder Hezekiah came again; and as I was then walking the floor, wiping the tears from my face, he ſat ſome time looking ſorrowful, and then ſaid—

"How does Thomas feel?"

I anſwered—I love the people, becauſe I love their fruits; and, after a minute or two ſilence, added, if I was naturally of a hard heart I would go off and leave you, (I meant on account of the little evidence I felt of this being the only way of ſalvation) but you overcome and conquer me with your love and kindneſs. This gave him ſome encouragement; he ſaid no more—but left me.

Early in the evening, a young believer, (Abraham Hendrickſon) came in, and after ſitting awhile ſilent, he aſked me, "If I wanted to ſee Elder Hezekiah." I knew well enough he was ſent by him, and what was meant by that queſtion; and as by this time I was much worn out, and felt very feeble in body and mind, I thought I muſt get rid of my trial and exerciſe one way or another, for it appeared to me that I could not live much longer under it;* I therefore anſwered him, You may tell him to come if he likes. He immediately left me to carry the good news—and in a few minutes my Elder came. The reluctance that I had felt, now increaſed; but I conſidered, if I did not comply with the gift I ſhould have no further privilege of proving the truth or fallacy of the faith, and as I wiſhed to abide until I was fully ſatisfied, and being over-perſuaded and conquered with their love and tenderneſs towards me, I concluded to comply. I walked the floor a few minutes after he came into the room, and then ſat down with intentions to open my mind, when I felt as if ſomething forbade me; directly I was ſurpriſed to find that I had loſt the power of ſpeech—and for near half an hour I was not able to ſpeak a word; I felt as if I was bound, and my

* "O, blindneſs of our earth-incruſted mind!
In what a midnight ſhade, what ſombrous clouds
Of error, are our ſouls immers'd, when thou,
O Sun ſupreme! no longer deign'ſt to ſhine!"

mouth closed as by an invisible power. Nor could I recollect one sin or evil deed that ever I had done; they were all completely buried in oblivion. In the time of my silence, Elder Hezekiah spake once, and said,

"I expect it is a greater cross now to confess your "sins, than it was when you first opened your mind."

For he thought the cause of my not beginning to open my mind, was because I was labouring to break through the cross; but he was greatly mistaken. I was not able to make any reply. When at the expiration of the time above mentioned, that something that bound me seemed to decrease, and I recovered the power of speech and recollection, when I began to open my mind—mentioning some particular sins, as swearing and intoxication, in my youth; for it was not much that I could recollect, and what I did recollect, or as it were forced into my mind, appeared like a dream, or something done a thousand years ago; and if he had not asked me questions relative to the sins of my past life, I could have recollected but little. In fact, I never felt such a sense of vanity, folly, and self-condemnation in telling any foolish story, or in any vain, idle conversation that ever I had in my life, as in thus opening my mind in obedience to the gift at this time

Afterwards in considering thereof, it appeared to me that this gift never came from God. For, thought I, I read that "the gift of God is life; that the spirit of God brings all things necessary for obedience to our remembrance, and gives light, life, peace, and power." But in my endeavouring to act in obedience to Mother Lucy's gift at this time, as far as I was able, it was all with me directly the reverse.

Next day I told Elder Hezekiah, that according to order, we are to open not only our sins, but every thing else with which we are exercised in our minds, or uneasy about; and that I had something on my mind with which I had been exercised, and perhaps I had better open it; he said,

"Yea, to be sure; what is it, Thomas?"

I answered—I believe our first Elders, namely, Ann Lee, (her half-brother) William Lee, and James Whittaker, were in the practice of drinking ſpirituous liquors to exceſs; and I likewiſe believe, that there has been inſtances of their quarrelling and fighting, the natural conſequences of intoxication. He appeared to be ſorrowfully ſtruck at this the confeſſion of my belief, and ſaid,

"Why, Thomas! what reaſon have you to believe "ſo?"

I anſwered—I have reaſon to believe ſo from the various well authenticated reports.

He then proceeded to endeavour to convince me to the contrary, ſaying, he had been with Mother at ſuch a time, and ſuch a time—and at different places he had ſeen her often; but had no reaſon to believe the truth of what I had ſtated—and ſpake ſome time reſpecting the firſt Elders. But all he ſaid did not convince me to the contrary; and I recollected how dancing naked had been denied, and ſurely, thought I, if they denied that truth they will this.

I replied—Well, I don't know as it need concern me what they did, even if what I have ſtated be true, as I do not believe any of the Elders, or members of the ſociety, are in thoſe practices now, but are an orderly, moral people—much more ſo now than what they were formerly; and I do not think I ſhould let their conduct hurt my faith, nor condemn the people now for what ſome have done heretofore. For if a perſon has been once bad or addicted to evil practices, but has become reformed, then ſuch a man ſhould not be condemned or thought worſe of for what he has done, but is worthy of reſpect and praiſe in having forſaken his evil ways; and it is juſt the ſame with a family or ſociety, nor neither are children to blame, nor ſhould they be deſpiſed for the bad conduct of their parents.

He replied—"Nay, Thomas; not ſo reſpecting the "children of the parents of the church. For the firſt "Elders, particularly Mother Ann, was *the ground-work,* "*foundation and pillar of God in the church;* and if ſhe and "they got drunk, quarrelled, and fought, as you ſay, "we are a deluded people, and on a ſandy foundation; "and I, though I ſtand as an elder and miniſter, would "leave them to-morrow morning."

From the candor with which he ſpake, I concluded he did not know or believe they were in ſaid practices. I thought if he had ſeen her act like an intoxicated perſon, he might believe as many did, that ſhe was bearing the ſtates of the people.

Now previous to this declaration, I was of a mind to ſet the firſt Elders entirely aſide, and not let their conduct hurt my faith; and as the people profeſs to be in a travail, ſo as ſoon as they ſee or come to a knowledge of their errrors, or wrongs in any reſpect, to put them away and mend—ſo I with them. But this won't do. If the firſt Elders were guilty of what I had ſtated, "we are a deluded people, and on a ſandy foundation." And he, even in his ſtanding with his faith, would renounce the ſame, and pack up in the morning and be off. Then, as I did believe ſaid conduct, what became of my poor little faith that had been ſo tried juſt before? Why, in one moment he gave it a fatal wound, viz. as to their having received the ſecond coming of Chriſt, and being in the only way of life and ſalvation. I made no reply, (as I avoided contradiction and controverſy, I having ſo propoſed and agreed as long as I continued with them) I believed he concluded I was ſatisfied, as he adviſed me to be obedient to the gift in ſettling my buſineſs, and to move up to Niſkeuna and gather my union with the believers, and at times of worſhip join in labour, i. e. dancing.

Next evening (about nine o'clock) I attended family meeting, which I had not done before ſince I had been here. But I was not obedient to the gift or order in labouring with them, as I could not join them therein when I felt ſo little faith, without acting the part of an hypocrite, which I abhorred. After the meeting, Elder Hezekiah aſked me why I did not labour. I made little or no reply. He ſaid,

"You ſhould take right hold of the gift that is for "you, and be obedient."

I ſaid nothing.

In the morning, ſeventh day of the week, after breakfaſt, I thanked them for their kindneſs, and bid them farewell, and returned home.

I now, in my own house, considered of all that had passed. But that which had the most weight on my mind was concerning first Mother being the "ground, foundation, and pillar of God in the church." I now recollected and considered more than I had done of what several old believers had told me respecting their faith in Mother Ann, and what had always been the faith of the church respecting her. That she suffered in spirit like unto Christ, and bore the different states of the people; and that they had seen her and also William Lee and James Whittaker, lie on the floor for several hours under that weight and suffering in spirit, to open the door and way of salvation—of which I could not form the least idea. Also of some who had suffered in spirit hundreds of years in a few minutes, or in a short time; or a thousand years in one day or hour, according to what we read, "one day with the Lord is as a thousand years, and a thousand years as one day"—2 Pet. iii. 8. I had also been informed that James Whittaker was in eternity in spirit several thousand years in a few hours, and in that time thousands of spirits confessed their sins to him. Thus I have often sat for hours hearing the mysteries and wonders of the faith, particularly concerning Mother and the first Elders. For with the old believers I never disputed nor contradicted what they said, but was rather disposed to ask questions and gain information. I now became convinced, that what I had stated in a discourse with the believers at Cornwall, as heretofore related,* respecting first Mother, was correct.

As further explanatory of their faith in her, I may here also remark, that according to the apostle, the woman, in its true, mystical, typical, and evangelical sense, is the glory of the man. In the Lord, the man is not (saved) without the woman, neither the woman without the man. For as the woman is of the man (i. e. saved by the man) so is the man also (saved) by the woman. But all things (i. e. the gift or power in them to salvation) is of God"—1 Cor. xi 7. xi. 12. "In Christ Jesus there is neither male nor female," in a car-

* See page 121.

nal sense; but both are one—Gall. iii. 28. This is what the apostle calls a great mystery, after he had been speaking concerning men and their wives. But I speak (says he) concerning Christ and the church—Eph. v. 32. Now as the mystery of God, relating to man's salvation, was not finished, until the woman (the second Eve) received that same power that Christ, the second Adam, did; therefore, she with him, is the subject of prophesy. And he who is curious enough, may examine the following passages: Psal. xlv. 2 to 8, speaks of Christ; ver. 9, to the end of the chapter, of Mother Ann. Jeremiah xxiii 6. and xxxiii 15. Christ; ver. 16. Ann: ib. xxxi. 22. Ann. Isa. lxvi. 7. Ann. Zech. vi. 13. Christ and Ann: ib. iv. 14. the same. Micah iv. 6, to the end, Ann: ib. v. 2. Christ; ver. 3. Ann. Zeph. iii. 10. xiv. Ann. Rev. xii. Ann and her children: ib. xix. 7. 8. Christ and Ann: ib. xxi. 9. Ann.*

They believe that the dispensation which they profess to be in, is "the marriage supper of the Lamb;" and those whom are called into it, are they whom St. John was told to "Write blessed." If those texts I have quoted, are prophetic of Mother Ann, as they say they are, then there are several more that are the same. Also many things under the Mosaic dispensation, were typical of her. It has also been asserted that the songs of Solomon, are prophetic dialogues between Christ and the Mother, and her and her virgins.

Much more might be said, concerning their faith, on this point; but as the subject was not further treated while I was among them, I shall not enlarge upon it. The Elders had said but little respecting their faith in Mother Ann, as it was then believed to be too strong meat to hand out to young believers. I had once told Elder Hezekiah, that when I first came among the people, I inquired why they did not publish their faith and doctrines to the world, as other societies had done I was then answered—There has not been any gift so to do.—But now I know the reason. He asked me—"What?" I answered—Publish your faith and doctrines in full, as

* See page 114—15.

other ſocieties have done; you will then have the whole world againſt you. He replied—"We know that: we "ſhould cut off all their ears."

Soon after I returned home from Lebanon, I had the following converſation with John Hodgſon, a young believer, (the heretofore mentioned R. Hodgſon's ſon,) who had belonged among the Quakers previouſly to his joining theſe people, and whom I have mentioned before. As we were pretty much of one mind on the main point heretofore controverted, we often converſed about the faith, doctrines, and practices of our brethren.

He ſaid—"I find the faith is very contrary to the idea "I had of it at firſt. I never expected ſuch an out- "ward obedience to the Elders would be preached, and "inſiſted on, in order to ſalvation, when they preached "at firſt to me ſo clear and plain the doctrine of the "Quakers, i. e. of an inward light, ſpirit, and word of "God in the heart, and obedience thereto, by not vio- "lating my conſcience."

I replied—If our church is right, or what they preach be the truth, the Quakers, as a body of people, and many others in every age of the world, who have borne teſtimony to the efficacy of the light that enlighteneth every man, have been, and are in this reſpect, much deceived; though I have often heard the Elders and old believers ſay, that the Quakers once had the power of God, and that they have been owned of God. That as John the Baptiſt was a forerunner of the firſt coming of Chriſt, ſo were the Quakers of the ſecond coming of Chriſt; but that they loſt their power by applying to the arm of fleſh, i. e. when they were perſecuted, repreſenting their ſufferings to the king and parliament, and petitioning a redreſs of their grievances. Now their acknowledging them to be the people of God, and loſing their power for their thus innocently repreſenting their ſufferings, is mere nonſenſe. For according to the faith of our church, if they had never thus applied to the arm of fleſh, they muſt inevitably have loſt their power, if ever they had any, by living in and after the fleſh; for they tell us this has been the cauſe of all people's loſing, or not retaining their power. As to their being a forerunner, preparatory, or opening the way for the second coming of Christ, it has not the least shadow of truth in it. For instead of their being any thing like this, they have been the principal people who have most effectually shut up the way; as they bore testimony an hundred years before this faith was preached, and at the time, and to this day, that salvation may be obtained without any outward ministration They have ever been crying out as if it were their intentions, or as if they were raised up to stop up this way—"Go not to man for teaching; look not to man. Whosoever goes to a man to be taught the way of life and salvation, goes to a wrong teacher;* but to the light within, to the seed, talent, word, and spirit of God in your own hearts." "O friends, turn in, turn in; go not after the lo heres, and lo theres; but to Christ who is spiritually present, as he promised he would be. Where the poison is, there is the antidote. There you want Christ, and there you must find him; and blessed be God, there you may find him."† "This, then, in thy heart, O man and woman! is God's gracious visitation to thy soul; which, if thou resisteth not, thou shalt be happy for ever."‡ And that "God had come to teach his people himself, and draw them off from all outward teaching."§ They have ever borne testimony against, and endeavoured to pull down all who set up for teachers above this inward principle, or the spirit of Christ in man As Wm. Penn's father told him on his dying bed, "Keep to your plain way of living, and plain way of preaching; you will make an end of the priests, to the end of the world:"‖ all much like John the Baptist, I confess, who said, "There is one cometh after me, hear ye him." Hear the Quaker, There are some who will come after us, saying, Lo here is Christ

* H Turford's Grounds of a Holy Life.

† William Penn's Preface to G. Fox's Journal.

‡ R. Barclay's Apology, p. 148.

§ G Fox

‖ Sewel's History, p. 651. Life of Wm. Penn.

among us; but believe them not.* Now I could show in many other respects how the Quakers have blocked up the way of the increase of this faith; and instead of crying like John the Baptist, "Make straight the way of the Lord"—John i. 23; they have made it exceeding crooked to us. I have thought that if I had never known the faith of the Quakers, I might have been more satisfied with the faith of the Shakers. It is harder for the Quakers to receive this faith, than any other society, as it is so pointedly against their fundamental principle.—If they had mentioned the French prophets as being forerunners of them, they would have come nearer the truth; but of these, they appear to know nothing, or at least, I never heard the brethren mention them

He replied—"I think thou hast given an exact and "true statement, and shown clearly the difference be-"tween the people called Quakers and Shakers; and "that the former, instead of being forerunners or pre-"paratory, have blocked up the way of the latter. And "now there is another subject occurs to my mind, which "I'll mention to thee, i. e. How my faith was hurt last "time I was at Lebanon, by Elder Stephen, who told "me, as he thought, to strengthen my faith, that though "they did not believe war was right, or that it was con-"sistent with the gospel to fight with carnal weapons, "nevertheless they conformed to the militia law, and pay "without compulsion, some hundreds of dollars a year. "But I considered their paying was aiding, assisting, "and supporting; therefore, no better than turning out, "preparing for, or fighting themselves. I can see no "material difference."

I replied—There is none; for he who prepares, or encourages one to murder another, is even in common law, considered as guilty with the murderer. And there is no difference in the crime of stealing myself, or assisting, or hireing another to steal for me; or in killing a man, or employing another to do it: and the same in every evil act whatever. As war, fighting, and killing of our fellow mortals, is contrary to the precepts, example, and

* G. Fox.

ſpirit of Chriſt; therefore, all who aid and aſſiſt in any way or manner whatever, act contrary to the commands and ſpirit of Chriſt. Therefore it is all a farce and ſubterfuge in their profeſſing to have nothing to do with the fighting kingdoms of this world, and belonging to a kingdom wich is not of this world, the ſervants of which cannot fight; neither aid, aſſiſt, encourage, nor ſupport, directly nor indirectly. This has been likewiſe a weighty conſideration with me, that they are not the people they profeſs to be. They affirm that the goſpel teaches them to beat their ſwords into ploughſhares, and their ſpears into pruning-hooks—(Mic. iv. 3.) Neverthelеſs, pay hundreds of dollars a year, for to help make them; to help build up the works of the devil, and ſupport the wrathful kingdom of ſatan. What inconſiſtencies!

The Quakers, in this reſpect, I think are before them, as they bare a publick teſtimony to the world againſt war, in practice, by not paying; and had rather ſuffer their moſt valuable property to be taken from them, than pay a cent willingly to the ſupport thereof. I mean them that are Quakers indeed. But thou knoweſt it is contrary to the gift for believers thus to open their minds and converſe together about matters that have been taught them, wherein they are not ſatisfied. A pretty Popiſh ſtory indeed, and much like the policy of the inquiſition, that we are not to examine for ourſelves the truth or falſehood of what is taught us by the Elders, however glaringly inconſiſtent and abſurd it may appear!

It had been now about three years ſince this young man had joined theſe people. Soon after this converſation, he told me he had ſuch evidence reſpecting the conduct of the firſt Elders, as heretofore mentioned, that he could not doubt the ſame. That he had many hours of deep exerciſe reſpecting this faith, whereby he became more and more uneaſy; and accordingly gave up his faith in an outward miniſtration lead, and left the people, and was ſoon again received a member by the Quakers;* and again (as he informed me) enjoyed peace of mind. His thus leaving this people was contrary to their expec-

* See page 183.

tation, as he was much efteemed by them, as well as by all who knew him, for his fincerity and honefty.

As I had confeffed fome of my fins, or as many as I could think of, when I was at Lebanon, therefore I was held in fome union; and as convenient, I went to Nifkeuna among the believers, and attended meeting; but did not labour (or dance) with them, though it was the gift from the Elders for me fo to do. As thofe who do not join in this part of their worfhip, ftand in a row with the fingers, I frequently turned my face to, and leaned againft the wall; and often fpent the meeting in folemn filence, and contemplation. After fome time, one of the Elders afked me, Why, and what was the reafon, I did not labour.' I made him little or no reply, as I had now done opening my feelings and doubts; for I received no help from them, in fo doing. They adminiftered no balm to cure my fick faith. Arguments were all in vain. I thought the truth of the faith muft be fubftantiated by more effectual means.

At our publick meetings, many fpectators, efpecially when the weather was pleafant, attended; and one of the brethren who had a gift, as they call it, from the Elders, would fpeak directly to them, teftifying the faith of the fociety. This preaching appeared to me to be, for the moft part, deftitute of pathos and feeling; and oftentimes fentiments were delivered, with which I could not unite. Alfo, exhorting the fpectators to civil behaviour, and cautioning them to keep their dogs out of the houfe, were repeated fo often as to become quite tedious.

It appeared to me that they exercifed but very little patience when they obferved any thing among the fpectators difagreeable. If any one fat with his hat on, the leaders of the meeting, or thofe who were the moft zealous, appeared to be much difpleafed. I afked fome of them, if they made fuch ado about fuch trifling things, and exercifed fo little patience, what they would do, if they fhould have dirt and ftones flung in at them, as had been the cafe with fome other fects, when affembled for publick worfhip. I obferved, that I believed they would bear it with much lefs patience than others had done, unlefs there was no poffibility of helping themfelves.— But what I moft difliked, was a fpeech of Iffachar Bates about this time, to a Methodift minifter, who fat on the fore feat. This man appeared to be very attentive to Iffachar's difcourfe, and moft of the time, he looked him in the face. At this, Bates appeared to take offence.— Accordingly, he left the fubject on which he was difcourfing, and ftretched out his hand toward the clergyman, and cried out—"*Brute, brute, brute, you are beneath "the beafts of the field.*" After meeting, the Methodift preacher went and ftood before the fire to warm himfelf. Bates went and ftood by the fide of him; and by his looks, I thought he was like a dog that was ready to fnap. Oh! thought I, what a fpirit you fhow.—"Ye know not what manner of fpirit ye are of." After meeting, I went home with the family, of which Seth Wells had the lead. To him, I expreffed my decided difapprobation of Bates' conduct; and told him that Bates had greatly infulted the man, and done enough to excite in the breaft of any one, the higheft feelings of refentment. I obferved that the Methodift preacher bore it with calmnefs, and fhowed the fpirit of a chriftian.— Whereas, Bates had exemplified the fpirit of the Devil.

All Seth faid in reply, was—"I don't know that we "have any right to condemn Iffachar's gift."

Aftonifhing! thought I, do you call fcurrility and abufe, a gift. But I muft not omit mentioning here, that, fometime afterwards, Elder Ebenezer received information of Iffachar's conduct, which I was informed he difapprobated, and fharply reproved him for it.— Stamping with his foot, he feveral times faid to him, in an accent of difapprobation—"What! do you abufe peo-"ple? What! have you no more fenfe of the order of "the gofpel, than to abufe people?"

I was pleafed to hear of this. It raifed Elder Ebenezer in my eftimation.

When I was in company with the believers, particularly before and after meeting, when they are fome hours together, I had but little or no converfation, but kept filent; yet they faw I was ftill deficient in my faith, by my not labouring with them in their meetings.

One of the believers (by name Frederick Wicker, naturally a fenfible man, and with whom I had had much converfation concerning the faith) faid—

"Thomas, I believe you will yet preach this gofpel "and faith. The doubts, reafons, and hard way you "have had to come into it, will be all for the beft, as "you thereby will be more able to help others through, "and out of the fame. Alfo, by much converfation and "controverfy you have had with the Elders and others, "on account of your many objections; and you having "heard anfwers thereto, whereby you have become much "more acquainted with the faith and doctrines than "you otherwife would have been: in confequence of "which, you will be more able to anfwer objections that "others may make, and vindicate the doctrines of the "gofpel."

I replied—I never can preach a faith, and vindicate doctrines, unlefs I fully believe in the fame, and have fufficient and fatisfactory evidence for that belief; and there appears to me fuch a deficiency and abfurdity in the ground work of the faith, (that you have never examined, nor known nothing of,) and fo many obftacles are in the way, that though poffibly I may continue with the people, yet I think I never fhall become fo firmly eftablifhed in the faith, as to preach and recommend the fame to others.

He replied—"All the Elders want of you, is for you "to take hold of the gift, and be obedient. And if you "would fo do, they know you would have that evidence "that you have but little idea of now; and thereby be- "come firmly eftablifhed in the faith; and you might "then go forth in obedience to a further gift and fer- "vice in the gofpel. They believe you would be of "great help to others. And what a pity it is, that men "to whom God has given five or ten talents, fhould bu- "ry them in the earth; and at laft, receive no other re- "ward but weeping and gnafhing of teeth But what "deficiency and abfurdity is there in the ground work "of the faith, which you fay has efcaped my knowl- "edge?"

I replied—You know it is contrary to the gift for young believers to open their minds to one another, wherein it will have a tendency to hurt their faith. But believers condemn me on account of my want of faith—Question, and draw words from me; and then all the blame falls on me for opening my mind, giving my reasons, and then hurting their faith.

I now had not been with the Elders since I was last at Lebanon (except with Elder Hezekiah a short time) though they had several times visited the believers at Niskeuna; but I did not request a privilege (as they call it) with them, for I had nothing to open; and was satisfied that they, by conversing with me, could not remove my doubts. But as all believers, according to order, must request, and have a privilege with them, and hear and receive the word individually, without which, they say no one can travail,* nor be held in union; I therefore, was advised by several believers to go to Lebanon to see the Elders; and I being still desirous of a further opportunity among the people, to prove the faith to the uttermost, and not suffer myself to be disowned, until I had done it. Also, that I might not afterwards be like some who had left the people, and had still fearful apprehensions remaining: and though my faith was less than a grain of mustard seed, nevertheless to Lebanon I went.

February 3, 1805. I now had new Elders to deal with me, as Elder John Meacham was gone to preach the faith in Ohio and Kentucky; and Elder Hezekiah Rowley had retired to private life in the church order at Niskeuna. Therefore, these men (whom I had never seen before) were appointed in the place of the others.

* I have stated and inquired of some of the elderly brethren as follows: Supposing a believer was taken away, as by a press-gang, against his will, and carried to some foreign part of the world, and could not return in a number of years, might he not while absent by living near to God in secret prayer and obedience, experience an increase in the divine life, or growth in religion. I was answered—"He could not gain at all in a travail; but as to that, "would stand still, though he might possibly keep his justification "by not committing actual sin."

A few minutes after the ſiſters had provided me ſomething to eat, one whom we called Elder Stephen, came and informed me that the Elders deſired to ſee me. I followed him into the room where they ſat. One of them ſaid—

"Thomas, you have been laboured with, and taught "from time to time; and as you have not been obedi-"ent, Elder Ebenezer ſays he has no further gift for you."

I ſaid—If you be the only people of God, and have the only way of life and ſalvation, I wiſh to abide with you.

One replied (in a tone, I thought, not chriſtian-like; but more like an angry man)—"If, if, if! you have al-"ways had your if's. We know that this is the only "way of God; and though others ſhould *ſwear the Lord* "*liveth, they know him not, and ſwear falſely.* It is a path "*the lion's whelp never trod, nor the vulture's eye never hath* "*seen.* You may cavil, diſpute, turn, and twiſt as much "as you will; you, nor all the world, can never over-"throw it; neither be ſaved any other way. Therefore, "if you wiſh to be found in the way of God, be obedi-"ent to your Elders, and not offer to diſpute with them, "as you have done; but do as they tell you, without any "heſitation; and when they tell you to confeſs your ſins, "*confeſs your ſins;* and when they tell you to labour, do "ſo: and whatever they tell you to do, that do; and "not wait until you feel and ſee it to be your duty with "your carnal feelings, and carnal eyes. You think you "know every thing; you think yourſelf very wiſe; your "Elders can't teach you any thing: then what do you "come here for? With all your knowledge, the moſt "ignorant and ſimple believer at Niſkeuna, who walks "in obedience to the gift of God from his Elders, is wiſ-"er than you are. But we have no more to ſay to you. "You have been taught ſufficiently already. We have "no *gift* for you but to be *obedient* to what you have been "*taught*, and to the *gift* that has been heretofore for you. "If you are ſo diſpoſed, you may go and ſee Benjamin, "and ſee what gift he has for you: may be you can

"agree with him. And you may cry to God on ac-
"count of your disobedience, and when God hears your
"prayers, the people of God will hear you."

I said—I hope I may have the privilege to speak a word, though I have not come here to dispute, or enter into any controversy with you.

One replied—"We won't hear any thing you have to "say, neither will we dispute with you:" and rose up to be going, when the one we called Elder Stephen, said—

"I would not have Thomas think, that these Elders "have spoken from any thing that has been built up in "them, or from any outward information, or from any "thing that has been told them; but from the present "revelation and gift of God to them."

An involuntary thought then struck me in an instant. My God! what a falsehood! Does the man think I am such a fool as not to know that these Elders have been told of all the labours of the former Elders with me, when they spake so pointedly to past transactions, naming the gifts for me heretofore; as, "When you are told "to confess your sins, confess your sins," &c. And then to be so barefaced as to say—"These Elders have not "spoken from any outward information," &c. I looked at the man with such astonishment, he might have read me in my countenance. There was a few more words passed to the same import as before, and my going to see Benjamin;* and one said—

"Be honest in your dealings, Thomas."

Then Elder Stephen spake again, and said to me—"Now you think this Elder means, to be honest in your "dealings with the world; but he don't mean so, as we "don't doubt but what you are."

* I did not know what Benjamin they meant; whether Benjamin Youngs, at Niskeuna (who had a spare house, into which the gift had been for me to move my family) or Benjamin Ellis, who had the *lead* of those in the backsliding order; and as they appeared to be so very short, I did not ask them. But if they meant the latter, I was not in the least disposed to go there, for I thought I had had trials enough in the fore order, without going into the back order, where I might meet with fresh ones.

As they were retiring, one ſaid—" Stay in the room " where you are, as long as you ſtay here."

A few minutes after they had left me, Elder Stephen* returned, and aſked me if I was going to ſtay all night; (which I took as a broad hint to be off. I thought it exceedingly unkind, as it was near ſun-ſet, and they ſaw I was ſo much fatigued with my journey, that I was hardly able to walk.)

I anſwered—I ſhall ſtay unleſs I am turned out of doors; and then, poſſibly I may worry through the ſnow unto the firſt world's houſe, which, I am ſure, will be no credit to you.

He replied—" If you ſtay, then ſtay in this room."

At the time of meals, evening and morning, after all the houſe had eat, I was called thereto, and ſat at table alone; neither had I, while I ſtaid there, the company of any one ſince the Elders left me, except one who came and ſpake a few words to me rather more mild.—And in the evening Abraham Hendrickſon, my old acquaintance and nephew, came and ſat with me a few minutes and ſeemingly ſympathiſed with me, and expreſſed a few words of his ſorrow and pity for me. I was fully ſatisfied that all others in the houſe, were told to have no converſation with me. About the time of my leaving them, i.e. eight o'clock in the morning (for I did not hurry to be off, as I thought I would not partake of their ſpirit, and ſhow any thing like reſentment,) I wiſhed to bid them farewell, particularly my nephew; but I ſaw no one. I was confident that they had all been ordered to keep out of my ſight as much as poſſible. Therefore, I bid no one farewell, nor any one me. But I thought I heard in the ſecret of my heart, farewell to Lebanon for ever; and returned home.

Elder Ebenezer, and one of the other Elders, left Lebanon an hour before I did, in a ſleigh, for Niſkeuna: and as I was there on foot, my wife aſked me when I return-

* He was not properly an Elder: his buſineſs was principally to attend upon the Elders.

ed, why I did not ride with the Elders; for ſhe had ſeen them go by the houſe four or five hours before I got home.

I replied—I ride with the Elders! You might as well aſk why common people don't ride with the Preſident of the United States!

She ſaid—" Well, it is a pretty ſtory indeed that they " ſhould ſet themſelves up ſo high as to come at the " ſame time, and from the ſame place, with a light ſleigh, " and not take thee in."

But I did not think much of my not riding with them, becauſe I knew it was contrary to order for believers to ride with the Elders.*

I was always adviſed by the believers to go to Lebanon to get my faith ſtrengthened; but every time I went (except the firſt) it was weakened—and now it was exceeding weak indeed; for in conſidering their treatment towards me, I could not feel union with them therein: though as to the words the Elders had ſpake to me, I had little or no diſunion with them barely on that account, as I knew I had not been obedient to the gifts (or orders) that had been for me, in believing and acting up to them in ſeveral reſpects. But it was the authoritative manner and ſpirit in which they delivered themſelves, that I could not have union with. Far, very far, I thought, from that meekneſs and mildneſs which they profeſs; more like officers of the Romiſh Inquiſition than diſciples of Chriſt; and I could not help recollecting a little of what I had read of ſimilar language delivered in an authoritative way of ſpeaking, and apparently like ſpirit to ſuch as they deemed heretics, or who diſbelieved in the only true faith, and were diſobedient to their orders: " Hold your tongue, you heretic! we don't want " to hear any thing you have to ſay. Do you think you

* The reader may now recollect, that I have heretofore ſaid, that my father rode from Cornwall to Lebanon, with the Elders: but this was mere condeſcenſion at that time, in order to gain him to the faith Like other young believers, he was dealt by as a child; as they ſuffer and bare with many things, until believers are brought into order, or until they know the order.

"can teach us? you think you are very wiſe, but you are
"in darkneſs and know nothing as you ſhould know—
"and all like you are loſt men, and fallen from the holy
"church. There is no ſalvation for you if you do not
"return" But that's the worſt of this reading, thought I, as it enables us to compare preſent things with paſt, therefore is a deſtruction to this faith.

But then, on the contrary, I endeavoured to put the moſt favourable conſtruction on their conduct. I thought it might be they only talked and uſed me thus unkindly to try me, or my faith, but having the ſame regard and tenderneſs in their hearts as the other Elders heretofore expreſſed. But I concluded the truth of the matter was, they were determined to be obeyed without regard to any believers' circumſtances in life, or excuſes that any one might make.

By this time I became more fully ſatisfied how the Elders came by their gifts, or knowledge in ſeveral reſpects, particularly of the unconfeſſed ſins of believers—it appeared to me it was not by revelation, as they have frequently ſaid, but by outward information. I conſidered that there is one called Elder Brother in each family, who preſides over it and takes the lead; all in the family look to the Elder Brother for counſel, and to him are obedient. Theſe Elder Brothers are oftener with the Elders than the others; alſo, when the Elders viſit the families, the Elder Brother has the firſt privilege with them; he often informs the Elders of the faith, life, and behaviour of thoſe with whom he lives and is daily converſant. Thus the Elders know all about each one in every family, almoſt as well as if they lived with them and daily converſed in each family themſelves.

When the believers are individually admitted into the company of the Elders, they can ſpeak to them according to their faith and conduct. Alſo ſome men and women, who have been intimate previouſly to joining them, one has confeſſed ſomething which the other has not, which perhaps one or the other had forgotten, or neglected to mention—whatever remains unconfeſſed they have a knowledge of by the information they have in this manner received. Now, after the miniſtration have received their knowledge of every individual, by the method I have mentioned, and every other outward method that can be devised, I thought it was not right for them to say, either publicly or privately, as I had often heard, "Don't think that any of you can come before us and keep your sins covered! The gift of God will search and find you all out. The Lord is searching Jerusalem as with a candle. We can see through and through you! Those of you who have not confessed your sins, we can pick out, we can call you by name." When I stood among them and heard all this, I thought, whether you can or not, you are enough to intimidate weak minds and make them confess all that they can remember.

In the next place, having taken into serious consideration the first and foundation principle of the church, which is, that Ann Lee, whom they call Mother Ann, was and will continue to be equal with Christ in the work of man's salvation; and that without a woman, who should be the second Eve, in the same sense that Christ was the second Adam, mankind could not receive salvation; and she being "the ground, foundation, and pillar of God in the church," I came to the following conclusions, viz. if what I had opened to Elder Hezekiah was true, then upon the obvious principles of their own faith, the great point would be settled to a certainty, in direct opposition to their being in the dispensation of the second coming of Christ, and in possession of the only means of salvation. Hence I determined to make more strict inquiry into the character of Mother Ann, of those who had been personally acquainted with her, many persons of this description being still living. Also, I now began to have some thoughts of publishing my singular life among this people; which if I should hereafter do, I considered that an account (more full, clear, and correct than I had received from the old believers) of the rise and practice of the church previously to my acquaintance with it would be necessary. Therefore I was the more determined to prosecute this inquiry by travelling and visiting those who bore a good character, from whom I might be able to obtain the information requisite for such an undertaking. This I thought to be the more necessary on account of the great profession of sanctity and order in outward deportment, which is made by this people, with their positive and solemn assertions of being in possession of the only means of salvation; in consequence of which, the minds of many had been and were still exceedingly tried and exercised. I had understood that several, who had been among them, in consequence of their many trials and much exercise of mind, had lost their senses; which I thought was very likely, considering what trials and exercises of mind I had passed through, and that it was a great mercy I had not been ruined in the same manner. I considered the scenes of trial and affliction passed through by many families, in consequence of only part of the family receiving the faith; especially when the husband believed and not the wife, which caused a separation. Many women have been left desolate and destitute.* It would take many pages to enumerate all the consequences resulting from a reception of the faith of this church; which, if not a true church, would be of no profit to the soul. Further, as the church is built on the divine mission of Mother Ann, I considered it very necessary (not only for my satisfaction, but for the satisfaction of many others hereafter) that a thorough inquiry should take place before all those who were personally acquainted with her, and with the church in its infancy, were in their graves; and then

* If the wife believes, and not the husband, according to the order of the church she must still abide with the husband, and take up her cross according to the faith. I considered the true cause was, because the church had not power to take her away. If the husband will voluntarily give her up, the church will then receive her to live among believers. But if the husband believes, and not the wife, he is counselled to forsake her, and to have no union with her; and if he pleases he can take his children from her.—Many have forsaken their wives and children. I had strenuously contended with several believers, that it was the duty of the husband to provide for his unbelieving wife and children, the same or better than he would have done if he had not believed. But this was disputed, and the following texts quoted to justify their conduct—Matt. x. 34 to 37. Luke xii. 52, 53.

no other account of her, nor of the origin of the church, could be obtained, except what the church itself might choose to give.†

Being now fully convinced, that the account I had received from those in the faith concerning Mother Ann, and the rise and practice of the church, was not altogether to be depended on, they being so partial and prejudiced in favour of the cause as to represent every thing in the most favourable light; besides, I knew that several things which they had told me were not true. But along at first, while prepossessed and prejudiced in their favour, I could not believe any thing bad of such great characters as Mother and the first Elders were considered to have been. Also, having heard so often (and been taught to believe) that "backsliders could not speak the truth," it was some time before I would hear them; and when I did happen in their company, I gave little credit to what they said. But, in process of time, I found many of them did speak the truth; as they gave the same account of many things that I had received from those in the faith. Likewise, some things I had read in Valentine Rathbone's pamphlet, before ever I saw these people, I found were true; as the old believers, when I came to converse with them, gave the same account.—Therefore, from incontestible evidence, I was obliged to give some credit to what several, to all appearance, impartially and disinterestedly declared they had seen and heard while they were among these people. For there are many of them scattered about the country, according to what some of the old believers have told me, i. e. they said they "believed there were as many who had fell off, from first to last, as there were now in the faith." I now

† A certain celebrated author observes, that "in the infancy of a new religion, the learned esteem the matter too inconsiderable to claim their attention or regard; but, after they have increased, many wish to know their origin, but the witnesses that might have given satisfaction have perished beyond recovery; and no means of information remain but those which must be drawn from those who wish to support it."

began to believe that many of them had ſufficient reaſon for ſo doing. Many of theſe I knew by name that I had not yet ſeen.

Shortly after the diſcourſe with John Hodgſon, of which I have given an account, he adviſed me to endeavour to ſee Daniel Rathbone, jun. who lived at Milton, near forty miles north of Albany—who had been of this faith ſoon after their firſt ſettlement at Niſkeuna. He thus adviſed me, he ſaid, becauſe he had ſeen and converſed with him, and that he appeared to him to be a candid man; and he believed that he could and would give me a further, correct, and ſatisfactory account reſpecting the firſt Elders, and the faith and practice of the people while they were living. By inquiring, I learnt that D. Rathbone ſupported a good character; I accordingly ſoon wrote to him, requeſting him when he came to town to call and ſee me. Accordingly, a few weeks after I returned laſt from Lebanon, he came and tarried with me nearly two days, in which time he gave me all the information he could, according to the beſt of his knowledge.

Reſpecting what I had opened to Elder Hezekiah, of the conduct of the firſt Elders, he ſaid he was perſonally and well acquainted with them; as it was his office, by the order of Mother Ann, to act for them, particularly for her, as Deacon in temporal concerns; therefore, he he was repeatedly with them, and had ſeen her ſeveral times in an intoxicated condition.

I aſked him if he was ſure it was occaſioned by liquor?

He replied—"I am ſure. I bought the liquor by her order—I ſaw her drink the ſame. I have ſeen her overcome by it, and I have ſeen her vomit; and I knew ſhe was affected by it, not only by ſight, but by ſmelling.—William Lee and James Whittaker, I have ſeen ſit and drink for hours—though I never ſaw Whittaker ſo much overcome by it, as I have ſeen Lee and his half-ſiſter Ann."

As to quarrelling and fighting, he gave me a particular and circumſtantial account of two inſtances; one of which was as follows:

"One day," ſaid he, "in the afternoon, William Lee, having drank very freely, fell aſleep; when he awoke, he ordered the brethren (in number about twenty) to be aſſembled, I being one with them William Lee then informed us, that he had a gift to rejoice—and ordered us to ſtrip ourſelves naked; and as we ſtood ready to dance, Mother Ann Lee came to the door of the room with one of the ſiſters William Lee requeſted her to ſtay out, as he had a gift to rejoice with the brethren. Still ſhe perſiſted. He ſaid to her again, *Mother, do go out—I have got a gift to rejoice with the brethren; and why can't you let us rejoice? you know if any of the ſiſters are with us, we ſhall have war*, that is, have to fight againſt the riſing of nature. But as ſhe would not retire, he puſhed her out, and ſhut the door againſt her. Then ſhe went round the corner of the houſe, and attempted to get in at a window. Lee prevented her. She came to the door again, with a ſtick of wood, and ſtove it open. Lee met her at the door. She ſtruck him with her fiſts in the face. He ſaid, the ſmiting of the righteous is like precious ointment. She then gave him ſeveral blows in quick ſucceſſion. At each of which he made the ſame reply. At laſt, the blood beginning to run, he loſt all patience, and exclaimed, before God you abuſe me; and preſented his fiſts and ſtruck her, and knocked her almoſt down. I immediately ſtepped in between them, and cried out, for God's ſake, Father William, don't ſtrike Mother! I had rather you would ſtrike me. The brethren, who had ſtood waiting the event, then gathered round and prevented further blows. There was hard threatening on both ſides. Thus ended the gift of rejoicing."

The other inſtance of quarrelling and blows, of which he gave me a particular account, was between William Lee, James Whittaker, and Ann Lee; which contention aroſe from a diſpute between Lee and Whittaker, which ſhould be firſt in the lead, and Mother interfered to ſettle the controverſy.

I aſked him how it was poſſible that he could retain his faith, after ſeeing ſuch conduct?

He anſwered—" We were infatuated, and taught to believe that they were bearing our ſtates, and that it was the evil nature in us imputed or transferred to them; and that they had to ſuffer thus on our account, and to act that evil ſpirit and nature out, that we might have a viſible ſight of that which was ſtill ſecret within us; and we were exhorted to dig deep and look into our hearts, and labour to put away every thing contrary to the goſpel; ſo the evil ſpirit and nature would be caſt out of the church, and all would live in peace and quietneſs. Notwithſtanding theſe plauſible reaſons for ſuch conduct, ſeveral from that time began to loſe their faith, and finally fell off, one after another. I continued until the death of Ann Lee; then, on account of what I have mentioned, and other inconſiſtent conduct, I left them, notwithſtanding the Mother had told me, that my name was written in the book of life, never to be blotted out."

He referred me to five or ſix perſons whom he named, as being preſent when the above mentioned quarrels happened, who had alſo left the people. One of whom he ſaid was Reuben Rathbone, who has ſince publiſhed a ſhort account of his life among them; in which publication he has given an account of the ſame conduct.* Alſo, ſaid he,

" My father, Daniel Rathbone, who was one of the ſociety five years, and who left them and publiſhed an account of the faith, teſtifies that he ſaw Ann Lee ſeveral times intoxicated."†

He further ſaid—

" If you leave the people, and publiſh your life among them, and you write concerning the conduct in any reſpect, which I have mentioned of Ann Lee and the firſt Elders, you may, if you chooſe, make uſe of my name; as I know I have told you nothing but the truth.

* Reaſons offered for leaving the Shakers—page 27.

† Daniel Rathbone, of Ballſton, a man of veracity and good moral character. The author has ſince made him a viſit, and received from him (as well as from ſeveral others) a circumſtantial account in confirmation of the above.

"About thirty years hence, the church may hold Ann Lee up to the world, according to what they believe of her, as a person of the greatest sanctity, perfection, and holiness; and no one who was personally acquainted with her will be living to contradict it."

The man appeared to be so candid and free from prejudice, that I thought if all the believers at Niskeuna had been present and heard him give the account of his life among the people, their faith, and conduct of the first Elders and others, they could not have doubted the truth of his relation. For my part I could not.

The account which he gave exactly corresponded, in several respects, with what I had heard from the Elders and others in the faith. I thought I had reason to believe his account of Mother and the first Elders, from what I had heard some of the old believers say of Mother's bearing the states of the people, even the state of the drunkard—and one had told me that he himself and several others had borne the same state.

I also knew, from what I had seen myself, that spirituous liquors were used by the church above six months after I joined it; when there came a gift, as the believers called it, from the ministration to use them no longer, except as a medicine. I told some of the believers, I thought that was a very good gift. I also now recollected what some old believers had told me, that previously to the above mentioned time the church had used spirituous liquors, and that it was often bought by the hogshead. Also, I had heard an esteemed old believer say, that spirituous liquors were used by the first Elders, and that it was necessary for a support under their sufferings and hard labours; as they had a great work to do to open and establish the gospel. But when I heard this, I was strong in the faith, and did not believe they used it to excess; though I even then thought that the use of spirituous liquor did not become gospel labourers. I now thought I had sufficient reason to be fully convinced, that the assertion which I had so often heard, that "backsliders cannot speak the truth," was absurd and inconsistent. I also considered, that I had reason to believe that there had been a want of rectitude of conduct in the first Elders and others in the faith, from what I had often heard from several of the society, which was more fully and clearly stated by B. Youngs; on my mentioning to him some reprehensible conduct that had been in the church, he said,

" We know there has been many things done and said " by the people, for want of a better understanding; and " we believe several have lost their faith and left us, who, " if they had been wisely dealt by, would have continu- " ed. Admitting it to be true, that the first or any of " the present leaders in the church, or any of the old be- " lievers, have done wrong, you should not let that hurt " your faith, and destroy your own soul; but you should " still travail on with the people, (as they profess to be in a " travail,) for as soon as they see they have erred, or done " wrong, they will put their errors away and mend; and " you know they are daily endeavouring to learn and " improve—and that they have travailed into a farther " increase of wisdom, understanding, and purity of con- " duct, is clearly manifested when we have compared " the church and the order therein with what it was in " first Mother's day. There were many things done then, " that the church has no union with now.* It was some- " time after the opening of the gospel before the church " was brought into order; and previous to that time " there was much confusion.

" The people or church of God, may properly be " compared to natural creation, which is believed to have " been from a chaotic state; and God is represented as " having been six days in creating and bringing all things " into order; it is also the same in creation, for nothing " grows to perfection in a moment; and it is also the " same in building a house, or constructing any machine, " each part naturally lies in apparent confusion till the " artist brings them together, and puts each one in its " proper place; then the beauty of the machinery and " the wisdom of the artist are apparent. Therefore, the

* I understood from one of the believers, that Elder Ebenezer Cooley had said, "That dancing naked and several other gifts " that had been in the church, were not gifts of God, but that " the people ran wild before they were brought into order."

" church is fitly compared to Solomon's temple: God " is the great artist and master-builder, the gospel is the " means, the ministration are his labourers, and are in-" struments under his direction, and we must labour in " union with them to cast away all rubbish out of, and " from around the building; and to labour to bring ev-" ery thing, both outward and inward, more and more " into order. Therefore, if a true written description " had been given of this building, i. e the church, and " faith and practice of the people, twenty years ago, it " would not be, in every respect, a true description in the " present day. Also, if a correct description of the pre-" sent standing of the church was now written, it would " not be, in all respects, applicable to it twenty years to " come, on account, as I said, of the church continually " increasing in wisdom, upright conduct, and order.— " Therefore, it is not wisdom in you to condemn the " church, and cast yourself off, for wrongs that have " been, or that you see now, in individuals, (or indeed " in the whole body) proceeding from a want of wis-" dom; when, at the same time, it is their intention, af-" ter they have attained more wisdom or a better under-" standing, to see wherein they have erred, or done wrong, " to renounce the error and put away all wrong, and la-" bour to do better for the time to come. Which you " must acknowledge is truly commendable and praise-" worthy; for creatures cannot travail out of errors and " wrong practices faster than God pleases to enlighten " them. Again, that may not be error or wrong prac-" tice in us at one time, which may become so at anoth-" er time, when we have attained to more light and un-" derstanding. The increase of light makes objects to " be more clearly seen; and this travail, of which I " have been speaking, will last eternally; for to suppose " a creature ever to arrive at a state in which he will not " err, would be to suppose him perfect, or infinite in wis-" dom, and therefore equal with God; which state of " equality no creature can ever attain."

When I heard this statement, I thought the most of it was very good. I considered, that to forsake every thing that is wrong, as soon as we come to a knowledge of its being ſuch, is all that can be required. I told them if this had been their fundamental principle, I believed I ſhould always have united with them; for, on the principles of the above ſtatement, they themſelves would relinquiſh an error as ſoon as they came to a knowledge of it as being ſuch—and I could not expect them to do it before. I thought that a ſociety could not poſſeſs better principles nor form a better plan to act upon, than as above ſtated. At the ſame time, I obſerved, that it was a pity they had ever laid any other foundation to build upon and find acceptance with God, but his grace, and a due improvement in the practice of good works. Further, on the principle of the above ſtatement I thought they might ſoon give up their faith in Mother Ann, as being equal with Chriſt, for a great error. I told them if they did, then all their practices in the infancy of the church might ſink into oblivion; becauſe, neither Mother Ann, nor any thing which had been tranſacted in time paſt, could affect their preſent faith, and need not be produced as evidence for or againſt it. But notwithſtanding, they tenaciouſly adhered to their faith in Mother Ann, as a foundation; and more and more increaſed in it as a doctrinal point.* Therefore, in direct oppoſition to the principles and reaſons in the above ſtatement, they would have it, that if what I had ſtated to Elder Hezekiah was the truth, they were, as he ſaid, a deluded people, and on a ſandy foundation. The principal reaſons which were offered in proof of the divine miſſion of Mother Ann, have been already mentioned, in page 180.

The following is the reſult of the converſations I have had with ſeveral; and my thoughts and concluſions reſpecting thoſe operations I had ſeen among the people, and ſome of which, as heretofore mentioned, I had had myſelf; as about this time I became ſatisfied reſpecting their cauſe, and from what they originated.

* In a book ſince publiſhed by the Shakers, entitled "The ſecond appearing of Chriſt," more than ſixty pages are taken up in endeavouring to prove and ſubſtantiate this doctrine. See pages 27 and 28, preface; pages 433 to 473, and 537 to 554.

I had, for some time past, thought that the Elders themselves did not believe those operations proceeded from the immediate power of God. The first time I had reason to think so, was about a year past—while Elder Ebenezer was preaching, one shook, stamped, and trembled so as to attract the attention of the audience; he made a stop in his discourse and said, in an accent of disapprobation, "The wild nature may stamp and tremble." Of this I took particular notice.

Sometime after, in conversation with Elder Hezekiah concerning these operations, I told him I did not believe that the Elders themselves believed them to be caused by the power of God.

He replied—"Nay, I do not believe they all are; but "I would not have you think none are."

I concluded he gave this answer from a fear that if he made a full acknowledgment of the truth of what I had told him, it would have affected my faith; because I had been taught to believe that they proceeded from the power of God—and had been under their influence myself.

When I became satisfied they were not caused by the power of God, I was desirous to know from what cause they took their rise. After much consideration on the subject, I came to the following conclusions:

Those who are subject to these operations have faith in them, and a strong belief that they feel the power of God operating to produce them; and the nerves, which are the organs of sensation and motion, become at once affected, which causes a trembling, or operations according to the affected state of the mind.*

Often the operations are only caused by the act of the will, which is wrought upon by a strong imagination of feeling the power of God.

I also became satisfied that even the extraordinary operation of turning round in the rapid manner in which I had seen several turn, was caused by the same power of imagination, zeal, enthusiastic fire, or rather religious

* "One reels to this, another to that wall,
'Tis the same error that deceives them all."

madneſs, whereby the nerves which proceed, and paſs from the brain to all parts of the body, are affected, and brought into contact with the mind, in its ſtrong imagination of feeling the power of God; and a ſtrong belief in this operation, with a paſſiveneſs of mind, or willingneſs to be thus affected, they begin to turn; and ſo long as the power of imagination and zeal remains, ſo long the perſon can turn. But as I had told ſeveral of the believers, it ought to be particularly noticed that this deſcribed ſtate of mind, aſſiſts them to learn to turn in this manner, and that they don't turn long at firſt, but according to the time and trials they have practiſed: and it is well known that long uſe and repeated trials, with a ſtrong imagination, will perform wonders.

Reſpecting ſuch as ſpeak in an unknown tongue, they have ſtrong faith in this gift; and think a perſon greatly favoured who has the gift of tongues; and at certain times, when the mind is overloaded with a fiery, ſtrong zeal, it muſt have vent ſome way or other; their faith, or belief at the time being in this gift, and a will ſtrikes the mind according to their faith; and then ſuch break out in a fiery, energetick manner, and ſpeak they know not what, as I have done ſeveral times. Part of what I ſpake at one time, was:—

Liero devo jirankemango, ad ſileabano, durem ſubramo, deviranto diacerimango, jaſſe vah pe cri evanigalio; de vom grom ſeb crinom, os vare cremo domo.

When a perſon runs on in this manner of ſpeaking for any length of time, I now thought it probable that he would ſtrike into different languages, and give ſome words in each, their right pronunciation. As I have heard ſome men of learning, who have been preſent, ſay, a few words were Hebrew, three or four of Greek, and a few Latin.

I had often heard of inſtances of the Elders taking the power away from individuals while under exceſſive operations. I inquired, if they were under the power of God, how could the Elders command that power?

I was anſwered—"The Elders have the greater, and "the leſs gives way to it, according to what we read— "The ſpirit of the prophets are ſubject to the prophets."

I likewise had been told, that "the Elders could give the power, as well as take it away."

But as I began to consider for myself, and reason on the propriety of every thing I saw and heard, it appeared to me that the truth was respecting the Elders giving and taking away the power, that as they have an implicit faith in the Elders, therefore, when they inform the believers that they must labour out of, and travail away from all those outward operations, and that there is no longer a gift therefor, they then cease, because then they believe the power of God ceases in those operations therefore, they have no desire nor will for them, knowing if they have, they will be out of the gift, and that the Elders will have no union with them therein; a acting in union with the Elders, is a fundamental point of faith.

The many other operations, with visions and miracles that are said to have been in the church from time to time, it appeared to me, as I calmly considered of them that they proceeded from the same cause as above described, i. e. in short, a strong belief and imagination, and oftentimes, a species of insanity; and with others as with myself, when I had those operations (and faith in those gifts and miracles) reason was entirely excluded.

I had now lost that which had caused me to think favourable of the first Elders, particularly of James Whittaker; namely, that beautiful and comprehensive description of christian experience,* said to have been written by him, as by this time I learnt that the letter which contained it, was not indited by him, but by William Skails, who was then a member of the society, and a man of much reading and education, who, soon after he indited the letter, left the society.

This work will exceed the limits at first prescribed yet I must not omit mentioning the result of some conversations with believers respecting the assertion which had been frequently made, that "the church did what "was just and right in all cases."† It appeared to me

* See page 40.

† See page 24, answer 11.

from what I had obſerved, that the church was faulty reſpecting the manner in which they had acquired much property; that is, by what they call a united intereſt I obſerved it was my belief, that, if any one loſt his faith, or for ſome cauſe choſe to leave the ſociety, the property he had depoſited, ought to be returned; and for the labour he had faithfully performed, he ought to be compenſated; that no one ought to be obliged to leave them poor and pennyleſs. I alſo told them, that the children of ſuch parents as had joined the church, whether they had been left with the world, or had gone forth into it after having been brought up in the ſociety, ought to have an equal, juſt, and lawful dividend of their parents' property, the ſame as they would have had, if their parents had never joined the ſociety. My reaſons for this, I obſerved, were, that it would be highly unjuſt, and might, with propriety, be deemed perſecution for any to ſuffer loſs of property on account of his belief or diſbelief in matters of religion.

Theſe points were controverted and diſputed in the uſual way.

They obſerved that—" All the church came together " into one joint body perfectly agreed, and thinking alike " in ſpiritual things; and in order that temporal things " might not interfere and diſturb them in their ſpiritual " and religious concerns, it was thought beſt, in conform- " ity to the example of the firſt chriſtians, to come into " what is called, a united intereſt. Therefore, of their " own free will and choice, all who had property, gave " it up; and each one, and all agreed to labour and " perform ſervices according to their ſeveral abilities, for " the common ſupport of the goſpel, without any pecun- " iary reward. Accordingly, they ſigned a written cov- " enant to that effect, binding themſelves not to bring " any debt or demand againſt the deacons or any mem- " ber of the church, for their property or ſervices."— Furthermore, they plead, that—" What had been freely " given, could not be remanded, or diverted from the " purpoſe for which it was given, without the free will " and conſent of the perſon or perſons to whom it had " been voluntarily reſigned." Alſo—" Thoſe who had

" left the way of God, for the world, had obtained what " they went after: they had chosen the pleasures of the " world, and that was enough for them. That if they " had carried their property with them, or had any thing " given them for their labours, it would have been to " consume it upon their lusts" And some of them said— " That it was no matter how poor they might become; " they ought to suffer for leaving the way of God. For " they have no right to any property, nor compensation " for their labours, which they have freely given up; " and they cannot, with any reasonable confidence, de- " mand it." Notwithstanding, they mentioned some who had been faithful labourers for ten, fifteen, or eighteen years; and that the church had given them something, i e. about ten dollars per year. But I believed, that even that was done, especially in some cases, to avoid contention, and a law suit with them, which some had threatened them, and in order to get from them a final discharge.

It is true these men had signed a covenant, as above mentioned, by which they had formally debarred themselves from receiving their property, or any compensation for their labours; but I considered, as they were not, and probably could not be incorporated under such a constitution, the covenant was null and void. I suspected the leaders were sensible of this, which was the occasion of their being allowed any compensation.

I contended that even admitting the covenant was binding in law, nevertheless, such as had been faithful labourers to support, and build up the society in temporal things, but could not continue in their belief of the doctrines of the church, ought in justice to be compensated for their labours. Though the covenant might be right so far as to debar any who left them from making unjust demands, or taking undue advantages of them, and I considered it just respecting property in no other point of light.

I reminded them, that in the early part of my faith, I was told several times that " people who joined them, " could live where they chose; and that man and wife " might live together, if they thought best so to do; and "in all civil things, act and think for themselves; and "that not any were disowned on any other account, "but by continuing in the practice of what they knew "to be sin."* Also, that "none were enjoined to en-"ter into a united interest and give up their property."† But now I know, said I, that they will not be held in union long, unless they move among believers, gather into a united interest, give up their property, and in all respects, act according to the counsel of the Elders.

I thought I should have been more satisfied, if I had had a deceitful memory. Though I united with them in several points of their faith, yet, in order to gather my union with the believers, as the Elders had counselled me, it was actually necessary for me to believe that I could be saved in no other way than by obedience to the Elders; and in order to this, I must believe, that the reign of Christ on earth had commenced in the way and manner which they had taught. But it appeared to me that the scripture prophecies on the subject of what is called the millennium, had no more reference or relation to this church, than to any other, even if first Mother, father William, and father James, as they call them, had been exemplary, pious persons. Therefore according to what I had once told Elder Hezekiah, the more I examined the scriptures, the more I doubted their being in the millennium; and that I had reason to believe that many of those who professed to be strong in the faith, even some of the leaders, had at times their doubts, exercises and trials about it, as well as myself and others.

Having thus considered all things appertaining to this faith, I now concluded and was satisfied, that this could not be that clear dispensation pointed out in the scriptures, in which God would pour out his spirit upon all flesh, and all should know the Lord, and no cause remain for doubts and exercise of mind respecting the truth of it. Nevertheless, I did not doubt but that those of

* See page 18, answer 5. Page 19, answer 6.

† Page 24, answer 10.

this ſociety, who ſincerely believed,* and were careful to forſake all evil, would, through the mercy of God, be ſaved. But I concluded I could not be ſaved by a religion, the fundamental points of which I did not believe, and thought it would be the higheſt wiſdom in me, to "take heed to the things" I believed to be right, for that only will bring a man peace at the laſt.†

It may here be obſerved, that many who had joined the ſociety, having firmly believed as I did, that they had entered the latter day glory, which had ſo long been the ſubject of propheſy and prayer; and afterwards having cauſe to believe to the contrary, met with a mortification and diſappointment, of which thoſe who never received this faith, can form no adequate idea. It appeared to me that ſome, rather than brook the diſappointment, were determined to believe,‡ and refuſed to hear any thing to the contrary,§ and appeared to be as happy as if they were really in the millennium.

Several who had been members of the ſociety, and who had left it, had obſerved to me, that it was with the greateſt reluctance. I had alſo heard the believers ſay, that when they were not reconciled, and had thoughts of leaving the people, they felt very diſtreſſed. I had experienced the ſame. One cauſe of which was, having heard ſo much of the direful conſequences of

* "Error," ſays Dr. Price, "when involuntary, is innocent; and all that is required of us, as a condition of acceptance, is faithfully endeavouring to find out and practiſe truth and right."—*Sermons, page* 265.

† "No way whatever," ſays Locke, "that I ſhall walk in againſt the dictates of my conſcience, will ever bring me to the manſions of the bleſſed. I may grow rich by an art that I take no delight in—I may be cured of ſome diſeaſes by remedies I have no faith in—but I cannot be ſaved by a religion I diſtruſt."

‡ "Sic ſentio, ſic ſentiam, i. e. ſo I believe, and ſo I will believe is the priſon of the ſoul for life time, and a bar againſt all the improvement of the mind."

§ "Some perſons are ſo confident they are in the right, that they will not come within the hearing of any notions but their own: they canton out to themſelves a little province in the intellectual world, where they fancy the light ſhines, and all the reſt are in darkneſs." *Watts on the Mind.*

resisting the testimony of the Elders, and of the woful state of backsliders; my mind had become so affected with it, and habituated to it, that I and others were filled with the most fearful apprehensions, which I found that nothing but an appeal to candid, fair, unbiassed reason, could conquer. But this reluctance and distress, and those fearful apprehensions, had been considered by the believers, as a proof that the dispensation they were under, was the only way of God. But I concluded the cause undoubtedly took its rise as above metioned: and also from having had a long acquaintance and intimacy with each other, and in the mean time, the Elders having used every exertion to unite them together in love and friendship, their affections had become closely attached to each other; and when that is the case, it is the same in other societies, or among other people when they part, or any thing takes place that thwarts their affections.

I shall now proceed a little further with my narration. Since I returned last from Lebanon, as I did not attend their meetings, nor manifest any further faith, therefore, in about three months after, the Elders testified to the believers, their disunion with me; and sometime after, when they found I showed no inclination to return, they charged them not to harbour, or welcome me in their houses, if I came to see them; nor to have any conversation with me, as I would hand out that which would be poison to their souls; and that as I had turned from the way of God myself, I would endeaour to lead others after me. They also forbid their stopping at my house in passing and repassing, as they had done before. These things I was informed of, soon after, by B. Youngs, Derick Veeder, Frederick Wicker, William Richardson, Hannah Train, my wife's sister Macee Everitt, and several other believers. I was also told by several, that those with whom the Elders have no union, the believers must have no union; and that as they wished to be obedient to every gift of God the Elders had for them, they were sorry that they could not fellowship me any longer; and wished me not to come to see them, or visit them: (these things were hard.) I was told that the

Elders believed that I knew it was the way of God I had turned from, and therefore, was the leſs excuſable. I was alſo told of my loſt, dark, miſerable ſtate and condition.

As to their teſtifying their diſunion with me (which is the way they diſown perſons from being conſidered as members of the ſociety) it was no great mortification to me, for which I did not blame them, as I thought it time we had parted, as to my making profeſſion with them; but then, as I ſtill had a friendly regard for the people, particularly thoſe with whom I had had a long and intimate acquaintance, and with whom I had had much converſation, believing moſt of them were ſincere, I wiſhed to part as friends, and if we could not agree in every point of faith and doctrine, I wiſhed to agree as neighbours, friends, and fallible mortals; and not by any means, deſpiſe, execrate, and ſhut doors againſt each other; but to endeavour to live in the conſtant exerciſe of love, pity, and kindneſs.

"To err is human; to forgive, divine."

Almighty God! creator of the univerſe: Father and friend of all the human race! look down on us, thine erring creatures. Pity us under our darkneſs and imperfections. Enlighten our minds. Enable us to ſearch and find out truth and right. Baniſh from our hearts the bitterneſs of cenſure. Cheriſh in our minds a diſpoſition to treat thoſe who differ from us, with kindneſs. Give us a ſpirit of forbearance and love towards all our fellow creatures. To our zeal, add knowledge; and to our, knowledge, charity. Make us humble under the difficulties that adhere to our faith; and patient under the perplexities which accompany our practice. *Lead and guide us by thy ſpirit;* and when all the viciſſitudes, changes and trying ſcenes of this life are over and done with, grant that we may all meet in ſome better ſtate of exiſtence.

END OF PART SECOND.

A BRIEF

# HISTORY

OF THE

# Rise and Progress

OF THE

# PEOPLE CALLED SHAKERS:

IN WHICH THE MOST SINGULAR OCCURRENCES
THAT HAVE TAKEN PLACE AMONG
THEM, ARE PLAINLY
DECLARED.

A BRIEF

# HISTORY, &c.

THE people called Shakers, who are the subject of this history, hold all churches that are under the protection of the civil power, to be churches of anti-christ, that is, all the established national churches in the world, without exception. They also hold, that the apostolic church gradually degenerated, and finally became a church of anti-christ, under the favour and protection of Constantine, the Roman emperor. But at the same time, they profess to believe that God has, in every age, raised up witnesses to bear testimony against sin and the power of anti-christ. These witnesses have been those who were called heretics, and who were persecuted as such by the established churches. When any of these heretics were suppressed by those churches, or lost their power by seeking the patronage of the civil authority, or forming a connexion with an established church, God raised up others in their place.

The people called Quakers, they assert, were raised up to be true witnesses for God, and to prepare the way for the second coming of Christ; and that they were the last of the witnesses who were put to death for their testimony. But that they also lost their power by petitioning the civil authority for a redress of grievances, and by coming under its protection. After them, they say, a people known by the name of the French prophets were raised up, and endued with the true spirit of prophesy; and that they were the two witnesses mentioned by St. John, who "after three days and an half," i. e. twelve hundred and ſixty years, " ſtood upon their feet,"* i. e. were not ſlain or perſecuted unto death. They alſo affirm that the prophetic teſtimony of the two witneſſes reſpecting the ſecond coming of Chriſt ended, as the time which theſe prophets had foretold ſoon commenced; for this reaſon, that is, becauſe the Shakers profeſs to believe that thoſe prophets were the laſt, and had the greateſt ſhare of the ſpirit of propheſy, and were particularly forerunners of, and preparatory to the ſecond coming of Chriſt, as profeſſed by them,† it may be neceſſary to give a ſhort account of the riſe of thoſe prophets, and their moſt noted proceedings.

They firſt appeared in Dauphiny and the Cevennes, in France, about the year 1688; in a few years, ſeveral hundred Proteſtants profeſſed to be inſpired; their bodies were much agitated with various operations. When they were receiving the ſpirit of propheſy, they trembled, ſtaggered, and fell down and lay as if they were dead. They recovered twitching, ſhaking, and crying to God for mercy for themſelves and for all mankind; not only in their aſſemblies, but at other times. After they had been under agitations of body, they would begin to propheſy, crying repent, the end of all things is near at hand. The Cevennes hills and mountains reſounded with their loud cries for mercy, and denunciations of judgments againſt all the churches and their prieſts, with predictions of the downfall of Popery. Their aſſemblies conſiſted of ſeveral hundreds, and ſome of them of two or three thouſand perſons. Theſe were the perſecuted Huguenots who were ſubdued in 1705, when three of them, namely, Elias Marlon, John Cavilier, and Durand Fage, repaired to London, where they alſo began to propheſy, with the like operations and ecſtacies, as in France. The French refugees, thinking themſelves ſcandalized at the behaviour of their countrymen, were authorized by the Biſhop of London, as ſuperior of the French congregations, to inquire into the miſſion of theſe prophets. They were declared impoſtors. Notwithſtanding this deciſion, which was confirmed by the Biſhops, they continued their aſ-

* See page 123. † See page 124.

ſemblies in Soho, under the countenance of Sir Richard Bulkley and John Lacy. They teſtified againſt the miniſters of the eſtabliſhed church. They denounced judgments againſt the city of London, and the whole Britiſh nation.

Marſon, Cavilier, and Fage, were perſecuted as falſe prophets and diſturbers of the public peace, and were ſentenced to pay a fine of twenty marks each, and ſtand on a ſcaffold with papers on their breaſts denoting their offence: A ſentence which was executed accordingly at Charing-croſs and the Royal Exchange. But theſe proceedings had no tendency to ſtop their progreſs: in about a year, there were ſeveral hundreds of both ſects, in and about London, who united with them. They had numerous meetings about the ſkirts of the city; there was to be ſeen the prophet proſtrate, as if expiring, or elſe like one out of his mind, mute, ſweating, trembling, at length beginning to rave and foam at the mouth, and uttering certain unintelligible expreſſions. Numbers of them had various ſigns on their bodies, particularly ſhaking and ſtaggering; and they declared that the impulſes of the ſpirit were ſuch, that they were forced to ſpeak, which ſeveral would do one after another—teſtifying againſt all the churches, and propheſying the downfall of Babylon, and near approach of the kingdom of Chriſt, or the millennium ſtate—that the Lord Jeſus was ſoon again to be revealed, (for which they would heartily pray) and that the whole creation ſhould appear in its primitive beauty, and man regain the perfection of Adam, and his immediate communion with God—and that this great reſtoration ſhould be brought about by the ſpirit of God—and that they were as a voice to bid the world prepare for the coming of the bridegroom, that they might get on the wedding garment, and ſo go in to the marriage feaſt, the ſupper of the Lamb. They ſpake of the new heavens, the new earth, the firſt reſurrection, and the New Jeruſalem deſcending from above. Alſo, that this great work was to be wrought by a ſpiritual power proceeding from the mouths of thoſe who ſhould, by the gift of the ſpirit, be ſent forth in great numbers to labour in the vineyard; and that their miſſion ſhould be atteſted by ſigns from heaven, and the deſtruction of the wick-ed univerſally, as by famine, peſtilence, and earthquakes; and that all the works of men being deſtroyed, there ſhould remain nothing but what was good, when there ſhould be one Lord, one faith, and one teſtimony among mankind.

They endeavoured to ſupport their predictions by the many ſcripture propheſies concerning the millennium, or reign of Chriſt, and univerſal peace on earth. This meſ-ſage, they ſaid, they were to proclaim to every nation under heaven, beginning firſt at England. In order to this, they profeſſed to have the gift of languages, and power to convey the ſame gift and ſpirit to others.—They alſo profeſſed to diſcern the ſecrets of the heart, and to have power to work miracles, even to the raiſing of the dead. They appointed a time for reſtoring a cer-tain Dr. Wells to life. Vaſt numbers crowded to the place, where they waited for the expected miracle till their credulity became a jeſt. They alſo predicted that they ſhould perform many other miraculous things.

They teſtified, that all the great things, of which they propheſied reſpecting the millennium, would be made known over all the earth within three years. They alſo declared, that if the power of God did not atteſt to the work before the twenty-ninth of April next, they would own themſelves deluded.

An anonymous author, who has written what he has entitled, an impartial account of the prophets, ſays, "they erred by fixing a time," as above mentioned, "which was not given them to know." The ſaid author was perſonally acquainted with them, though not one of them; and he appears to have taken much pains to examine in-to their miſſion, lives, and characters. He ſays,

"They were ſuppoſed to be mad when they had their extatic fits; but then they would argue with brighter reaſon than out of them; deliver diſcourſes very elegant and long; aſk or anſwer queſtions with wonderful pro-priety and wiſdom, even exceeding their natural capaci-ty." Alſo that "they were men of ſober lives and con-verſations, and of good characters among their neigh-bours." They were generally ſuch as had been accounted plain, honeſt, well-meaning people." "That they all practiſed in private what they performed and taught in public, viz. a zeal for God and his holineſs, and conſtant prayers and praiſes to him." "They were deſpiſed and perſecuted, but they appeared to be humbly reſigned to the will of God, and to have a ſincere love to their neighbour."

Several of theſe prophets went from London to Scotland, and afterwards to Holland, where the magiſtrates committed them to priſon.*

James Wardley (a taylor by trade) and Jane, his wife, perſons of obſcure birth and contracted fortune, lived at Bolton, county of Lancaſhire, in England, and belonged to the people called Quakers; but receiving the peculiar ſpirit of the French prophets, they joined with them in teſtifying againſt all the churches then in ſtanding. Like thoſe prophets, they profeſſed to have viſions and revelations of the downfall of the kingdom of anti-chriſt, and that the ſecond coming of Chriſt, or millennium, as propheſied of in the ſcriptures, was then actually commencing.

However ſingular this might have appeared, yet there were not wanting perſons of credulity enough to believe it, particularly ſuch as had been with, or who believed the predictions of the French prophets. Several of theſe and others were added to them; and in 1747,†, they were formed into a ſmall ſociety, without any eſtabliſhed creed or particular manner of worſhip, as they profeſſed to be only beginning to learn the new and living way of complete ſalvation, which had long been the ſubject of propheſy; and therefore they profeſſed to be reſigned, to be led and governed, from time to time, as the ſpirit of God might dictate.

* Smollet's Hiſtory of England—Cunningham's Hiſtory of Great Britain—Chauncy's work. Impartial Account of the Prophets—H. Adams' View of Religions—Dr. Calamy's Commentaries on the New Prophets—J. Moſer's Anecdotes.

† See page 122.

The principal members of this infant sect were John Townley, by trade a mason, of Manchester, and his wife, and John Kattis. John Townley was wealthy, and very liberal in helping the needy of his society, most of whom were poor. Kattis was said to be a scholar; but did not long retain his faith. The others were illiterate. Shortly after Townley and his wife joined the society, Wardley and his wife, being poor, removed from Bolton, twelve miles from Manchester, and lived with Townley. Meetings were frequently held under the ministry of Wardley and his wife. Wardley's wife was called Mother; to her confession of sins were made, though it was not so much yet insisted upon. She had the principal lead in their meetings, which were generally held at Townley's. At which meetings they sometimes sat silent a short space, then they would be seized with violent and tremulous motions, during which they would express their detestation against sin, and its contrariety to the divine nature. Sometimes their whole bodies would shake as if forcibly agitated by a strong hand; then they would sing and shout for the downfall of the anti-christian powers, and make signs, and walk swiftly and jostle against one another; they would jump violently, and shiver for a considerable length of time. Hence, as appropriate names for them, they were called shiverers by some, and jumpers by others.

In the year 1757, Ann Lee joined their society, by confessing her sins to Jane Wardley. She was the daughter of John Lee, blacksmith, of Manchester, (who was brother to Charles Lee, a celebrated general in the American army in the revolutionary war with Great Britain. He also had a brother who was alderman of Algate Ward, and sheriff of London.) She was born about the year 1735. There is no cause to believe that her childhood or youth was marked with any uncommon event, or that she joined any religious society, till the period above mentioned. A short time before, she was married to Abraham Standley, a blacksmith, who had worked at the same trade with her father—her occupation was a cutter of hatter's fur.

She had eight children, who all died in infancy, moſtly occaſioned by hard labour; her laſt child was extracted by forceps; after which, for ſeveral hours, ſhe lay with but little appearance of life. After ſhe recovered, on account of her thus ſuffering, and the unkind treatment of her huſband, who was much given to inebriety, ſhe declared that ſhe would never have any more carnal intercourſe with man. And ſoon after ſhe profeſſed to receive, by revelation, a knowledge of the man of ſin, the root of all evil; the gratification of which nature, ſhe ſaid, was the ſin and cauſed the fall of Adam and Eve. Then ſhe began her teſtimony againſt marriage and ſexual intercourſe. Here it may be obſerved, that previouſly to this they had held to marriage; but as they had no union with the reſt of mankind in any of their proceedings, ſeveral were married by Jane Wardley, or declared to be man and wife by her, after their promiſes to each other before her and others of the ſociety; Wardley having retained ſomething like the mode of marriage which they had learnt of the Quakers, ſome were married afterwards according to law, to render their children legitimate.

Theſe people uniting with Ann in her teſtimony againſt the luſt of the fleſh, (as they called it) acknowledged ſhe had received the greateſt gift; and from that time, which was about the year 1771, ſhe was owned as the ſpiritual Mother, and took the lead of the ſociety.

Four or five years before that time, John Partington, of Mayor-town, received their teſtimony and joined the ſociety; and alſo John Hocknell, of Cheſhire, (twenty-four miles from Mancheſter) who was brother to Townley's wife. They were both illiterate men, but poſſeſſed conſiderable property, and being zealous in the cauſe, they did conſiderable towards ſupporting the poor of the ſociety. Hannah, Hocknell's wife, at firſt was much oppoſed, but after ſome time alſo joined the ſociety.—Partington and Hocknell had both been noted men among the French prophets.

The believers,* as they were now called, in paſſing and repaſſing from Mancheſter to John Hocknell's, often held meetings at Partington's, and likewiſe at Hocknell's.

Ann Standley, now called Mother Ann, profeſſed to have the gift of languages, the gift of healing, and profeſſed to diſcern the ſecrets of the heart, and to be wholly actuated by the inviſible power of God; and that ſhe had attained a ſtate of ſinleſs perfection She aſſerted that ſhe was the one ſpoken of in the twelfth chap. of Rev.; and that ſhe had immediate revelations for all ſhe delivered. She teſtified that then was the eleventh hour, and all thoſe who rejected her teſtimony would reject the counſel of God againſt themſelves, like unto the unbelieving Jews.

After ſhe was acknowledged Mother, various operations increaſed, (like thoſe which had been among the French prophets, who by this time had become extinct.) Their exerciſes in their meetings were ſinging, dancing, ſhouting, ſhaking, ſpeaking tongues, (or ſpeaking what no one underſtood) and propheſying of the downfall of all the anti-chriſtian churches, and the increaſe of that kingdom in which they profeſſed to be. Alſo, teſtifying againſt ſin, and preaching up the neceſſity of confeſſion of ſins, which were now principally made to Mother Ann.

Shortly after ſhe took the lead of the people, ſhe was taken from one of their meetings by a number of people, at the head of whom was a civil officer, who committed her to the dungeon of the priſon-houſe; the next day ſhe was taken out and put into Bedlam, where ſhe was confined ſeveral weeks and then diſcharged.†

About this time William Lee, Ann's half-brother, a blackſmith by trade, James Whittaker, a weaver, and James Shepard, a ſhoemaker, likewiſe joined them — Lee and Whittaker were very zealous in the cauſe, and

* Called Believers becauſe they believed in a new diſpenſation, or the ſecond coming of Chriſt.

† See page 46.

ſoon became pillars with Mother Ann in the work; and were firſt called Elders, and ſometime afterwards were acknowledged as Fathers.

In theyear 1772, there were about thirty perſons who belonged to this ſociety, though there had many more joined it, but they had fell off. There then appeared to be no proſpect of any further increaſe, as the people in general diſbelieved in their teſtimony. About that time Mother Ann profeſſed to receive a gift, or revelation from God to repair to America. She propheſied of a great increaſe and permanent eſtabliſhment of the church and work of God in this country. Accordingly, as many as firmly believed in her teſtimony, and could ſettle their temporal concerns and furniſh neceſſaries for the voyage, concluded to follow her. They procured a paſſage at Liverpool, and arrived at New-York, Auguſt, 1774. Thoſe who came with the Mother were her huſband, Abraham Standley, though he did not believe in the miſſion of his wife, and of courſe was not a member of the ſociety, William Lee, James Whittaker, John Partington, and Mary his wife, John Hocknell, James Shepard, and one Ann Lee the Mother's niece.

John Townley, before mentioned, loſt his faith of the ſecond coming of Chriſt, as did ſeveral others; and ſhortly after the above named perſons left England, James Wardley and his wife removed from Townley's and rented a houſe, but not being able to ſupport themſelves, were taken into the alms-houſe, where they ended their days. Thus the ſociety in England was broken up.

After their arrival at New-York, being ſtrangers in the country, and rather deſtitute in their circumſtances, they made application to ſome of the ſociety called Quakers, for counſel and advice, and received for anſwer, that the beſt thing they could do would be to repair to Albany, and leaſe a tract of land ſome where near that city, and ſettle on it. After this, Hocknell, Whittaker, and Partington, made an excurſion to the northward in order to take a view of the country, and to find a place of ſettlement. They at laſt concluded to ſettle at Niſkeuna, ſince named Watervliet, though generally known by the firſt name. Partington and Hocknell contracted each for a ſmall farm, already ſettled.

The early part of next year, Hocknell embarked for England—and returned with his wife and four children, (namely, Richard, Francis, Mary, and Hannah; Francis was his youngeſt and laſt child he had, born Sept. 15, 1767; he had ten children, ſix of whom he left in England.)

By the ſpring of 1776, Hocknell with his family, and all thoſe who came over firſt, became ſettled at Niſkeuna, except Standley, Ann's huſband, who left her while ſhe tarried at New-York. They had alſo leaſed in perpetuity ſeveral hundred acres of unimproved land joining Hocknell's farm; and by the fall of the ſame year they had built a log-houſe, where their principal ſettlement now is—where Mother Ann, Elders Lee, Whittaker, and Shepard, fixed their place of reſidence, and where they held their meetings. Here they abode in the wilderneſs, much unnoticed and unknown, three or four excepted, who were mechanics and neceſſitated to ſeek employment abroad in order to provide ſuſtenance for their common ſupport. William Lee worked at the trade of a blackſmith, and James Shepard at ſhoe making, in Albany, until they became better circumſtanced at Niſkeuna; in the mean time, thither they reſorted, particularly on the Sabbath, to attend meetings.

In the year 1779, at New-Lebanon and adjacent parts there was much of a religious awakening; and many believed the millennium, or Chriſt's ſecond coming, was near. They had various operations, and profeſſed to have viſions and revelations of the glory of that day. Hence the minds of many were ſomewhat prepared to receive the faith of theſe people. In the winter of 1780, Talmage Biſhop, of that place, by ſome means became acquainted with them, and received a meaſure of faith. Elated with joy he returned to Lebanon, bearing tidings of a ſtrange people* at Niſkeuna, having the power of

* When they came to America, they bore the name of "a ſtrange people," which name in four or five years after, on account of

God! A number of the ſubjects of the revival at Lebanon, appointed Calvin Harlow to go and ſee the people at Niſkeuna, and bring an account of them. Harlow returned; and not knowing what to think of them, went again in company with Joſeph Meacham and Amos Hammond, (both Baptiſt preachers) and Aaron Kibbe; theſe four believed that what they ſaw and heard was the work of God, and confeſſed their ſins. They returned to Lebanon and reported accordingly. Various and vague reports began to be ſpread abroad concerning them; multitudes ſoon flocked from Lebanon and thereabouts to ſee them, and many joined them; in conſequence of which there ſoon became a ſettlement in that place, which, for ſome time paſt has been the reſidence of the miniſtration. The moſt noted characters that joined them about this time, beſide thoſe above mentioned, were David Darrow, Valentine Rathbone a Baptiſt preacher, Daniel Rathbone, and Reuben Rathbone. Valentine renounced his union with the ſociety within a few months after he joined them, and ſoon publiſhed a pamphlet againſt their faith and practice.

There were (and had been for ſome time) a ſect in Harvard, Maſſachuſetts, whoſe ſentiments bore ſome affinity to the Shakers; of courſe their minds were a fit receptacle for the faith of theſe people. This ſect were called Shadrach Irelands, from Shadrach Ireland their leader. The principal tenets of this peculiar ſect were renouncing connection with their wives, and like the Shakers, teſtifying againſt, and renouncing the works of the fleſh, in order to become perfectly free from ſin. As ſoon as they arrived at this ſtate of perfection they might marry ſpiritual-wives, from whom were to proceed holy children, which were to conſtitute the New Jeruſalem or millennium. Shadrach Ireland put away his firſt wife, and married Abagail Logy for his ſpiritual wife. He profeſſed to be Chriſt in his ſecond coming. He likewiſe believed that he ſhould not die, or if he did, that he

their plain dreſs and addreſs and their refuſing to bear arms, was changed to the name of Shaking Quakers; but for ſome years paſt they have been called only Shakers.

should be raised to immortal life the third day. He however died, and his followers waited the three days, expecting to see him rise at the end of them; but as he did not, they supposed they had mistaken the meaning of his prophecy, and that a day was to be considered a prophetic year. Under these impressions, they laid him in a close cellar of his own house, as in a vault, where he remained until the Shakers visited and preached to them a better understanding of their principles of faith; they then caused Shadrach Ireland to be buried, and Abagail Logy, his wife, with several of his followers, joined the Shakers. It has been said the Mother spake of these people before she left England; and asserted they were near and ripe for the gospel.

Many now from Lebanon, Hancock, Harvard, and other eastern parts, convened at Niskeuna—believers for counsel, and others for curiosity. Such numbers resorting thither, the country being then engaged in the war with Great Britain, drew upon them a suspicion that they had some secret machinations in embryo prejudicial to the liberties and good of the public. In consequence of this jealousy, in July, 1780, David Darrow, who had lately received faith, as he was driving a flock of sheep from Lebanon to Niskeuna, was stopped and brought back before the authority at Lebanon, by whom he was tried under suspicion of treason. His sheep were taken from him, and he, in company with Joseph Meacham a believer, was sent under guard to be tried by the commissioners at Albany; before whom they were both ordered to promise obedience to the laws. With this they could not conscientiously comply; as part of their laws were of a military nature and totally repugnant to their principles, they could make no such concessions, lest in obedience they should be compelled to violate their consciences; therefore they, with Elder John Hocknell, who had appeared in their defence, were committed to prison. The suspicion of their being enemies to their country continuing to gain ground, Hezekiah Hammond, Joel Pratt, Mother Ann, John Partington, Mary Partington, William Lee, James Whittaker, Calvin Harlow, and Elizur Goodrich, all principal leading characters, were ſoon after impriſoned with Darrow and Meacham; but in a ſhort time Mother Ann,* with her companion, were taken out with intent to baniſh them to the Britiſh at New York. Having conveyed them as far as Poughkeepſie, they there impriſoned them, till a more favourable opportunity ſhould offer for their tranſportation. Here many viſited them, and ſome received a meaſure of faith in their teſtimony. And after being confined above three months, Governor Clinton, who then reſided at Poughkeepſie, hearing of their impriſonment ordered them to be releaſed. Thoſe impriſoned in Albany were viſited by many, and through the grates of the priſon they preached to multitudes. Many exclaimed againſt the perſecution and impriſonment of theſe people, which was believed to be merely for conſcience ſake. After about four months confinement they were releaſed.

This uſage, far from anſwering the deſign of their perſecutors in diminiſhing, ſerved to augment their numbers. Out of the many hundreds who viſited the church and Elders at Niſkeuna and Lebanon, many received faith in their teſtimony, principally in the ſtates of Maſſachuſetts and Connecticut; they returning and teſtifying their faith, proved a means of gathering more.

In the year 1781, ſometime in May, the Mother, with a female companion (Hannah Kendall) and James Whittaker, in company with another Elder, took a journey to the eaſtward, travelling from place to place, viſiting thoſe who had received faith. Being famed for their religious ſingularity, great numbers reſorted to ſee and hear them from the different parts adjacent to the places they viſited. After a tour of about two years, in which time they held a number of meetings and preached; and having prevailed upon many to believe that they were ſent of God, and to confeſs their ſins to them, they returned to Niſkeuna. In this journey they did not eſcape abuſe, calumny and detraction, which was heaped upon them from time to time by the malevolence of perſecutors. As nearly two thouſand had received faith in their

* See page 120.

teſtimony and joined them, the Elders were encouraged to perſevere in the work. Whittaker ſpent no idle time.

There had always been among the Shakers more or leſs operations, contortions and agitations of body, but they now became exceſſive, eſpecially at their meetings, ſuch as trembling, ſhaking, twitching, jirking, whirling, leaping, jumping, ſtamping, rolling on the floor or ground, running with one or both hands ſtretched out and ſeemingly impelled forward the way one or both pointed; ſome barked and crowed, and imitated the ſound of ſeveral other creatures—theſe were gifts of mortification. Alſo hiſſing, bruſhing and driving the devil or evil ſpirits out of their houſes; often groaning and crying on account, as they ſaid, of the remains of the evil nature in them, or for the wicked world; at other times rejoicing by loud laughter, ſhouting and clapping their hands. There were ſeveral inſtances of ſome of them even profeſſing to have gifts to curſe ſuch as cenſured their conduct; if they were reproved for it, they would juſtify themſelves by referring to the inſtance of Eliſha curſing the children in the name of the Lord; and alſo, to tell certain perſons to "go to hell," particularly ſuch as had been of their faith and turned againſt them, (for whatever is ſaid or done in the gift is right, though out of the gift it would be a ſin.) Every thing they ſaid or did they had ſome reaſon or ſcripture for; ſo for this ſpeech they would quote Pſalm lv. 14, 15, ſaying, "David even prayed that death might ſeize upon ſuch as had been his companions, and with whom he had taken ſweet counſel, and that they might go down into hell quickly Alſo the apoſtle ſays, Let them be *anathema maranatha*, i. e. curſed when the Lord comes, (if they will not then be obedient.) He further ſays, In the name of our Lord Jeſus Chriſt, that is, in the gift of God, we are to deliver ſuch to Satan for the deſtruction of the filthy fleſh."

Their ſuperfluous furniture, ſuch as ornamented looking glaſſes, &c. in a number of inſtances, were daſhed upon the floor and ſtamped to pieces; ear and finger-rings were bitten with all the ſymptoms of rage, and then ſold for old metal. All this was done to teſtify their abhorrence of that pride which introduced theſe things among mankind—and likewiſe as a type of the deſtruction of Babylon. They ſaid, "all *outward adorning and putting on of coſtly apparel* were the works of the fleſh." Among ſome, all books that they had, except the Bible, they called anti-chriſtian, and were burnt or otherwiſe deſtroyed. Some of them deſcribed circles on the floor, around which they would ſtamp, grin and perform all manner of grimace, and every act of diſdain; they then jumped within the ring and ſtamped with the utmoſt vehemence, making a hideous noiſe. They conſidered the circle as repreſenting ſin in the world, and their actions round and in it marked their diſpleaſure and abhorrence againſt ſin; and likewiſe their ſtamping in the ring with a noiſe was figurative of the deſtruction of ſin and paſſing away of the old heavens, according to the ſcripture expreſſion, "as with a great noiſe." In ſhort, theſe extraordinary proceedings were carried to a height ſcarcely to be conceived They were alſo continued with but little intermiſſion till the church was brought into order, as will be ſeen in the ſequel. I may here obſere, many profeſſed to have viſions and to ſee numbers of ſpirits as plain as they ſaw their brethren and ſiſters; and alſo to look into the inviſible world, and to converſe with many of the departed ſpirits who had lived in the different ages of the world, and to learn and to ſee their different ſtates in the world of ſpirits. Some they ſaw, they ſaid, were happy and others miſerable. Several declared that they often were in dark nights ſurrounded with a light, ſometimes in their rooms, but more often when walking the road, that they could ſee to pick up a pin; which light would continue a conſiderable length of time and enlighten them on their way. Many had gifts to ſpeak languages, and many miracles were ſaid to be wrought, and ſtrange ſigns and great wonders ſhewn by the believers.*

* Several who have ſince left the ſociety, with whom the author has converſed, ſtill declare they ſaw ſights and things done, for which they have not been able to aſſign a natural cauſe.

In order to mortify the carnal mind, their dances were excessive; and the various methods they practised to mortify and try that which they called the root of all evil, were truly astonishing. Several things which took place, for the sake of modesty, are here omitted. But I may observe thus far, that they stopped every avenue of their houses, so that the world's people, as they called them, could not see them, and had one or two of the brethren out to watch; they then stripped themselves and danced naked, when the gift or order came from Mother Ann so to do; those who would not be obedient had to walk out of the room, and such were generally mortified by being called "fleshly creatures—full of the flesh."

Notwithstanding their care not to be discovered by the world's people, this conduct by some means leaked out, and it was noised about that the Shakers danced naked. It appears that Daniel Rathbone, sen. was the first who was questioned concerning the truth of it. He gave no direct answer, being unwilling to expose his brethren and sisters; he opened the matter to Whittaker for counsel in such cases; Whittaker told him he might deny it—For the first leaders held that they might deny the truth, and at the same time speak the truth; for instance, they were not naked in one sense, being clothed with spiritual garments, "clothed with salvation"—2 Chron. vi. 41; "with righteousness"—Ps. cxxxii. 9; "If so be that being clothed, we shall not be found naked"—2 Cor. v. 3. Though Elder Whittaker did not fully unite with their stripping naked, and would often leave the room, he said those gifts of Mother which he could not fully see into, he would not condemn. Several were whipped, and some were ordered to whip themselves, as a mortification to the flesh. A young woman by the name of Elizabeth Cook, was stripped and whipped naked, by Noah Wheaton, for having desires towards a young man.—Abiel Cook, her father, hearing of it, prosecuted Noah Wheaton for whipping his daughter naked. Hannah Cook, sister to Elizabeth, who was present at the time, was called for a witness. She went to Elder Whittaker and asked him what she should say.

He anſwered—" I cannot tell you what you muſt ſay, " for I don't know what queſtions will be aſked you; " but," ſays he, " ſpeak the truth, and ſpare the truth, " and take care not to bring the goſpel into diſrepute."

She accordingly teſtified before the court that her ſiſter, who was whipped, was not naked. Thus ſhe obeyed Whittaker's orders; for ſtrictly ſpeaking ſhe was not naked, for ſhe had at the time a fillet on her head. It alſo may be here proper to obſerve, that it was alſo ſaid by the firſt leaders, " That no practice is wrong nor any " oath falſe, which is made to gain the cauſe of the truth, " or to defend the goſpel againſt error; though it might " appear directly oppoſite to truth in the eyes of the " world, yet as done for the cauſe of the goſpel it is con- " ſidered as true."

Some time after Whittaker's laſt journey, that I have mentioned, he went another and travelled from place to place above ſix months, in company with Daniel Rathbone, ſen. who alſo often preached.

Elder William Lee ſeldom travelled to gain proſelytes, being ſevere in his temper and harſh in his manners; his preaching was not fraught with that mildneſs and urbanity which is neceſſary to draw the attention and win the affections of the hearers, and render a man beloved. It once happened as he was ſpeaking to a public congregation, one of the ſpectators, a young man, behaved with levity and diſreſpect; upon this Lee took him by the throat and ſhook him, ſaying, " when I was in England " I was ſergeant in the King's life-guard, and could then " uſe my fiſts; but now ſince I have received the goſ- " pel I muſt patiently bear all abuſe, and ſuffer my ſhins " to be kicked by every little boy; but I will have you " know that the power of God will defend our cauſe."

Whittaker was more mild in his temper and ſoft in his manners, and accommodated his preaching to the feelings and ſentiments of his hearers. He ſaid he connived at many things of which he did not approve; but as believers came forward in the faith he was careful to correct, obſerving, that " any man muſt lack wiſdom " who ſhould attempt to threſh his grain as it ſtands in "the field. Nay," said he, "first reap it, then bind it "in bundles and fetch it into the barn, and then thresh "and winnow it at leisure."

Mother Ann seldom spake in public congregations, but often testified her faith to individuals in conversation. She was a woman of much confidence and boldness, and one who spake her mind freely on all occasions, whether in commendation or disapprobation. There were several instances similar to the following, which the believers called her sharp testimony against sin. As she with some of the Elders was disputing with two or three opposers, (who contradicted with some acrimony) she at length told them they were dogs, dumb dogs, damned dogs! One of the opposers replied to the Elders, "What will you make of that? do you call that the language of a woman of God?" He was answered that "it was sim-"ilar to the language of scripture. St. John says, *all* "*without are dogs and sorcerers, and he that believeth not is* "damned *already* And David says, speaking of Christ, "*Dogs compassed him about.* Also, Christ calls such *ser-*"*pents and vipers*, and that they could not *escape the dam-*"*nation of hell:* and he likewise says, "*He that believeth not* "*shall be damned.*"

For sometime past William Lee and James Whittaker had been called Fathers by the believers; and they had always understood that Lee stood in the lead next to the Mother, and Whittaker next to him. But as Whittaker had been the principal instrument in gaining proselytes, there arose a dispute between them in the latter part of the year 1783, which should be first, and Mother Ann interfered to settle the controversy—and the contention arose to such a height that it was the cause of several losing their faith. But the dispute finally terminated in the death of William Lee, which was on the twenty-first of July, 1784, in the forty-first year of his age. This was a great trial to many; but it was soon absorbed in another of greater magnitude. The head and Mother of the church, Ann Lee, that extraordinary personage, who was esteemed and admired by her followers, and for her singularity was a curiosity to many others—who (for a woman) had travelled much to propagate the faith, and had from time to time suffered scenes of insult and abuse from inconsiderate people, was now called upon to resign up her charge. She died at Niskeuna, on the 8th day of September, the same year that Lee died. Her funeral was attended by a large concourse of people, not only believers, but by many from the city of Albany and adjacent parts. The people were moderately served with wine, and returned home generally satisfied with having been at the funeral. She was buried near William Lee, in their burying-ground, about a quarter of a mile from their meeting-house at Niskeuna.

The most of her followers were much grieved on account of her death; and to many it was an unexpected event, for they had entertained an idea that she would never die, or at least that she would abide on earth a thousand years. She had given some such intimations, but Whittaker never inculcated such a belief.

Shortly after her death, many lost their faith and fell off. But by the unremitting exertions of Elder Whittaker, upon whom the lead then devolved, the believers were reconciled to the death of Mother Ann; and were taught that it was necessary for her to enter the world of spirits, in order to their further increase in the gospel. He often prophesied of a great spread of the gospel, and of an ingathering to the church, which was soon to take place.

About six months after Mother Ann's death, on account of so many falling off one after another, he denounced heavy judgments against those who should hereafter leave the church. His words were these—"Whosoever from this time forsakes the blessed work of God, "will never prosper in this world nor in the world to "come, nor die the natural death of other men; if they "do, God never spake by my mouth!" He sent out several to preach the gospel in different parts of the country; one of these was Reuben Rathbone, with a companion, who for his testimony in Connecticut was imprisoned four months in New-London jail.

In 1785 and 6, the church by order of Elder Whittaker, built a ship of two hundred tons, called the Union, at the town of Rehoboth, principally for the purpose of ſpreading the goſpel among foreign nations. It was an excellent ſhip, well built and completely finiſhed When, in conſequence of a contention which aroſe between Morrel Baker and Noah Wheaton, which ſhould be captain, the deſign of circulating the goſpel was relinquiſhed.—She was fitted out for Hiſpaniola, with a cargo of horſes, flour and other articles in her hold, and commanded by Morrel Baker, who, with moſt of the hands, were Shakers. From Hiſpaniola they ſailed to Havanna, from Havanna back to Hiſpaniola, from thence to Charleſton, from Charleſton to Savannah, and then to Hiſpaniola again, and from thence to Boſton, where ſhe was ſold. The building of the ſhip, with theſe ſeveral voyages, produced no gain to the church; and the conduct of Baker and the hands did not, while following a ſea-faring life, comport with their profeſſion.

About this time Daniel Rathbone, ſen. before mentioned, and his wife left the ſociety. Soon after he gave the public his principal reaſons for ſeparating in a printed pamphlet, containing about an hundred pages. Alſo, by this time Richard Hocknell and Ann Lee, the niece of Mother Ann, (before mentioned) had left them He and this Ann Lee were ſhortly after joined together in matrimony.

Auguſt, 1786. Elder John Hocknell and John Partington went to New-York to ſeek a paſſage for England. James Whittaker had been oppoſed to their going; but when they left Niſkeuna, he with Joſeph Meacham were at Tyringham on a viſit among the brethren. Information ſoon reached Whittaker that they were gone—he immediately took horſe, in company with Meacham, and proceeded to New-York in order to ſtop them, but did not arrive before they had ſailed. Some days before their departure they wrote to the church at Niſkeuna for a few articles of proviſion, which letter was received by the church September 5. The next day they wrote to them expreſſing a deſire that they would remember them, and pray for them that they might "proſper in the way of everlaſting life;" and alſo, that they ſincerely wiſhed that they, while gone, might "proſper both in ſoul and body." The letter with ſundry articles of provision was sent by Elder James Shephard, but he did not reach New-York till they were gone. He there met Whittaker and Meacham; they returned in company to Niskeuna. In about a year Hocknell and Partington returned from England. Partington soon after his return separated from the society.

And some time after James Shephard also left the society. He had presided as an inferior Elder, and had been a considerable support to the society in its infant state. Therefore Elder Whittaker said, if he should be unfortunate or live to be old, the church must not let him suffer, whether he should continue in the faith or not. The author visited said Shephard in the year 1807, and found him to be in very low circumstances and advanced in years; but an honest man. He said he had spent the best part of his days in the service of the church, and that it was their duty to help him. Shortly after, he visited the church at Niskeuna for that purpose; and the author was pleased to hear that they liberally afforded him relief. As he had no antipathy against them, but on the contrary, still manifested a regard for the society, he was invited to return and live in it, as he could live more comfortable than in the situation he was. He accepted the invitation, and was accordingly placed in the backsliding order * This usage to a man worn out, mostly in the service of the society, was considered as a credit to it.

It was also near this time that William Skails left them. He had been liberally educated and had read much; had belonged to the society several years, and for awhile had been zealous in the cause. At one time he stripped himself naked and testified his faith before Lucy Wright, the present Mother of the church, Samuel Fitch, John Truesdell and several other believers, saying, "Naked came I into the world, and naked must I go out; "and naked must my soul stand before God, as naked "as my body now stands before you. It is my faith "that sin has been the cause of shame, and my soul must "become divested of shame, and as completely stripped

* See note page 58.

"of ſin as my body is now ſtripped, or I can never ſtand "before you in the world of ſpirits." Afterwards he diſcovered as great zeal againſt them and their faith; ſeveral times he went among them and exclaimed againſt them. He wrote ſeveral pieces concerning the faith and practice for publication, but they never appeared in print. It is ſaid he afterwards became ſomewhat delirious

Elder Whittaker continued indefatigable in his endeavours to ſpread the goſpel; he almoſt continually employed his time in travelling and preaching, and viſiting the believers and endeavouring to build them up in the faith; and though many fell off from time to time, yet many were gathered. By the year 1787, Elder Whittaker, with the aſſiſtance of ſeveral others who had travelled with him, had gained more or leſs believers, beſides thoſe at Niſkeuna and Lebanon, at the following places; Hancock, Richmond, Pittsfield, Shirley, Harvard and Tyringham, in the ſtate of Maſſachuſetts; at New-Enfield, Canterbury and Loudon, ſtate of New-Hampſhire; at Enfield, ſtate of Connecticut, and at Alfred in the province of Maine. The whole number of believers at theſe different places amounted to near three thouſand.

A long ſtatement of facts might be given, which the limits of this work will not admit, reſpecting the abuſe and perſecution which the Elders and many of the believers ſuffered. Let it ſuffice to ſay, they were often whipped out of towns and villages, and ſeverely threatened to prevent their return. Sometimes they did return, and were again inſulted and abuſed. Mobs frequently gathered round their houſes, broke their windows and doors, dragged them into the dirt through the ſtreet, and kicked, whipped and ſeveral other ways abuſed them. At one time, Mother Ann was ſo beaten that her body was black and blue—and at the ſame time Whittaker had two of his ribs broken. The church having increaſed, as above mentioned, while America was in a war againſt Great Britain, many of them were preſſed and taken from their dwellings to bear arms, which they would not do; when a gun was forced into their hands they would immediately let it fall, on account of which they were often pricked with bayonets, whipped, kicked and beaten. In ſhort, they ſuffered almoſt every thing, the loſs of their lives excepted.

The church had now begun to aſſume the appearance of proſperity, when it was again called upon to part with its principal pillar Elder James Whittaker, who had been out upon a religious journey in company with Reuben Rathbone, (who had been ſeveral journeys with him before) returning home was taken ſick at Enfield, (Con.) in March, 1787, where he remained until he died, which was on the morning of the 20th of July following, aged about thirty-eight years. In the evening before he died he ſent a believer to give information to the church at Lebanon that he was going to die, with orders for a few of his brethren, whom he named, to come and ſee him; but before they reached Enfield he was dead.— His death was a great trial to moſt of the believers, for he was much beloved by them.

Thus the church had loſt its three principal leaders, who had nurtured it in its infant ſtate, and whoſe foſtering care had protected it through all its imbecilities and various trials, and had raiſed it to a degree of maturity. They had been the principal pillars to ſupport its fabric, which more than once had been threatened by the rage of oppoſition and perſecution to be annihilated. I ſhall here ſuſpend further narration, while I give the faith of the church in, and a few characteriſtic traits of, theſe three extraordinary perſonages. Their faith in Mother Ann was great; and they ſtill believe though ſhe is abſent in body, yet ſhe is preſent in ſpirit. They believed that ſhe was wholly actuated by the power of God; and that ſhe, with Chriſt, had been the ſubject of propheſy; and that ſhe was equal with Chriſt and ſuffered in ſpirit like unto him in a death to a fallen nature, in order to finiſh the work of man's final redemption.* They believe ſhe was the woman propheſied of by St. John that fled into the wilderneſs, and that Niſkeuna was the place; and that in this place of retirement ſhe was nouriſhed for a time, times and half a time, i. e. three years and an

* See pages 271, 272.

half, when ſhe became known by opening and preaching the goſpel as before related. Many of them believed that the man child, ſpoken of in the Revelations, was James Whittaker; and that he, or rather that ſpirit which he poſſeſſed, was as a rod of iron againſt ſin, which in the progreſs of the work would rule all nations. Ann Lee, when addreſſed with the title of miſtreſs or madam, ſometimes remonſtrated againſt it, ſaying, "I am Ann the word," meaning to ſignify that ſhe was the word in the ſame ſenſe that Chriſt is called the word in the firſt chapter of the goſpel according to St. John. She was ſometimes called the Elect Lady,* but the believers have generally called her Mother, and Whittaker and Lee Fathers; becauſe through or by them they were begotten in the goſpel, brought forth into a new creation or birth, and empowered from babes to become men in the work of their redemption.

Ann Lee was a woman rather ſhort and corpulent. Her countenance was fair and pleaſant, but often aſſumed a commanding, ſevere look; ſhe ſang ſweetly, with a pleaſant voice, but would frequently uſe the moſt harſh, ſatirical language, with a maſculine, ſovereign addreſs. Her natural genius was reſplendent, with a quick and ready turn of wit, but entirely deſtitute of ſchool education. She was exceeding loving and kind to the believ-

* About the ſame time Ann began her teſtimony in America, Jemima Wilkinſon, a Quaker's daughter, who was born in Cumberland, ſtate of Rhode-Iſland, alſo began to teſtify that Chriſt had made his ſecond appearance in her. She, like Ann, declared ſhe had immediate and ſpecial revelation from God for all ſhe delivered. Her profeſſion and preaching were in moſt reſpects the ſame. She alſo gained a number of followers. Jemima was called, by many people, the Elect Lady; and as the ſame title was ſometimes applied to Ann Lee, this, when one of them was ſpoken of, has ſometimes rendered it difficult to diſtinguiſh which of the two was meant. Jemima and ſome of the leading characters among the Shakers have had conferences on the ſubject of their religion; though their profeſſion was nearly alike, yet each party believed they had a revelation ſuperior to the other. But the author has heard the Shakers ſay, that Jemima acknowledged them to be before her. For a further account of Jemima Wilkinſon, ſee H. Adams' View of Religions, p. 458, third edition.

ers; ſhe often called them her children, and ſometimes her dear children, and recommended them to love one another as ſhe loved them. Thoſe people who came to ſee her and her followers, that did not oppoſe them, but on the contrary manifeſted a friendly diſpoſition, ſhe alſo treated with much kindneſs, eſpecially if they manifeſted any inclination to receive the faith.

William Lee had been married and had two children by his wife He was for a time a non-commiſſioned officer in the King's life-guard; while in it his wife proved falſe to him, and had a child by another man; after which (ſome time before he came to America) he entirely forſook her. He was large in ſize, ſtrong and robuſt, ſtern and commanding, in his conduct generally harſh and ſevere, and was called by the believers "a ſon of thunder." It has often been ſaid that he was more fit to have the command of a ſhip of war than of a church of Chriſt.

Whittaker was a man of a lively diſpoſition, and a bright turn of mind; he had a penetrating eye, and a majeſtic, commanding, authoritative look, at the ſame time pleaſant and complacent. He was of a fair complexion, the picture of health, and a man of conſiderable information, and generally reſpected and believed to be ſincere even by thoſe who were not members of the ſociety. The author has heard ſeveral ſay who have ſeparated from the ſociety, that they "really loved Whittaker."

Mother Ann and William Lee often drank freely of ſpirituous liquors, and were ſometimes intoxicated.*— She ſometimes ſaid that ſpirituous liquor was one of God's good creatures James Whittaker was, for the moſt part, a ſober man and ſeldom drank to exceſs.

* Other reports have been in circulation concerning theſe firſt leaders, particularly that Ann Lee was a laſcivious and lewd woman; this has been publiſhed in the Theological Magazine—and that ſhe was a woman of ill fame in England But any thing which has been reported or heretofore publiſhed reſpecting her or her followers, that has not been ſufficiently authenticated, is diſcarded from this work.

They ſometimes obſerved, that *to the pure all things were pure*, but to the *defiled and unbelieving nothing is pure, their minds and conſciences* being *defiled*—Titus, i. 15.—Such they ſaid were damned in all that they ate and drank, becauſe they did not do it in faith; *for whatever is not of faith, is ſin*. But with reſpect to themſelves, whatſoever they did was done in faith with a pure conſcience, therefore they felt no condemnation in that which they allowed—Rom. xiv. 22, 23. Thoſe things in which they found no evil, might appear evil to the wicked, being ſeen by them with an evil eye, and examined with a wicked heart. Further it was ſtated, that no man was able to judge them in their conduct with a right judgment, any more than men formerly were able to judge Chriſt when he did that in a number of inſtances which appeared to the evil-minded to be ſin—as his breaking the Sabbath, as they ſaid; but as Chriſt was Lord of the Sabbath and Lord of all things, ſo were the Elders, particularly Mother Ann. Alſo, when they ate or drank, or whatever they did, they did all to the glory of God; and they expected to be evil ſpoken of for that, for which they gave thanks—1 Cor x. 30, 31. The teſtimony of theſe perſons, particularly Ann and Whittaker, was invariably at all times againſt ſin and the gratification of the carnal mind, and the neceſſity of purity in heart and life. They profeſſed to have many viſions and revelations of the ſpiritual world, and concerning things in the preſent life. They ſaid they often converſed with angels and departed ſpirits. They aſſerted that often when they were preaching, they ſaw many ſpirits who appeared to be attentive to hear and receive the word; alſo many believers declared they ſaw the ſame Ann and Whittaker often propheſied of a great increaſe and ſpread of the goſpel in the next opening; and that it would break out in ſome place far diſtant.

The author has made much inquiry concerning the ſtate of mind in which they appeared to die, but he never could learn that they bore any particular teſtimony in ſupport of their faith, or expreſſed any happy ſenſations or comfortable hope. Mother Ann was peeviſh, and even croſs. Lee died in excruciating pain. Whittaker, ſome months before he was taken ſick, ſaid that he ſhould not live long; and ten or twelve hours before he died appeared to have a ſenſe that his end was near, and alſo appeared to be calm and reſigned.

The vacancy occaſioned in the miniſtration by the death of Whittaker was filled by Joſeph Meacham, who had travelled and preached much with Whittaker. His uſeful, active zeal had procured him the eſteem and veneration of the church A ſhort time previous to this, preaching to the world had been almoſt ſuſpended, or as they term it, "the goſpel was cloſed or ſhut up, and withdrawn from the world, that the church, as a body, might gather into order and increaſe in its own ſpiritual ſtrength, and travail into the ſubſtance of what they profeſſed."

Elder Meacham was indefatigable in his exertions to collect the believers into families, to ſupport a joint intereſt and union and to hold all things in common, (for which Whittaker had begun to make ſome preparations previouſly to his death.) He ſignified the departure of Elder Whittaker was neceſſary in order that they might travail into a deeper work, and for the further increaſe of the goſpel. In order to this increaſe, he laboured to convince the believers of the neceſſity of travailing out of a fleſhly relation or union according to the ties of nature, and of being gathered into a church or ſpiritual relation, and of becoming purified from every principle proceeding from a carnal nature, and then they would be prepared to miniſter the goſpel to others. They were taught that in order to become truly a church of Chriſt, a joint temporal intereſt ſhould be abſorbed in one common and indiſtinct property.

The firſt gathering commenced at Lebanon, in the year 1788, where ſeveral hundreds both male and female were collected from the different places where there were believers; ſome on account of their mechanical ingenuity; ſome for their property; ſome for helpers and aſſiſtants in temporal things, and others for ſpiritual teachers and helpers, and ſome on account of their own protection and ſalvation. All theſe entered into a verbal covenant, the ſubſtance of which was, to maintain and ſupport a joint intereſt, and a promiſe not to bring one another into debt for any ſervices or property they ſhould beſtow on the joint intereſt of the church. Alſo an agreement to be under the order and government of the Deacons in all their temporal concerns. All the Deacons and Elders, together with the people, were under the guardianſhip and direction of Meacham.

Though the teſtimony and labours againſt the fleſh had hitherto been ſevere, yet now they were increaſed with redoubled energy The exerciſes of thoſe who were gathering into a family, united intereſt and order, were extreme beyond conception. They conceived that by the power of God they could labour completely out of that natural inſtinct implanted in mankind for the purpoſe of procreation. They believed this to be the moſt weighty and important work they had to do; to which they were ſtimulated by their Elders, who told them that ſuch a ſtate had been attained by ſome in the faith, particularly by Mother Ann and Elder Whittaker. They now preſſed forward in the work of mortification and ſuffering with cheerfulneſs and reſolution, and endeavoured by every poſſible means to root out and deſtroy this inherent propenſity. Imagination was exhauſted by inventing, and nature tortured in executing this arduous work. They often danced with vehemence through the greateſt part of the night, and then inſtead of repoſing their wearied bodies upon a bed, they would, by way of further penance, lie down upon the floor on chains, ropes, ſticks, in every humiliating and mortifying poſture they could deviſe! This work continued with ſuch unabated zeal, that ſeveral who were the moſt faithful and zealous, laboured into ſuch a degree of mortification as to travail out of the fleſh ſure enough; the ſpirit took its departure out of its emaciated and ruined tabernacle—and being thus purged from carnal propenſities, was conſigned to the dark receſſes of the ſilent tomb! And it was ſaid, ſuch gave up their lives for Chriſt's ſake and died on the croſs.

This work was not limited wholly to Lebanon, but preachers were appointed and ſent by Elder Meacham, to kindle the ſame flame among believers in the different parts where they lived, and to gather them in the ſame order. The next gathering commenced at Hancock, in the year 1791; the direction of which was aſſigned to Calvin Harlow. They thus proceeded in this work from one place to another till moſt of the believers were gathered, and the ſame order eſtabliſhed at Niſkeuna and moſt of thoſe places, before mentioned, where Whittaker and others had planted the faith. Thoſe who were gathered into this order and united intereſt ſtood in what was called church relation, i. e. related to the church at Lebanon, which was called the mother church, and firſt goſpel church; thoſe private or individual families who were not yet gathered, ſtood in what they called fleſhly relation; and all were taught that thoſe who ſtood in church relation could travail further out of the fleſh in one week, than thoſe who ſtood in fleſhly relation could in a year. This work they ſay was effected and confirmed by the year 1792, when they believe Daniel's thirteen hundred and thirty-five days ended.*

Some time before this, thoſe various operations I have mentioned began to abate and now came quite to an end, i. e. with thoſe who were gathered into this order.

It may here be obſerved, that the laſt inſtance of ſtripping naked and of corporeal puniſhment, was at Niſkeuna about the year 1793: two young women, by name Abigail Lemmons, Saviah Spires and another who has ſince left the people and had rather her name ſhould not be publickly mentioned, amuſed themſelves by attending to the amour of two flies in the window: they were told by Eldreſs Hannah Matterſon for thus gratifying their carnal inclinations, and as a mortification to the ſame, they muſt ſtrip themſelves naked and take whips ſhe had provided and whip themſelves, and then whip each other; two happened at once to ſtrike the third, when ſhe cried *murder!* they were then ordered to ſtop and to plunge into a brook near by: all this was done in the preſence and under the approbation of Elder Timothy Hubbard, and Jonathan Sloſſon one of the brethren.

* See page 124.

Shortly after, Elder Meacham came from Lebanon, and being informed of it, he ſaid, the gift for ſtripping and labouring naked, and uſing corporeal puniſhment, had entirely run out: for as they could not keep ſuch conduct ſecreted from the world, the church had already ſuffered much perſecution on account of it, therefore there muſt be no more ſuch proceedings.

It may be now proper to take notice of ſeveral things that had been, and are ſtill reported of this people.— Thoſe reports that have been the moſt circulated are, that they not only ſtripped and danced naked in their night meetings, but ſometimes put out the candles and went into promiſcuous intercourſe; and that the Elders had connexion when they pleaſed, with ſuch women as they choſe; and that they concealed the fruits of it by the horrid crime of *murder!* It was alſo reported, that many of the Shakers, by order of the Elders, were caſtrated.

The intention of the author in this hiſtory is to ſtate things in a true light; and from the pains he has taken to procure a correct accout of the practices of this people, he is able *confidently* to aſſert, that not any of theſe reports, except ſtripping and dancing naked, have any foundation in truth. A few ſolitary inſtances of ſexual intercourſe might be mentioned; but the parties were ſhut out of union and not received again without confeſſions and profeſſions of repentance and contrition ſimilar as in other churches.

James Seton, who had been among the Shakers, aſſerted before a collection of people, that he could imitate the Shakers in every thing but burning children. Being aſked if they burnt children, he anſwered in the affirmative. He then was taken before a magiſtrate, and made oath, that he ſaw David Chauncy, his wife, and Roxey Chauncy, burn a child. A warrant was iſſued immediately, and the accuſed being brought before court, when the trial commenced, Chauncy, with a ſtern, impreſſive look, demanded of Seton if he had ever ſeen any of them burn a child. Seton, conſcious of his wickedneſs in thus accuſing the innocent, replied he had not. The persons arraigned were consequently discharged, and Seton punished by the court for his perjury.

In the course of a few years after they had verbally agreed and covenanted to support a joint interest, numbers who were not able, or would not abide the fire of Zion as they called it, fell off from them; and some afterwards brought charges against the deacons whom they had been under for their services, and some of their claims were unjust. The leaders therefore found it expedient for all to enter into a written covenant, which they did in the year 1795, with an intention to invest the church with power to do what they thought right in such cases.

Before and after this covenant was signed, the deacons endeavoured to settle with, and take receipts of those who had renounced the faith, and who had made a demand for their services. But it was believed the time would come when those who went away would not be allowed any thing; and it was not long before this belief was realized. This measure was considered by many as unjust; by Reuben Rathbone in particular, who at this time had the lead of a family of believers at Hancock. He opened his mind to the ministration upon the subject, who told him that those who left the church had no more right to receive any temporal property out of the church as a compensation for any labour, or any interest they had brought in, than Judas had to an inheritance with the apostles, after he had betrayed Christ.— It was alledged, that the interest or service that was given, was given to God, and to take that away would be committing sacrilege; and it was signified that the wicked did not deserve any thing but judgment, and they that went away from the church to the world, had what they went after; they had the flesh, and that was enough for them. However, some time after the leaders of the church concluded to give those who left the church, an hundred dollars as a sacrifice for peace sake, and in order to get a final discharge from them; likewise to avoid a controversy in law.

When the covenant was ſigned it only included a mutual promiſe the ſame as was verbally made in the year 1788. But about the year 1800, one of the aſſiſtant deacons obſerved before a number of his brethren, that as they were not an incorporated ſociety, any one who left them might by law recover wages for his ſervices, or remuneration for the property he had depoſited: for this he was chaſtiſed by the Elders. They told him it was an attempt to corrupt the minds of his brethren, and to bring that covenant into diſrepute which had been given to Elder Joſeph Meacham by immediate revelation from God. He was accordingly ſhut out of union, and had to kneel down in the preſence of the brethren and ſiſters, and to confeſs, that he had done wrong, in order to be received into union again. However, the covenant was ſhortly after renewed, and they mutually bound themſelves to the deacon or deacons, and his or their ſucceſſors. The new covenant was to this effect, viz. To give up all to the care and diſpoſal of the deacons and their ſucceſſors for the good of the goſpel, and to ſubject themſelves as brethren and ſiſters, to the order and government of the church; to adhere to juſtice and equity both with reſpect to themſelves and others; and endeavour to ſupport a joint intereſt; and never to make any demand or to bring any debt or charge againſt the deacons, or againſt any member of the church for their ſervices or property.

In teſtimony of which, both brethren and ſiſters ſubſcribed their names in the preſence of each other.

Elder Calvin Harlow before mentioned continued in his work of gathering the believers into order at Hancock, until he died, which was on the 21ſt of December, 1795.

It would take up too much room in this work to give an account of the gatherings, and of the Elders that were appointed to the work, at Tyringham, Enfield, and at ſeveral of the other places I have heretofore mentioned. It may ſuffice to ſay, that the work was all ſimilar to that at Lebanon and Hancock, and that all thoſe Elders were under the direction of Elder Meacham, who was firſt Biſhop and Father of the church. Theſe Elders had to receive the word and counſel of God (as they believed) from Elder Meacham, and communicate the ſame to thoſe who were placed under their care. Elder Meacham (who was believed to be the Son of man ſpoken of by Ezekiel, that was to deſtroy Gog and Magog) became reduced in his health, and the 16th of Auguſt, 1796, he was called upon to bid an everlaſting adieu to all ſublunary things, and enter that "world from whoſe bourn no traveller returns." Some time before his death, he ſaid, that "before this generation paſſed "away all nations would acknowledge this goſpel."

The next in ſucceſſion was Lucy Wright, whom they call Mother Lucy, who had ſtood in the lead with Elder Meacham the latter part of his miniſtration. Her name by marriage was Goodrich: there had been ſeveral gifts of mortification to ſeparte the affections of Goodrich from his wife Lucy.

According to their faith, natural affection muſt be eradicated; and they ſay they muſt love all equally alike as brothers and ſiſters in the goſpel. It would exceed the limits of this work to give a particular account of the various ſchemes that have been contrived to deſtroy all natural affection and ſocial attachment between man and wife, parent and child, brothers and ſiſters, eſpecially towards ſuch as have left the ſociety. Two inſtances that occurred about this time as ſpecimens of others may ſuffice. A mother, who had renounced the faith, came to Niſkeuna to ſee her daughter. Eldreſs Hannah Matterſon told the daughter to go into the room to her carnal mother and ſay—"What do you come here for? "I don't want you to come and ſee me with your car- "nal affections."

The mother being grieved, replied—"I did not expect that a daughter of mine would ever addreſs me in that manner."

The daughter in obedience to what ſhe was taught, replied again—"You have come here with your carnal, "fleſhly deſires, and I don't want to ſee you," and then left her mother.

Some time after, one Dunham Shapley, who had belonged to the ſociety, called to ſee Abagail his ſiſter at

Niskeuna, whom he had not seen in six or seven years; but he was not admitted; he waited some time, being loth to go away without seeing her; at last she was ordered to go to the window and address him in the language of abuse and scurrility. The words she made use of, it would be indecent to mention. For this she was applauded, and that in the author's hearing when he belonged to the society.

Elder Henry Clough who had laboured in the ministry as an assistant to Meacham, now stood next in oder to Mother Lucy. He was esteemed a wise man, and it was believed he had a great work to do in relation to the further opening of the gospel.

The church had now been enclosed, or shut up nearly ten years from the world, and there was but little preaching to any but the believers. A few during this time had joined them, and those who did (as they said) were born out of due time and could not travail as those did who came in when the gospel was open, and could not gain much in a travail, until it was opened again.—Among those who during this time received faith, were Benjamin Youngs and his wife, Abraham his son, and a daughter.

A short time previously to Meacham's death, it was believed and spoken of, that the time was near for the opening of the gospel again to the world. Not long after Clough took the lead, ministers were appointed and sent forth. The gift for those who were sent out, was to go and preach the gospel to the world, and hear them confess their sins. They went forth according to their direction; visited divers private families far and near, and occasionally preached publickly, and great hopes were entertained, which was a matter of rejoicing. However, as it was to little purpose, it was thought they had not a right gift, and another was given, viz. To go and preach the gospel, and invite all to come to the church; but in this method they were as unsuccessful as before. It was then thought that the lack was in the ministers: accordingly they were suspended, and others sent out, but all yet to little effect. At Niskeuna, Peter Cocanut and Abraham Youngs received the gift to go and preach. They accordingly went forth; travelled about an hundred miles, and returned home void of any fruit

Some time after, John Scott, then an assistant Elder, accused Youngs of a shameful sin, and ordered him to confess it. Youngs denied the charge, and for his denial, was shut out of union. It was some time after believed that he was innocent of the crime alledged against him. Elder John Meacham told the author of this work, that " he had not been wisely dealt by, and if he would " return, it should not be required of him to confess it, " as he believed that he was innocent of the charge."—The author being then in the faith, and anxious to gain Youngs back again, informed him of what Elder Meacham had said; to which he replied, " that they professed " to know all things by revelation; and he in this among " other instances, had discovered the fallacy."

While they were labouring to open and spread the faith, Elder Henry Clough, who was much admired for his wisdom and abilities, and considered by them as a splendid ornament to the church, and who (they believed) was raised up for the increase and spread of the gospel, was taken sick, and departed this life some time in March 1798.

The next in succession as the first Minister or Bishop, was Abiathar Babbat, who also was in subordination to the Mother Lucy Wright.

Jan. 1798. The author having heard many singular reports of them, was induced to go and see them: he conceived a favourable opinion of them, and was prevailed upon to join them. He returned to the place of his residence, and persuaded several to go and visit them. Some of these received faith and joined them. He likewise represented them in such a favourable manner among his acquaintance at Albany, that several were prevailed upon to visit them: some received faith and confessed their sins. About the same time the author joined them, Seth Wells, schoolmaster in the city of Albany, did the same; and shortly after his five brothers and two sisters from Long-Island; many also from different parts of the country, so that by the year 1805, nearly a hundred young-believers were added to the church at Niſkeuna, and moſt of them gathered into a united or family intereſt.* Alſo B. Youngs, before mentioned, who had lived with his wife and family ever ſince he had joined the ſociety, and had tranſacted buſineſs on his own account, now in obedience to the Elders, with his wife and two daughters who were believers, went into one of the families that ſupported a joint intereſt, and gave up the greateſt part of his property into common ſtock, the remainder he gave to his three unbelieving ſons.

But it has almoſt always been the caſe, while ſome are joining the church, others are falling off. One of theſe was Reuben Rathbone before mentioned, who belonged to the church at Hancock eighteen years. He having become diſſatisfied in ſundry reſpects with the faith and conduct of his brethren, ſeparated from them 24th of July, 1799; and ſoon after publiſhed a pamphlet, entitled, "Reaſons offered for leaving the Shakers."

This pamphlet being examined by the leaders of the church, was declared to be full of corruption and falſehood. The believers were charged not to read a ſyllable in it, nor to touch it. If any perſons offered to lend one, they were told not to receive it, for it would poiſon their ſouls.

The pamphlet appears to be written with candour, and ſeveral who were believers when the author of ſaid pamphet was, who have alſo left the ſociety, have obſerved that the ſaid pamphlet is a candid ſtatement of facts.

The author of this hiſtory, when he was a member of the ſociety, underſtood from ſeveral of the believers, that the church had procured many of theſe pamphlets and burnt them. Daniel Rathbone's pamphlet, before mentioned, alſo ſhared the ſame fate.

In the time of the above mentioned increaſe, five perſons left the church at Niſkeuna, who had been members of it many years.

* It may here be obſerved, that it is not abſolutely required of thoſe who join them to give up their property and enter into a united intereſt till ſome time has elapſed, according to their faith, ſituation, and circumſtances in life.

Elder John Hocknell, mentioned in the beginning of this history, departed this life February 26, 1799, aged seventy-six years and nearly six months He had not been much of an officiating character; his faith was not so much in the present ministration as in the first. He was spoken of as the last of the four living creatures mentioned in Ezekiel chap i. ver. 5. Also, the last of the four beasts mentioned in Rev. chap. iv. According as some of the leaders have explained these texts, that the first, namely, Mother Ann, "was like a lion," or according to Ezekiel ver. 10, "had the face of a lion." William Lee had the face of an ox; James Whittaker "had the face of a man," and John Hocknell "had the face of an eagle," or "like an eagle."

Some time in the fall of the year 1795, after the yellow fever had subsided in the city of New-York, the church at Lebanon, Hancock, and Niskeuna, by order, (or gift as they term it) of the ministration, by and with the approbation of Mother Lucy Wright, carried twenty-seven waggon loads of provision to Albany and sent it from that place by water to the corporation of the city of New-York, for the relief of the poor, who had been in great distress during the sickness, and were at that time, in want of the common necessaries of life. Again in the year 1803, some time in the month of November, they made the following liberal donation to the said corporation for the relief of the poor who were in similar circumstances, viz. 300 dollars in specie, 853 lb. of pork, 1951 lb. of beef, 1794 lb. of mutton, 1685 lb. of rye flour, 52 bushels of rye, 24 bushels of beans, 197 bushels of potatoes, 34 bushels of carrots, 2 bushels of beets, 2 barrels of dried apples, and 26 dollars and 50 cents intended for the payment of freighting the articles from Hudson to New-York.

The corporation of the city presented the church with their thanks for its well-timed generosity, which was published in some of the newspapers

In the years 1803 and 4, but few joined the church, but in 1805 a rapid increase commenced, and many were added to the society Before I give a particular account of this increasing work, I conceive it necessary and intereſting to the reader, to ſtate a few brief ſketches of an extraordinary revival and awakening in the minds of people, in what is uſually denominated the Kentucky revival, out of which this gathering was made. It may be alſo obſerved, that previouſly to people's receiving this faith, their minds have been ſomewhat prepared by receiving ſentiments ſimilar to the Shakers, and profeſſing to have viſions and revelations of the near approach of the millennium; and in particular, by becoming diſſatisfied with all other denominations, and imbibing an unfavourable opinion of ſexual intercourſe. The firſt extraordinary work I have referred to, began under the preaching of John Rankin, miniſter of the Preſbyterian church at Gaſper, Logan county; from thence it began in Chriſtian county. In the ſpring of 1801, the ſame work appeared in Maſon county, upper part of Kentucky, under the exhortation of thoſe who had received the ſpirit of the work, and believed in a full and free ſalvation, and that it was attainable. From theſe ſmall beginnings the work ſpread extenſively. News circulated through the country of a marvellous nature, which bro't many to ſee the novel ſcene. The aſſemblies ſoon became too numerous for the houſes to contain them, and to avoid being crowded, they found it expedient to encamp in the open air, in convenient ſhady places.

Camp-meetings, one after another, were held in various places in the ſtates of Kentucky and Ohio. To theſe meetings, people of both ſexes reſorted on foot, on horſeback, and in carriages, with tents and camp equipage proportioned to the number, which was from three to twenty thouſand. They generally continued from three to five or ſix days and nights. A great proportion of thoſe who attended were diſtinguiſhed from the reſt by new and ſtrange operations which were believed to be a ſpecial effect of divine power. Many fell and lay as if they were either dead or entranced, and were ſometimes collected together to ſecure them from danger, and laid out ſide by ſide like ſo many corpſes. At one of theſe meetings, the number who fell were computed to be three thouſand. Others diſcovered the moſt ardent zeal in the cauſe, and laboured for the ſpread of what they called, the ſpirit of the work, by their vociferations, prayers, and exhortations. They ſang, ſhouted, clapped their hands, and leaped for joy; in ſhort, the ſcene was novel beyond deſcription. This work ſpread through the whole country like a contagious diſtemper.' Seven Preſbyterian miniſters attended one of theſe camp-meetings, four of whom were oppoſed to it, and ſpake againſt it about three days, when one of them addreſſed the aſſembly, acknowledged his convictions, and ſaid that "that they had wickedly oppoſed the anſwer of their "own prayers."

All thoſe camp-meetings, and others in the revival, muſt have appeared to an unprejudiced ſpectator, like the greateſt confuſion, ſcarce to be deſcribed by human language. They uſually commenced with a ſermon, near the termination of which many would break out in an unuſual outcry. Some vociferated their feelings in fervent ejaculations; others with the language of exhortation, would addreſs their careleſs friends, beſeeching them with the pathos of affection, to repent and forſake their ſins. Some terrified at theſe awful proceedings, ſought to extricate themſelves from the group that ſurrounded them, and fled precipitately from the crowd.—Some in the agony of conviction and poignancy of grief, deprecating the wrath and imploring the mercy of God, continued under theſe impreſſions till the ſymptoms of approaching diſſolution appeared prominent in every feature: others cheering their almoſt expiring nature with prayer and praiſe. Some collected from theſe complicated maſſes, cenſuring and diſputing; others applauding and defending; and though the meetings were held at ſo many different places, and the operations exhibited ſuch a variegated ſcenery, yet one and the ſame ſpirit ſeemed to actuate the whole.

The Preſbyterian New Lights having received the ſpirit of the revival, cauſed a ſeparation from that church in 1803. The principal official characters that ſeparated were, Robert Marſhall, John Dunlavy, Richard M'Nemar, Barton W. Stone, and John Thompſon.* Many of

* See an apology for renouncing the juriſdiction of the Synod of Kentucky, page 24, 26.

the subjects of the revival united with those who separated from the Presbyterian church, who were called schismatics. These people renounced all old established creeds, forms of worship, and church government;* therefore, each one had liberty to exercise his own faith and proceed as he believed the spirit of God might dictate; and it was, they said, to the spirit they sought for light to open the sense of scripture; particularly those prophecies of things which were to take place in the millennium which they believed was now about to commence. They had liberty to act and pray as they believed was right; and by the boldest, most energetick, and loudest gift of prayer the cause was commonly decided. In this way, says the author of the Kentucky Revival, "they generally settled their controversies of every kind. One would begin to preach or exhort, and if his doctrine was judged unsound or uninteresting, he would be presently matched with a prayer, and which ever collected the greatest warmth, and manifested the most lively sensations of soul, gained the victory, and interested the general shout on that side."

Not any thing among any people professing religion, has ever appeared more singular, than those various operations and contortions of the body that now prevailed principally among those called schismatics.

Those exercises which were believed to have been of an involuntary kind, were rolling, jirking, and barking, and were thought by some who were much engaged in the cause, to be substituted by the spirit, in the room of the falling.

In the rolling exercise, as it was called, they appeared to be forcibly thrown down, and to roll over and over like a log, or in a kind of double posture to turn like a wheel. Sometimes they went in this manner through mud and dirt which was considered very degrading In the jirking exercise the head appeared to be violently moved towards one shoulder, then the other, and backwards and forwards. Here it may be observed, that

* See observations on church government by the Presbytery of Springfield.

during the time they were under these operations, though they were often exposed to imminent danger, yet few received any hurt. It also seemed to be out of the power of the person thus affected to prevent it. One instance among many others was related to the author by Lorenzo Dow, a well known itinerant preacher; while he was preaching in Kentucky, one of his hearers appeared to be jirked about the house in a violent manner; after repeated attempts, he at last got out of the meeting-house; he attempted to mount his horse, but his feet were jirked every way so that he could not get them into the stirrups, when all his efforts proved ineffectual, two men set him on his horse, but he was immediately jirked off on the ground, where he lie under the operations of violent twiches and jirks for some time, yet he escaped without any hurt. People of every age, sex, sect, and condition, appeared to be more or less affected with the disagreeable operations of these exercises, not only at their meetings, but in their daily employments.

Lorenzo Dow also informed the author, that about twenty Quakers in those parts who attended one of his meetings, were, just as he was beginning to preach, all taken with twitching and jirking, which to them was a great humiliation. The jirking exercise was sometimes accompanied, and often succeeded the barking. In this exercise both men and women personated and took the position of a dog, moved about in a horizontal posture upon their hands and feet, growled, snapped their teeth, and barked as if they were affected with the hydrophobia. But notwithstanding their suffering under these spasmodic or affected exercises, they had frequent intervals, in which they vociferated, that the work of God was increasing and that his blessed kingdom was about to appear. Sometimes they said they had been absent from the body, during which time they had visited their departed friends, and seen their situation in the invisible world. They professed to hear the musick of the heavenly choir, and to be flung into rapturous extacies by the melodiousness of the sound. In short, the visions they professed to have had, and the strange operations they saw of things upon earth, would take up too much room to admit a particular relation in this work. They firmly believed this was the time prophesied of by Joel ii. 28 to 31; and they were more confirmed in their faith from a number of signs which are recorded to have been seen; as the extraordinary phenomena of the shooting stars and trains of fire that illuminated the whole hemisphere as far as the extension of the horizon, accompanied by a hissing noise and several loud reports, particularly by the shower of blood that fell in the summer of 1804, seven miles from Turtle creek meeting house.

Their exercises were often succeeded, and sometimes relieved by dancing. The following singular instance of dancing, which is said to have first taken place, was at Turtle creek in 1804 J. Thompson, a preacher and a man of parts and education, danced above an hour at the close of a camp meeting, in a regular manner, all the time repeating with a low voice, "This is the Holy Ghost—Glory." Shortly after dancing was discovered to be a remedy for the jirks and barks, and considered by many as a part of religious worship. About the beginning of the year 1805, praying, shouting, jirking, twitching, barking, rolling, dreaming, dancing, prophesying of the near approach of the millennium, accompanied with violent shaking hands, and sacred promises to continue in the work until their prayers were answered, pervaded many parts of the state of Ohio, Tennessee, and Kentucky Information of these things being circulated in the public papers, many of which are taken by the Shakers and read by their leaders, particularly by the deacons; through this medium the Elders at Lebanon, state of New-York, received the intelligence. They took the matter into consideration, and the ministration came to the following conclusion, viz. That the minds of many of those who were thus wrought upon, were in a prepared state to receive their faith. Accordingly, on the 1st of January, 1805, the ministration at Lebanon sent Elders John Meacham, Benjamin S. Youngs, and Issachar Bates, to visit the subjects of the revival, and open their testimony to those who were able to receive it.

The ministration did not select them for their literary talents or abilities. Elder John Meacham was the son of

Joſeph Meacham. He was born in the year 1769, and being brought up among them, his mental faculties received but little improvement from ſchool education, as by theſe people it is conſidered ſuperfluous. He was ſtrong in the faith; his appearance was harmleſs, innocent, and ſolid, and his deportment exemplary.

Youngs was born 1773, and received the faith in 1794. He was a ſmall man, and had much the ſame appearance as Meacham, with common ſchool education.

Bates had but little literary information, but ſomewhat of a poetical genius. He was ſtrong in the faith, and ſo very zealous as often to incur the cenſure of thoſe to whom he ſpake.

They arrived in Kentucky about the 1ſt of March, and ſtopped at Paint lick, where they were kindly received. From thence they proceeded to Caneridge, and tarried a few days with the ſubjects of the revival, by whom they were treated with reſpect They then paſſed into Ohio, and firſt viſited a few inhabitants at Springfield. They did not aſſume the characters of publick ſpeakers at any of theſe places; but only converſed with individuals, endeavouring to diſcover their ripeneſs for the faith, and to open their teſtimony accordingly. They journeyed till they arrived at Turtle creek near Lebanon, on the 22d March. They firſt ſtopped and tarried the night at Malcham Worley's, and converſed with him concerning the revival, and partly opened their teſtimony The next morning they viſited Richard M'Nemar, and ſpent the day with him, opening and converſing on their faith and practice. Worley and M'Nemar conceived a favorable opinion of them, and were more diſpoſed to aſk queſtions and learn, than to controvert and oppoſe them. They received encouragement to open their teſtimony to the inhabitants of Turtle creek, either in publick or in private, as they felt diſpoſed. Next day being the Sabbath, Bates and Youngs attended their meeting, and at the concluſion, opened their miſſion and teſtimony, by treating briefly on, and expreſſing their union with the work of God that had been among the people in thoſe parts of the country, and informed them that the time was now come for them to enter into actual poſſeſſion of that for which they had been praying. In order thereto, they infomed them, that they muſt confeſs and forſake their ſins by ſelf-denial and taking up a full croſs againſt the world, fleſh, and all evil, and follow Chriſt by walking as he walked, and by becoming in all things conformed to him as their pattern, &c. Great agitations of mind, and much inquiry then commenced concerning them and their doctrines, by this means their faith was inveſtigated at Turtle creek, and numbers who had been leading characters, and others, ſoon united with them.—Malcham Worley, a man of liberal education, independent fortune, and of good character, was the firſt who confeſſed his ſins.

Various and vague reports of theſe people and their faith, were now circulated. The agitations of mind occaſioned by them, may be gathered from part of a letter written by B. W. Stone, a leading character in the revival, to R. M'Nemar, dated,

*Caneridge, April* 2, 1805.

"The churches thus, quid dicam? Neſcio:—What ſhall I ſay? I know not. My heart grieves within me. Certain men from afar whom you know, inject terror and doubt into many; and now religion begins to lament in the duſt among us. Some, as I ſuppoſe, will caſt away the ordinances of baptiſm, the Lord's ſupper, &c. but not many as yet. Moſt dear Brother, inform me what you think of theſe men among us and you, from a diſtant region."

The letter from which the above extract is made, was ſent by I. Bates who had been to ſee Stone, and partly opened their teſtimony to him.

Meacham, Youngs, and Bates travelled from place to place with unremitting zeal and aſſiduity teſtifying their faith, which in a few months obtained ſo much credit that R. M'Nemar, Matthew Houſton, John Dunlavy, Eliſha Thomas, and a few others, all of whom had been officiating characters in the revival, embraced and preached the faith of the Shakers, teſtifying that the time which had been predicted, and which thouſands had been praying for in the revival, had now actually commenced, and by confeſſing their ſins and taking up their croſs againſt all ſin in thought, word, and deed, they received that overcoming power which ſaved them from their ſins."

In a few months numbers received the faith at Turtle creek, Eagle creek; and on the ſouth ſide of Kentucky, at Mercy, Shelby, Paint lick, and Long lick; and likewiſe John Rankin before mentioned, Preſbyterian miniſter, and ſeveral of his congregation joined them.

Though many leading characters and ſubjects of the revival had now embraced the faith, yet there were ſeveral officiating characters, and hundreds of the ſubjects of the ſame revival* who as violently oppoſed them. The reader may form ſome idea how high oppoſition ran by the following extracts, and a few verbal ſpeeches reſpecting the Shakers, and conduct towards them. John Thompſon in a letter, dated,

*Springfield*, *April* 5, 1805,

Says—"It matters not to me who they are, who are the devil's tools whether men or angels, good men or bad, in the ſtrength of God I mean not to ſpare. I would they were even cut off who trouble you. I mean in the name and ſtrength of God to lift his rod of Almighty truth againſt the viper. I ſee the mark of the beaſt on that church as plain as I ſee this paper while I write, and I know that I ſee it by the light of God."

B. W. Stone ſays in his letter of July, 1806—"They are a ſet of worldly-minded, cunning deceivers, whoſe religion is earthly, ſenſual, and deviliſh."

The Shakers had intimated that ſuch who rejected their teſtimony, and oppoſed and perſecuted them on account of it, would loſe the light and power with which they had been favoured; therefore ſays Stone in the ſame letter—"Now the work of God goes on in ſpite of all the Calviniſts, Shakers, and devils in hell. Now

* Many through the progreſs of the revival joined other ſocieties, particularly the Baptiſt, who received an addition of ſome thouſands.

we know your prophets are liars."* "Think seriously and soberly of the shocking conduct of your revelling mock-worship, and tremble!"

Great opposition arose on account of their dancing, though many of them had practised dancing themselves. "What! (say they) go forth in the dance without being jirked? and say they are praising God in the dance. The dances too of them that make merry—of them that serve the devil Take their dances to serve God.—Christians, read your Bibles, and you will see that these fellows are not of God, for they keep not the Sabbath."

Stone in the postscript of his reply to Campbell's strictures, says—"You have heard no doubt before this time of the lamentable departure of two of our preachers, and a few of their hearers, from the true gospel into wild enthusiasm, or Shakerism. They have made shipwreck of faith, and turned aside to an old woman's fables, who broached them in New-England about twenty-five years ago. These wolves in sheep's clothing have smelt us from afar, and have come to tear, rend, and devour."

Much opposition was raised against them on account of their professing to be in a new dispensation, and their testifying that Christ had come the second time, though it was that for which they had been praying; but they would not believe this was the way of his coming. John Thompson, at a camp meeting at Turtle creek on the 27th of April, 1805, entered into a publick investigation of their doctrines, and in the close of it, with a loud voice, exclaimed, "They are liars! they are liars! they are liars! According to the fable, a liar is not to be believed when he speaks the truth."

At a general meeting held at Concord the second Sabbath in August, B. Youngs, M. Worley, M'Nemar, and Dunlavy, were all forbidden to speak, and threatened with being prosecuted as disturbers of the meeting if they did. On the last day of the meeting, J. Thompson, B. W. Stone, R. Marshall, D. Purviance, J. Stockwell, and

* "Christians of almost every denomination appear at times to have forgotten that harshness widens rather than closes the breaches which the diversity of sentiment may have occasioned." *Evan. Reflections.*

A. Brannon, alternately delivered each his opinion of the Shakers in a publick address; in which they were pronounced liars, false Christs, false prophets, wolves in sheep's clothing, deceitful workers, dumb dogs,* and every opprobrious scripture name they could think of. These discourses gave the ignorant class of people encouragement to abuse and persecute the Shakers. Accordingly, at one of those meetings, a professed Christian said to Issachar Bates, "Go to hell;" while a certain man followed J Meacham spitting in his face, and hallooing to the people to make a fire and burn these false prophets. Some christian professors laughed and encouraged him.†

The same reports that have been mentioned, page 336, were about this time also circulated in these parts, respecting this people.

Mobs beset their houses in the night and broke their windows by flinging in clubs, stones and dirt; they then pulled down their fences, and turned in cattle to destroy their grain. They disfigured their horses, and beat and abused them. They disturbed them in their worship by

* "Oh that great men and good men, should ever quarrel and not be willing to bear and forbear. If one is our master, even Christ, to him let us be content to be responsible; follow the best dictates of our conscience, and be happy to indulge our brethren with the same liberty." Stone and Thompson, when they arrive "at the right hand of the great Shepherd and Bishop of souls, must then be ashamed of their harsh spirit and harsh speeches It is a mercy for us all, that we have such a compassionate High Priest, who knows how to pity our infirmities, and to pardon our iniquities" *Haweis.*

"While we wrangle here in the dark, we are dying and passing to that world which will decide all our controversies, and the safest passage thither is by *peaceable* holiness." *Baxter.*

† "Mark the man that abuses, hates, and injures his brother for his opinions: he is a murderer, in whatever church he is found."

"Those who persecute always bear the brand of anti-christ; the persecuted have presumptive evidence in their favour that they follow at least the dictates of conscience" *Haweis.*

"He who hates another man for not being a christian, (or because he believes him not to be such) is himself not a christian.— Christianity breathes love, peace, and good will to man." *Littleton.*

throwing in sticks, dirt and stones, by pushing, laughing, mocking, threatening, railing, collaring, tearing and pulling them about.*

I. Bates returned some time in the latter part of the same year to Lebanon and Niskeuna, and brought marvellous accounts of wonderful operations and miracles in Kentucky, as proof of the truth of their faith. Bates, after a few weeks visiting among the brethren, returned to the southward. Likewise, some time after, John Meacham visited his brethren and sisters at Lebanon and Niskeuna—and returned to his allotted work. The ministration likewise sent from Lebanon a few other men and women to be helpers in the work, among which was David Darrow, before mentioned, who was appointed with Meacham to take the lead of the believers in Ohio, &c.

In the year 1807, Richard M'Nemar, (before mentioned, one of the leading characters in the revival, and one of those who joined the Shakers) published an account of the Kentucky revival. In the same publication he gave a brief account of the entrance and progress of what the world calls Shakerism, among the subjects of the revival. This publication I have partly followed in compiling this history respecting the revival and of the Shakers in Ohio and Kentucky. This is the first publication that has ever appeared from any of the members of this society, except a small pamphlet written by Joseph Meacham, entitled A Concise Statement, &c. with a letter annexed,† and published in the year 1790.

A further idea of the beginning and increase of the Shakers in Ohio and Kentucky, and of the opposition they met with, may be obtained by an extract from a letter written by B. S. Youngs to his brethren at Niskeuna, dated,

" *Miami County, Ohio, 10th of the 9th Mo.* 1807.

" What the number of believers are at present I can-
" not positively tell; but to speak as I suppose within
" bounds, they may be rising three hundred adult per-

* "Ye fools and blind," why could ye not "let them alone?"

† See page 33.

" sons—two-thirds of these in Ohio and the others in " Kentucky, scattered abroad from each other for the " distance of two hundred and thirty miles, principally in " a north and south direction. The largest body is at " what is (improperly) called Turtle creek, four miles " west of Lebanon, and are about one hundred or up- " wards; here doubtless a meeting-house will be built. " The first meetings of the believers were kept in private " houses, and that very secretly on account of persecu- " tion. After a few of these private meetings were held, " the believers continued for some time to assemble at " their old Presbyterian meeting house, to hear preach- " ing after the old form. At a certain time after preach- " ing, the believers commenced singing and dancing— " such a racket, perhaps, was never heard before; op- " position was then high; some singing, dancing and " shouting with all their might, because the day of re- " demption had come—others cursing, swearing, threat- " ening, laughing and mocking—some praying and ex- " horting—others yelling and screaming—some weeping " from conviction, (for the scene was solemn on the part " of the believers)—others crying from pity to see the " people carried away with such awful delusions. From " this some judgment may be formed what a scene and " tumult there was; and such we had many—sometimes " in houses, sometimes in the field, and sometimes in the " woods. The first public place of meeting was built in " the woods. It was a platform without cover, twenty- " two feet by eighteen, and two feet from the ground, " surrounded with banisters; this was burnt by persecu- " tors in September, 1805, after it had been used about " two months. Another like building was afterwards " erected between two houses, about thirty by twenty- " five feet, under cover, which has continued in use to " this day. At Beaver creek, twenty miles north of Leb- " anon, are about eighteen or twenty believers, who like- " ly will continue there; and at Eagle creek, sixty-five " miles east of Lebanon, are about seventy, under the " care of John Dunlavy, these will likely continue there. " At Shawney run, twelve miles north of Danville, are " about thirty believers, under the care of Elisha Thom-

"as; here the first gathering in Kentucky will doubtless
"be. At Paint lick, forty miles south of Lexington,
"are about thirty believers, under the care of Matthew
"Houston. At Shelby, sixty-two miles north-west of
"Danville, are about ten, who will soon remove. At
"Long lick, four miles south of Salt river, are about
"twenty believers, these are the youngest in the faith.
"And sixty miles north-east of Lexington and near
"Washington, are a small number more, who will likely
"soon remove from that place."

Since the date of the above letter, they have built several meeting-houses in Ohio and Kentucky; two at Turtle creek, one fifty feet long and forty wide, and well finished, the other not quite so large. Many have become gathered into the same order and joint interest as at Lebanon and Niskeuna, under the particular ministration of David Darrow, a man destitute of science, but strong and zealous in the faith. Several more of their zealous brethren and sisters have been sent from the church at Lebanon to their assistance, to build up and strengthen the believers in the faith. And likewise the same church has assisted the leaders at Turtle creek in building and purchasing lands for the use of the brethren. There are now Shakers in several other places in Ohio, Kentucky and Tennessee; and though many since their first increase at Turtle creek, have separated from the society, nevertheless they are now in number near two thousand.

The following is an extract from the Western Citizen, written by Col. James Smith, a gentleman of public character well known in Pennsylvania, and who has lately resided in Kentucky and Ohio He says,

"About five years ago, three Shakers, viz. Issachar Bates, John Meacham and Benjamin S. Youngs, came to Kentucky where I then resided, but I was abroad in Tennessee. On my return to my son James Smith's in Kentucky, where I had my home, I found he had joined the Shakers; I knew very little about them; but soon after, they having collected a party on Turtle creek, in the state of Ohio, I asked the above mentioned Bates if I might go and live with them for some time, to see what sort of people they were; to which he agreed. I accordingly went, and from that time to the present, I have diligently endeavoured to find them out, (which is truly difficult) and I think I have succeeded in a good degree My son James Smith, after joining the Shakers, appeared to be divested of natural affections towards his wife Polly and other connexions, and appeared determined to sell his plantations in Kentucky and remove to the Shakers on Turtle creek—which at length he did, contrary to his wife's consent. But before he removed, (which was in October, 1809) he promised to Polly if she would go with him, he would not take her among the Shakers, but buy a place three miles from them.—Notwithstanding he had left her bed a long time before this, and slept in a separate one from his wife, she bore this, and upon these terms she consented to go rather than to be separated from her children. Notwithstanding this, he took her directly among the Shakers, where she was constantly perplexed with their urging her to confess her sins, and telling her if she would not do so and receive their testimony, she would surely go to hell! About the first of March, 1810, they ordered Polly from the house she lived in while among them, and took her children from her. The fifth day of the same month, my step-son, William Irvin, and I, went with Polly to Shaker-town ; she asked of James the privilege of seeing her children. He told her where they were, and said she might go and see them, but refused to go with her. William Irvin and I went with her to the house where the children were, and asked to see them. We were told by John Woods and Malcham Worley that James had committed the children to their care, and she should not see them. We used entreaties and finally threatened Woods and Worley with the civil law, but all in vain. That night we retired, the tender mother in deep distress, bereft of her children, not knowing whether she ever should see them again. March sixth, we returned to Shaker-town to try if by any means Polly could be admitted to see her children. A short interview was granted, on condition that she must not converse with them except in the presence of the Shakers When she was about to take leave of her children, her eldest son laid hold on his dear mamma and wept bitterly. O mournful scene! The feelings of my heart I cannot describe! My son, before he received their testimony, was kind to me and affectionate to his wife; he received me into his house, and gave me every reason to expect his succour in my declining age"

The author, knowing of several instances of similar conduct towards relatives, particularly such as have been taught the principles of their faith, or as they word it, "have had the offer of the gospel," and refused to receive the same, has been more ready to receive the above account as a correct statement.

According to another account, dated Cincinnati, September first, on the twenty-seventh of August several companies of militia from the counties of Warren and Butler, accompanied by a large number of citizens, amounting in all to about a thousand, assembled before the Shaker settlement at Turtle creek, for the purpose of compelling them to deliver up the three grand-children of Col. J. Smith, and some other persons who were said to be detained by them against their inclinations. Committees were appointed on both sides to confer on matters in dispute. The conference being had, it was reported by the Shakers that the children were gone to Lebanon with their father; and finding none who wished to be liberated, the multitude after threatening the Shakers, dispersed.

In the year 1809, the church published a book, printed in the state of Ohio, and next year re-printed at Albany, state of New-York, entitled "The Testimony of Christ's Second Appearing" In this work there is a display of learning and erudition; the author appears to have been instructed in the Latin and Greek languages, but the men whose names are subscribed to the work as authors, it is well known are not men of education; and it is generally believed, and has been asserted by several members of their church, that the reputed authors wrote it by divine inspiration. In this work "the tenets" of that "blunt and illiterate" woman, Ann Lee, "expressed in a rude, confused and ambiguous manner," are "digested, dressed up and presented under a different form by" ſome more "maſterly hands" than Darrow, Meacham and Youngs, ſo "that they aſſume the aſpect of a regular ſyſtem. And hence it is that theſe writings (ſaid to have been compiled by Darrow, Meacham and Youngs) are more recommended than thoſe of" the prophets and apoſtles *

The worſhip of the church at firſt conſiſted in dancing, occaſionally preaching, ſometimes kneeling in ſilence, and always when aſſembled they ſang tunes without words; but ſoon after their increaſe in Ohio and Kentucky, hymns were compoſed by I. Bates and other members of the ſociety, which they often ſang in their meetings inſtead of thoſe tunes. By the year 1811, they had near an hundred compoſed on the different ſubjects of their faith, part of which were printed only for the uſe of the ſociety; ſome of which I have ſelected for an appendix to this work.

After a number have believed, the next principal labour of the leaders is to gather them into a united intereſt and order, like unto the church at Lebanon and Niſkeuna, the order of which is ſuch that it would take up many pages to give a particular account.† A few ſketches in addition to what has already been mentioned in the courſe of this work, may ſuffice. They aſſemble together every Sabbath in their public meeting-houſe—at Niſkeuna there are two orders, i. e. the church order called ſometimes old believers, and the younger order called young believers; the latter aſſemble in the forenoon, and the former in the afternoon. They walk to the meeting-houſe in order two and two, and leave it in the ſame order. Men enter the left hand door of the meeting-houſe, and women the right hand. In each dwelling-houſe is a room called the meeting-room, in which they aſſemble for worſhip every evening; the young believers aſſemble morning and evening, and in the afternoon of the Sabbath they all aſſemble in one of

* See Second Appearing, p. 397, ver. 28 and 29.

† In caſe there ſhould be a demand for a ſecond edition of this work, I may give a full account of the order of the church, and alſo treat this hiſtory more at large.

these rooms in their dwelling-houſe, to which meeting ſpectators or thoſe who do not belong to the ſociety, are not admitted, except friendly viſitors.

Their houſes are well calculated and convenient. In the great houſe at Lebanon, there are near an hundred; the men live in their ſeveral apartments on the right as they enter into the houſe, and the women on the left—commonly four in a room They kneel in the morning by the ſide of the bed, as ſoon as they ariſe, and the ſame before they lie down; alſo before and after every meal. The brethren and ſiſters generally eat at the ſame time, at two long tables placed in the kitchen, men at one and women at the other; during which time they ſit on benches, and are all ſilent. They go to their meals walking in order, one directly after the other; the head of the family or Elder, takes the lead of the men, and one called Elder Siſter takes the lead of the women. Several women are employed in cooking and waiting on the table—they are commonly relieved weekly by others. It is contrary to order for a man or woman to ſleep alone, but two of the brethren ſleep together, and the ſiſters the ſame It is contrary to order for a man to be alone with a woman—alſo to touch one another. If a man preſents any thing to a female, or a female to a male, due care muſt be taken by each one not to touch the other. It is contrary to order for a woman to walk out alone, or be alone A man and woman are not allowed to converſe together, except in the preſence of ſome of the brethren and ſiſters. They ſometimes have what they call union meetings, when ſeveral of the brethren and ſiſters meet together, ſit and converſe and ſmoke their pipes. If a man is on the road from home alone in a carriage, it is contrary to order for him to admit a woman to ride with him on any account whatever. It is contrary to order, or the gift as they call it, to leave any bars down, or gates open, or leave any thing they uſe out of its proper place, conſequently they ſeldom have any thing loſt. It is according to the gift or order, for all to endeavour to keep all things in order; indolence and careleſſneſs they ſay is directly oppoſite to the goſpel and order of God; cleanlineſs in every reſpect is ftrongly enforced—it is contrary to order even to fpit on the floor. A dirty, flovenly, carelefs or indolent perfon, they fay, cannot travail in the way of God, or be religious. It is contrary to order to talk loud, to fhut doors hard, to rap hard at a door for admittance, or to make a noife in any refpect; even when walking the floor they muft be careful not to make a noife with their feet.—They go to bed at nine or ten o'clock, and rife at four or five; all that are in health go to work about fun-rife; in-door mechanics, in the winter work by candle-light; each one follows fuch an employment as the Deacon appoints for him. Every man and woman muft be employed, and work fteadily and moderately. When any are fick, they have the utmoft care and attention paid to them. When a man is fick, if there is a woman among the fifters that was his wife before he believed, fhe if in health, nurfes and waits upon him.

If any of them tranfgrefs the rules and orders of the church, they are not held in union until they confefs their tranfgreffion, and that often on their knees, before the brethren and fifters.

Each church in the different fettlements has a houfe called the office, where all bufinefs is tranfacted, either among themfelves or with other people; each family depofit in the office all that is to be fpared for charitable purpofes, which is diftributed by the Deacon to thofe whom he judges to be proper objects of charity; he never fends the poor and needy empty away.

## CONCLUSION.

I have refrained from expreffing my belief of this people, their doctrines or practices, in this work, or making digreffions on what I have written, but have left the reader to form his own judgment. But I may obferve thus far, that I am not of the opinion of many, that they will foon become extinct. Their general character of honefty in their temporal concerns, and their outward deportment and order being fuch, that many may be induced to join them; and as induſtry and frugality are two great points in their religion, it is likely they will become a rich people.

Theſe inferences may be deduced by a parity of reaſoning—If we conſider their primitive ſtate under the miniſtration of a penurious James and Jane Wardley, whoſe days were terminated in an alms-houſe—view them in their migration from Europe and ſettlement at Niſkeuna, conducted by the imbecility of a femanine leader—view them in their humble receſs, obliged to perform ſervile drudgery to procure the morſel that ſupported their being—ſee their whole attenuated force collected under the roof of a log-hut, ſurrounded with the towering pines—obſerve them through all their multiplied operations and trials, calumniated and ſtigmatized, reproached and deſpiſed—in ſhort, follow them through all their complicated ſcenes of poverty and difficulties, and then behold the preſent contraſt! See the once uncultivated wilderneſs waſte of Niſkeuna and other places, now turned into fruitful fields—ſee their neat public edifices towering amidſt the ſurrounding elegancy and neatneſs of their more private habitations—ſee their ability in their munificent donations to the poor in New York. After canvaſſing and weighing their paſt increaſe, beginning under ſuch embarraſſed circumſtances, and having a zeal without knowledge, or lack of wiſdom and experience, (as they confeſs) which cauſed them to run into many practices which they have now diſcarded; and judging of their future proſperity from their preſent flouriſhing ſtate, and from their being a much more orderly people, it is poſſible they may increaſe in number and acquire a prevailing influence in the future deſtinies of the country.

# APPENDIX,

Containing HYMNS composed by several members of the church called Shakers—a few of which are given, as they are explanatory of their faith, and several upon subjects entirely new.

*The Gospel from England to America; its first opening and increase therein.*

THE gospel, clear as the noon-day,
From England to America,
On eagle's wings did soar away,
Unto the place appointed.

2 Then came to pass, as the prophet said,
My church I will convey away,
The wilderness shall be her stay,
Until the time appointed.

3 And when the time was fully come,
Swift as the rays of morning sun
The gospel-fire began to run,
Which brought on Satan's trial.

4 At Watervliet, that blissful seat,
From whence the law went forth to greet,
With the last trumpet to repeat
Salvation found in Zion.

5 Now consternation seized on all!
They saw their towers must surely fall,
The great, the mighty and the small,
Began to quake and quiver.

6 Some unto whom the sound did come,
Knew that it was the morning sun;
They seiz'd the kingdom as they run,
Which kingdom stands for ever.

7 Lo Achor's valley ſpreads in ſight,
The doors of hope diſpell'd the night,
And thouſands brought their deeds to light,
And waſh'd in the pure river.

8 Like Pentecoſt, new ſcenes unfold;
With tongues and ſigns as Jeſus told,
And gifts of God, more rich than gold,
Had every true believer.

9 This was not in a corner done,
But ſpread towards the riſing ſun,
And became the glory of New-Lebanon,
Which God had firſt prepar'd.

10 From Lebanon, towards the eaſt,
With beams of burning light increas'd,
And thouſands called to the feaſt
Of hidden glory, ſhare.

11 Thoſe whom the goſpel call obey'd,
Then felt a ſure foundation laid,
Whereon the righteous never ſtray'd,
Nor can they be miſtaken.

12 The work which God had promis'd long,
Hath now appear'd, at laſt ſo ſtrong,
'Tis verify'd with a new ſong,
With dancing and with ſhaking.

13 Some twiſt and turn, and back they ſtart!
With idols fixed on their heart,
They hated from their ſins to part,
So call'd the work deluſion.

14 Now void of ſenſe—how God will break
The proud, the lofty and the great;
At once cry out, ye miſchief make—
Ye Shakers make confuſion.

15 So in their rage they turn away,
And never think what God did ſay,
That ſhaking in the latter day
Should ſeize all earth and heaven.

16 The little ſtone is now cut out—
The trump of God ſpeaks with a ſhout,
Awake, thou ſleeper, and come out,
And have thy ſins forgiven.

17 O glorious resurrection day!
The mountains skip, the hills do play;
The islands too are fled away,
And waters back are driven.

18 Hail nations, hail! the great I Am
Hath plac'd his kingdom now in man—
The virgins, followers of the Lamb,
Have found their seat in heaven.

---

*Second Appearing.*

CHRIST'S second appearing was in Mother Ann,
Whose soul cry'd to God for salvation for man;
And God heard her cries for the good of the whole,
And sent the true comforter into her soul:
Zion, O break forth into singing!
Her gospel is ringing—'tis true
With Mother, three Elders like angels did stand,
With her cross'd the ocean and came to this land;
They gave us the gospel which stained our pride,
And for us these saviours all suffer'd and dy'd:
Zion, to bless your dear Saviour
Is your due behaviour—'tis true
Then our Father Joseph, whom God did prepare
By faith and obedience, became the true heir,
Our bless'd Mother's mantle did cover his soul,
And a faithful Elder he was to the whole:
Zion is daily possessing
Our dear Father's blessing—'tis true.
Then our Mother Lucy, who now is our guard,
Became a true helper with him in the Lord;
A Father and a Mother we children then found,
From fleshly relation our souls they unbound:
Zion then cloth'd in beauty,
Felt thanks was her duty—'tis true.
In regeneration their souls swiftly run,
And true church relation by them was begun;
They planted the church and establish'd its laws,
Devoted their lives in support of its cause:
Zion in regeneration,
Does find church relation—'tis true.
Two pillars in Zion they truly remain'd,
And by faithful labour church order they gain'd,
And then Father's work on the earth was all done,
Whose soul now in glory does shine like the sun.
Zion his suffering regretted,
And still feel indebted—'tis true.

Now brethren and ſiſters let us all agree,
In thanks for a Mother whom daily we ſee,
Whoſe ſoul is a temple for God's only Son,
Whoſe ſecond appearing is truly begun :
 Zion, O bleſs your protector,
 For God does reſpect her—'tis true.
Ann our bleſs'd Mother, who came from afar,
And the lovely Elders who travell'd with her,
Our Father and Mother who roſe in this land,
Whoſe ſouls all unſpotted in union do ſtand :
 Zion, through theſe came the bleſſing,
 Which thou art poſſeſſing—'tis true.
The heavens of glory did ſmile on the earth
When theſe bleſsed worthies received their birth;
We bleſs the good days when theſe worthies were born,
And bleſs God who kept them till the ſecond morn :
 Zion, through their interceſſion,
 Is ſaved from tranſgreſſion—'tis true.
We bleſs our dear Mother, the chief corner-ſtone,
Which God laid in Zion, his anointed one;
We bleſs all the faithful who then did embark
With Mother to come and help build us an ark :
 Zion, God thy maſter-builder,
 With wiſdom had fill'd her—'tis true.
The ark was a ſhelter to ſave us from ſin,
And this they erected and left us within,
With Father and Mother of the choſen race;
Since Father deceas'd, Mother fills up the place :
 Zion, by Mother protected,
 Does not feel neglected—'tis true.
Are we truly thankful for what we've receiv'd?
Through their faithful labours we all have believ'd;
And ſtill by their labours protection we've found—
O brethren and ſiſters, may our thanks abound!
 Zion, while thanks are progreſſing,
 You're gaining the bleſſing—'tis true.

---

*The Pillar of Truth.*

LET names and ſects and parties,
 Accoſt my ears no more;
My ever bleſſed Mother
 For ever I'll adore;
Appointed by kind Heaven
 My Saviour to reveal,
Her doctrine is confirmed
 With an eternal ſeal.

She was the Lord's anointed
To ſhew the root of ſin,
And in its full deſtruction
Her goſpel did begin.
A fleſhly, carnal nature,
With all its deep diſguiſe,
She ſtript entirely naked
Before the ſinners' eyes.
Sunk in your baſe corruptions,
Ye wicked and unclean!
You read your ſealed Bibles,
But know not what they mean;
Confeſs your filthy actions,
And put your luſts away,
And live the life of Jeſus,
This is the only way.
Ye haughty kings and beggars,
Come learn your equal fate!
Your carnal, fallen nature,
You've ſurely got to hate;
Whatever your profeſſion,
Your ſex or colour be,
Renounce your carnal pleaſures,
Or Chriſt you'll never ſee.
The way of God is holy,
Mark'd with Emmanuel's feet,
Luſt cannot reach Mount Zion,
Nor ſtain the golden ſtreet;
If you will have ſalvation,
You firſt muſt count the coſt,
And ſacrifice that nature,
In which the world is loſt.
At Mancheſter in England,
This bleſſed fire began,
And like a flame in ſtubble,
From houſe to houſe it ran.
At firſt a few receiv'd it,
And did their luſt forſake,
And ſoon the word in power
Brought in a mighty ſhake.
The rulers cry'd "Deluſion!
Who can theſe Shakers be?
Are theſe the wild fanatics
Bewitched by Ann Lee?
We'll ſtop this noiſe of ſhaking,
It never ſhall prevail;
We'll ſeize the grand deceiver,
And thruſt her into jail."
Before their learned councils,

Though oft ſhe was arraign'd,
Her life was uncondemned,
Her character unſtain'd;
And by her painful travail,
Her ſuffering and her toil,
A little church was formed
On the European ſoil.
This little band of union,
In apoſtolick life,
Remain'd a while in England
Among the ſons of ſtrife,
Till the Columbian Eagle,
Borne by an eaſtern breeze,
Convey'd this little kingdom
Acroſs the rolling ſeas.
To mark the ſhining paſſage,
Good angels flew before
'Towards the land of promiſe,
Columbia's happy ſhore.
Hail! thou victorious goſpel!
And that auſpicious day,
When Mother ſafely landed
In Hudſon's lovely bay
Near Albany they ſettled,
And waited for a while,
Until a mighty ſhaking
Made all the deſert ſmile:
At length a gentle whiſper,
The tidings did convey,
And many flock'd to Mother,
To learn the living way.
Through ſtorms of perſecution,
The truth ſhe did maintain,
And ſhow'd how ſin was conquer'd,
And how we are born again:
The old corrupted nature,
From place to place ſhe trod,
And ſhow'd a new creation,
The only way to God.
About four years ſhe labour'd
With the attentive throng,
Confirm'd the young believers,
And help'd their ſouls along:
At length ſhe cloſ'd her labour,
And vaniſh'd out of ſight,
And left the church increaſing
In the pure goſpel light.
How much are they deceiv'd
Who think that Mother's dead!

She lives among her offspring,
Who just begin to spread;
And in her outward order,
There's one supplies her room,
And still the name of Mother
Is like a sweet perfume.
Since Mother sent the gospel,
And spread it in the west,
How many sons and daughters
Are nourish'd from her breast!
How many more conceiv'd,
And travailing in the birth!
Who yet shall reign with Mother
Like princes on the earth.
I love that testimony
That shows me what to do:
I love my precious Mother,
I love the Elders too:
The Brethren and the Sisters,
I love them and their ways,
And in this loving spirit
I mean to spend my days.

*The Believers' Appeal.*

MAN, at his first creation,
As he was made upright, you know;
While in that situation
He walked in the light you know.
As he was male and female,
The man must be the head you know;
And by his wholesome counsel
The woman must be led you know.
The woman was beguiled
And got the serpent's seed you know;
And though she was defiled
The harlot took the lead you know.
Then from his head old Adam fled,
And cleav'd unto his wife you know;
And for his fall he never shall
Eat of the tree of life you know.
And in his flesh relation,
He lies beneath the curse you know;
And every generation
Has still been growing worse you know.
But God decreed another seed
Of a superiour birth you know;

Whose feet should tread the serpent's head
And people all the earth you know.
The time has been predicted,
And this must be the day you know;
And he that is convicted
Will quit his former way you know.
The carnal life of man and wife
Cannot appear so right you know.
Now the old man's offended,
Unwilling yet to die you know;
He says he was commanded
To go and multiply you know.
He argues still he can fulfil,
The all important trust you know;
But this pretence is his defence
To gratify his lust you know.
The serpent now in fetters,
Though he's but a thief you know;
To Paul's mysterious letters
He'll hasten for relief you know.
Permission blind he there can find,
But no express command you know.
That some forbid to marry,
The carnal man can read you know;
Whatever sense they carry,
Upon this word he'll feed you know.
Seducers boast he now can trace
With Shakers in his eyes you know,
And boldly say that these are they,
But carnal men will lie you know.
The protestant reformers,
The Roman priests condemn you know;
And this forbidding marriage
They've charg'd upon them you know.
Whoever might the civil right
Prohibit or forbid you know;
We do not say it might be they,
But Shakers never did you know.
The lust his father gave him,
The carnal man seduc'd you know;
And marriage cannot save him
But from a worse abuse you know.
It comes to bind the carnal mind,
And nail it to the cross you know.
The cross he will not carry,
But at the truth will spurn you know;
Though Paul says let him marry,
It's better than to burn you know.
If he's in pain and can't contain,

And will not ſerve the Lord you know,
Then ſure he muſt live in his luſt
And take his juſt reward you know.
Old Adam in vexation,
May ſearch the ſcripture through you know,
And find a large relation
Of Gentile and of Jew you know.
But he that would be truly good,
A woman will not touch you know;
This is the one that God will own,
And Paul himſelf was ſuch you know.

---

*Hymn of Love.*

LOVING Brethren, loving Siſters,
Middle ag'd and blooming youth,
Lay aſide your Sirs and Miſters,
Love the plain and ſimple truth.
Love's the ſpring of our communion,
Life and breath of the new man;
Never was ſuch love and union,
Never ſince the world began.
From our bleſsed, loving Mother,
Firſt the loving tidings came;
That her children love each other,
And that love's their father's name.
Loving Elders brought the meſſage,
Loving New-lights gave it paſſage,
Till it ſpread both far and wide.
Let us then not be miſtaken,
As to what we're call'd to love;
Whether things that may be ſhaken,
Things below or things above.
Firſt divide the fleſh and ſpirit,
Good from evil ſeparate;
Then the thing that's void of merit,
We muſt love not, we muſt hate.
Love not ſelf that muſt be hated,
Love not ſatan, love not ſin;
And to the fleſh though you're related,
Love not fleſh nor fleſhly kin
Love not riches, honour, pleaſures,
Love no earthly, vain delight;
But the goſpel, hidden treaſure,
You may love with all your might.
Love your parents in the ſpirit,
Love them freely though unſeen;

Love the kingdom they inherit,
  Love whatever's pure and clean.
Love your Elders in their calling,
  Love their counſel to obey;
Love to ſee old Babel falling,
  Love the new and living way.
Love the croſs, love ſelf-denial,
  Love to labour day and night;
Love that faith that ſtands the trial,
  Love with brethren to unite.
Love the ſouls yet bound in fetters,
  Love to help them on to God;
Love to feel yourſelves their debtors,
  Love the preachers ſent abroad.
Love the inward, new creation,
  Love the glory that it brings;
Love to lay a good foundation,
  In the line of outward things.
Love a life of true devotion,
  Love your lead in outward care;
Love to ſee all hands in motion,
  Love to take your equal ſhare.
Love to love what is belov'd,
  Love to hate what is abhorr'd;
Love all earneſt ſouls that covet
  Lovely love and its reward.
Love repays the lovely lover,
  And in lovely ranks above,
Lovely love ſhall live for ever,
  Loving lovely loved love.

THE END.

CPSIA information can be obtained at www.ICGtesting.com
Printed in the USA
LVOW092139301012
305169LV00007B/4/P